Women Playwrights of Diversity

Women Playwrights

of Diversity

A Bio-Bibliographical Sourcebook

Jane T. Peterson and Suzanne Bennett

Greenwood Press
Westport, Connecticut • London

Library of Congress Cataloging-in-Publication Data

Peterson, Jane T.
  Women playwrights of diversity : a bio-bibliographical sourcebook
/ by Jane T. Peterson and Suzanne Bennett.
     p.   cm.
  Includes bibliographical references (p.) and index.
  ISBN 0–313–29179–9 (alk. paper)
  1. American drama—Women authors—Bio-bibliography—Dictionaries.
2. Women dramatists, American—20th century—Biography—
Dictionaries.   3. American drama—Minority authors—Bio-
bibliography—Dictionaries.   4. Lesbians' writings, American—Bio-
bibliography—Dictionaries.   5. American drama—20th century—Bio-
bibliography—Dictionaries.   6. Minority women in literature—
Dictionaries.   7. Ethnic groups in literature—Dictionaries.
8. Minorities in literature—Dictionaries.   9. Lesbians in
literature—Dictionaries.   I. Bennett, Suzanne.   II. Title.
PS338.W6P48   1997
812'.54099287'03—dc20   96–27388
  [B]

British Library Cataloguing in Publication Data is available.

Library of Congress Catalog Card Number: 96–27388
ISBN: 0–313–29179–9

First published in 1997

Greenwood Press, 88 Post Road West, Westport, CT 06881
An imprint of Greenwood Publishing Group, Inc.

Printed in the United States of America

The paper used in this book complies with the
Permanent Paper Standard issued by the National
Information Standards Organization (Z39.48–1984).

10 9 8 7 6 5 4 3 2 1

Contents

Preface

RATIONALE/PURPOSE

Women Playwrights of Diversity is a reference book designed to highlight briefly the careers and work of selected women playwrights who are writing from and about the ethnic and cultural diversity in America in the 1990s. However, the Latina, Asian American, African American, and lesbian voices are too frequently underrepresented on our stages and in our classrooms. By focusing on these playwrights, both established and emerging, we hope to bring these women to the attention of wider audiences.

This guide is intended as a practical resource for theatre practitioners seeking plays to produce in the professional, community, or academic theatres and will also serve as a supplement for educators teaching dramatic literature or courses in women's studies. Our purpose is to facilitate those producers, scholars, and students who wish to locate, read, write about, and produce plays by women of color and by lesbians.

SCOPE

This book includes playwrights who self-identify as (1) African American, (2) Latina, (3) Asian American, (4) a combination of these ethnicities, and/or (5) lesbian. To make this resource as contemporary and up to date as possible, the majority of a playwright's works had to be written since 1970.

To ensure the inclusion of established as well as emerging playwrights (playwrights whose work was sufficiently developed to warrant their recognition and support by a professional theatre), we solicited recommendations from four sources: (1) theatres that are members of the Theatre Communications Group and are consequently listed in *Theatre Profiles*; (2) theatres listed in the *Dramatists Sourcebook*; (3) essayists who are expert in their respective areas; and (4) selected scholars and pedagogues whose academic work supports marginalized women playwrights. Letters outlining our purpose and response forms were sent; we asked that they recommend at least two but no more than five playwrights who had been associated with their theatre or organization and whose work deserves to be given wider attention. To protect their relationships with individual playwrights, the theatres' and scholars' names would be included in an index of contributors but would not be affixed to specific playwrights. The response was overwhelmingly supportive and spoke volumes of the need for such a resource book.

A list of playwrights was compiled from the recommendations submitted. Two key criteria were used in selecting playwrights for inclusion: (1) the existing production record of the writer or (2) the potential for production of the plays. Our own professional experiences (Suzanne as a director, literary manager, and artistic director in the nonprofit theatre, and Jane as a dramaturge, a professor of dramatic literature, and an advisor to departments about multicultural, multiethnic plays) accustomed us to consider production values in the selection of plays and playwrights and to ask a series of questions: Is the subject of the play likely to be of interest to a diverse audience (i.e., women, men, younger adults, older adults, straight, gay, white, and audiences of color)? Will audiences respond to the characters? Does the playwright understand the demands of, and have a sophistication about, the stage? Will the play attract directors, designers, and actors? Is it "worth" doing? That is, given the hard reality of the cost of producing a play, does it have a distinctive voice, a fresh perspective, an authenticity, honesty, "soul" to warrant an investment of time and money?

We excluded plays that were unlikely to be performed by artists other than the original creators. This eliminated the work of many solo or performance art performers who work exclusively in those forms and plays developed by a collective of artists centered exclusively on their personal histories. With the welcome interest in publication of collections of work by women, records of many of these solo performance art pieces and collectively created texts are available.

The playwrights (or their agents) were contacted directly for the following information: a complete biographical narrative; a list of published plays and the publishers; a list of unpublished plays available from some source (a specific theatre, agent, New Dramatists, the playwright); one or two manuscripts representative of their work, if the plays were not readily available; a production history; and critical assessments not available in major newspapers or periodicals. While the overwhelming response from the playwrights was generous and supportive, a few playwrights, unhappily, did not respond to repeated entreaties for information. We were forced to omit entries for those playwrights or, if the information was available from other sources, to provide the best information we could.

In order to contextualize the individual playwrights within their own contemporary ethnic or cultural theatrical history, we selected an expert scholar or practitioner from each major category to write an overview chapter.

FORMAT/ORGANIZATION

All entries are listed alphabetically. Separate lists identifying the playwrights as African American, Asian American, Latina, and/or lesbian are included at the end of the volume; obviously, some playwrights will appear in more than one list. A separate list of playwrights who do not receive an entry but whose work bears consideration is also included.

Stylistically, all playwrights whose names appear in **boldface** on first mention in the chapters and entries have a separate entry in this book. While we have made every effort to be as accurate and inclusive as possible in our information, we make no claim to being definitive. Our intention, rather, is to provide a brief overview of the playwright and her work; we hope to stimulate interest and suggest resources for further consideration rather than provide a comprehensive study.

Each entry consists of the following information:

1. *A brief biographical narrative.* To ensure equity among the playwrights, the biographies highlight similar information for all: date and place of birth; education; other nondramatic writing; and careers apart from playwrighting. Any undocumented quotes within the entries are from biographical information provided by the playwright.

2. *Description of plays.* The play descriptions, when at all possible, were written after reading or viewing the plays. On occasion we relied on a playwright's own description of her play.

3. *A selected production history of each work.* For many of the established playwrights, a complete production history is too extensive and serves no purpose for the intention of this resource book. For those plays and playwrights, usually only the first professional, most important productions or major subsequent productions are included. In the case of emerging playwrights, we have frequently included a more extensive production history; often these works have not yet had a major production, and the history provides documentation of the circuitous route that many new works must take in their journey to be seen by a larger audience.

4. *Play availability.* In addition to listing the published plays and the publisher, other resources (playwright, agent, New Dramatists, and so on) for obtaining the manuscripts are provided.

5. *Awards.* The major playwriting awards and grants earned are listed for each playwright.

6. *A selected bibliography of critical and review articles.* This bibliography

is not intended to be complete or comprehensive. It is, rather, a tool to begin further inquiry and research into the individual playwright. We have also tried to limit the resources to those available at a full-service public library; we have intentionally avoided reference for obscure or hard to obtain publications wherever possible. Page numbers often had to be omitted if the reviews sent by playwrights had been clipped without the page numbers.

Acknowledgments

The resources of The Women's Project and Productions and the generosity of Julia Miles enhanced this resource guide immeasurably. The literary manager of the Women's Project during the crucial period of our research was Susan Bougetz, and her assistance was particularly valuable and always prudent and encouraging.

The optimism and advice of writer friends, in particular Broeck Wahl Blumberg, Cindy Cooper, and Mary Wings, made the work seem possible.

Susana Meyer was patient, listened, and kept her promises.

A special thanks goes to essayists Jill Dolan, Tiffany Ana Lopez, Chiori Miyagawa, and Sydné Mahone, who not only provided provocative essays but also offered help, advice, and stimulating conversation.

My deepest appreciation is for my mother, Miriam Savage Bennett, whose belief is an enormous gift.

Suzanne Bennett

A special thank you goes to the following graduate students who added invaluable research to this project during the course of various independent studies: Michael Hilger, who is committed to infusing diverse drama into community productions in New Jersey and Long Island; Joe Wolgemuth, whose interest in lesbian drama is a welcome reminder that voices resonate beyond the boundaries of sex and gender; and Barb Short, whose newly tapped interest and enthusiasm remind me why I got into theatre in the first place.

A big thank you goes to Cliff Gillman in Academic Computing at Montclair State University for his expertise and vast patience and to Faith Roberson for facilitating all our computer issues.

Thanks is owed to Jenny Clarke for her willingness to take time away from her own research to help fill in some of the gaps. And Tom Veenendall will be remembered for his generosity in typing when the converting and scanning failed.

An enormous debt of gratitude is owed to those who provided moral support and encouragement. Thanks to Cindy Cooper for talking me through the roughest of times and especially to Suzanne Trauth whose gentle prodding and calm reason were always there when I needed them.

Words alone are not enough to thank Eileen McGurty without whom this book would not be a reality. It was her faith in me and the project that kept me going, and it is her love that makes it all worthwhile. Her typing contributions and computer know-how helped immeasurably, too. I owe you a big one!

Jane T. Peterson

We are particularly grateful to Greg Kunesh who, at the beginning, encouraged our collaboration, and near the end, gave us timely help with the title.

Finally, a special thank you is due to all the nominators and playwrights who supplied us with recommendations, advice, and information.

Abbreviations

ACT	American Conservatory Theatre
ATHE	Association for Theatre in Higher Education
AUDELCO	Audience Development Committee, Inc.
BACA	Brooklyn Arts and Cultural Association
CAPS	Creative Arts Public Schools
CETA	Comprehensive Employment and Training Act
CSC	Classic Stage Company
EST	Ensemble Studio Theatre
HOLA	Hispanic Organization of Latin Actors
IATI	Instituto De Arte Teatral Internacional
INTAR	International Arts Relations, Inc.
La Mama ETC	La Mama Experimental Theatre Club (also referred to as La Mama)
LATA	Latin American Theatre Artists
L.E.N.D.	Lesbian Exchange of New Drama
MAP	Multicultural Arts Program
PEN	International Association of Poets, Playwrights, Editors, Essayists, and Novelists
P. S. 122	Performance Space 122
TDR	The Drama Review
WOW Cafe	Women's One World Cafe

Introduction: The Challenges of Diversity

Suzanne Bennett

Contents on the drama shelves in bookstores, libraries, and our studies have altered radically in the last several years. When we conceived this project three years ago, the paucity of collections and anthologies of plays by women of varied ethnicities and cultures severely limited the possibilities for production and study. We now have valuable anthologies of African American, Asian American, and Hispanic women and lesbian playwrights and, to date, at least one collection of plays by women of color. Further, the work of playwrights most often confined to the margins of alternative spaces and ethnic specific theatres has appeared under separate cover. For professors assembling a reading list, and theatres searching for plays of women playwrights writing outside the mainstream, these collections are invaluable aids. Just as important, when a drama book customer searches the shelves of a bookstore, she or he will see for the first time plays representing the diversity of life in America.

Change continues, too, in the language used to describe peoples who are not Caucasian, not heterosexual—partly an outcome of the rapid and confusing assimilation by nonwhites and homosexuals into mainstream culture. "Minority" and "third world" have long been regarded as insulting words by black, Hispanic, and Asian people who, worldwide, outnumber white people. Certainly, many hours of conversation have ensued between ourselves and our colleagues, essayists, nominators, and editors, and many words have been considered in relation to the wording of the "categories" in this guide as well as its title. When we began, African American was de rigueur; three years later, "black" has reemerged as an acceptable and, by some, preferable choice. Where "queer" was once as derogatory as "nigger," now many younger homosexuals have appropriated a designation previously regarded as inflammatory. The language we use in these pages represents the advice of those who contributed to this book coupled with our own preference for words in common use for several years. After listening to the playwrights included here, we decided to use lesbian, as well as bisexual. We alternate the use of black and African American as both at this writing are in frequent use. Latina has a more specific reference than Hispanic and seems to be more appropriate for the majority of playwrights included here; however, in more generalized discussions, Hispanic is also employed (see Tiffany Ana Lopez's chapter for a thorough discussion of Latina). In short, our uneasiness about who we are ethnically and culturally in the United States is best expressed in the ever-shifting way we name our racial and sexual identities.

In the introductory essays, Jill Dolan, Tiffany Ana Lopez, Sydné Mahone, and **Chiori Miyagawa** highlight the accomplishments and trace concerns occurring within the lesbian, Latina, African American, and Asian American communities. From their essays and a reading of the plays some similarities emerge: the women protagonists more often find ways to control their destinies; more women write outside the realistic style prevalent on stages in the 1970s and early 1980s; and, interestingly, a significant number of diverse playwrights are constructing character by multiple factors and often excluding race or sexual preference as a defining feature.

One of the most challenging nontraditional protagonists of the playwrights discussed here is the porno film actress Etta Jenks, from **Marlane Meyer**'s play *Etta Jenks*. Meyer takes the familiar story of the naive, aspiring actress who makes pornographic films in order to achieve Hollywood fame and shows her manipulating the system she is in rather than drowning in its dehumanizing way of life. Etta achieves power and economic success without losing her ability to recognize and fight the more pernicious evils of the pornography business. The workers in the **Five Lesbian Brothers** satiric farce *The Secretaries* also assert their independence untraditionally—each month they eliminate a lumberjack by a chainsaw. Other memorable examples include: Desdemona seeking excitement and sexual pleasure in **Paula Vogel**'s *Desdemona* or **Cherríe Moraga**'s bodiless Cerezita extolling farm workers in *Heroes and Saints*. The central figures in plays by women of diversity are asserting themselves in often bizarre and compelling ways.

Realism continues as the dominant mode in American drama for all playwrights; however, a surprisingly large proportion of the playwrights included here depart from the realistic form. **Adrienne Kennedy** is one of the earlier experimenters and the playwright she influenced, **Suzan-Lori Parks**, shares with her predecessor the ability to stretch the boundaries of language on stage. The four Asian American playwrights discussed in the chapter by Chiori Miyagawa—**Diana Son, Eugenie Chan, Naomi Iizuka**, and **Sandra Rodgers**—in the majority of their plays utilize a nonrealistic, stylized mode. Playwrights **Claire Chafee** and **Kia Corthron** use a heightened realism, lyrical and sparse in Corthron's *Come Down Burning*, lyrical and epigrammatic, in Chafee's *Why We Have a Body*. Vogel, **Lisa Loomer, Split Britches**, and the Five Lesbian Brothers are all very different playwrights, yet they all enrich the language of the stage by their insistence on theatricalism and an irreverent playfulness.

Many of the playwrights in this volume eschew racial definition of character. **Maria Irene Fornes, Lynne Alvarez**, and **Caridad Svich** are three Latina playwrights who have written major plays without Hispanic characters. In fact, Fornes never specifies ethnicity in her plays and, as Lopez tells us, feels that specifying race will set up expectations by which audiences will less thoughtfully experience a work. Lopez makes an insightful, persuasive argument for reading a "racialized cultural identity" in *Fefu and Her Friends*; however, Fornes gives little clues by character descriptions or names that her characters belong to any one ethnic group.

Is a play written by a lesbian playwright without any lesbian content (or a play with lesbian content by a heterosexual) a lesbian play? As Jill Dolan admits, "definitions of 'lesbian playwright,' 'lesbian play,' or even 'lesbian' are complicated to attempt." (We have included **Martha Boesing** who, in the Adrienne Rich mode of definition, could be described as lesbian and whose seminal work in the 1970s and 1980s at the radical feminist theatre At the Foot of the Mountain in Minneapolis makes her plays of historical note for this reference.) In **Phyllis Nagy**'s more recent work, lesbian characters are, at times, peripheral or their sexuality is not the subject of the play. In *The Strip*, for example, the only lesbian encountered on this wildly imaginative odyssey across America is a secondary character whose sexuality is incidental to the exploration of the damaging effects of the pursuit of fame. *Baltimore Waltz*, one of lesbian playwright Paula Vogel's most familiar and most often performed plays, portrays the female character as a heterosexual dying from AIDS (couched as ATDS, Acquired Toilet-Seat Disease Syndrome) and having one last fling in Europe while her brother conscientiously searches for an ATDS serum.

Mahone cites **Anna Deavere Smith**'s best known works, the solo performances *Fires in the Mirror* and *Twilight: Los Angeles 1992*, which have black-and-white racial divisiveness at their cores, but present an array of characters from a wide ethnic spectrum. Class and gender as well as race are decisive factors in the characters Kia Corthron creates. Diana Son questions the need to write from her cultural viewpoint exclusively and as Chiori Miyagawa concludes in her essay, the new generation of Asian American playwrights are unlikely to satisfy "mainstream's appetite for the exotic." Thus, for a playwright to be classified as Latina, Asian American, African American, or lesbian, must her drama have characters who are racially delineated with sexual preference made explicit? Must multicultural theatre speak only of racial and sexual politics? Must it serve what Miyagawa believes is a demand for the exotic?

The largess of the major foundations toward a multicultural agenda have certainly helped to increase the number of diverse voices in the theatre. Have they also created a situation in which theatres competing for ever-diminishing amounts of money will commit to plays by nontraditional writers only if they demonstrate an ethnic or cultural identity? In her one act play *Pidgin Hole*, **Linda Faigao-Hall** satirizes a grant writer at a Filipino theatre company who is trying to devise a project that will receive funding. The grants person is appalled when the resident Filipina director wants to do a "straight" production of *Romeo and Juliet*. She tries to convince the group that a Hawaiian Juliet speaking Taglish, a combination of English, Spanish, and Tagalo (Filipino English), opposite a Romeo from Iowa is the most fundable. "You don't want to be too exotic," explains the grant writer, "you will want to remain accessible" in order to attract Caucasians as well as the "ethnics." By the end, the group of women comply leaving the Filipina playwright to ask: "Where did it go wrong? It was such a good idea . . . multiculturalism . . . cultural diversity."

Artists are more forward-thinking (and amusing) than administrators. The many multicultural collaborations of playwrights and directors point the way toward truly diverse artistic marriages. The example of Liz Diamond with **Suzan-Lori Parks** is well known; **June Jordan** credits Peter Sellars with "steady motivation and reward" as her director of *I was looking at the ceiling and then I saw the sky*; Anna Deavere Smith has worked with white directors Christopher Ashley and Emily Mann; Chiori Miyagawa has worked with Juliette Carrillo (Latina), Max Mayer (white, male), and Karin Coonrod (white, female) in the development of her autobiographical pieces about a Japanese American female's assimilation within American society. These and other models confirm that many playwrights welcome diverse collaborations.

Issues surrounding diversity are further confused by ethnic configurations that are more complicated than any categories are capable of representing. Several of the playwrights included here remind us how varied a multicultural-multiethnic menu can be: **Caridad Svich** lays claim to Cuban, Croatian, Argentine, and Spanish parentage; **Milcha Sanchez-Scott**, Balinese, Chinese, Dutch, Columbian, and Mexican; **Velina Hasu Houston**, black, Native American, and Japanese; Marlane Meyer, Polynesian, Native American, German, and Swedish; and **Sandra Rodgers**, Indian and Scottish. However, in order to promote and educate people about multicultural-multiethnic playwrights, "naming" is useful. It is a way of being counted. As Lopez explains, using the phrase "Latina drama" is helpful for practitioners and critics to "distinguish and characterize playwrights and their works." The danger is when categories become excuses to limit inclusion in specialized circumstances, such as festivals of ethnic plays. The plea of women playwrights to be recognized simply as playwrights is compounded by nontraditional writers who want to be recognized not as lesbian, Asian American, Latina, or black women playwrights but simply as writers who choose to write for the stage.

A further complication is that ethnic and lesbian theatres, while important in developing, cultivating, and building an audience for diverse playwrights, remain essentially ghettoized—artists writing for their own audiences in what Jill Dolan calls "site specific" venues. All too frequently the writers who work and hone their crafts in these alternative spaces never make the journey uptown to off-Broadway, much less Broadway, theatres. Maria Irene Fornes has done much of her work at the Theatre for a New City; **Split Britches** and **Holly Hughes** at WOW Cafe, La Mama, and P. S. 122; and numbers of others at HERE, One

Dream, Duo, or the Nuyorican Poets' Cafe, all removed from off-Broadway's greater visibility.

Recently, however, we have seen important exceptions: the Five Lesbian Brothers at New York Theatre Workshop; Paula Vogel at Circle Repertory; **Claire Chafee, Pearl Cleage, Cassandra Medley**, and **Kate Moira Ryan** at the Women's Project and Productions; **Cheryl West** at Manhattan Theatre Club; **Lynn Nottage** at Second Stage, **Lisa Loomer** at the Vineyard, and Suzan-Lori Parks at the Public Theatre. And many of these playwrights are well represented on the major regional stages. Theatre that has been clearly polarized is beginning to pollinate.

The alphabetic ordering which comprises the primary structure of this book is one way of saying that what brings these playwrights together is that they are women who work without a recognized theatrical tradition and who, because of the dominance of white males historically and contemporarily, still are underrepresented on the stage. An informal survey of the Theatre Communications Group theatres in 1995 revealed these figures: out of over 1,000 plays presented, 26 percent, or a little over 300, were written by women; of these plays, 60 (approximately 18 percent) were written by lesbians or women of color. These 60 plays, however, represent only 38 playwrights, or approximately 5 percent of the total number of playwrights. (These figures include children's and young adults' theatre.)

We all like to see ourselves reflected on stage. And we deserve to see our cultures and issues occupy a meaningful place in our contemporary mirrors—television, film, and the theatre. While television and film have begun to accommodate, often begrudgingly, the new demographic realities, the theatre is slower to make changes. Our hope is that this resource book will compliment the recent recognition that increased publication and productions at mainstream theatres have afforded women of color and lesbians. Clearly, the statistics tell us that our stages have a long way to go in equitably representing our new demographics. Still, the influence of strong feminist theoretical writing by women in theatre and their presence in our classrooms has provided a foundation from which we will continue to see change. There will be more anthologies and collections of diverse women's plays: a new audience is being educated in ways almost unimaginable 20 years ago when the plays we were reading in American drama classes and seeing on our stages did not speak directly to the lives of the audiences. The playwrights included in this volume challenge existing norms and accepted definitions of our drama of diversity.

June Jordan, poet, essayist, and playwright, who has written so cogently about race and gender for decades, reminds us: "Focusing on racial *or* class *or* gender attributes will yield only distorted and deeply inadequate images of ourselves. Traditional calls to 'unity' on the basis of only one of these factors—race or class or gender—will fail, finally, and again and again . . . because no single one of these components provides for a valid fathoming of the complete individual" (Jordan, June. *Technical Difficulties*. New York: Vintage, 1994, p. 163).

The Sista Masses (1970s–1990s): African American Women Playwrights

Sydné Mahone

I write as a sista witness/ a woman of african descent living in north america/ who came of age and came to artistic and political consciousness in the mid to late 1970s/ in the aftermath of the 1960s civil rights movement/ as a young adult(hood)/ looking out at the world/ the decade of the 1970s was an era that delivered promise of New Art from black women/ 1974/ these times delivered/ a bright comet crossed the cultural landscape/ **ntozake shange**, author of *for colored girls who have considered suicide/ when the rainbow is enuf*: a choreo-poem.

com.et—a heavenly body in the solar system, having a starlike nucleus with a luminous mass around it, and, usually, a long, luminous tail that points away from the sun: comets follow an elliptical or parabolic orbit around the sun

Before *for colored girls*, I would never have thought to punctuate the opening paragraph of a critical essay using a slash (solidus) in place of a period. I borrowed elements of the author's style to recollect the impact of **Ntozake Shange** on the written word from which her revolutionary choreopoem emerged. Influenced by poetic structure, two of many stylistical and syntactical reinven-tions of the dramatic text were the use of the slash mark in place of the period, the use of lower case letters to subvert the capitalization of words, and the attendant value judgments that afford some words and not others the status of proper nouns. In literature and in performance, Shange freed herself from West-ern convention and claimed the space of cultural sovereignty for African Amer-ican playwrights.

Ntozake Shange delivered on the promise of a liberated and liberating black female voice. Within the context of the African American female dramatic canon, this choreopoem was the theatrical event of the decade. It was developed in the early 1970s through workshops in the West Coast women's collectives in 1974. Woodie King, Jr. produced *for colored girls* at his New Federal Theatre in New York City, where it won the Obie Award in 1974. The show moved to Joseph Papp's Public Theatre en route to its Broadway opening at the Booth Theatre on May 17, 1976, where it ran for 747 performances.

Cultural history is shaped by the experience and documentation of events that galvanize (or perhaps illuminate) the masses of people, signifying a collective physical, psychological, or spiritual shift. In the religious context, Mass is a collective celebration or service, often expressed in part through music. A prominent civil rights veteran recently commented that the civil rights movement, typically considered a political mass movement, succeeded because it harnessed the spiritual energy of the black masses. If contemporary theatrical art bears any trace of its roots in African and Greek rituals, which were designed to honor or communicate with ancestral or other deities, perhaps the texts that create mass movements in the contemporary theatre are the secular liturgies of our times. From the 1970s to the 1990s, two major theatrical events have been created on Broadway by African American women: Ntozake Shange's choreopoem, *for colored girls* (1976), and **Anna Deavere Smith**'s *Twilight: Los Angeles* (1994).

A mass movement, however, does not occur in a vacuum. It is the culmination of a series of events that create a groundswell of thought and activity in small communities. The number of African American women playwrights has steadily increased over the past two decades. Their growing presence in the field reflects their significant contribution to the American theatre in both form and content.

In order to appreciate fully the progressive actions taken by women theatre artists during the 1970s, one must glance back on that revolutionary decade of the 1960s which spawned the "*colored girls* phenomenon," that unique convocation—the collective assertion and voicing of "the black women's community."

During the 1960s, the ideals of freedom, equality, peace, and justice were translated through the civil rights movement into the particularly empowering ideas of black pride, black beauty, and black power. The use of psychedelic drugs and sexual freedom was also a part of the social revolution of the 1960s. However, it was the tactics and strategies of nonviolence—the marches, sit-ins, and songs of the civil rights movement—that created the model for the peace and women's movements to emerge formally.

Similarly, the dramatic art of Ntozake Shange created a bridge from the black agenda to the women's agenda. Among the many things that *colored girls* reflected, it symbolized a collective mind change for many black women—a leap in consciousness, a discovery of voice. It became clear that women's dramatic texts could be different from men's texts, and it also became evident that there was a tremendous diversity within the chorus of black women dramatists. A lot of sistas did not like the play; however, whether one liked it or not, one had to see it and take a stand on it.

In addition to mainstream audience support, *for colored girls* was powerfully supported by both the masses of black women and the masses of feminists. Heretofore, these groups were not identified as interest or consumer groups, but given the economic success of the work, they would never again be dismissed by theatre producers and marketers.

But turn to the text. The final beat of the choreopoem rang triumphant and transcendent in all its gorgeous piety, its sounding of a private battle cry—a new anthem; a victory prayer song, a moan, and a shout; a testimony:

> I found god
> in myself/and I loved her
> fiercely

Ensconced in the lyric was the pure holiness of women loving women—a dangerous concept for a patriarchal society dependent upon the control of women. Within the thought was the deed: we heal when we let ourselves love each other. We overcome the sickness. We take care of ourselves. We tell the truth. It heals us. It frees us. For me, *for colored girls* did that.

Ntozake Shange's voice shook up the theatre world, not only because she disrupted the syntax with candid and complex poetry, but perhaps most profoundly because she changed the face of heroism. Unlike Alice Childress, Lorraine Hansberry, and Adrienne Kennedy, her dramatic foremothers, Shange made herself—a black woman—the subject of the drama. Consequently, the intellectual, erotic, and spiritual dimensions of black women were rescued from stereotype, represented for the first time in the matrix of character and identity. The self-defined, redefined renderings of character continue to emerge with variety in the texts of African American women playwrights.

Like Lorraine, who was twenty-eight years old when she arrived on Broadway, Ntozake was twenty-eight when she arrived, bringing the voice of youth. Like Lorraine, Ntozake is a world literature/world art scholar and intellectual. We see in both women the gift of political analysis and the ability to articulate evolved thought on political events of the day, extending their artistic visions to the interpretation of social and political realities. Both women were children of upper middle-class families, and both were influenced by famous black leaders who were family friends.

Incorporating poetry and dance, the piece was also distinguished by its beauty. The spectacle of seven beautiful black women on a stage, furnished only with a large flower suspended upstage center, unleashed a new aspect of performance from the cage of Western convention. This newly designed space allowed black women to take center stage. The elements of Western theatre—character, plot, action, time, and place—were thrown off for a more fluid, poetic, ritualistic experience of theatre. In support of the poetry, this style required live music and live dance.

The sista masses in the theatre began with **J. e. Franklin**'s *Black Girl*, which was produced by Woodie King, Jr., at his New Federal Theatre in 1971 (231 performances). Then, in 1972, came Alice Childress's *Wedding Band* and Vinnette Carroll and Micki Grant's Broadway musical hit, *Don't Bother Me, I Can't Cope*, which began at the Urban Arts Corp (1,032 performances). This was followed, in 1976 (the same year as *colored girls*), by Judi Ann Mason's comedy, *Livin' Fat* (61 performances), which was produced by the Negro Ensemble Company, and Carroll and Grant's *Your Arm's Too Short to Box With God*. Neither before nor since that collaboration have black women had such a foothold in that elite class of commercial theater. Black musicals were popular, rising in parallel with blaxploitation films. In 1977 **Aishah Rahman**'s *Unfinished Women Cry in No Man's Land While a Bird Dies in a Gilded Cage* was produced by Joseph Papp at the New York's Public Theatre.

Throughout the 1970s, black artists continued the work of the agendas set by Martin Luther King, Jr., and Malcolm X—they integrated the professions and established black institutions. Both activities enabled black artists to exert greater influence over the production of black theatre. Inspired by the success of the New York theatres that began during the 1960s, NEC and New Federal Theatre, regional black theatres were founded: Crossroads in New Brunswick, New Jersey, in 1978; Penumbra in Minneapolis, Minnesota, in 1976; St. Louis Black Rep in 1976; Jomandi in Atlanta, Georgia, in 1979; and San Francisco's Lorraine Hansberry Theatre in 1980.

The impact of *for colored girls* on performance is also noteworthy. Because it liberated dramatic form, solo performance lured many artists of all cultures to this aesthetic frontier. During the 1980s, stand-up comedy grew in popularity and performance art flourished on the cabaret circuits in all the major cities. Whoopi Goldberg, who emerged from this scene, made a Broadway debut that ultimately led to Hollywood.

Although the 1970s commenced as a decade of promise, by the end of the decade, the backlash against civil rights and women's rights had begun. Nevertheless, Ntozake Shange had opened the door wide for black women playwrights to enter professional theatre. And come they did along with their audiences.

The writers who entered the professional theatre during the 1980s collectively brought stylistic diversity to the exploration of the black women's point of view as translated through drama. Some chose Western convention as a base on which to improvise with form. However, they were not confined to writing about women's experiences. They took the liberty of writing about whatever they chose.

The list of writers who reigned during the 1980s or enjoyed multiple productions includes **P. J. Gibson**, more from J. e. Franklin, **Cheryl L. West**, **Pearl Cleage**, **Endesha Ida Mae Holland**, **Karen Jones-Meadows**, and **Cassandra Medley**. Performance artists, including Laurie Carlos, **Robbie McCauley**, Judith Jackson, and Danitra Vance, enjoyed a cult following among the alternative theatre artists and audiences. Some crossed over to the mainstream, as did Danitra Vance, who was the first sista to join the ensemble of television's innovative comedy show, "Saturday Night Live."

During the 1980s, the public debate on gender had reached a highly engaged level of expression. Sexuality became the obsession of the media which simultaneously broadcast the war on women while domestic violence rates soared. On the flip side of the rising violence and deteriorating economy of the 1980s stood Oprah Winfrey, leading daytime talk show host turned producer, with her television adaptation of *The Women of Brewster Place*, based on Gloria Naylor's most successful novel of the same title. In the 1990s, Oprah Winfrey was one of the principal producers of the off-Broadway revival and touring production of *From the Mississippi Delta*, by Endesah Ida Mae Holland, the most produced black play of the 1994 season.

Black playwriting in the 1980s was dominated by two brothas: August Wilson and George C. Wolfe. In the 1990s, they shared the spotlight with Anna Deavere Smith and **Suzan-Lori Parks**. While Wolfe and Wilson maintain their presence on Broadway, African American women playwrights remain outsiders. After Whoopi Goldberg's launch to stardom in the 1980s, Anna Deavere Smith is the only African American woman playwright to visit Broadway in the 1990s with the brief run of her one-woman show, *Twilight: Los Angeles*, in 1994.

In the same way that Ntozake Shange's work encouraged the inclusion of women writers in the theatre and brought perspective to the current debates on racism and sexism in the 1970s and 1980s, Anna Deavere Smith brought new perspective to the same issues within the context of the distinctly 1990s pursuit of true multiculturalism in America. In her groundbreaking, one-woman show, supported by the use of slides, film footage, and simple but multiple sets and costumes, she focused on a major event, the Los Angeles uprising that followed the Rodney King verdict, to bring the verbatim words of people from different walks of life into one dramatic event. She crossed the boundaries of race, culture, gender, and class to present the poetics of personal testimony on the stage.

Suzan-Lori Parks has a strong but elite following fostered largely by her productions of the *America Play* and *Venus*, coproduced by Yale University Theatre and the New York Shakespeare Festival's Public Theatre. (The Public Theatre is the producing common denominator in the works of the three black women playwrights who have had a major impact on the American theatre.) Parks has also written the screenplay for *Girl 6*, the first film produced by Spike Lee that was written by someone other than himself.

Other writers who are gaining momentum in the 1990s are **Kia Corthron**, **Lynn Nottage**, Karen Jones-Meadows, Kathleen McGhee-Anderson, and **Marian X**.

The encouraging reality is that there are so many sista playwrights out there who may be called upon to deliver the next good work, who stand ready to galvanize the next sista mass motion in theatre, to once again reinvent the theatre as a site of transformation, healing, and regeneration.

Brave, Bold, and Poetic: The New Generation of Asian American Women Playwrights

Chiori Miyagawa

Taking risks with their language, form, and message, Asian American women playwrights are breaking down the walls of small living rooms and kitchens that accommodated many of the Asian American plays of the previous generation. Their characters are not culturally displaced and defeated women anymore but are culturally displaced and agitated warrior women. Sometimes they are not even Asian. Unlike **Wakako Yamauchi**'s beautiful classic, *And the Soul Shall Dance* (1977), which focuses on the intricate emotions deeply rooted in the specific Japanese American and Japanese sentiments, playwrights today do not simply experience their culture internally or display it for the audience but demand the world to put it in context. And their "culture" goes beyond what is traditionally expected; it is no longer simply about some ancient Chinese folktale told by a grandmother or about a rude white customer at a laundromat. Yes, it is often still about identity or oppression, but the new generation is looking at a larger picture. Who is out there? To whom are we talking? How would they understand our "language"? How do we fit into or disturb our surroundings? How do we understand ourselves? What truly makes us Asian *American*? Today the questions are more complex, and the search is perhaps more dangerous because our plays take away the comfort of stereotypes from the audience.

SINGULAR VOICES

Four women on this front line are **Eugenie Chan**, **Naomi Iizuka**, **Sandra Rodgers**, and **Diana Son**: young women who range in age from their late twenties to mid-thirties, with Chinese, Japanese, Indian, and Korean backgrounds, respectively. Though their personal missions as playwrights differ from one another, they share a common ground: these women are not interested in satisfying the audience's appetite for exotica; they have assumed the big job of finally making Asian Americans human and real in American theater. In the fall of 1995, I conducted telephone interviews with each playwright and asked questions about their artistic influences and intentions.

Sandra Rodgers grew up in England and started writing plays in Berkeley, California. Her passion for the theater began at a boarding school where she encountered a teacher who left her with a lifelong love for Shakespeare's *King Lear*. John Steinbeck's love for America first attracted Sandra to the United States, and she finds her inspiration for writing in a wide range of artists from Balzac to Elvis Costello. Sandra believes that theater should make you uncomfortable. "Unless it really hurts, unless I cry, I know it's not the truth," she says. Sandra's plays have a political tone, although she considers herself social-political, because she does not want to "take the humanities away and lose the important connection to the community with politics alone."

In her *Owning Half the Dog*, the reality of Neela, an Asian woman, is on a balancing bar between her family and her lover Samuel. Their relationship is a strange dance of trying to make sense of the positions, physical and emotional. Neela's family is tangled up in the wool that the mother is endlessly knitting. Neela has succeeded in getting away from that cobweb, but she is still torn between her lover and her family. Sandra Rodgers feels that in contemporary society we all come from somewhere else. Today our identity has less to do with our birth place, the town we grew up in, or our family. In this play she explores what a new American is—she is both who she is now and where she came from; she embraces the lover and the family. The title comes from Sandra's belief that rejecting part of who you are is like owning half a dog. You can have a richer life by admitting all that you are. In *Ram Ram*, Sandra examines the same issue in a different circumstance. The play revolves around a relationship between two women, Lourdes Mary, an East Indian, and Kay, an American. Lourdes Mary's mysterious past is revealed through ghostly visitations by a man from her political life in India. Inspired by Kay's selfishness to make her own decisions rather than to accept the ones made generations before, Lourdes Mary is transformed into a new person, a union of Eastern and Western strengths.

Eugenie Chan also investigates all aspects that personally make her Asian American. For her, writing plays is a way to sort out the different threads of being a fifth-generation Chinese American, a descendant of the Old Country people, and a product of the contemporary West where Asians and Latinos have lived side by side for many years. "I like to mine the breadth of races, cultural identities, dreams, and aesthetics that shape my real and mythological American landscape," she says. Eugenie, who lives in San Francisco, says that the most important influence on her has been Maxine Hong Kingston's novel, *Woman Warrior*, which was also an inspiration to David Henry Hwang. Some years later, when Eugenie saw a production of David's *FOB*, she thought, "I could do it, too—that is write and be free and be Chinese American, too."

Unlike Sandra, comedy is Eugenie's forte. Her autobiographical stories are set against surreal landscapes. *Rancho Grande* is about a Chinese American girl's coming of age. The main character, Mamie, who is stuck in a Hollywood-like dream-desert land, grows up in a family who lives the "cowboy" life of men going off and women staying home in pretty red dresses and cooking. Mamie's sexual awakening occurs with her discovery of the gender rules. Eugenie's characters are "odd balls in the native land," she says. She ventures into the loneliness and alienation of the American cultural landscape with her characters. Writing is her cultural vote for a personal truth, against the stereotypes, laundromats, living rooms, and railroads. In *Emil, A Chinese Play,* Eugenie brings together a mother and a daughter in a highly structured and repressed world. Emil, a young South American man, is thrown into the mix, and this forms a strange love triangle. Eugenie says, "They are each stuck in their own worlds and idiosyncrasies of identity and sexuality, yearning to break free."

Naomi Iizuka is also a West Coast playwright whose influences include not only eclectic artists such as Gertrude Stein, Emily Dickinson, Sam Shepard, and Cindy Sherman, but also certain geographies such as California and Tokyo. She believes education about expectation is important. What she means by expectation is not just cultural, but is also about form, language, time, and space. "Time and geography concern me," she says about her pursuit to understand the future in relationship to the past and present. Out of the four writers, Naomi's work is the riskiest because she abandons all attachment to naturalism. She does not necessarily think that the language should mean what it means. It is more important to find a voice of expression. "How do you find the language for the dead? How do you live with ghosts?" Naomi asks herself. Realistic storytelling is distorted, she believes, because human experiences are complex, mysterious, and nonlinear.

Coxinga, her adaptation of Chikamatsu's *The Battles of Coxinga,* takes place on a large canvas and combines different political themes on the environment, consumerism, nuclear horror, and others. This epic happens in multiple locations, mainly Japan and China. Naomi, like Eugenie and Sandra, is interested in the cultural displacement that occurs in this society. "Racial identity colors my work," she says. Her main characters are "almost like a black hole, their nationality and parentage uncertain." In *Carthage,* Naomi explores the female identity through two characters called SHE and Patricia V. There is also a chorus of Arab women, inspired by the women terrorists of Palestine: conservative, religious, circumscribed, and veiled, yet at the front line of the battle. "The Arab women are as 'other' as women can get for us," she says, hoping to find a language for their paradox. She likes to build a landscape of sound. "Language is not only meaning, but sound," she says, much like music.

The rhythm of language is also important to Diana Son, the most realistic and ethnically unspecific playwright of the four. "If the rhythm is right, the language choice, content, and meaning are right, and I trust that things are in sync," says Diana. The first professional theater production Diana saw was

Joseph Papp's *Hamlet* in 1983 with Diane Venora as Hamlet. She saw herself in Diane Venora's portrayal of Hamlet, played as a man but with her presence as a woman, creating a perfect androgyny. Her second profound theater experience occured while she was a student at New York University: Anne Bogart's direction of *South Pacific,* which was a production about a production of *South Pacific* performed by actors who are playing patients in a Vietnam veterans' hospital. She continues to be excited and challenged by Anne's work twelve years later.

Stealing Fire, her adaptation of the myth of Philomela, is a tapestry of tightly woven moments of outrageous comedy and heartbreaking tragedy. Disappointed in localized and small contemporary sensibilities, she chose a classic theme. "Americans don't believe in myth and spirituality," Diana says. "I struggle to believe in something." She found her own voice in her play *Boy.* How much freedom do we really have in this society? Diana examines this question by challenging gender rules. The character Boy, who is really a girl, is raised by her parents as a boy. She grows up with contrasting impulses that are organic and socialized. "This story can take place in every culture, not just Asian," stresses Diana. "I'm hesitant to write from just my cultural point of view. When I go to the theater, I'm often excluded socially and culturally." The last thing she wants to do is alienate the audience; theater should look like the world. She also feels a responsibility to provide opportunities for artists of color. "Community for me is individuals bound by a common goal." Diana is uncomfortable in any situation that is one demographic.

THE WARRIOR PATH

It is not easy to place yourself in the unfamiliar universe and leave the comfort of the familiar. By going beyond what is traditionally expected of Asian American playwriting, these four playwrights risk discomfort from producers and audiences. None of these playwrights writes a family drama which comes to a climax at a dinner table where a woman, wearing a kimono, commits suicide. They do not satisfy the mainstream's appetite for the exotic. They write about human beings, not exclusively Asians, risking accusations of self-hatred. They divert from the naturalistic style and dialogue that have characterized the melodramatic structure of traditional Asian American plays. I believe that, by being exposed to a spectrum of stimulation and by exposing themselves to the possibilities of rejection and acknowledgment, these playwrights are enriching the new "American" culture with plays that are explosive, embracing, hard edged, multicultural, multidimensional, real, surreal, funny, and heartbreaking all at the same time. These are four playwrights, who will inspire yet another generation of playwrights because they are not afraid to claim who they are; are not only women playwrights, but also playwrights; not only Asian Americans, but also Americans. We will move forward.

Beyond the Festival Latino: (Re)Defining Latina Drama for the Mainstage

Tiffany Ana Lopez

What is Latina drama? Are Latina dramatists only those who explicitly identify themselves as Latina? Do all Latina dramatists have Spanish surnames? Is Latina drama thematically limited to political issues, such as bilingual education, barrio violence, or class struggle? Must actors have clearly recognizable "Latin" features and a "z" in their last names in order to communicate to an audience that a play is a Latina dramatic work? Ultimately, how—and more important, why—use the category "Latina"?

A recent conversation I had with the playwright **Migdalia Cruz** illustrates a common scenario for Latina dramatists and the need to open up existing categories. Cruz had submitted one of her works to a literary director only to have it returned with the comment that the theater had already made its selections for its Latino theater festival. Cruz had not specified that she was a Latina dramatist. Rather, the "z" in her last name prompted a series of assumptions on the literary director's part about the category "Latina." The director assumed that Cruz had submitted her work for the festival; furthermore, she or he assumed that Cruz's work could be read *only* within that particular context. Why was Cruz's work not also (or better yet, first) considered for the main stage during the regular season?

The term "Latina drama" is useful inasmuch as it helps practitioners, critics, and writers distinguish and characterize playwrights and their works. However, the term is often used to limit readings of Latina dramatic works and, consequently, production possibilities. While many Latina/o-authored plays will be considered for the Festival Latino, few will be given staged readings, and even fewer main stage productions. In this era of scarce funding for the arts, many theaters fear that subscribers will not support Latina/o drama. Such fears stem from misperceptions about who Latinos are and what, exactly, constitutes Latina/o drama. Historically, popular culture has portrayed Latinas as domestic servants, beautiful señoritas, Latin spitfires, and self-sacrificing madres. Latina actresses are seldom allowed to perform beyond these roles. Many readers assume that Latina/o plays are limited to race and social protest issues. Most often, the dominant culture employs the term ''Latino'' as a convenient catchall in reference to anyone seemingly linked to a Spanish-speaking culture.

''Latina'' and ''Latino'' are, however, not terms of ethnicity, but rather of political and cultural affiliation. The term ''Latino,'' which evolved from 1960s-based identity politics, is used to indicate alliances among those cultural groups—predominantly Chicanos, Puerto Ricans, and Cubans—who find themselves sharing common political, as well as cultural, concerns. Feminists from these various and intersecting groups established the term ''Latina'' to distinguish the political interests of women that more often than not conflict with the patriarchal politics that characterize cultural nationalism. Not all Chicanos, Puerto Ricans, or Cubans consider themselves Latinos, and certainly the term Latina/o is not limited solely to these groups. In my work, I use the term in reference to a very specific group of writers either who have chosen explicitly to identify themselves as Latina or whose works have directly impacted the direction of the contemporary Latina dramatic movement.

HISTORICAL AND CULTURAL OVERVIEW: WRITERS, THEATERS, AND PERFORMANCE

Theater has become an important artistic arena for Latinas working through the issues of women's identity and cultural development, particularly in regard to their representation of two marginalized groups in American society—women and people of color.

Crucial to the development of a specifically Latina theatrical space is **Maria Irene Fornes**, the author of more than two dozen works for the stage. Born in Havana in 1930, she emigrated to New York in 1945. Her first play, *Tango Palace*, was produced in 1963; shortly after, she was directing all of her own work. Fornes is one of a handful of Latina dramatists whose plays have been collected and published (*Promenade and Other Plays* and *Maria Irene Fornes: Plays*, both published by PAJ Publications). Among her most critically recognized plays are *Promenade* (1965), *Fefu and Her Friends* (1977), *The Danube* (1982), *Mud* (1983), and *Sarita* (1984). *Fefu and Her Friends*, one of Fornes's most produced plays, concerns eight women who reunite for a weekend's retreat and unveil their hopes, regrets, and yearnings.

In addition to her prominence as a playwright and director, Fornes has been most instrumental as a teacher and mentor of a generation of Latina dramatists at INTAR (International Arts Relations, Inc.) in New York City. Fornes began the Hispanic Playwrights' Lab during the early 1980s in hopes of fostering new voices that would revitalize the American theater. Latina dramatists who worked under her direction at the lab include **Lynne Alvarez**, Migdalia Cruz, Lorraine

Llamas, **Cherríe Moraga**, **Dolores Prida**, **Milcha Sanchez-Scott**, Ana Maria Simo, and **Caridad Svich**, among others.

Other important Latina voices of this generation include **Denise Chávez**, **Josefina López**, **Edit Villarreal**, **Evelina Fernandez**, Diana Sáenz, and Laura Esparza. All of these playwrights have contributed to a body of work that deals with culturally specific issues and the empowerment of women. Many recurring central themes include political oppression (Sáenz, Esparza, Sanchez-Scott), the relationships women have to traditional customs so often rooted in patriarchy (Moraga, Cruz, López, Prida), the proscription of familial and cultural roles that constrict one's sense of self (Fernandez, Svich, Simo), and the need to create a woman-centered spirituality (Villarreal, Chávez).

Cherríe Moraga's work has been groundbreaking in her exploration of lesbianism, the effect of male influences on women's relationships, and the politics of the working class. Her work has premiered at the Theatre Rhinoceros, the Eureka Theatre, and BRAVA! for Women in the Arts, where she is playwright in residence and conducts writing workshops for Latina and Native American women and teaches writing for performance to gay and lesbian youth. *Shadow of a Man* won the Fund for New American Plays Award in 1990. Her first play, *Giving Up the Ghost* (1986), has been critically acclaimed for its portrayal of Chicana lesbians. In this work, Moraga literalizes the symbolic ways in which Woman is constructed as the boundary of culture and thus challenges the myths of patriarchy that promise that father figures will protect female members. *Heroes and Saints* (1992) explores the effects of pesticides, from rare cancers to birth defects, on Chicana women farm laborers. *Heroes and Saints* has received numerous awards for best original script, including the Will Glickman Prize, the Drama-logue and Critic Circles awards, and the Pen West Award. In 1994 West End Press published a collection of Moraga's work, *Heroes and Saints and Other Plays*.

Caridad Svich's plays have been performed in the United States and Europe, including the Cincinnati Playhouse, Latino Chicago, INTAR, and the Women's Project of New York. Her works include *Brazo Gitano*, *Any Place but Here* (published in Theatre Communication Group's Plays in Process Series) and *Scar*. *Gleaning/Rebusa* (1992) explores the relationship of two Cuban American women whose thoughts and superstitions reflect the inheritance of their mothers' myths. *Alchemy of Desire/Dead-Man's Blues* presents a poetic telling of a woman's loss of her husband on a battlefield in an unnamed foreign land. In her solo piece, *Scar*, which may be performed by a man or a woman, a character embarks on a quest to redefine the American landscape in an end-of-the-millennium journey.

Milcha Sanchez-Scott's plays consistently address feminist issues. *Latina* (1980, produced by the New Works Division of Artists in Prison and Other Places), was critically acclaimed for its demonstration of differences as well as similarities among women from different parts of Latin America. *The Cuban Swimmer* (1984) deals with a woman who is striving to succeed in swimming from Long Beach to Santa Catalina Island. *Dog Lady* (1984) features a female runner who has been given a potion by a *curandera* (spiritual healer) that makes her run faster than any other woman in the race. The catch, however, is that she must run on all fours. Sanchez-Scott's most produced work, *Roosters* (1986), explores the dynamics of a Chicano family when the father returns home from prison to find his two children in the midst of coming-of-age crises.

Many Latina dramatists address issues of family life with particularly nuanced attention to the effects of patriarchal authority on the development of female family members. *Going to New England* (1991), by Cuban-born Ana Maria Simo, charts the accelerating tensions in a Puerto Rican family caused by each individual's history of oppression. Evelina Fernandez's *How Else Am I Supposed to Know I'm Still Alive* (1989) deals with the friendship of two women, one whose child has grown, the other who is thrown into a crisis when she believes she is pregnant in her middle age. In 1989 the play won the Nuevo L. A. Playwriting contest and was adapted into a screenplay and filmed for the American Film Institute and Universal's Hispanic Film Project. Fernandez is a founding member of the Latino Theater Lab where she cowrote *August 29* with other lab members. Josefina López, one of the youngest and most important voices in this generation of playwrights, wrote her first play at the age of seventeen. Her work includes *If My Mother Knew*, *Real Women Have Curves*, *Food for the Dead*, and *Simply María or the American Dream* (1988), which deals with the myths of the American Dream and the development of a Mexican woman in the United States.

Dolores Prida, one of the most important figures in Latina drama, consistently employs a comedic approach to the issues of transculturation, community politics, and feminism. Her works have recently been collected in a volume published by Arte Publico Press, *Beautiful Señoritas & Other Plays*. Her first play, *Beautiful Señoritas*, uses music to present a feminist satire of beauty pageants. In *Pantallas*, Prida explores the notion of soap opera literacy in the Latino community. *Botánica* focuses on a young Latina about to receive her degree in business from an ivy league college and the painful decisions she must make between her desire to work in corporate America and her family's wish that she return and run her mother's botánica (a small community-based store that specializes in spiritual objects). *Coser y Cantar* is one of Prida's most produced plays. The two characters are She, who speaks English and represents American assimilationist politics in the extreme, and Ella, who speaks Spanish and clings to traditional cultural objects and values. This work provides a powerful illustration of the struggle to incorporate both sides of self in claiming a U.S.–Latina identity.

Migdalia Cruz's *Rushing Waters* (1992) is a community-centered project for the Cornerstone Theater Company whose goal is to work in collaboration with ethnically diverse communities across the United States. The play addresses the community of Pacoima, a predominantly African-American and Latino community in Los Angeles, and their shared history, which includes colonization, drug wars, the L. A. riots, and the emerging multicultural family amidst a changing California population. There are forty-six members in her cast, the majority of whom are members of the community. By writing local concerns into the script and rehearsing local actors into the roles, Cornerstone and Cruz work to involve people of all backgrounds in the creative process necessary to build a new, inclusive American theater. Cruz has written more than twenty plays and musicals, including *Miriam's Flowers, Telling Tales, Lucy Loves Me, The Have-Little, Fur*, and *Cigarettes and Moby Dick.* Cruz's work has been produced in London, Montreal, New York, and other cities in the United States. In 1995 the Latino Chicago Theater produced a season of her work. *Latins in La-La Land* appeared in the 1994 Bay Area Playwrights' Festival and in the 1995 New Works Festival at the Public Theater.

Performance art plays an important role in Latina drama because it provides a means by which artists can act out history in an autobiographical format, as exemplified by *L. A. REAL.* This one-woman show by Theresa Chavez and Rose Portillo (in collaboration with About Productions of Los Angeles) explores the Mestizo/Mexican (mixed Indian and Spanish) history of Los Angeles during the period from 1774 to 1900 and how this history is remembered. The history is retold through Portillo, a Mestiza who warns, "Don't reinvent me on your salsa bottles, your wine labels, your tract home logos." Alina Troyano, in New York City, is a Cuban comic voice whose character and stage persona, **Carmelita Tropicana**, tells the story of her emigration from Cuba to become one of the famous dancing girls of Miami's Club Tropicana, which provides a cheeky look at stereotypes associated with Latina woman. *Milk of Amnesia/Leche de Amnesia* explores the central role memory plays in the lives of Cuban Americans. Troyano developed her Carmelita Tropicana persona at the WOW Cafe. Her early performance pieces were performed at P. S. 122, La Mama, and other alternative theater spaces in New York City. *The Boiler Time Machine*, a musical commissioned through INTAR's Musical Theater Workshop, with music by Fernando Rivas, had a staged reading in 1986 and was later adapted for solo performance. Troyano regularly collaborates with her sister and filmmaker Ela Troyano. The two wrote the screenplay for Ela's film *Carmelita Tropicana: Your Kunst Is Your Waffen* (1993), which has been widely shown in the United States and Europe and has received numerous awards.

Los Angeles–based Rose Sanchez and Ofelia Fox use theater to promote social awareness and have written extensively in both English and Spanish for radio, television, and the theater. They combine comedy with serious themes, particularly those that affect women and Latinos. In their plays, they bring to the surface homosexuality and AIDS among Latinos, as well as the difficulties encountered by immigrants and their expectations and fears. Marga Gomez and **Monica Palacios** use comedy to discuss cultural issues, particularly those related to sexuality. Palacios performs comedy and develops scripts that promote positive images of people of color, women, and gays and lesbians. She is one of the founding members of Teatro Viva in Los Angeles, a performance-based group that uses theater to raise awareness in the Latino community about AIDS-related issues. Gomez's *Memory Tricks* has been workshopped at numerous performance spaces, including the Solo Mio Festival and Josie's Cabaret in San Francisco, and subsequently seen at the Public Theater in New York City. *Marga Gomez Is Pretty, Witty, and Gay* has been produced at numerous venues including P. S. 122, the Whitney Museum's Biennial Performance Series, Highways Performance Space in Santa Monica, California, and the Edinburgh Fringe Festival.

READING ISSUES OF CULTURAL IDENTITY IN THE WORKS OF MARIA IRENE FORNES

Almost without exception, each of the Latina dramatists discussed above at some point in her career worked under the mentorship of Maria Irene Fornes. Her workshops at the Hispanic Playwright's Lab fostered the development of a new generation of Latina dramatists. Interestingly, Fornes, a Cuban-born playwright, has never made reference to her ethnicity as significant to the reading of her work. She is most widely and critically discussed as one of the foremost voices in feminist avant-garde theater in the United States. She is the first Latina dramatist to have received national recognition for her work.

Throughout her career, Fornes has always distanced herself from those questions that have been understood as defining identity affiliation. For example, when David Savran suggested her position as a role model, she responded, "I don't believe in role models because I don't believe in that expression" (Savran, 51–69). Another interviewer asked if she found "a tension between being feminine and being a feminist"; Fornes replied, "I never thought that I should not do certain work because I'm a woman nor did I think I should do certain work because I'm a woman" (Cummings, 51–56). When asked to comment on the woman's voice in U.S. drama, Fornes described how such preconceived notions of identity limit the readings of her work:

Often, there are misunderstandings about my work because it is expected that as a woman I must be putting women in traditional or untraditional roles. . . . When contradictions occur, the critics never question their initial premise. Instead, they see it as a fault in the play.

The same thing happens if you have a non-white character or actor in a play. Immediately people assume the play is dealing with racial questions. One can almost hear people asking, "If you want to deal with a person, why don't you put a 'person' on stage?" ("Creative Danger." *American Theater*, September 1985, 13–15)

The prevailing assumption is that because Fornes is a woman, her writing on female characters is always for the purpose of advancing feminist politics. Critics' assumptions—whether in regard to gender, class, or race—stem from their imposition of categories on Fornes's work rather than from reading how identities function for her *or* function in the context of her plays. Significantly, they are categories which Fornes prefers to complicate.

Though Fornes acknowledges shared characteristics among a culturally identified group of writers, she resists the use of categories (such as feminist, lesbian, woman of color) because in her words, "Just as you go to McDonald's and expect a certain kind of meal, you come to expect a certain kind of writing from a chosen category of writers." Fornes does find it important to talk about differences because it is important to be able to define them; however, she finds language limiting when differences are used to establish rigid categories and expectations that imprison the writer and the reader. For example, Fornes is puzzled about why people do not read her work in a Hispanic context because she sees evidence of common concerns shared with other writers of the culture, primarily in regard to the use of Spanish, the influence of Catholicism, the employment of particular aesthetic images, and a focus on what she perceives as shared cultural definitions concerning morality.

The issue of identity in Fornes's own work, as critics have imposed it on their readings to date, does not correspond at all to the complicated ways in which Fornes has dealt with the issue of cultural identity. Uniformly, mainstream theater scholars read Fornes's work as exemplary in its feminist presentation of the female body as a critique of patriarchal power structures. For Bonnie Marranca, the female body in her work functions as a specifically female body of knowledge. Gayle Austin applauds Fornes's use of the madwoman image to spotlight women as active subjects; similarly, Stephanie K. Arnold praises Fornes's intimacy among women in her texts. Additionally, critics, too numerous to cite, applaud her plays as feminist theater because of their focus on female characters and "the transformation of the personal."

Each of these critics defines female identity in Fornes's work as positioned only along an inclusionary/exclusionary axis of gender. Significantly, critics rarely consider racialized or other cultural experiences as integral to the identity formation of women or as part of their various relationships to power. Though critics will cite the fact that Fornes was born in Cuba, this is used to inform a reading of her work in very essentialist ways. For example, M. Elizabeth Osborn included Fornes in her anthology *On New Ground: Contemporary Hispanic Playwrights*. Yet, Osborn did not include a context for the reader as to what it is about Fornes's work that is culturally "Hispanic," or what issues permeate her work and clarify her writing as belonging to a culturally specific arts community. The problem I see with this is that if no efforts are made to define Latina drama historically in terms of its various contexts, issues, and movements, then the mention of race/culture alone appears to be all that is needed to understand writers as Latina playwrights. Furthermore, it ghettoizes the literature and does not open up the work to a clearly comparative notion of identity among the dramatists in a way that expands conceptualization of identity and difference, not to mention aesthetics, language, form, and technique.

Fefu and Her Friends

Fefu and Her Friends focuses on eight women who come together on a 1935 spring afternoon in New England to discuss plans for a fund-raiser vaguely described as having something to do with education. The scenes in the play focus on the movements of the friends through the various spaces in Fefu's home; tensions around Julia, who is in a wheelchair and recovering from a hunting accident; and the group's plans for their fund-raiser, which is the reason for their coming together.

One typically would not think that race is a part of *Fefu and Her Friends* because Fornes does not explicitly describe any of the characters racially. However, I want to posit that the play does flesh out social tensions about the need to render difference as visibly readable, specifically through skin color. Although Fornes does not say so in her character descriptions, the text of the play makes it clear that two of the characters are lovers. There is also a long monologue in which one of the characters expresses how she often felt separated from her friends because of the issues of class difference. The question I want to turn to now is, where do readings of race fit into this play?

Shortly after Cindy introduces the story about Julia's hunting accident, the women gather together in Fefu's living room to plan the order in which they will speak at the fund-raiser. Emma begins by suggesting, "We should do rehearsal in costume. What color should each wear? It matters. Do you know what you're wearing?" The women offer suggestions to one another about the colors they think are best suited for one another and conclude that "we'll speak in order of color." It is then judged that "the treasurer should wear green" and that Julia should wear "Purpurra." When it is suggested that the color for Fefu is "all the gold in Persia," Fefu asserts, "There is no gold in Persia." Emma, who has just returned from a trip to Peru, corrects, "In Peru. I brought my costume. I'll put it on later." Fefu questions, "You're not in costume?" Emma replies, "No. This is just a dress. My costume is . . . dramatic. I won't tell you any more about it. You'll see it." She says, "I had no idea we were going to do theater." This verbal play about color ends on Emma's note that "Life is theater. Theater is life. If we're showing what life is, can be, we must do theater" (Part 1).

Throughout the scene, no one names her own color preference; the judgment about color comes from someone else's association of color with profession and personality. Color is read along rigid and stereotypical categories: the treasurer shall wear green; gold is associated with an exoticized third-world country from which a privileged first-world woman has just returned from vacation. The focus on color as a costume calls attention to the artificial use of color as the basis for organization and underlines its reality in group practice.

This scene raises some interesting questions about identity and the use of fixed categories. How can each of the women play this game of naming? How is the audience then able to join in on the fun? Each already knows how to make the connection between color and identity; she has to or she would not be able to participate. Furthermore, what makes this scene work in the play, either in terms of the reading I am offering or in terms of it being read "lightly" (as a playful verbal exchange) is that the audience, too, must know how to make the connections.

As playwrights and audiences have become better readers, so must directors. If a script does not mention all the defining points of a character's identity, does this automatically mean that the character is white, middle-class, and heterosexual? What kind of meanings emerge in an all-white casting of *Fefu and Her Friends*? How would multiracial casting add to or change such a reading of the play? If one were to cast multiracially, would that mean that the play would have to be politicized as being specifically about race?

To avoid categorizing, Fornes almost never names her characters' racial identities. Interestingly, although theater practitioners recognize Fornes's Cuban birth, they assume her characters are not Latino unless explicitly named as such in her character descriptions. One might read Fornes as completely ignoring the issues of identity. However, I read her work as reworking the notion of Latina identity in a way that asks readers to see Latinas in all shades and class affiliations and more importantly to see Latinas first and foremost as persons. Not all Latinas are from Manhattan, not all are brown, not all have "z"'s in their last names. And some are named Julie and Cindy.

Lesbian Playwrights: Diverse Interests, Identities, and Styles

Jill Dolan

Although earlier periods in American culture saw any hint of so-called deviant sexuality reviled when it was portrayed on stage (*The Captive* by Edouard Bourdet might be one early example), post-Stonewall theatre in the United States has gradually opened to gay and lesbian content. The feminist and gay and lesbian liberation movements of the 1960s through the present in the United States have also allowed theatre critics to call attention to playwrights' gender and sexual identities in positive cultural ways. By the 1990s, the success of gay and lesbian activism in promoting a civil rights discourse around sexual identity has yielded a more open dialogue not only about the content of dramatic literature in the United States, but also about the sexuality of the playwrights.

Following on the heels of similar debates over whether a playwright's gender makes an integral impression on his or her work, issues of sexuality and authorship have more recently been noted by theatre professionals, critics, and scholars. In many ways, the relationship between sexual identity and artistry is more vexed than that of gender, since sexual practice can remain invisible in ways that the relatively clear announcement of gender precludes. As a result, definitions of "lesbian playwright," "lesbian play," or even "lesbian" are complicated to attempt.

The early second wave of U.S. feminism brought with it new definitions of lesbian identity. Adrienne Rich's early article, "Compulsory Heterosexuality and Lesbian Existence" (*Signs* 5.4, 1980), proposed a continuum of woman identification, which allowed some feminist women to claim lesbian identities not necessarily based on sexual practice. From 1980 to the early 1990s, a more fractious lesbian criticism developed multiple, contradictory definitions of lesbian identity, some explicitly along sexual lines. These debates of necessity haunt any discussion of lesbian playwrights and the production and reception of their work.

Playwrights affiliated with feminist theatres early in the feminist and lesbian movement of the 1960s and 1970s occasionally wrote lesbian plays. For example, **Martha Boesing**, founder of At the Foot of the Mountain Theatre (Minneapolis), wrote *Love Song for an Amazon* (1976) as a ritual ceremony to celebrate women's friendships. The one-act play, performed by two women, used transformational theatre techniques. Each performer played many roles meant to encourage the female-only audience's identification with the multiple, positive aspects of their gender. Although not specifically written as a lesbian drama, its criticism, in the Rich mode, describes it as "woman-identified."

Another feminist theatre group that produced lesbian drama in the 1970s and early 1980s was the Women's Experimental Theatre (WET) in New York, whose trilogy *The Daughters Cycle* includes the play *Electra Speaks* (1980). Playwright **Clare Coss** worked with director Roberta Sklar and performer Sondra Segal to create an interactive, mythic, feminist theatre piece that called on its spectators to witness a rereading of their own lives as women. By revising the myth of the House of Atreus to ask, "What happened to the women?" the WET implicitly describes a lesbian possibility as Electra leaves her father's house to commit her life to women. Although the play could be read as a veiled coming-out narrative, Electra's sexual identity is allied with women and is not specifically marked as lesbian. Critics and historians, however, tend to read the WET's productions as lesbian-feminist. Lesbian-feminist poet **Judy Grahn**'s play *The Queen of Swords* (1987) is also a literary, mythic piece grounded in the ideologies and contents of 1970s feminism.

The first U.S. playwright to enter mainstream theatre discourse as a self-identified lesbian was the late **Jane Chambers**, whose play *A Late Snow* was produced by Playwrights Horizon in New York in 1974. The play details the conflicting relationships between a college professor and her ex-lover, new lover, and potential lover as they inadvertently meet at an isolated cabin. The play marks the sometimes conflicting demands of gay liberation and feminism.

Chambers, who died in 1983, remains a frequently discussed, frequently published lesbian playwright. Her play *Last Summer at Bluefish Cove* (1980) enjoyed a long run in an off-off-Broadway New York theatre. Chambers's last play, *Quintessential Image* (1983), indicates her move toward a more complicated, layered theatre form, in its references to the construction of lesbian identity through the conflicting discourses of heterosexuality, the media, and the family.

While Chambers has achieved something of a cult following since her death, other lesbian playwrights have taken up her mantle. Although Chambers's work was cast in popular, conventional formulas and pitched to presumptively gay and lesbian audiences, many later lesbian playwrights have worked with new forms and have generated contents that begin with lesbian experience to make their claim toward understanding contemporary social and sexual relations.

Paula Vogel has perhaps achieved the most success on regional theatre circuits with plays that wickedly resist theatrical and social pieties. Vogel's work transgresses conventional boundaries of form and content by focusing on sexual practice and its infinite, inventive variety. For example, *Baltimore Waltz* (1992), Vogel's most frequently produced play, both addresses and skirts commonly held assumptions about emotional and social responses to AIDS by writing a fantasy travelogue in which the heroine, suffering from the dreadful ATDS (Acquired Toilet-Seat Disease Syndrome), tours Europe with her brother, indulging in nonstop, flamboyant promiscuity. Their roles finally reverse, and the text admits that it is the brother who is dying of AIDS.

Vogel has described the subcultural grumblings that responded to this play's success in New York and in regional theatres. Some lesbians critized Vogel for not writing about lesbians and AIDS, or for not writing about lesbians at all. These complaints miss the power and poignancy of Vogel's writing: through her command of theatricality and her nuanced critique of social systems, each of her plays writes a solid, wry, biting satire of the ideologies that deny full sexual, emotional, and political expression for women, lesbians, and gay men. Vogel's plays (including *Desdemona: a play about a handkerchief* [1993], her rewriting of Shakespeare's *Othello*) inevitably begin with sex, as the foundational (if sometimes foolish) interaction of social and political life. *And Baby Makes Seven* (1987) and *The Mineola Twins* (1995) are similarly absurdist investigations into the complacencies of heteronormative life, disrupting its facades with wild sexual practices performed in unlikely places.

Paula Vogel is one of the few out lesbian playwrights who also heads a creative writing program (**Julie Jensen** is another). Vogel's program at Brown University has fostered the talent of lesbian playwrights such as **Madeline Olnek**, who has adopted Vogel's disregard for standard theatrical conventions. Olnek's quirky play *Spookyworld* (1995) is set in a floundering horror-amusement park. Its nonlinear, non-sequitor style and the lesbian seductions that motivate its fairly inconsequential action clearly show the influence of Vogel's teaching. **Claire Chafee** also briefly studied at Brown. Her play, *Why We Have a Body* (1993), is a literate, wry, monologue-driven story of a lesbian, whose sister and mother have rejected conventional social roles, and her new, married lover. A lesbian romance and coming-out story are central to the play's action, but also afford opportunities for Chafee to reflect on many different kinds of human relationships.

Other lesbian playwrights employ antirealist forms and emphasize sexual practice as a site of social relation and control, rather than emphasize lesbian identity and experience per se. **Maria Irene Fornes** is a Cuban American playwright whose work has long focused on relations of domination and imperialism that congeal around sexuality. Her best known plays, *Conduct of Life* (1985), *Mud* (1983), and *Sarita* (1984), among others, although not explicitly lesbian in their content, are persuasive for their analysis of gender as a power relation intimately connected to colonizing private and public practices. Sexuality becomes a means of nation building in Fornes's plays, a Foucauldian site of power relations. In her one-act *Springtime* (1989), Fornes shows the dissolving of a lesbian relationship after a woman poses for pornographic pictures to pay for her lover's medical treatment.

The relationship of sexuality and gender to state power forms the content of many forceful lesbian plays, many of which find their expression in postmodern, anticonventional structures. **Joan Schenkar**'s early play *Signs of Life* (1979) uses intertextual references to characters in American literature to create a savage critique of the medical establishment's power over women's bodies. Her play *Between the Acts* (1989) borrows famous lesbians from history—including Natalie Barney and Renee Vivien—to enact a fantastical morality tale in which Barney's wealthy capitalist father dies seven different ways in the second act. Schenkar's subjects range from Nazi Germany, to Typhoid Mary, to theatrical representations of historical literary figures, in plays whose perspective is more overtly materialist and feminist than lesbian. On the other hand, *Burning Desires* (1994), her deconstruction of the Joan of Arc mythologies, is rife with lesbian seductions along with pointed social and literary satire.

Experimental forms and contents infuse the work of many contemporary lesbian playwrights. Chicana critic, theorist, poet, and playwright **Cherríe Moraga**'s play *Giving Up the Ghost* (1984) is a fragmented, episodic, poetic script that evokes a split in its main character, as she traces her desire through her past relationships in ways that complicate the play's representations of gender and ethnicity. Moraga's later work *Shadow of a Man* (1985), which returns to a well-made, realistic play format, places its emphasis on sexual choices in the context of Chicano family; *Heroes and Saints* (1989) is a political play with expressionistic features.

Tina Landau, a playwright also trained as a director, typically works in experimental production sites; her play *Stonewall* (1994), chronicling the events leading up to the Stonewall riots of 1969, was commissioned by En Garde Arts in New York, a production company that solicits site-specific work. *Stonewall* was presented on a pier along the Hudson River.

While some commentators trumpet the 1990s as the glorious age of gay theatre, one cannot help but be frustrated that lesbian work has not moved to Broadway alongside Terrence McNally's or Tony Kushner's. Gender politics have left lesbians lingering behind in reputable regional theatres or avant-garde performance spaces. Lesbian playwrights still receive their most passionate response from lesbian communities, particularly in New York and San Francisco, at vital performing venues such as the WOW Cafe and P. S. 122 (in Manhattan) and Josie's Cabaret (in the Castro).

The WOW Cafe, on the Lower East Side of Manhattan, has developed its own mythology as a development site for lesbian playwrights and performance artists. WOW, which began as a storefront space on East 11th Street, now makes its home, without any private or public sector support, in a warehouse building on East 4th Street, across from La Mama and down the block from the New York Theatre Workshop. WOW was established through the labor of Peggy Shaw and Lois Weaver, a couple many would call the grande dames of lesbian performance and playwrighting in the United States. Shaw and Weaver, along with Deb Margolin, formed the **Split Britches** company, which wrote, performed, and produced influential lesbian and feminist performance for nearly fifteen years, beginning with their signature piece *Split Britches* in 1982. Shaw, Weaver, and Margolin performed together in *Upwardly Mobile Home* (1984), *Beauty and the Beast* (1982), and *Little Women* (1988); Margolin wrote and Shaw and Weaver performed *Lesbians Who Kill* (1992); and Shaw and Weaver collaborated with **Holly Hughes** on *Dress Suits to Hire* (1987). These productions, with their combination of oral history, personal experience, wild theatricality, intertextual reference, and rowdy, bawdy, seductive direct addresses to lesbian and other audiences, have remained the touchstone of lesbian performance and playwrighting since the early 1980s. Shaw and Weaver have also collaborated on *Lust and Comfort* (1995), an absurdist-inflected description of the complications of power and desire in lesbian relationships which, in some ways, extends, with a hint of wistfulness and melancholia, from their early performance *Anniversary Waltz* (1989), which celebrated the beginnings of their long-term relationship. Shaw has also produced her own solo piece, *You're Just Like My Father* (1995)—about the development and complications of her own butch lesbian identity—which she tours around the United States.

Many popular lesbian playwrights started in performance spaces such as the WOW Cafe, some serendipitously. Performance artist and playwright Holly Hughes's piece *Cat 'o Nine Tales* (1996) recounts her search for "the mystery space" that will pull her longing life together, a space that turns out to be, of course, the WOW Cafe. Hughes's *The Well of Horniness* (1983) is a parodic romp through the lesbian subculture that quotes the conventions of radio drama, murder mysteries, soap operas, and melodrama. Her performance piece *World without End* (1989) is a solo piece that chronicles her family relationships in her hometown, Saginaw, Michigan—a theme that is pursued in *Clit Notes* (1994).

The one-woman show or solo performance art format has been appealing for lesbian writers who also embody their work. Along with Hughes, lesbian performers **Carmelita Tropicana**, Babs Davy, Dominique Dibbell, and Lisa Kron began at the WOW Cafe and later spun off their own solo productions. Carmelita Tropicana (the persona of playwright and performer Alina Troyano) is a Cuban American character whose work *Milk of Amnesia* (1995) revolves around the in-betweenness of her ethnic and social identity, using fantasy and memory to frame a journey back to an irretrievable cultural home.

In addition to their solo work at WOW and other New York and national performance spaces, Davy, Dibbell, and Kron work with performer-writers Peg Healy and Mo Angelos as the **Five Lesbian Brothers**, whose three productions since 1990 have further challenged normative gender and sexuality thoroughly transgressed in most WOW performances. The Five Lesbian Brothers (whose name alone inspires either despair or delight) produced their first play, *Voyage to Lesbos* (1989), at WOW; their subsequent productions, *Brave Smiles* (1992)—

a perfect parody of theatre and film genres that have demonized or specularized lesbian characters through the twentieth century—and *The Secretaries* (1994)— about a cult of murderous office workers at a lumber company—were both presented at the New York Theatre Workshop.

Other lesbian performer-writers continue to work primarily alone, traveling their solo pieces to lesbian community spaces and performance venues around the United States and sometimes in Europe. **Susan Miller**, whose play *Confessions of a Female Disorder* (1973) was one of the first lesbian pieces to be anthologized, recently won an Obie for her performance piece *My Left Breast* (1994), which describes her experiences with breast cancer. Tallahasse-based artist **Terry Galloway** has toured her piece *Lardo Weeping*—whose seering focus on the female body is moving and evocative—around the United States and has also developed other solo pieces, while creating community-based political theatre troupes in Tallahassee (Mickee Faust) and in Austin, Texas (Esther's Follies). Los Angeles–based Latina performance artist Marga Gomez also performs solo work around the country, including her memorial to her father, *A Line around the Block* (1996), in San Francisco and New York.

Not surprisingly, New York, San Francisco, and to some extent Los Angeles appear to be the most fertile sites for lesbian playwrighting and performance. Despite its current reach toward the mainstream, lesbian theatre work continues to grow from the sexual subcultures that on some level provided its first impetus. The most visible, most active, largest lesbian and gay communities are those able to foster and support work by lesbian playwrights and performance artists. These cities are also the most racially and ethnically mixed, which allows lesbian artists to work within the interstices of sex/race/gender communities. **Dolores Prida**, for example, in New York, works with Latina lesbians but also collaborates on Latino and African-American work in other community spaces (for example, her collaboration with Anita Gonzalez, *Hola Ola* [1996]). Five of Prida's ten plays are published in a volume called *Beautiful Señoritas and Other Plays*. **Janis Astor del Valle**, a Puerto Rican lesbian playwright, crosses multiple community borders with her work. Working in large cities with large gay and lesbian populations also allows lesbians to work with gay men. At the Theatre Rhinoceros, in San Francisco, for instance, lesbian playwright Adele Prandini serves as the artistic director and sponsors both gay and lesbian work.

The explosion of interest in gay and lesbian writing in the 1990s bodes well for the future of lesbian playwrighting. Major trade houses are publishing lesbian fiction; major university presses are publishing lesbian and queer theory; and mainstream media have called attention to new lesbian lifestyles, suddenly popularized through the newly stylish term, ''queer.'' Much of this interest could simply be faddish, and some of it devolves into convenience, rather than a clear comprehension of a political challenge to dominant ideologies. The current fashionable use of ''queer'' also runs the risk of making lesbians invisible, under the all-inclusive yet not quite specific enough embrace of its nomenclature.

Nonetheless, strictures against lesbian visibility, especially in large coastal cities, seem to be loosening. More lesbian writers and readers and spectators can be open about their identities, and more demand is created for fiction, films, and plays about lesbian experience and perspectives. Lesbian characters now show up frequently on major network television series, such as ''Seinfeld,'' ''Friends,'' ''N.Y.P.D. Blue,'' and ''Roseanne.'' The perpetuation and circulation of lesbian drama and performance depends on such heightened interest and visibility. Without a significant production, it remains very difficult to publish a play. Without publication and the criticism that promotes interest, lesbian writing and performance will remain site specific, tied to relatively insular local communities. Lesbian playwrights deserve wider attention and acclaim.

PLAYWRIGHTS

ROSANNA YAMAGIWA ALFARO

(1939–)

BIOGRAPHY

Rosanna Yamagiwa Alfaro was born in Ann Arbor, Michigan, where she attended the University School. Her BA is from Radcliffe College and her MA in English is from the University of California-Berkeley. Although she has lived in California and Nova Scotia, most of her adult life has been spent in Cambridge, Massachusetts, where she currently resides with her husband, Gustavo Alfaro, and her two children.

Alfaro began her writing career in the mid-1970s with short stories, but by 1980 she had switched to plays. While she continues to publish short stories and poems, her creative output in the past fifteen years has focused on drama.

In 1992 Alfaro wrote, narrated, and coproduced a thirty-minute documentary, *Japanese American Women: A Sense of Place*, which was part of the Smithsonian Institution's traveling exhibition, "Strength and Diversity, Japanese American Women 1885–1990." Directed by Leita Hagemann, the film is distributed by Women Make Movies. Alfaro's short stories and poems are available in various literary publications.

PLAY DESCRIPTIONS

Rosanna Alfaro's plays explore the full range of dramatic genres and cultural themes. *Behind Enemy Lines* traces the disintegration of a Japanese American family as it moves from an assembly center to a relocation camp during World War II. *Going to Seed* concerns a Japanese American professor who is coming up for tenure during the Vietnam War. The one-act *Dimsumzoo* is a dark comedy about two friends discussing shared lovers over dim sum.

Alfaro's theatrically compelling *Mishima* traces the events leading to the suicide of Japan's flamboyant and excessive novelist Yukio Mishima (1925–1970). Set in Tokyo in the last year of his life, the play utilizes flashbacks and narration to create a collage of Mishima's struggle: the disparity between the perfection of artistic vision and the imperfectability of life, the passionate desire for a return to traditional Japanese imperial values and the increasing Westernization of Japan, and his candid homosexuality and his obligatory marriage. The character of Mishima assumes three essences: a narrator of past events, a participant in the action, and a voyeuristic audience member as he watches the action unfold on stage. Alfaro crafts an accessible image of this singular artist, based on Mishima's week-long visit to Alfaro's Japanese father in Michigan. Since its 1988 production by the Los Angeles–based East West Plays, Alfaro has reworked the play to include a young American admirer and has retitled it *The Art of Dying*.

Cowboy Samurai depicts the stormy relationship of a Japanese American stand-up comic and his childhood sweetheart who are reunited after a ten-year separation. Tom's comedy act derives its material from his childhood adventures with, and feelings for, Sally. When Sally attends one of his performances and thereby reenters his life, the characters' disparate life choices are explored. Both raised by internment camp survivors in suburban America, the two young people have taken decidedly different attitudes toward their cultural heritage. While Tom accepts Americanization and embraces Japanese tradition, Sally rebels on both counts: she resents Americans for her parents' treatment during World War II and despises the Japanese for their acceptance of their fate. The play employs incarnations of the characters' younger selves who simultaneously inhabit the same stage space as their older counterparts. This juxtaposition of past and present allows the audience to witness the effect of childhood circumstances on adult behavior.

Alfaro's *Matters of Life and Death* depicts a naive woman's attempts to cope with her husband's indifference, her mother's early symptoms of Alzheimer's, and the selling of the family home. The political arena replaces the domestic sphere in *Barrancas*, a play that involves the tricky alliance between an American ambassador and the dictator of an imaginary Central American country. A bit closer to home but no less political is *Martha Mitchell*, a gritty characterization of the "Cassandra of Watergate" that traces the trajectory of Mitchell's life from a privileged Southern belle to the colorful and charismatic wife of Attorney General John Mitchell to a pitiful, pill-popping paranoiac unwilling or unable not to tell the truth about the Nixon White House.

In *Pablo and Cleopatra*, Alfaro again utilizes historical figures in a love triangle that centers on the competition between Cleo, who is forty-nine years old, and her niece Danielle, who is nineteen, for the attentions of the seventy-three-year-old Pablo Picasso. Set in Paris of the 1950s, this realistic drama explores the relationship between aging and creative renewal. When Pablo and Cleo's longtime affair becomes increasingly abusive and bereft of love, the menopausal Cleo is no match for the lithe, young Danielle. When her niece becomes the painter's model and lover, Cleo seeks solace in the arms of her friend, Jean. As her new relationship flourishes, Cleo's own artistic career is revitalized, and her battered self-esteem is renewed. Pablo and Danielle's relationship quickly deteriorates; the temperamental Picasso beats the young woman so severely that she loses the baby she is carrying. When Cleo goes to retrieve her niece, she is forced to confront Pablo once again.

Alfaro is "interested in characters who walk into a room and use up all the oxygen. . . . Perhaps that is why I have written about historical figures like Picasso, Martha Mitchell, and Yukio Mishima. I like to alternate political and personal plays though I hope that my political plays are also personal and that my kitchen sink plays keep a window open to the world."

SELECTED PRODUCTION HISTORY

Under Siege (one-act radio play, coauthor)
  Audio Stage, CBC Radio, Canada, 1979

Behind Enemy Lines
  Reading, Pan Asian Repertory Theatre, New York, 1980
  Production, People's Theatre, Cambridge, Massachusetts, 1981
  Production, Pan Asian Repertory Theatre, New York, 1982
  Workshop, East West Players, Los Angeles, 1982

Going to Seed
  Reading, Playwrights' Platform, Boston, 1982
  Staged Reading, Group Theatre Company, Seattle, 1985
  Staged Reading, Playwrights' Platform Fall Festival, Cambridge, Massachusetts, 1989

Mishima
  Reading, Pioneer Square Theatre, Seattle, 1986
  Production, East West Players, Los Angeles, 1988

Over the Hill (short monologue)
  Production, Playwrights' Platform Workshop One-Act Festival, Boston, 1986

Matters of Life and Death
  Staged Reading, New Voices, Boston, 1987
  Staged Reading, Theatre in the Works, Amherst, Massachusetts, 1987

Tea (one-act play coauthored with Leita Hagemann)
  Staged Reading, Theatre in Process, Cambridge, Massachusetts, 1987

If the Truth Be Told (one-act play)
  Staged Reading, Theatre in Process, Cambridge, Massachusetts, 1987
  Production, Twelfth Night Club, New York, 1989

Fresh from Detroit (one-act play)
  Production, Playwrights' Platform, Cambridge, Massachusetts, 1987

Barrancas
  Staged Reading, New Play Cafe, Lyric Stage, Boston, 1988
  Production, Asian American Playwrights' Festival, Magic Theatre, San Francisco, 1989

Martha Mitchell (one-act monologue with music by Jean Ives Ducornet, Marie Buigues, and Joan Faber)
  Production, Showcase Festival, Theater Center Philadelphia, 1988
  Production, Theater Center Philadelphia, 1988
  Production, Theatre Lobby, Boston, 1989
  Production, Calton Studios, Edinburgh Fringe Festival, Edinburgh, Scotland, 1989
  Videotape, Boston Cablevision (Channel 23), December 1989

Prologue/Epilogue (for Three Noh Plays by Yukio Mishima)
  Production, Harvard-Radcliffe Drama Club, Cambridge, Massachusetts, 1988

Pablo and Cleopatra
  Reading, Unit II and Playwrights' Platform, Cambridge, Massachusetts, 1990
  Workshop, Cleveland Public Theater, Cleveland, Ohio, 1991
  Reading, East West Players, Los Angeles, 1994

The Second Coming (one-act play)
  Staged Reading, Unit II, Cambridge, Massachusetts, 1990
  Workshop, Cleveland Public Theatre, Cleveland, Ohio, 1992

Cowboy Samurai (formerly titled *Solo Flights in the Confessional Mode*)
  Reading, Next Stage (the Kentucky Project), Boston, 1991
  Reading, East West Players, Los Angeles, 1992
  Staged Reading, New Federal Theatre, New York, 1993
  Workshop, NeWorks Festival, New Theater, Boston, 1993

Eppur Si Muove (one-act play)
  Workshop, Cleveland Public Theatre, Cleveland, Ohio, 1992

Accompanist for a Seduction (one-act play)
  Production, Playwrights' Platform, Cambridge, Massachusetts, 1992

Dimsumzoo (one-act play coauthored with Rikki Ducornet)
  Reading, Women's Theater Guild, Cambridge, Massachusetts, 1992
  Production, Changing Scene Theater, Denver, Colorado, 1993

Coyote Gulch
  Reading, Playwrights' Platform, Cambridge, Massachusetts, 1993

PLAY AVAILABILITY

The Cleveland Public Theatre has agreed to make available all plays listed above. Please contact the Cleveland Public Theatre, 6415 Detroit Avenue, Cleveland, Ohio 44102.

AWARDS

The American Minority Playwrights' Festival, Group Theatre Company, Seattle, Finalist, *Going to Seed*, 1985

The Clauder Competition, Finalist, *Matters of Life and Death*, 1987

The Lois and Richard Rosenthal New Play Prize, Cincinnati Playhouse in the Park, Finalist, *Matters of Life and Death*, 1989

Actors Theatre of Louisville, National Ten-Minute Play Contest, Finalist, *The Second Coming* and semifinalist, *Eppur Si Muove*, 1991

The Ann White New Playwrights Competition, Ann White Theatre, Finalist, *Pablo and Cleopatra*, 1992

Actors Theatre of Louisville, National Ten-Minute Play Contest, Finalist, *Dimsumzoo*, 1992

Cleveland Public Theater Festival of New Plays, Finalist, *Coyote Gulch*, 1994

Massachusetts Cultural Council Artists' Grant for Playwriting, 1995

DESCRIPTIVE AND CRITICAL RESPONSES

Gladstone, Mary. "Martha Mitchell." *The Scotsman*, 23 August 1989.

Loynd, Ray. "East West Players Offer Premiere of *Mishima*." *Los Angeles Times*, 9 April 1988, VI4.

Marx, Bill. " 'Pablo': Unflattering Portrait of Picasso." Review of *Pablo and Cleopatra*. *Boston Globe*, 16 April 1996, 86.

Nelson, Nels. " 'Showcase Festival' Debuts 5." *Philadelphia Daily News*, 2 May 1988.

Tran, Tony. "East West Players' *Mishima* Impressive: Relates Life, Death of Celebrated Modern Japanese Writer." *Daily Bruin*, 3 May 1988, 16, 20.

———. "*Mishima*." *AsiAm*, July 1988, 54.

Weiner, Bernard. "Latin Concept Breeds Familiarity in Plot." Review of *Barrancas*. *San Francisco Chronicle*, 11 August 1989, E14.

CLAUDIA ALLEN

(1954–   )

BIOGRAPHY

Allen is a playwright in residence and teacher at Chicago's Victory Gardens Theater, which has produced four of her plays on its main stage. She has received several Joseph Jefferson Awards for new plays, and two of her plays have been produced on radio, including *Deed of Trust*, starring Sharon Gless and Tyne Daly. A Chicago resident, Allen teaches playwriting at the University of Chicago, the Newberry Library, as well as at Victory Gardens. Her plays have been produced in a number of cities in the United States. An essayist as well, Allen has been published in the *Chicago Tribune Sunday Magazine*. Her collection of lesbian plays, *She's Always Liked the Girls Best*, was a finalist for the American Library Association Gay/Lesbian Book of the Year and was nominated for a Lambda Award.

PLAY DESCRIPTIONS

A popular Chicago playwright, Allen writes consistently about lesbian experiences, and she is valued for her strong portrayal of women. *Roomers* is an intimate contemporary play set in small-town Michigan. The front porch of Ida's rooming house provides a focal point for the exploration of relationships among a diverse group of townspeople and visitors. The worldly Ida is the mother confessor for the tenants, who include June (a Black woman who is escaping the violence of Detroit), Ed (a salesman), Ernest (who owns a string of Motel 6s), and Ida's precocious daughter, Letty. When June's lesbian daughter visits, Letty recognizes the first stirrings of love.

Hannah Free tackles the issue of rights in the lifelong lesbian relationship of Hannah and Rachel, who are both confined to the same nursing home. When

Hannah is prevented from visiting Rachel by Rachel's daughter, she is consoled by a visit from the spirit of a young Rachel. A young woman who comes to research Hannah helps her to see her lover for a final good-bye.

The fantasy play *Movie Queens* is about being closeted in Hollywood. Two older actresses, Adele and Meg, are reunited during the rehearsals of a new Broadway play. By weaving 1980s rehearsal scenes with flashbacks to 1930s Hollywood, the cause of the feud that separated the two women is revealed. Adele's efforts to keep her sexuality hidden from the world conflicted with Meg's desire for greater openness. The play tells about love found, lost, and found again in the closeted world of Hollywood.

SELECTED PRODUCTION HISTORY

Movie Queens
 Production (one-act version), Stonewall Repertory, New York, 1986
 Production, Zebra Crossing Theatre, Chicago, 1990

The Long Awaited
 Production, Victory Gardens Theater, Chicago, 1989

Still Waters
 Production, Victory Gardens Theater, Chicago, 1991

Gays of Our Lives
 Production, Celebration Theatre, Hollywood, California, 1992

Hannah Free
 Production, One in Ten Theatre Company, Tucson, Arizona, 1993
 Production, Victory Gardens Theatre, Chicago, 1996

Deed of Trust
 Production, Victory Gardens Theater, Chicago, 1993

PLAY AVAILABILITY

Ripe Conditions is published by Dramatic Publishing, P. O. Box 129, Woodstock, Illinois 60098.

Roomers, *Raincheck*, *Hannah Free*, and *Movie Queens* are collectively published in *She's Always Liked the Girls Best*. Chicago: Third Side Press, 1992.

Acting editions of *The Long Awaited* and *Movie Queens* are available from Chicago Plays, Inc., 2632 N. Lincoln, Chicago, Illinois 60614.

AWARDS

Joseph Jefferson Award for Outstanding New Work, *The Long Awaited*, 1988–1989

Joseph Jefferson Award for New Work, *Still Waters*, 1991

American Library Association Gay/Lesbian Book of the Year Award Nomination, 1992

DESCRIPTIVE AND CRITICAL RESPONSES

Christiansen, Richard. "Losers Look for Love in Gusty *Ripe Conditions*." Review of *Ripe Conditions*. *Chicago Tribune*, 28 May 1993, 26.

Cooper, Jeanne. "Tenderness, Comedy in a Search to Be 'Free'." Review of *Hannah Free*. *Boston Globe*, 30 March 1995, 46.

Grahnke, Lon. "Promise of *Trust*." Review of *Deed of Trust*. *Chicago Sun Times*, 17 December 1993.

Koehler, Robert. "Gays of Lives Is a Soapy Spoof." Review of *Gays of Our Lives*. *Los Angeles Times*, 21 August 1992, F21.

LYNNE ALVAREZ

(1947–   )

BIOGRAPHY

Lynne Alvarez was born in Portland, Oregon, but was raised in Michigan from the time she was about five years old. After graduating from high school in Detroit, Alvarez attended the University of Michigan where she majored in Italian, Romance languages, and history. She graduated at the age of nineteen and went to Mexico where, from 1966 to 1973, she served as a newspaper reporter in Veracruz and also taught journalism and English at the university. She met her husband in Mexico.

Her experience during that very tumultuous time in Mexico politicized Alvarez. When the couple returned to the United States, she joined the Urban Coalition in Detroit and later the Puerto Rican Legal Defense Fund in New York.

Alvarez, who had written poetry since her childhood, moved to New York and decided to write full-time. In 1978 the Puerto Rican Traveling Theatre invited her to join a playwriting workshop under the direction of Fred Hudson. During her two years in the workshop, she wrote three plays. It was through her plays that Alvarez explored her own Hispanic background. Although her parents were Argentinean, the family had suppressed their Latino background while living in the very Anglo areas of Michigan. Lynne's experience with the Hispanic culture came primarily from her residence in Mexico.

Lynne Alvarez is the author of two volumes of poetry, *The Dreaming Man* (1984) and *Living with Numbers* (1987). She lives in Cooperstown, New York, where she writes poetry and drama and translates plays by Arrabal and Tirso de Molina.

PLAY DESCRIPTIONS

Lynne Alvarez looks at contemporary life through the eyes of a poet. The language of her plays is dense with rich, vivid imagery; her stories are complex and transporting. *The Guitarron*, a tragic tale based on the lives of common people she knew in Mexico, is rendered in her uniquely poetic manner. Through a number of scenes, we are introduced to the characters who populate the beach near Veracruz, Mexico. Calorias, a middle-aged fisherman, and Julio, his friend and lover, eagerly await the completion of their fishing boat promised by the Master Builder, an old Cuban boat builder, and Guicho, his seventeen-year-old apprentice. Antonio, a good-looking but crippled street beggar, does business with all of those on the beach. In the background, often dressed in full concert attire, is the Maestro, an elderly cellist who plays music on the beach day and night. All of the villagers dream for what is just outside of their reach. Guicho has visions of getting out of the village to make a life for himself and taking Micaela, the young prostitute, with him. The Master Builder dreams of returning to Cuba in the boat he is building for Calorias. Calorias and Julio fantasize about a fishing fleet; Antonio wants to steal the Maestro's cello for the money it will bring. Although Guicho wants no part of stealing the cello, he agrees to talk with the musician. Sensing the young boy's intentions, the old man teaches Guicho how to play a few notes so that he will know the true value and meaning of what he is stealing. When Calorias and Julio's fishing trip fails, they are seduced into Antonio's plan to steal the cello, and Calorias slits the old man's throat. To revenge the Maestro's death and to retrieve the cello, Guicho stabs Calorias during a violent knife fight. Alone on the beach, the young apprentice escapes the realities of life and death by teaching himself to play the instrument while the spirit of the old musician begins to transform into a native fisherman.

If *The Guitarron* is about the price of dreams, Alvarez's *The Wonderful Tower of Humbert Lavoignet* is a whimsical and poignant exploration of the rewards and drawbacks of vision and faith. Humbert Lavoignet, an unemployed postal worker, awakens from a six-month stupor convinced that God has told him to do something wonderful. His wife's initial joy at having Humbert back is soon tested when he reveals that the "something wonderful" is to build a tower of trash. While Connie tries to make financial ends meet by selling homemade pies and canned goods, Humbert is consumed with the empty cans, broken window frames, and other debris that provide the material for his tower. He is joined by Johnny Snowalker, an itinerant Indian fiddle player, who wants to climb the tower to find his people who were killed years ago in an act of racial hatred and bigotry. As Humbert's obsession with his construction mounts, his family's needs are not being met. Connie leaves, seeking solace in the arms of Humbert's best friend, Arnie. When Humbert's celebrity status increases, his son also walks out because he is no longer able to tolerate his father's eccentricities. The day before the grand opening of the tower, however, Arnie and Mike arrive to tell Humbert that Connie has died. Believing in Johnny's theory that things come back from the dead according to their nature, Humbert and Johnny leave in search of Connie. When Mike climbs the tower to see which way his father went, he is awed by ''God's view of nature, '' the legacy of his father's unique vision and unflagging faith.

SELECTED PRODUCTION HISTORY

Graciela
  Production (radio), WBAI, New York, 1979

Latinos (musical collaboration with Manuel Martin and Omar Torres)
  Production, INTAR, New York, 1981

Mundo
  Production, IATI, New York, 1982

Hidden Parts
  Production, Monomoy Theatre, Chatham, Massachusetts, 1983
  Production, Primary Stages, New York, 1987

The Guitarron
  Production, St. Clement's Theatre, New York, 1984

The Wonderful Tower of Humbert Lavoignet
  Production, Capitol Repertory Theater, Albany, New York, 1985

The Red Madonna: A Damsel for a Gorilla (translation of a play by Fernando Arrabal)
  Production, INTAR, New York, 1986

The Reincarnation of Jamie Brown
  Staged reading, Women's Project and Productions, New York, 1987–1988
  Production, New Plays Program, American Conservatory Theatre, San Francisco, 1994

Greed (one-act play in *The Seven Deadly Sins*)
  Production, DUO Theatre, New York, 1987

Don Juan of Seville (translation of Tirso de Molina's *El Burlador de Sevilla*)
  Production, CSC, New York, 1989
  Production, Source Theatre Company, Washington, D.C., 1989

Thin Air: Tales from a Revolution
  Reading, Women's Project and Productions, New York, 1989
  Production, San Diego Repertory Theatre, San Diego, California, 1989

Voices in the Dark
  Reading, Women's Project and Productions, New York, 1995
  Workshop, ACT, San Francisco, 1996

PLAY AVAILABILITY

Don Juan of Seville, Alvarez's translation of the play by Tirso de Molina, is published by *Plays in Process*, vol. 10, no. 6. New York: Theatre Communications Group, 1989.

The Guitarron is published in M. Elizabeth Osborn, ed. *On New Ground: Contemporary Hispanic-American Plays.* New York: Theatre Communications Group, 1987.

On Sundays is published in Daniel Halpern, ed., *Plays in One Act.* New York: Ecco Press, 1991.

The Reincarnation of Jamie Brown is published in Marisa Smith, ed., *Women Playwrights: The Best Plays of 1994.* Lyme, New Hampshire: Smith and Kraus, 1995.

The Wonderful Tower of Humbert Lavoignet is published by Broadway Play Publishing, 56 East 81st Street, New York, New York 10028–0202.

Other scripts are available through the agent: Joyce Ketay, 1501 Broadway #1910, New York, New York 10036.

AWARDS

National Endowment for the Arts Fellowship, *The Guitarron*, 1982

Kesselring Award for New Plays, *Hidden Parts*, 1983

Le Compte du Nouy Prize, *The Wonderful Tower of Humbert Lavoignet*, 1984

FDG/CBS Award, Capitol Repertory Company, Albany, New York, Winner Best Play, *The Wonderful Tower of Humbert Lavoignet*, 1985

Drama League Playwrights Assistance Award, *Thin Air*, 1987

New York Foundation Grant, 1994

DESCRIPTIVE AND CRITICAL RESPONSES

Alvarez, Lynne. "Lynne Alvarez." In *On New Ground: Contemporary Hispanic-American Plays*, edited by M. Elizabeth Osborn. New York: Theatre Communications Group, 1987.

"Drama League Awards to Go to 7 Playwrights." *New York Times*, 14 December 1987, III, 22.

Stasio, Marilyn. "Play Has Poetry but Needs to Get Physical." Review of *The Guitarron*. *New York Post*, 29 June 1983.

JANE ANDERSON

(n.d.–)

BIOGRAPHY

Jane Anderson grew up in northern California. After two years in college, she moved to New York City to pursue an acting career, and in 1975 she appeared in the New York premiere of David Mamet's *Sexual Perversity in Chicago*. She begin writing in 1979 when she founded the New York Writers Bloc with playwrights Donald Margulies and Jeffrey Sweet. In the writers' group, Anderson developed a series of character sketches and, subsequently, performed as a comedienne in New York clubs and cabarets. In 1982 her act was discovered by Billy Crystal, and she was brought to Los Angeles to be a regular on "The Billy Crystal Comedy Hour," which ran for three weeks. Anderson continued to perform in Los Angeles, where she received critical acclaim for her one-woman show, *How to Raise a Gifted Child*. She also worked as a writer for television on the staff of "The Wonder Years," and she created *Raising Miranda* for Grant Tinker.

Her playwriting career began with *Defying Gravity*, which premiered in Los Angeles and was later produced at the Williamstown Theatre Festival in Williamstown, Massachusetts. Anderson, who has continued to write plays, received particular attention for *The Baby Dance*, which, after several regional productions, had a commercial run in New York. She has found a theatrical home at the Actors Theatre of Louisville, in Kentucky, which has produced and commissioned a number of her plays. Her television writing netted her an Emmy (along with director Michael Ritchie and stars Holly Hunter and Beau Bridges) for the Home Box Office movie *The Positively True Adventures of the Alleged Texas Cheerleader-Murdering Mom*. Film work includes *It Could Happen to You* (Tristar) and *How to Make An American Quilt* (Amblin/Universal) from the novel by Whitney Otto.

Jane Anderson is a member of the Dramatists Guild and lives in Los Angeles.

PLAY DESCRIPTIONS

The nonrealistic, lyrical style of *Defying Gravity*, which paid homage to the painter Matisse, gave way to a more realistic mode with contemporaneous social themes in *The Baby Dance* and *Food and Shelter*.

Her second full-length play, *Food and Shelter*, gains much of its strength from the way in which the subject of homelessness is treated humanely yet humorously through the story of one homeless family who decides to spend their lottery winnings on a trip to Disneyland to give their four-year-old daughter "something to feed her soul." After illegally spending the night camping in the theme park, the husband is arrested. Following his release, he departs to find work but has to leave his wife and young daughter behind. While they wait for word and money, the child develops miraculous, mystical powers. When the father returns, he has saved some money and it appears that their circumstances will improve. *Food and Shelter* does not pretend to offer solutions to the problem of homelessness; in fact, the play is more a love story between two people in highly straitened circumstances than it is an issue play. The playwright suggests a Japanese simplicity for the staging and, revealingly, asks the director/designer to "go easy on the chain link fencing" and to leave room for the "possibility of angels."

The Baby Dance, the story of selling and buying a baby, is more firmly situated as an issue play; like *Food and Shelter*, however, it is distinguished by strong characterizations and dialogue. Wanda and Al are dirt poor, living in a trailer, and are unable to pay the phone bill when Wanda gets pregnant with her fifth child. She suggests to her husband that they answer an ad in the paper that offers to help with expenses in exchange for their child. Not surprisingly, when affluent Californians Rachel and Richard enter the territory of these "white trash" Louisianans, a culture clash ensues. As misunderstandings grow, conflicts escalate and the assumptions and values of Rachel and Richard are challenged. While the morality of buying a baby is never overtly debated, the widely differing economic situations and educational levels of the two couples result in arguments over class privilege and prejudice. The choice Rachel and Richard make when the baby appears likely to have brain damage indicts the characters whose intelligence and background should allow for greater humanity and generosity.

The Last Time We Saw Her, a short one act, was written after Anderson and her partner took part in the 1993 Gay March on Washington. When an older, Catholic businessman propositioned her on the plane while she was returning to California, Anderson said, "I shut my eyes and wrote a play." When Fran, a division manager, tells her boss that she is a lesbian and intends to tell her office about her partner, Judith, he attempts to dissuade her. He compares homosexuality to alcoholism and claims that it is no more than sexual behavior. The play ends in a stalemate for both characters.

SELECTED PRODUCTION HISTORY

The Baby Dance
Production, Pasadena Playhouse, Pasadena, California, 1990
Production, Williamstown Theatre Festival, Williamstown, Massachusetts, 1990
Production, Long Wharf Theatre, New Haven, Connecticut, 1991
Production, Lucille Lortel Theatre, New York, 1991
Production, Theatre 40, Beverly Hills, California, 1994

Food and Shelter
Production, American Conservatory Theatre, San Francisco, 1990
Production, Vineyard Theatre, New York, 1991

The Pink Studio
Production, Humana Festival, Actors Theatre of Louisville, Louisville, Kentucky, 1990

Lynette Has Beautiful Skin (one act)
Production, Actors Theatre of Louisville, Louisville, Kentucky, 1990

Defying Gravity
Production, Williamstown Theatre Festival, Williamstown, Massachusetts, 1991

Hotel Oubliette
Production, Williamstown Theatre Festival, Williamstown, Massachusetts, 1992

Lynette at 3 A.M. (one act)
Production, Humana Festival, Actors Theatre of Louisville, Louisville, Kentucky, 1992

The Last Time We Saw Her (one act)
Production, Humana Festival, Actors Theatre of Louisville, Louisville, Kentucky, 1994

Tough Choices for the New Century
Production, Actors Theatre of Louisville, Louisville, Kentucky, 1995
(As *Smart Choices for the New Century*, a section was performed at the McCarter Theatre, Princeton, New Jersey, 1994)

PLAY AVAILABILITY

The Baby Dance and *Food and Shelter* are published by Samuel French, 45 West 25th Street, New York, New York 10010-2751.

The Last Time We Saw Her is published in *Humana Festival '94: The Complete Plays*, edited by Marisa Smith. Lyme, New Hampshire: Smith and Kraus, 1994.

Lynette at 3 A.M. is published in *More Ten Minute Plays from Actors Theatre of Louisville*. New York: Samuel French, 1992.

Lynette Has Beautiful Skin and *The Last Time We Saw Her* are published in *Ten Minute Plays: Volume Three from Actors Theatre of Louisville*. New York: Samuel French, 1995.

The Pink Studio (monologues) is published in *One Hundred Monologues for Women* and *One Hundred Monologues for Men*. Newbury, Vermont: Smith and Kraus, 1991.

Unpublished plays are available through her agent: Martin Gage, The Gage Group, 9255 Sunset Boulevard, Suite 515, Los Angeles, California 90069.

AWARDS

W. Alton Jones Grant, *Defying Gravity*, 1991

Susan Smith Blackburn Prize, *Hotel Oubliette*, 1992

Heideman Award, cowinner, *Lynette at 3 A.M.*, 1992

Heideman Award, cowinner, *The Last Time We Saw Her*, 1994

DESCRIPTIVE AND CRITICAL RESPONSES

Brandes, Philip. " 'Baby' a Tangle of Commerce, Parenting." Review of *The Baby Dance. Los Angeles Times*, 2 September 1994, F2.

Drake, Sylvie. "*Defying Gravity* in the Challenger's Wake." Review of *Defying Gravity. Los Angeles Times*, 17 June 1987.

Gussow, Mel. "Disneyland as Antidote for Poverty." Review of *Food and Shelter. New York Times*, 2 June 1991, 65.

Koehler, Robert. "Jane Anderson's Human Comedy." *Los Angeles Times*, 12 February 1986.

Mason, M. S. "Louisville's Window on New Plays." Review of *Lynette at 3 A.M. Christian Science Monitor*, 2 April 1992, 12.

Rich, Frank. "A Couple Try to Buy What They Can't Make." *New York Times*, 18 October 1991, C5.

VALETTA ANDERSON

(n.d.–   )

BIOGRAPHY

Born and raised in Chicago, Illinois, Valetta Anderson has made her home in Atlanta since 1983. She began her theatre training at Atlanta's Academy Theatre School of the Performing Arts and continued her playwriting under the mentorship of Barbara Lebow. She served as Literary Manager at the Academy Theatre during the 1989–1990 season. In 1989 Anderson was awarded an Artist Initiated Grant from the Georgia Council for the Arts enabling her to begin work on the first play in a trilogy on the Montgomery family of Mississippi, part of an ongoing project to document black history.

Anderson is the executive director of the Southeast Playwrights Project (SEPP) and an active member of AlternateROOTS. She teaches playwriting to high school students through the Alliance Theatre Young Playwrights Program. In 1994 she coedited the anthology *Alternate Roots: Plays from the Southern Theatre* (Heinemann).

She continues to live and work in Atlanta.

PLAY DESCRIPTIONS

Valetta Anderson's work is characterized by strong, black female characters trying to make sense of the world in which they live. Lively dialogue and a sense of humor are employed to explore her themes. The playwright uses language to depict subtle nuances of regionalisms, class, ethnicity, and gender and to evoke vivid poetic images. *She'll Find Her Way Home* is the first play in a historical trilogy in which she explores the founding of the first all-black township of Mound Bayou, Mississippi. Set in Vicksburg, Mississippi, in the early 1870s, the play tells of the emerging relationship between Martha Robb and

Isaiah Montgomery. Through the intervention of Martha's mother, Gussie, the young woman is introduced to the successful young entrepreneur. At first Martha is not attracted to Isaiah's dark black skin and big ears, but as the young man gains her trust and confidence, her opinion begins to change. Also vying for Martha's attentions is Thomas Siefred, Martha's light-skinned boyfriend since childhood. Thomas holds Martha to her youthful promise of marriage, and, despite her growing affection for Isaiah, she feels compelled to honor her earlier pledge. Thomas forces the issue, and at the same time, reveals that his intention is for them to pass for whites in their new lives away from the South. Martha, refusing to ignore or cover up her ancestral roots, rejects him. When she aligns herself with Isaiah, she has clearly fulfilled her mother's dream of coming home to her African heritage.

In *Today*, Anderson explores the stormy terrain of life's masculine and feminine forces. Alice arrives at Brenda's home with Dave, a man claiming to be one of Brenda's lovers from her past. When they become trapped in a blizzard, the boundaries of reality and magic are tested in this flirtation with the supernatural.

Anderson is currently working on a script about the late black actress Dorothy Dandridge.

SELECTED PRODUCTION HISTORY

Today
> Reading, Southeast Playwrights Project, Stone Mountain, Georgia, 1990
> Workshop, Women's Project and Productions, Atlanta, 1991
> Production, Jomandi Productions, Atlanta, 1991

She'll Find Her Way Home
> Production, Jomandi Productions, Atlanta, 1991
> Production, Jomandi Productions, Atlanta, 1993 (this remounted production subsequently toured nationally)

AWARDS

Artist Initiated Grant, Georgia Council for the Arts, 1989

Georgia Theatre Conference, First Prize, *Today*, 1990

AT&T Awards, *She'll Find Her Way Home*, 1991

DESCRIPTIVE AND CRITICAL RESPONSES

"4 New Plays Win AT&T Awards." *New York Times*, 30 October 1991, C20.
Freeman, Egypt. "Playwright Finds Her Voice, Tells of Human Nature." *Atlanta Journal Constitution*, 8 January 1995, N2.
Hulbert, Dan. "Atlanta's Rising Playmakers." *Atlanta Journal Constitution*, 16 January 1994, N1.

————. "Black Playwrights Listening to the Past." *Atlanta Journal Constitution*, 17 February 1991, N4.

Murray, Steve. "Valetta Anderson: Playwright Finding Her Way as Jomandi Premieres Script." *Atlanta Journal Constitution*, 30 December 1990, K8.

JANIS ASTOR DEL VALLE

(1963–   )

BIOGRAPHY

Janis Astor del Valle is a Bronx-born second-generation Puerto Rican, lesbian playwright, actor, and producer. At the age of seven, Janis was uprooted from her beloved Bronx barrio and transplanted to New Milford, Connecticut. On the family's weekend trips back to the Bronx, Janis wrote and directed scenes in which she and her cousins performed. Her first play, *Jackie, Lee and Chicky*, written at the age of nine, depicted the trio's struggle to survive in the South Bronx. In 1986 she returned to her native New York to attend Marymount Manhattan College, where she earned a BA in theatre.

Astor del Valle was a member of the Primary Stages Writers' and Directors' Project and the Latino Writers Lab at the Public Theatre. She is a founding member of She Saw Rep, a lesbian feminist troupe which made its debut at the National Lesbian Conference in Atlanta in 1991. She is also a cofounder of Sisters on Stage (S.O.S.), a multicultural trio of lesbian theatre professionals dedicated to fostering the development of aspiring lesbian playwrights. She works closely with her mentor **Dolores Prida**, who has directed several of Astor del Valle's productions. Janis is currently employed by New York University as an actor and teacher with the Creative Arts Team. She was commissioned to write a ten-minute play, *Mi Casa Es Tu Casa*, for Primary Stages New York Project.

PLAY DESCRIPTIONS

Janis Astor del Valle's plays are gritty yet humorous depictions of the various worlds the playwright inhabits. Her characters poignantly reflect her Puerto Rican heritage, the multicultural reality of the Bronx, and her lesbian/gay lifestyle as they struggle through the everyday tribulations and joys played out in living rooms and kitchens. The one-act coming-out play *I'll Be Home Para la Navidad* takes place as Christmas Eve approaches and Cookie and her mother prepare food for the festivities. Cookie reveals that she has invited her "friend" to stay for the holiday and makes it clear that she will leave if her lover is not welcomed by the family. Mother and daughter reach a quiet understanding, and Mami agrees to help placate Cookie's father.

The emphasis on family, in all of its permutations, is evident in Astor del Valle's full-length play *Where the Señoritas Are*. This touching play is a love story with a twist. Maxie and Luli have been best friends since adolescence, even though Maxie does not fully approve of Luli's lesbian lifestyle. On a weekend jaunt to Cherry Grove Beach, Fire Island, Maxie's homophobia is challenged as she comes to know and care for Luli's gay friends. Maxie is also beginning to realize that her relationship with her boyfriend is abusive—a far cry from the love and caring demonstrated by the people she is meeting. Having missed the ferry back to Long Island, the two friends find themselves spending the night together at a friend's beach house. What had been a platonic love blossoms into a physical relationship. Although their path is frequently rocky and circuitous, the two friends find a newer, more deeply rooted love.

Fuchsia extends Astor del Valle's earlier emphasis on family and her distinctive "Spanglish" dialogue into a humorous and touching portrait of love and caring. As Nina's uncle is dying of AIDS, she finds strength and comfort from her "other family," a unique and lovable trio of gay men: Red, Nina's best friend, is an honest, dependable black male Diva; Manny is a papi chulo, an irresistibly cute and charming gay Puerto Rican; and Alonzo is a gay Cuban man who is a bittersweet realist with a proclivity toward elitism.

SELECTED PRODUCTION HISTORY

Where the Senoritas Are (one-act version)
  Production, Duality Playhouse, New York, 1992
  Production, Women Playwrights' Collective, Lesbian and Gay Community Center, New York, 1992
  Production, Madison Avenue Theatre, New York, 1993
  Production, Nuyorican Poets' Cafe, New York, 1994

I'll Be Home Para la Navidad
  Production, Village Playwright, New York, 1993
  Production, Nat Horne Theatre, New York, 1994
  Staged reading, Latino Writers Lab, Public Theatre, New York, 1994
  Production, INTAR Latino Actors Base, New York, 1994
  Production, 42nd Street Collective, New York, 1995
  Production, Nuyorican Poets' Cafe, New York, 1995
  Production, 42nd Street Collective Summerfest, Samuel Beckett Theatre, New York, 1995

Production, Do Gooder Productions, Theatre on Three, New York, 1995

Where the Señoritas Are (full-length version)
    Production, Nuyorican Poets' Cafe, New York, 1994
    Production, Perry Street Theatre, New York, 1994

Trans Plantations: Straight and Other Jackets Para Mi (one-woman show written and
performed by Astor del Valle)
    Production, Nuyorican Poets' Cafe, New York, 1996

Fuchsia
    Production, Nuyorican Poets' Cafe, New York, 1996

PLAY AVAILABILITY

I'll Be Home Para la Navidad is excerpted in Rosemary K. Curb, ed., *Amazon All Stars:*
    Thirteen Lesbian Plays. New York: Applause, 1996.

I'll Be Home Para la Navidad and *Where the Señoritas Are* are published in one-act
    versions in Sue McConnell-Celi, ed., *Torch to the Heart: Anthology of Lesbian Art*
    and Drama. Red Bank, New Jersey: Lavender Crystal Press, 1994.

Plays are available through her agent: Joaquin J. Ramon, Joaquin J. Ramon Agency, 157
    West 88th Street, Suite 2, New York, New York 10024; (212) 877–3811.

AWARDS

Van Lier Playwriting Fellow at Mabou Mines, 1994–1995

Samuel French/Love Creek One-Act Play Festival, Semifinalist, *I'll Be Home Para la*
    Navidad, 1994

Mixed Blood Theatre National Playwriting Contest, Cowinner, *Where the Señoritas Are*,
    1995

JEANNIE BARROGA

(1949–   )

BIOGRAPHY

Jeannie Barroga was born into a musically inclined family in Milwaukee shortly after the end of World War II. She graduated from the University of Wisconsin, Milwaukee, in 1972 with a degree in fine arts. After graduation, Barroga moved to northern California where she "felt a sense of relief" because she blended into the multiethnic population.

She wrote her first play in 1979 as a response to her father's death. It was not until later in her playwriting career, however, that she began to explore her own Filipino background. In 1983 Barroga founded Playwright Forum in Palo Alto to encourage new works written by California playwrights. It has since become the Discovery Project after it merged in 1986 with Palo Alto's TheatreWorks. She has served as literary manager for the Oakland Ensemble Theatre and currently serves in that capacity for TheatreWorks. In 1990 she was the temporary associate artistic director for the San Francisco–based Filipino youth theatre, TnT (*Teatro ng Tanan* or Theater for the People).

Barroga, who teaches playwriting in the Bay Area, conducted a playwriting class at Colorado College in 1995. Among her more than fifty plays, Jeannie Barroga has written five cable television plays and has had numerous commissions. She is a member of the Dramatists Guild and the Theatre Communications Group.

PLAY DESCRIPTIONS

Barroga's ability to "play with theatrical styles" is reflected in *Walls*, her investigation of the controversy surrounding the Vietnam Memorial. Structured as a collage of characters and stories, the play explores the myriad attitudes the memorial evokes in those who are left to understand that tumultuous time in American history. The characters include the angry, patriotic vet who lost half of his company in the war; the army nurse stationed in San Diego who is riddled with guilt because she was not sent to Vietnam; the 1960s protester who lost friends in the war but still believes that protest was justified; and others who were maimed or killed or who lost loved ones. As each tries for a catharsis and understanding, the play pivots around the memorial's architect, Maya Lin, who strives to clarify the memorial's message.

Barroga explores the Filipino experience in *Talk-Story*. Dee, a first-generation Filipino American, writes a series of newspaper articles featuring the stories of her father and uncle in the Philippines and California. Dee also gives voice to the Filipino sense of frustration at their lack of unique identity: despite being the largest Asian group in California, they are often confused with Chinese and Japanese. By mixing reality and fantasy that freely traverse time and space, Jeannie Barroga is able to parallel the experiences of her family and herself—racial prejudice directed at Filipinos in the 1930s with current anti-Asian racism and the uses (and abuses) of fantasy.

The bittersweet short play *Kenny Was a Shortstop* also uses the device of the newspaper reporter as the impetus for the plot. Cora, a young reporter, tries to get the "personal angle" on Kenny, a young Filipino who has been killed in a gang incident. When she interviews Kenny's mother and father, Cora uncovers the hidden angers and resentments that seethe within the ostensibly quiet family as well as her own painful memories.

Jeannie Barroga returns to her own Filipino American experience in *Rita's Resources*. Set in the 1970s, this comedy of the immigrant experience explores a Filipino household's struggle in pursuit of the American Dream.

SELECTED PRODUCTION HISTORY

Pigeon Man
Staged reading, Playwrights' Center, San Francisco, 1982
Production, Teletheatre Channel 60, San Jose, California, 1984

When Stars Fall
Staged reading, Playwright Forum, Palo Alto, California, 1985
Production, Playwright Forum, Palo Alto, California, 1986

Batching It
Staged reading, Playwright Forum, Palo Alto, California, 1985
Staged reading, Playwrights' Center, San Francisco, 1986

Paranoids
Staged reading, Playwrights' Center, San Francisco, 1985

Lorenzo, Love
Staged reading, Playwrights' Center, San Francisco, 1985
Production, Foothills College, Los Altos Hills, California, 1986

Eye of the Coconut
  Staged reading, Playwright Forum, Palo Alto, California, 1986
  Production, Northwest Asian American Theatre, Seattle, 1987
  Production, Asian American Theatre Company, San Francisco, 1987 and 1991
  Staged reading, East West Players, Los Angeles, 1991
  Production, East West Stage, Berkeley, California, 1993
  Production, Asian American Repertory Theatre, Stockton, California, 1995

Angel
  Staged reading, Playwright Forum, Palo Alto, California, 1987

Sistersoul
  Production, TheatreWorks, Palo Alto, California, 1988
  Production, Bay Area Playwrights Festival, San Francisco, 1989

Adobo
  Staged reading, Seattle Group Theatre, Seattle, 1988

Family
  Production, Northside Theatre Company, San Jose, California, 1988

The Game
  Staged reading, Playwright Forum, Palo Alto, California, 1988

Walls
  Production, Asian American Theater Company, San Francisco, 1988
  Production, New World Theatre, Amherst, Massachusetts, 1991
  Production, Asian American Repertory Theatre, Stockton, California, 1993; Modesto,
    California, 1994

Musing
  Staged reading, Asian American Theater Company, San Francisco, 1989
  Staged reading, Eureka Theatre, San Francisco, 1992

My Friend Morty
  Workshop, Playwrights' Center, San Francisco, 1989

Kenny Was a Shortstop
  Staged reading, New Traditions Theatre Company, San Francisco, 1990
  Production, BRAVA! for Women in the Arts, San Francisco, 1991

Talk-Story
  Staged reading, Bay Area Playwrights' Foundation/Magic Theater, San Francisco,
    1990
  Staged reading, Mark Taper Forum, Los Angeles, 1992
  Production, TheatreWorks, Palo Alto, California, 1992
  Production, Kumu Kuhua Theatre, Honolulu, 1995

Kin
  Production, Teatro ng Tanan, San Francisco, 1991

The Revered Miss Newton
  Production, San Francisco State University, San Francisco, 1991

Letters from Dimitri
  Staged reading, American Conservatory Theater, San Francisco, 1992
  Staged reading, TheatreWorks, Palo Alto, California, 1992

Rita's Resources
  Workshop, Pan Asian Repertory Theatre, New York, 1992
  Production, Pan Asian Repertory Theatre, New York, 1995
Shades
  Staged reading, BRAVA! for Women in the Arts, San Francisco, 1993
  Staged reading, East West Players, Los Angeles, 1994
A Good Face . . . for Writers
  Reading, Working Women Annual Theatre Festival, San Francisco, 1996

PLAY AVAILABILITY

Kenny Was a Shortstop and *The Revered Miss Newton* are published in *Jeannie Barroga, Two Plays*. San Francisco: CrossCurrents Publications, 1993.

Walls is published in Roberta Uno, ed., *Unbroken Thread: An Anthology of Plays by Asian American Women*. Amherst: University of Massachusetts Press, 1993.

Jeannie Barroga's other plays are available through her agent: Helen Merrill, Ltd., 435 West 23rd Street 1A, New York, New York 10011; (212) 691–5326.

AWARD

Bay Area Playwrights Festival, San Francisco, *King of Cowards*, 1993

DESCRIPTIVE AND CRITICAL RESPONSES

Coates, Mari. " 'Women Times Three': A Showcase of Women Directors." Review of *Kenny Was a Shortstop. San Francisco Sentinel*, 16 May 1991.
Harvey, Dennis. " 'Women Times Three' from Brava!" Review of *Kenny Was a Shortstop. San Francisco Weekly*, 15 May 1991, 22.
Peifer, Deborah. "Women Direct." *Bay Area Reporter*, 16 May 1991.
"Playwright Jeannie Barroga to Debut in New York with 'Rita's Resources.' " *Headline Philippines*, 19 December 1994—1 January 1995, 9, 25.
Runion, Dianne. " 'Walls' Helps Break Down Divisions between Us." Review of *Walls. Stockton Record*, 20 June 1993.
Sussman, Diane. "A Proud and Angry Woman." *Palo Alto Weekly*, 27 May 1992, II 26.
Uno, Roberta. "Jeannie Barroga." In *Unbroken Thread: An Anthology of Plays by Asian American Women*, edited by Roberta Uno, 201–5. Amherst: University of Massachusetts Press, 1993.

MARTHA BOESING

(1936–   )

BIOGRAPHY

Playwright, director, performer, and theatre administrator, Martha Boesing was born in New Hampshire in 1936. She began her forty-year career in the theatre at the age of sixteen as an apprentice in summer stock. After graduating from Connecticut College for Women in 1957 with a BA in English, Boesing went on to the University of Wisconsin, where she earned an MA in English literature in 1958. While she was at Wisconsin, Boesing became "radicalized politically," a choice that has shaped her subsequent life and work, with its feminist perspective and lesbian overtones.

In the early 1960s, Boesing moved to Minneapolis where she worked with the fledgling Minnesota Repertory Company and the Moppet Players (later the Children's Theatre) and was one of the core group of the Firehouse Theatre (1964–1968) and a founder of the Earth Family Theatre (a collective that performed in Minneapolis and Cambridge, Massachusetts). She also performed as a folksinger.

After serving a brief stint at the Academy Theatre in Atlanta (1972–1974), Martha and her husband, Paul Boesing, returned to Minneapolis. Seeking to create a theatre collective with a feminist perspective, Boesing became one of the founding members and the artistic director of the radically feminist At the Foot of the Mountain (1974–1991), a theatre that had the distinction of being "the oldest continuously producing professional women's theatre in America." Although Boesing departed from At the Foot of the Mountain in 1984, she has been involved with numerous other projects, including the Playwrights' Center (1983–1987), writing and directing for In the Heart of the Beast Puppet and Mask Theater of Minneapolis (1986 and 1989), the Minneapolis Environmental Theater Project (1990–1991), the multimedia project *The Cicada Journals*

(1994), and San Francisco's A Traveling Jewish Theater. The mother of three children, Martha Boesing currently resides in Minneapolis.

PLAY DESCRIPTIONS

Martha Boesing has devoted her playwriting career to creating plays with a radical voice and an iconoclastic aesthetic. *Pimp* is an imagistic play about three women who sell out each other and themselves for men. Its companion piece, *The Gelding*, is a play for three men: the father (Eban), his son (Jules), and the father's mute shadow-self (Beethoven). The play chronicles Eban's attempts to break through the barriers of convention and frozen emotion in order to establish connections with his son. The friendship between two women is revealed and celebrated in *Love Song for an Amazon*. In Boesing's prismlike series of images, we see the two women in various roles: school chums, career women, mothers, daughters, teachers, students, lovers, amazon warriors, and visionaries. *Moontree* is a modern Bluebeard tale in which each woman looks behind a secret door to find, not the corpses of former wives, but their mad reality. During the play, set in an insane asylum for women, each of Schooner's previous wives discovers her own independence as a lunatic, or one who lives under the influence of the moon. *Junkie!*, a collaborative creation with At the Foot of the Mountain, is a participatory ritual event that scrutinized addictions of all types (food, chemicals, sex, love, money, work, and others). Following the path of recovery, the stories that begin in pain and denial move into the sharing of experience and on to communal renewal.

The Web interweaves past and present to explore Abigail Sater's life. Childhood memories of her gay uncle's suicide, her own resentment of a wealthier cousin, and her brother's rape of her cousin all merge with the reality of the adult Abigail's life. We see Abigail's lectures on feminist aesthetics interspersed with her theatrical career and interrruptive phone calls from her two teenage daughters. It is this web of past and present, joyous and painful, that makes up the tapestry of one's life. *Ashes, Ashes We All Fall Down* is a ritual drama about nuclear madness and the denial of death, which Boesing created with At the Foot of the Mountain. During the play, set in the household of a "normal, nuclear family," the family members try to come to terms with the impending death of the mother. By playing off the mother's hallucinations of historical and contemporary mass deaths, the play explores the mortality of the earth in light of the buildup of nuclear arms. *Antigone Too: Rites of Love and Defiance* is an adaptation of the Sophocles text. By interweaving the Greek original with the words of women who have committed civil disobedience (Mother Jones, Rosa Parks, Fannie Lou Hammer, and others), Boesing creates a celebration of women whose names may have been forgotten but who have played a vital role in bringing about social change.

Martha Boesing's more recent work retains her characteristic feminist perspective and social activist stance. In *My Other Heart*, she creates a poignant tale of two women's evolving friendship, which eventually allows them to escape from traditional roles to explore their own individuality and freedom. Set in the fifteenth-century home of Anton Quintero, a young shipbuilder and navigator, the play traces the love and friendship that emerges between Pilar Quintero, Anton's young wife, and Guacarapita, the Tainos slave girl whom Anton presents to his wife when he returns to procure supplies for Christopher Columbus's fleet to go to the New World. Guacarapita's refusal to conform to European culture and religion eventually prompts Pilar to acknowledge her own Jewish heritage, even at the risk of her life before the Inquisition. Together the two friends escape the confining society of fifteenth-century Spain to find a society where they can dare to be themselves. *Hard Times Come Again No More* is based on the stories and essays of Meridel LeSueur, a writer who chronicled the very human lives of Midwesterners during the Depression years. Set in a boarding house during the Minneapolis truckers strike in July 1934, Boesing's play captures the nuances that structure the lives of these people who are unexceptional in all but their struggle to survive. It is through the games of checkers, the stolen glasses of milk, and the flowers pilfered from the garbage can to give to a loved one that the Depression is measured. The political issues of the era take a back seat to the human drama, which is framed by The Pregnant Woman, who defies logic to bring another life into the world, and The Dying Woman, a Cassandra-like figure whose rantings mix wisdom with weariness. In *The Cicada Journal*, Boesing has created a text taken from the memoirs and journals of European and American women that combines the new physics with the Neolithic mythology of the aboriginal goddess cultures. The text, together with a vocal score composed by Lisa Carlson and paintings created by visual artist Nancy Randall, depicts the stages of a woman's spiritual journey into her own mind and soul.

SELECTED PRODUCTION HISTORY

Because Martha Boesing's dramatic output is so extensive, only the premiere productions are listed below.

The Wanderer (opera libretto with Paul Boesing)
Production, Minnesota Opera Company, Minneapolis, 1970

Earth Song (musical with Paul Boesing)
Production, American Friends Service Committee, Midwest Tour, 1970

Shadows, a Dream Opera (collaborative creation)
Production, Academy Theater, Atlanta, 1972

Journey to Canaan
Production, Academy Theater, Atlanta, 1974

Pimp (one-act play)
Production, Academy Theater, Atlanta, 1974

The Gelding (one-act play)
Production, At the Foot of the Mountain, Minneapolis, 1974

River Journal
Production, At the Foot of the Mountain, Minneapolis, 1975

The Moontree
Production, At the Foot of the Mountain, Minneapolis, 1976

Love Song for an Amazon (one-act play)
Production, At the Foot of the Mountain, Minneapolis, 1976

Mad Emma (one-act play)
Reading, The Loft, Minneapolis, 1976

The Story of a Mother (collaborative play)
Production, At the Foot of the Mountain, Minneapolis, 1977

Trespasso (one-act play)
Production, At the Foot of the Mountain, Minneapolis, 1977

Labia Wings (one-act play)
Production, At the Foot of the Mountain, Minneapolis, 1979

Dora Du Fran's Wild West Extravaganza or The Real Low-Down on Calamity Jane
Production, At the Foot of the Mountain, Minneapolis, 1979

Song for Johanna (radio play)
Production, KSJN Radio, Minneapolis, 1980

Junkie! (collaborative play)
Production, At the Foot of the Mountain, Minneapolis, 1981

The Web
Production, Trinity Square Repertory Company, Providence, Rhode Island, 1981

Ashes, Ashes All Fall Down (collaborative play)
Production, At the Foot of the Mountain, Minneapolis, 1982

Antigone Too
Production, At the Foot of the Mountain, Minneapolis, 1983

Las Gringas
Production, At the Foot of the Mountain, Minneapolis, 1984

The Nightingale (adaptation)
Production, In the Heart of the Beast Puppet and Mask Theater, Minneapolis, 1986

The Business at Hand (one-act play)
Production, Actors Theater of St. Paul, St. Paul, 1988

Snake Talk (with Naomi Newman)
Production, A Traveling Jewish Theater, San Francisco, 1988

The Reaper's Tale
Production, In the Heart of the Beast Puppet and Mask Theater, Minneapolis, 1989

Heart of the World (collaborative play)
Production, A Traveling Jewish Theater, San Francisco, 1989

Standing on Fishes
Production, Environmental Theater Project, Minneapolis, 1991

My Other Heart
  Production, Northlight Theater, Evanston, Illinois, 1993

Hard Times Come Again No More
  Production, Illusion Theater, Minneapolis, 1994

The Cicada Journals (multimedia collaborative project)
  Production, Pathways, Minneapolis, 1994

PLAY AVAILABILITY

The Business at Hand is published in *Slant Six: New Theatre for Minneapolis Playwrights Center.* Minneapolis: New Rivers Press, 1990.

The Gelding, Love Song for an Amazon, and *River Journal* are published in Martha Boesing, *Journeys along the Matrix: Three Plays by Martha Boesing.* Minneapolis: Vanilla Press, 1978.

Pimp is published in Rachel France, ed., *A Century of Plays by American Women.* New York: Richards-Rosen Press, 1979.

The Web is published in *Plays in Process*, 4. 1. New York: Theatre Communications Group, 1981.

Other scripts are available through the playwright Martha Boesing, 3144 10th Avenue South, Minneapolis, Minnesota, 55407; (612) 825–2820.

AWARDS

Martha Baird Rockefeller Foundation Grant for Experimental Opera, 1972–1973

National Endowment for the Arts, Music Fellowship, 1979–1980

Playwright Festival, Winner, Women's Theatre, Seattle, 1979

Playwright Festival, Winner, Women's Theatre, Seattle, 1980

Twin Cities Mayors' Public Arts Award, 1981

YWCA, Outstanding Woman Artist of the Year Award, 1982

McKnight Playwriting Fellowship, 1983

Bush Foundation, Fellowship in Playwriting, 1983–1984

Houston Film Festival Award, *Junkie!*, 1984

Minnesota State Arts Board, Individual Artists Grant, 1985–1986

National Endowment for the Arts, Playwriting Grant, 1987

Fund for New American Plays, Kennedy Center, *My Other Heart*, 1993

DESCRIPTIVE AND CRITICAL RESPONSES

Greeley, Lynne. "Martha Boesing: Playwright of Performance." *Text and Performance Quarterly* 9, no. 3 (July 1989): 207–15.
Leavitt, Dinah L. "Martha Boesing." In *Notable Women in the American Theatre*, edited by Alice M. Robinson, Vera Mowery Roberts, and Milly Barranger, 71–74. Westport, Conn.: Greenwood, 1989.

Stephens, Judith L. "Subverting the Demon-Angel Dichotomy: Innovation and Feminist
    Intervention in Twentieth-Century Drama." *Text and Performance Quarterly* 9,
    no. 1 (January 1989): 53–64.
Terry, Clifford. "Right from *My Other Heart*." Review of *My Other Heart*. *Chicago
    Tribune*, 13 February 1994, 7.
Vaughan, Peter. "*Hard Times Come Again*: Play Captures the Depression, LeSueur Tales
    about the Times." Review of *Hard Times Come Again No More*. *Star Tribune*
    (Minneapolis), 5 April 1994.

CLAIRE CHAFEE

(1959–   )

BIOGRAPHY

Chafee grew up in New York City where she studied acting and directing. She also studied in London and spent time in San Francisco studying drama therapy while working in theatre. For Theatre Rhinoceros, she was one of the composers for **Judy Grahn**'s *Queen of Swords*. Chafee spent a year in the master of fine arts (MFA) program at Brown University, where she studied with **Anna Deavere Smith** and **Paula Vogel**, but she returned to San Francisco where she became an associate artist at the Magic Theatre. Her play *Why We Have a Body* ran there for six months prior to New York and Los Angeles runs.

About the lack of a political agenda in her plays, she states, "I resist topics. Topics don't interest me and I resist speaking for any one other than myself. I'm from the school of thought that if you're willing to go deeper into what you don't know about yourself, it's more interesting than expressing what you think you do know about other people" (Milvy, D26).

Chafee taught playwriting at San Francisco State University while completing *A Practical Guide to the Night Sky*, a commission from the Berkeley Repertory Theatre. She is adapting *Why We Have a Body* for film and completing an MFA in fiction at Brown University.

PLAY DESCRIPTIONS

Why We Have a Body ruminates on the lives of four women: an absent mother who is off exploring exotic lands; her youngest, psychotic daughter Mary, who robs only 7-Elevens; her oldest daughter Lili, a lesbian private detective who specializes in divorce cases; and the married woman Renee, whom Lili seduces. The mother is an archeologist, Renee is a paleontologist, and Mary is obsessed with Joan of Arc. While all of the women have investigative careers or obsessions, their primary exploration in the play is interior, as they journey into their own natures and their relationships with each other. The play is character and language driven, and the fragile plot hangs on the success of Lili's affair with Renee. Direct audience address is interspersed with dialogue, and the language of the play is distinguished by its epigrammatic, witty qualities. Chafee believes that our memories go back centuries and that the body, particularly for women, is its conscience, "the unremembered memories of fierce assaults and slow betrayals" (*Body*, II, 8).

Even among These Rocks, Chafee's first play, was written while she was at Brown University. The play follows three lesbians who are drawn together by their friendship with Maxwell, a gay man who is dying from an AIDS-related illness. The play is about their romantic involvements and the way they must let go of their friend Maxwell. The title of the play comes from a line in the T. S. Eliot poem, "Ash Wednesday": "Teach us to care and not to care/teach us to sit still even among these rocks."

SELECTED PRODUCTION HISTORY

Even among These Rocks
   Production, New Plays Festival, Brown University, Providence, Rhode Island, 1992
   Production, Magic Theatre, San Francisco, 1994

Why We Have a Body
   Production, Magic Theatre, San Francisco, 1993
   Production, Women's Project and Productions, New York, 1994
   Production, Tiffany Theatre, Los Angeles, 1995
   Production, Alice B. Theatre, Seattle, 1995
   Production, Ensemble Theatre of Cincinnati, 1996

PLAY AVAILABILITY

Even among These Rocks is available from her agent: Joyce Ketay Agency, 1501 Broadway, #1910, New York, New York 10036.

Why We Have a Body is published in Marisa Smith, ed., *Women Playwrights: The Best Plays of 1993*. Newbury, Vermont: Smith and Kraus, 1994.

AWARDS

Bay Area Critics Circle Award, *Why We Have a Body*, 1993

Cable Car Award, *Why We Have a Body*, 1993

Dramalogue Awards, San Francisco, *Why We Have a Body*, 1993–1994

Oppy Award (*Newsday*), New York, *Why We Have a Body*, 1995

DESCRIPTIVE AND CRITICAL RESPONSES

Bougetz, Susan. "Humor on the Brink: Claire Chafee on *Why We Have a Body*." [The Women's Project] *Dialogues* 11, no. 1 (Fall 1994): 1–2.

Erstein, Hop. "Feminist Builds Strong *'Body'* of Humor." Review of *Why We Have a Body*. *Washington Times*, 25 April 1993, D5.

Holden, Stephen. "A Surreal Dissection of the Lesbian Brain." Review of *Why We Have a Body*. *New York Times*, 8 November 1994, C22.

Milvy, Erika. "Chafee on Passion, Zen and Lesbian Life." *San Francisco Chronicle*, 12 June 1994, D26.

Solomon, Alisa. "Body Language." *Village Voice*, 1 November 1994, 96.

Weiner, Laurie. " 'Body': Women Who Have No Need for Men." *Los Angeles Times*, 13 April 1995, F8.

Winn, Steven. "Why Gay Theatre Is Taking Off." *San Francisco Chronicle*, 3 June 1993, C1.

JANE CHAMBERS

(1937–1983)

BIOGRAPHY

Jane Chambers, who was born in South Carolina and died at age forty-six of a brain tumor, was considered one of the most significant lesbian playwrights because of her depiction of the love between women as nonpathological. She was a novelist and poet who wrote for television as well. Chambers grew up in Orlando, Florida and then attended Rollins College for a year, then studied acting at the Pasadena Playhouse for two years; later in life, she graduated from Goddard College. Before becoming a full-time writer, Chambers worked for a literary agent, acted, directed, was a staff writer for a television station in Poland Spring, Maine, and was the director of avocation for the Job Corps in Jersey City. It was there she met Beth Allen, who became her life partner and manager. In 1972 she founded the Women's Interart Theatre in New York City with Margot Lewitin.

A Late Snow was one of the first plays with positive lesbian characters to be professionally produced. Chambers faced many difficulties with the production, beginning with auditions, when women refused to read for a lesbian role, and culminating when a cast member dropped out the day before the opening because her boyfriend convinced her she would not get any more commercials if she appeared on stage as a lesbian. Chambers later described the experience as a "hideous nightmare" which abruptly changed when the play was a hit and "suddenly the cast and crew adored each other" (Hoffman, xii). The Broadway option was dropped, however, after six months when no backers were interested in a play about lesbians.

Her playwriting career continued with a series of one acts performed at the Interart Theatre, *Last Summer at Bluefish Cove* at the Shandol Theatre in New York City, and *My Blue Heaven*. During rehearsals for *Kudzu*, Chambers became ill with what was subsequently diagnosed as a brain tumor. Chambers has said about her writing: "I have always felt a strong identification with the underdog and much of my work is set in minority or ethnic subcultures." However, when *Bluefish* was criticized for its lack of radical lesbian characters, she asserted, "I'm a middle-aged, middle-class, WASP dyke. That's what I know" (*Contemporary Authors*, 103). The Women in Theatre Program, an organization within the Association for Theatre in Higher Education (ATHE), created the Jane Chambers Playwriting Award in her honor to encourage new plays about women's experiences that have a majority of principal roles for women.

PLAY DESCRIPTIONS

The bodies of Chambers's plays are realistic, domestic-comedy dramas whose characters are self-examining women struggling with their relationships. The plays resemble good situation television scripts with their distinct characters and amusing repartee mixed with psychological revelations and romantic sentiment; the only difference is that the protagonists are lesbians. *A Late Snow* uses an effective comedic formula of unexpected meetings among a group of present, former, and future lovers who become trapped together in a cabin by a snow storm. There are the usual confrontations, confessions, and realignments until the central character, Ellie, a professor, acknowledges that the young woman she's with "doesn't ring her chimes" (a metaphor throughout for true love) and finds real love at last in the arms of a well-known, jaded writer who is tired of living alone and wants a life partner. Chambers treats this relationship in the time-honored way of entertainment romances: there is an instant attraction and, in the space of a weekend, an old lover is discarded and the professor and writer decide to live together. Only societal mores prevent the play from ending in a wedding, the classic comedy resolution.

Her most frequently performed play, *Last Summer at Bluefish Cove*, again uses an isolated setting, a lesbian resort, to segregate her characters. The device of the straight outsider who, because of her otherness, naturally incites an analysis of the lesbian lifestyle (Ellie's former roommate, Peggy, in *Snow*) becomes central to the plot in *Bluefish*. Eva is fleeing an unworkable marriage (as is Peggy) and unknowingly rents a cabin among a group of women who vacation together every summer. Her presence immediately provokes tension among the group, most notably from Dr. Kitty Cochrane, the best-selling author of a book on women's sexuality who fears being outed by Eva, and from Lil, who worries that her attraction to Eva will turn out badly. Not surprisingly, Eva and Lil have a hot romance, which is shattered by the return of Lil's cancer, an illness she had kept from Eva. Following the funeral, the women gather to pack up and distribute Lil's belongings, and Chambers makes it clear that Eva has become strong and independent through her association with Lil and the other women. The characters and couples (one, a young-old/rich-poor relationship; another, two white-collar professionals; and another, a stereotypically butch-fem pair) represent a diversity of types within the framework of white, middle-class women. They find their sustenance in their friendships with each other; as Lil explains near the end of Act I, "We gays are kind of like hobbits . . . we thrive in Middle Earth . . . we straddle both worlds and try to keep our balance."

Quintessential Image, a two-character one-act play, set in a television studio, departs from Chambers's domestic comedy-dramas in its conflict between Margaret Foy, a closeted television talk show host, and Lacey, the out photographer she is interviewing. Although the interviewer appears to "win" because she reveals that she can control the interview by cutting and editing, at the play's end, Lacey exits to tell her story to a writer who happens to be Foy's lesbian lover.

SELECTED PRODUCTION HISTORY

Tales of the Revolution and Other American Fables
  Production, Eugene O'Neill Memorial Theatre, New York, 1972

Random Violence
  Production, Interart Theatre, New York, 1973

Mine and *The Wife* (one acts)
  Production, Interart Theatre, New York, 1974

A Late Snow
  Production, Clark Center for the Performing Arts by Playwrights Horizons, New York, 1974
  Production, Theatre Rhinoceros, San Francisco, 1983 and 1987

The Common Garden Variety
  Production, Mark Taper Forum, Los Angeles, 1976

Last Summer at Bluefish Cove
  Production, Shandol Theatre by The Glines, New York, 1981

My Blue Heaven
  Production, Shandol Theatre by The Glines, New York, 1981
  Production, Theatre Rhinoceros, San Francisco, 1982

Kudzu
  Workshop (pre-Broadway), Playwrights Horizons, New York, 1981
  Production, Theatre Rhinoceros, San Francisco, 1988

Quintessential Image
  Production, Town Hall, New York, 1982
  Production, Theatre Rhinoceros, San Francisco, 1984

The Eye of the Gulf (written in 1971; revised by Vita Dennis)
  Production, Footsteps Theatre, Chicago, 1991

PLAY AVAILABILITY

Last Summer at Bluefish Cove is published in Lillian Faderman, ed., *Chloe Plus Olivia: An Anthology of Lesbian Literature from the 17th Century to the Present*. New York: Viking, 1994; and by JH Press, New York, 1982 (TN'T Classics).

A Late Snow is published in William M. Hoffman, ed., *Gay Plays: The First Collection*.

New York: Avon/Bard, 1979; and by JH Press, New York, 1970, 1989 (now TN'T Classics).

My Blue Heaven is published by JH Press, New York, 1982 (TN'T Classics).

Quintessential Image is published in Rosemary Curb, ed., *Amazon All Stars: 13 Lesbian Plays.* New York: Applause, 1996.

Unpublished plays are available from Beth Allen, 402 5th Street, Greenport, New York, 11914; (212) 580–9999.

AWARDS

Connecticut Public Television Award for Best Original Religious Drama, 1971

Rosenthal Poetry Award, 1971

Eugene O'Neill Playwright, 1972

CAPS Grant, New York State, 1977

Dramalogue Critics Circle Award, *Bluefish Cove*, 1980

Fund for Human Dignity Award, 1982

Los Angeles Drama Critics' Circle Award, *Bluefish Cove*, 1983

Dramalogue Critics Circle Award, *Kudzu*, 1988

DESCRIPTIVE AND CRITICAL RESPONSES

Case, Sue-Ellen. *Feminism and Theatre.* New York: Methuen, 1988; 77–78.

Contemporary Authors. Vol. 85–88. Detroit: Gale Research, 1980, 76–78.

Coss, Clare. "On Jane Chambers: An Interview with Beth Allen and Jere Jacob." *Heresies* 17 (1984): 83–84.

Dace, Tish. "For Whom the Bell Tolled." *New York Native*, 24 October–6 November 1983, 47.

Dolan, Jill. *Presence and Desire.* Ann Arbor: University of Michigan Press, 1993, 169–72.

Feingold, Michael. "The Good Little Girl Grows Up." *Village Voice*, 15 August 1989, 93.

Helbing, Terry. "Jane Chambers: A Reminiscence." *New York Native*, 11 April 1983, 14.

Hoffman, William, ed. "Introduction." *Gay Plays: The First Collection.* New York: Avon, 1979, x–xii, xxxvii–xxxviii.

Landau, Penny M. "Jane Chambers: In Memoriam." *Women and Performance* 1, no. 2 (1984): 55–57.

Rich, Frank. "*Last Summer at Bluefish Cove.*" Review of *Last Summer at Bluefish Cove. New York Times*, 27 December 1980, 13.

Sisley, Emily. "Playwright Jane Chambers: The Long Road to *Last Summer at Bluefish Cove.*" *Advocate*, Los Angeles, 13 November 1980, 31–32.

Stasio, Marilyn. "A Warm 'Summer' at the Glines." *New York Post*, 3 July 1980, 27.

EUGENIE CHAN

(1962–   )

BIOGRAPHY

Eugenie Chan, who was born and raised in the San Francisco Bay Area, is a fifth-generation Chinese American. In 1984 she received her BA in literature from Yale University. Her MFA, awarded in 1993, is from New York University's Tisch School of the Arts where she won the Graduate Achievement Award in Playwriting and Screenwriting.

Before turning to dramatic writing, Chan worked as a dramaturg at various regional theatres, including Berkeley Repertory and the Magic Theatre in San Francisco, where she also served as literary manager from 1988 to 1991. She taught writing and English literature at the Chinese University in Hong Kong, as a Yale-China Teaching Fellow, and at Skyline Community College in the Bay Area.

In addition to her dramatic works, Eugenie Chan works as a screenwriter. Her screenplay *Paradise Plains* was filmed in 1993, and *Street X*, a street soap opera which she coauthored, was filmed in 1992. *Willie Gee!* was a finalist in the Academy of Motion Picture Arts and Sciences' Nicholl Fellowship. Other screenplays include *Athena Adrift*, *Communion*, and *Winnie's World*.

PLAY DESCRIPTIONS

Eugenie Chan has stated that she "seek[s] to explore different aspects of Chinese American experience in the hopes of uncovering some kind of personal myth or logic that will make sense of it." This process of uncovering began with her choreopoem *The Fan*, which is a parody of a "fan dance." In a dance using Chinese and Japanese movement and fans, three Asian women assume caricatures of Asian women through time to play out their rage and desire. *Tour*

Sino is a radio play that depicts one day in the life of a tour guide in China after the Tiananmen Square uprising.

Closer to her own roots is *Rancho Grande*, a surrealistic coming-of-age play. Set in the middle of the Southwestern desert, Mamie, a precocious young Chinese-American girl, dreams of becoming the Great American Kissin' Cowgirl. Dream is confused with reality, however, as Mamie and her brother Sammy attempt to keep the disintegrating family intact, and Mamie asserts her own identity as a woman. Chan mixes Eastern and Western images symbolized most poignantly in the juxtaposition of Mamie's dime-store cowgirl outfit and her mother's traditional Chinese wedding dress. The dramatic parable is an exploration of cultural and gender issues, a tale of growing up made more difficult by living out a strange version of the Chinese legend of Moon Lady and Oxboy.

The free blending of reality and fantasy is also characteristic of the short play *Novell-aah!*, a send-up of the Spanish soap opera form. A Chinese mother and daughter enact a love/hate relationship that focuses on the same Latino lover. Marlene, an aging grand dame in peignoir and bleached blond 'do, embraces Izzy, a young tuxedoed Casanova, who is revealed to be Marlene's daughter. Both await the arrival of Carlos, their shared object of lust and passion. In a series of interruptions to the games played by Marlene and Izzy, Olga, the maid, reveals first that Carlos is stuck in traffic, then that he is sick and ultimately dead. Their quick recovery into another "routine" brings into question the reality of their suitor.

Chan's quirky, unique voice also reflects a multicultural landscape in her *Emil, a Chinese Play*. Emil, a South American man, undertakes a picaresque journey in America in search of "home." He is snared by Mother in Chinatown, who brings him home to Maggie, her virginal, resistant daughter. Although Mother wants heirs, she also wants Emil. The ensuing love triangle is worked out during the remainder of the play.

Chan says her objective in these plays is "to mine the breadth of races, cultural identities, dreams and aesthetics that have shaped and continue to shape the real and mythological American landscape. Mostly, the plays are comedies that deal with serious issues. In formal terms, I use a lot of imagery and wordplay."

SELECTED PRODUCTION HISTORY

The Fan (one-act play)
  Production, Yale University, New Haven, Connecticut, 1983

Emil, a Chinese Play
  Staged reading, East West Players, Los Angeles, 1990s (exact date not available)
  Staged reading, Pan Asian Repertory, New York, 1990s (exact date not available)

Tour Sino (radio play)
  Aired, WBAI, New York, 1992

Novell-aah!

Staged reading, Public Theatre, New York, 1993
Production, BRAVA! for Women in the Arts, San Francisco, 1994

Rancho Grande
Staged reading, Bay Area Playwrights Festival, San Francisco, 1994

PLAY AVAILABILITY

Eugenie Chan's plays may be obtained directly from the playwright: 1479 Terrytown Street, San Mateo, CA 94402; (415) 341–9396 or (415) 453–4878.

AWARDS

Graduate Achievement Award in Playwriting and Screenwriting, New York University, Tisch School of the Arts, 1993

DESCRIPTIVE AND CRITICAL RESPONSES

Ahlgren, Calvin. "Diversity Grows in Plays by Asian Americans." *San Francisco Chronicle*, 16 July 1989.
Stein, Ruthe. "Playwrights on Edge of Discovery." *San Francisco Chronicle*, 2 August 1994, E1.
Yang, Jeff. "Critical Mass." *Village Voice*, 16 March 1993, 92.

DENISE CHÁVEZ

(1948–   )

BIOGRAPHY

Denise Chávez was born in Las Cruces, New Mexico, in 1948. She took theatre classes while going to high school in Mesilla, New Mexico, and attended New Mexico State University where she studied under Mark Medoff. After graduating with a BA in 1971, Chávez attended Trinity University in San Antonio, Texas, where she earned an MFA in theatre. In 1984 she received an MA in creative writing from the University of New Mexico.

As an educator, Chávez has taught various courses in theatre, playwriting, and creative writing at the College of Santa Fe, the American School of Paris, Northern New Mexico Community College, and the University of Houston. She has worked extensively with the bilingual theatre La Compania de Teatro de Albuquerque and Sante Fe's Theater-in-the-Red. Denise Chávez is also active in many organizations that promote and employ the arts in the community, especially among senior citizens and at-risk youth.

In addition to her work as a playwright, Denise Chávez is an actress, poet, essayist, short story writer, and novelist. *Face of an Angel*, a novel, was published in 1990, and her short stories and other writing are frequently anthologized in *The Norton Anthology of American Literature*, *Breaking Boundaries*, *Chicana Creativity and Criticism*, and numerous other collections and periodicals.

Denise Chávez has returned to her hometown of Las Cruces, New Mexico, where she continues to write.

PLAY DESCRIPTIONS

One of Denise Chávez's goals as a writer is to give voice to those people who traditionally have had no voice. Her plays focus on the lives of people one does not generally see as characters in plays: the old men who occupy the benches of the town plaza, bag ladies, waitresses, and others. They are all survivors in the harsh, dry background of her native Southwest. *Plaza* is representative of her subjects and style. Set on a typical day in Santa Fe's plaza, the play is populated with "regular folk": a retired janitor-handyman, who watches all the comings and goings in the plaza from his bench (Benito); a slightly retarded paper boy (Wilfred); a waitress of forty years standing at the Plaza Cafe (Minnie); a real estate broker and insurance salesman, who is running for reelection to the state senate (Tommy); the thirtyish owner of the Turquoise Tepee gift shop (Iris); and a teenage breakdancer spending the summer with her divorced father in Santa Fe (Cris). Chávez weaves their individual stories into a colorful tapestry of Southwestern life as their paths crisscross throughout the day. Amid the finely crafted character detail, Chávez is able to raise important issues: traditional versus contemporary values and the true meaning of friends and family.

SELECTED PRODUCTION HISTORY

Novitiates (one-act play)
  Production, Dallas Theatre Center, Dallas, 1971

Elevators (one-act play)
  Production, Munn Theatre, Santa Fe, New Mexico, 1972

The Flying Tortilla Man (one-act play)
  Production, Northern New Mexico Community College, Espanola, 1975

The Mask of November (one-act play)
  Production, Northern New Mexico Community College, Espanola, 1977

Nacimiento (one-act play)
  Production, Kimo Theatre, Albuquerque, New Mexico, 1979

The Adobe Rabbit (one-act play)
  Production, Taos Community Auditorium, Taos, New Mexico, 1979

Plaza (one-act play originally produced under the title *Santa Fe Charm*)
  Production, Santa Fe Armory for the Arts, Santa Fe, New Mexico, 1980
  Production, Kimo Theatre, Albuquerque, New Mexico, 1984

Si, Hay Posada (one-act play)
  Production, Kimo Theatre, Albuquerque, New Mexico, 1980

El Santero de Cordova (one-act play)
  Production, Fiesta Artesana, Albuquerque, New Mexico, 1981

How Junior Got Throwed in the Joint (one-act play)
  Production, Penitentiary of New Mexico, Santa Fe, New Mexico, 1981

Hecho en Mexico (one-act play written with Nita Luna)
  Production, El Sancturario de Guadalupe, Santa Fe, New Mexico, 1982

The Green Madonna (one-act play)
  Production, Armory for the Arts, Santa Fe, New Mexico, 1982

La Morenita (one-act play)
Production, Immaculate Heart of Mary Cathedral, Las Cruces, New Mexico, 1983

Francis! (one-act play)
Production, Immaculate Heart of Mary Cathedral, Las Cruces, New Mexico, 1983

El Mas Pequeño de Mis Hijos (one-act play)
Production, Kimo Theatre, Albuquerque, New Mexico, 1983

Novena Narratives (one-woman show)
Production, Our Lady of Guadalupe Church, Taos, New Mexico, 1986

The Step (one-act play)
Production, Museum of Fine Arts, Houston, 1987

Language of Vision (one-act play)
Production, Albuquerque Convention Center, Albuquerque, New Mexico, 1987

Women in a State of Grace (one-woman show)
Production, Museum of Fine Arts, Houston, 1989

The Last of the Menu Girls (one-act play adapted from author's short story of the same title)
Production, Main Street Theatre and Teatro Bilingue de Houston, Houston, 1990

PLAY AVAILABILITY

Novena Narrativas y Ofrendas Nuevomexicanas is published in Maria Hererra-Sobek and Helena Maria Viramontes, eds., *Chicana Creativity and Criticism: Charting New Frontiers in American Literature.* Houston: Arte Publico Press, 1988.

Plaza is available in David Richard Jones, ed., *New Mexico Plays.* Albuquerque: University of New Mexico Press, 1989.

AWARDS

Best Play Award, New Mexico State University, *The Wait*, 1970

New Mexico Arts Division Grant, 1980

National Endowment for the Arts Grant, 1981

Rockefeller Foundation, Playwriting Grant, 1984

Arts Council of Houston Grant, 1989

Cultural Arts Council of Houston, Creative Artist Award, 1990

DESCRIPTIVE AND CRITICAL RESPONSES

Gray, Lynn. "Interview with Denise Chávez." *Short Story Review* 5, no. 4 (Fall 1988): 2–4.
Heard, Martha E. "The Theatre of Denise Chávez: Interior Landscapes with 'sabor nuevomexicano.' " *The Americas Review: A Review of Hispanic Literature and Art of the USA* 16, no. 2 (Summer 1988): 83–91.

Moran, Julio. " 'My Dream Was to Work at the Dairy Queen.' " *Los Angeles Times*, 9
        November 1994, E1.
Sowers, Leslie. "A Spicy Slice." *Houston Chronicle*, 12 October 1994, D1.
Valdes, Alisa. "La Girlfriend Denise Chávez." *Boston Globe*, 30 September 1994, 61.

THERESA CHAVEZ

(1957–   )

BIOGRAPHY

Theresa Chavez is a writer, director, producer, and interdisciplinary artist with a background and training in performance/theatre, dance, photography, music/voice, and the social sciences. She received an interdisciplinary BA in the social sciences from UCLA in 1979. This was followed by a BFA and an MFA in photography from the California Institute of the Arts in Valencia.

Chavez served as assistant to the artistic director of the Los Angeles Theatre Center and with the Latino Theatre Lab of the Los Angeles Theatre Center. In 1987 she became a cofounder and artistic codirector of About Productions, a nonprofit interdisciplinary arts organization which produces works challenging traditional assumptions about history, gender, and cultural and sexual identity.

Her photographic and curatorial work has appeared in various art spaces including the International Arts Relations (INTAR) Gallery in New York, the Los Angeles Center for Photographic Studies, Beyond Baroque, and others. As an associate with Community Arts Resources (CARS), Chavez helps in the management and production of festivals (Santa Monica Arts Festival), concerts, art bus tours, and conferences. Chavez is active on numerous arts committees and advisory groups that promote the work of women and multicultural artists.

Theresa Chavez is currently on the faculty of the School of Art and School of Film at the California Institute of the Arts where she teaches courses in the interdisciplinary, collaborative process, performance art, and interdisciplinary critique.

PLAY DESCRIPTIONS

Theresa Chavez's work encompasses a wide range of topics and issues that challenge the assumptions (ethnic, cultural, gender) dominating our contemporary heritage. *The Musical Chairs*, an interactive theatre game-ritual, examines the role of ritual in contemporary culture while *Mektoub* is an intermedia performance piece that combines a panel with theatrical scenes to reconstruct the story of Isabelle Eberhardt. The collaborative performance piece *Job* is structured by four authors in search of a script dealing with the history of labor and the labor of acting.

Vox combines historical record with contemporary technology to examine the nature of speech, gender, and language. Structured around the historical fifteenth-century trial of Joan of Arc, *Vox* fluidly moves from past to present as it explores war and women's relationships to war. Using transcripts of the trial proceedings, Chavez highlights the disparity between Joan of Arc's testimony and the official record of the trial. Joan's accounts were eclipsed in favor of the version generated by the male clergy and transcribers; this discrepancy between the two versions is only one of the several juxtapositions between public and private voice. As the play moves into the twentieth century, Joan of Arc becomes Lt. Col. Joan Purcell who is court-martialed for her outspoken opposition to the violence and destruction of war. Joan's inquisitor becomes a television talk show host while other figures become reporters. Employing the technology of the theatre, Chavez multiplies, divides, and distorts the voices of her characters as they struggle to be heard and understood. The roles of historical record, translation, and the media in the construction of the public voice are scrutinized as is the conflict between finding one's voice (especially for women) and the persistent attempts to silence that voice.

In *L.A. Real*, Chavez explores her own family tree (the Lugo clan) and its place in the history of Los Angeles. In the interdisciplinary work (both as a single-person performance piece and as a six-person piece), Chavez attempts to reclaim the history of the city through a collage-like exploration of cultural roots and identity. By combining text, music, dance, painting, photography, and video, Chavez excavates the real history from the myth and the romanticized nostalgia under which it is buried. The journey is overseen by two twentieth-century mestiza narrators: Rachel, the great-great-great-granddaughter of the Spanish Lugos who helped settle the valley in the 1770s, and Joe Gabrielino, a native California Indian. The conflicting ways in which property was perceived by the three dominant cultures that have inhabited Los Angeles (the native Indian, the mestizo/Mexican, and the American/European) become a yardstick of the cultures' values. The contemporary real estate agent is the epitome of the fast-talking salesman whose versions of Mexican and Indian history are incorporated into plasticized tract homes. Chavez is not afraid to ask who or what is the "real" Los Angeles in her attempt to salvage her heritage from fast-food restaurants and superhighways.

The Correct Posture of a True Revolutionary, a fictional performance piece in progress, is concerned with how Americans define revolution and how it is affected by language and imagery. Angela Davis, Sandino, Che Guevara's mother (Celia de la Cerna), and a Nicaraguan woman who is a poet/soldier are characters who all must grapple with their identities as revolutionaries.

SELECTED PRODUCTION HISTORY

The Musical Chairs (interdisciplinary, interactive theater game-ritual)
  Performance, Theater II, California Institute of the Arts, Valencia, 1986

Vozes (one-person performance piece; earlier version of *Vox*)
  Performance, Lhasa Club, Hollywood, California, 1986

Mektoub (intermedia performance)
  Performance, California Institute of the Arts, Los Angeles, 1988

Vox (interdisciplinary performance piece)
  Performance, Skylight Theatre, Los Angeles, 1988

Job (collaborative performance piece)
  Performance, Beyond Baroque, Venice, California, 1989
  Performance, Flight Theater, Los Angeles, 1990

L.A. Real (six-person interdisciplinary performance piece)
  Performance, Los Angeles Contemporary Exhibitions (LACE), Los Angeles, 1990
  Performance, Highways Performance Space, Santa Monica, California, 1990
  Performance, Gene Autry Western Heritage Museum, Los Angeles, 1993
  Performance, Armory Center for the Arts, Pasadena, California, 1993

L.A. Real (one-person interdisciplinary performance piece)
  Performance, National Women's Theatre Festival, UCLA, Los Angeles, 1992
  Performance, Mark Taper Forum, Los Angeles, 1992
  Performance, ARLIS Conference, San Diego Museum of Contemporary Art, San Diego, California 1992
  Performance, Public Theatre, New York, 1992
  Performance, California State University, Northridge, California, 1993

The Correct Posture of a True Revolutionary (performance piece)
  Performance, Poetry Center, San Francisco, 1994
  Performance, Highways Performance Space, Santa Monica, California, 1994
  Performance, Macondo Espacio Cultural, Los Angeles, 1994
  Performance, Los Angeles Theatre Center, Los Angeles, 1995

Vox
  Reading, Telluride Theatre Festival, Colorado, 1996
  Reading, Los Angeles Theatre Center, Los Angeles, 1996

PLAY AVAILABILITY

Scripts are available through the playwright: Theresa Chavez, 2018 Griffith Park Boulevard, Apt. #120, Los Angeles, California 90030; (213) 664–9602.

AWARDS

National/State/County Partnership Multicultural Artists Consultancy Grant, 1987

Pasadena Arts Commission, Artist in Residence, 1992

Artist in the Community, City of Los Angeles Cultural Affairs Department, 1992–1993

DESCRIPTIVE AND CRITICAL RESPONSES

Agalidi, Sanda. "Notes on *Vox*." *Oversight Magazine* (Spring 1990): 22–23.

Breslauer, Jan. "A Funny Thing Happened at the Forum." *LA Weekly*, 16–22 October 1992, 33.

Burnham, Linda Frye. "Alternative Histories: Artists Challenge the Official Story." *High Performance* (Winter 1992): 57–59.

Drake, Sylvie. "Women Continue Empowerment Theme." *Los Angeles Times*, 1 August 1992, F12–13.

———. "A Bigger *L.A. Real*." Review *L.A. Real*. *Los Angeles Times*, 3 April 1994, F4.

Winer, Laurie. "A Revolutionary's Dilemma." Review of *The Correct Posture of a True Revolutionary*. *Los Angeles Times*, 10 April 1995, F3.

Zellen, Jody. "Theresa Chavez *Vox*." *High Performance* (Summer 1989): 52.

KITTY CHEN

(n.d.–)

BIOGRAPHY

Kitty Chen was born in Shanghai, China, and raised near Philadelphia. Chen came to New York City after receiving a BA in math from Brown University. Chen received a scholarship at the Martha Graham School in New York, where she studied modern dance. Her career as a dancer led Chen into acting and the theatre where she has performed on stage, screen, and television. The dearth of interesting parts for Asian women compelled her to write.

Kitty Chen is a member of the Dramatists Guild, Women's Project and Productions Playwrights' Lab, and the Asian Pacific Alliance for Creative Equality.

PLAY DESCRIPTIONS

Kitty Chen's work deals with serious issues in a humorous, often playful manner. Through witty dialogue and lively characters, she gives the audience entertaining and enlightening glimpses into family relationships and Chinese American culture. For example, in the domestic comedy *Rosa Loses Her Face*, a mother and daughter learn to accept and respect each other in new ways. Amy Loo, a poet in her thirties, goes home to visit her overbearing mother, Rosa. The single-minded Rosa is determined that Amy marry a wealthy Asian and has promised Larry Tanaka, her accountant, that Amy will marry him. Amy, on the other hand, is waiting for a call from Gregor, the Polish poet and locksmith to whom she has lost her heart. When Amy realizes her mother's scheme, she forces a confrontation that culminates in an exciting Peking Duck toss.

Family is again the focus in *Eating Chicken Feet*, Chen's bittersweet look at a daughter's coming to terms with her parents' separation and ultimate divorce. Betty Sung, a young woman of eighteen, is in a coma in the hospital after her ploy to bring her parents together has gone awry. Chen juxtaposes the comatose Betty with her conscious alter ego who narrates the story and directs some of the action from the vantage point of her hospital room. Gathered into her world are her parents, her brother Lowell, his friend Peter, and Peter's feminist girlfriend, Diane. Betty's fantasies allow her to create, if only for a moment, the kind of "Father Knows Best" family for which she longs. When her efforts fail to reunite her parents, however, Betty is forced to wake to the reality of her familial situation. She and Diane commiserate over chicken feet soup (a symbol of women's second-class status in Chinese culture), and Betty begins to understand the quiet strength it takes for her mother to leave her verbally abusive husband. Chen's successful blending of seriousness and compassion with playful absurdity in her examination of the complexities of family life transcends cultural boundaries.

SELECTED PRODUCTION HISTORY

On Good Terms
  Reading, Second Stage, New York, 1985

Rosa Loses Her Face
  Reading, Hudson Guild Theatre, New York, 1989
  Reading, Double Image Theater, New York, 1990

Eating Chicken Feet
  Reading, East West Players, Los Angeles, 1991
  Workshop, Playwrights Theatre of New Jersey, Madison, 1993
  Production, Women's Project and Productions/Pan Asian Repertory Theatre, New York, 1993

A Change of Heart, So to Speak
  Production, Nat Horne Theatre, New York, 1994
  Production, Pegasus Theatre, Houston, 1994
  Reading, La Mama La Galleria, New York, 1995

She's Not My Relative
  Reading, Tandem Acts, Women's Project, New York, 1994
  Reading, La Mama La Galleria, New York, 1995

I See My Bones (previously titled *Old Folks*)
  Workshop, Playwrights Theatre of New Jersey, Madison, 1995
  Reading, Women's Project, New York, 1995
  Tour, Urban Stages (Playwrights Preview Productions), New York, 1996

Taking It on the Chin
  Staged reading, Tandem Acts, Women's Project, New York, 1995

Rowing to America
  Staged reading, Tandem Acts, Women's Project, New York, 1996

PLAY AVAILABILITY

Eating Chicken Feet is published by Dramatic Publishing Company, P.O. Box 129, Woodstock, Illinois 60098.

All unpublished plays are available from the playwright: Kitty Chen, 152 West 94th
Street, Apt. 1, New York, New York 10025; (212) 666–1104.

AWARDS

Fellowship, Blue Mountain Center, 1987

Fellowship, New York Foundation for the Arts, 1989

National Endowment for the Arts, Playwriting Fellowship, 1992–1993

Fellowship, Edward Albee Foundation, 1992

Humana Festival, Actors Theatre of Louisville, finalist, *Eating Chicken Feet*, 1992

DESCRIPTIVE AND CRITICAL RESPONSES

Bruckner, D.J.R. "*Eating Chicken Feet.*" *New York Times*, 9 November 1993, C22.
Daniels, Robert L. "*I See My Bones.*" *Variety*, 30 October–5 November 1995, 178.
Evans, Greg. "*Eating Chicken Feet.*" *Variety*, 22 November 1993, 36, 37.
"Kitty Chen on *Eating Chicken Feet.*" [Women's Project and Productions] *Dialogues*
10, no. 1 (Fall 1993): 1, 3.

PEARL CLEAGE

(1948–)

BIOGRAPHY

Pearl Cleage was born in Springfield, Massachusetts, but grew up in Detroit, Michigan. She studied playwriting at Howard University for three years and then completed her undergraduate education at Spelman College in 1971 with a BA in theatre. Later she pursued Afro-American studies at Atlanta University and creative writing at the University of the West Indies.

Cleage has worked at a variety of jobs in the Atlanta area, including working at the Archival Library of the Martin Luther King Memorial; serving as the director of communications for Atlanta's first black mayor, Maynard Jackson; and emerging as media personality by hosting "Black Viewpoints" on a local television channel and interviewing, writing, and producing "Ebony Beat Journal" for another station.

Pearl Cleage's multifaceted writing career includes poetry, essays, and fiction, in addition to her plays. Her most recently published collections include *Mad at Miles: A Black Woman's Guide to Truth* (1990), *The Brass Bed and Other Stories* (1991), and *Deals with the Devil: And Other Reasons to Riot* (1993). She is also a regular contributor to *Essence*, and her essays are published in numerous journals and magazines.

Amid all of her writing and journalistic endeavors, Cleage continues to write plays and to create and perform a repertoire of performance pieces, many done in collaboration with other artists. Her best known play, *Flyin' West*, commissioned by the Alliance Theatre, has had many regional productions. From 1983 to 1987, she was playwright in residence at Atlanta's Just Us Theatre Company where she took over the artistic directorship in 1987. She founded the magazine *Catalyst* in 1987, is a columnist for the *Atlanta Tribune*, and teaches creative writing at Spelman College.

PLAY DESCRIPTIONS

Pearl Cleage's plays feature black women who, either by choice or circumstance, take their lives into their own hands. Her keen ear for dialogue and her strong, earthy characters provide a powerful insight into the struggles of the disenfranchised. *Hospice* is a domestic drama that pits the cancer-ridden Alice Anderson against her thirty-year-old pregnant daughter, Jenny. Reunited for the first time since Alice left Jenny at age ten to live the life of a bohemian poetess in Paris, mother and daughter have separately sought refuge in the house previously occupied by Alice's mother and Jenny's grandmother. They warily circle each other, giving voice to their own angers and fears. Alice, wracked with pain and facing the inevitability of her own death, is forced to justify her effort to achieve her own identity, both as a woman and as a poet. Jenny, struggling to become a writer herself and confronting the impending birth of her child, comes to terms with the reality of her mother's love.

Chain is the first in a series of plays that Cleage refers to as morality plays which seek a redefinition of sisterhood and survival. This short piece is essentially an extended monologue that delineates sixteen-year-old Rosa Jenkins's struggle to get off drugs. She is chained to the radiator in her Harlem living room by her well-meaning parents, and her physical confinement powerfully objectifies the more abstract imprisonment of young people seduced by drugs on the street. During the seven-day period of the play, we see Rosa live through a process of transformation. As the drugs ebb from her body, she moves from being a caged animal instinctively fighting her tether, to an angry young woman—angry at the society that shaped her choice. Slowly her anger is replaced with defiance, then complacency, and at last, hope. As she finally opens the door to the outside world, the audience is left to wonder if her new resolve to live a drug-free life will remain steadfast.

A transformative process also provides the action of *Late Bus to Mecca*. Set two nights before Mohammed Ali's return to boxing in 1970, Cleage's play shows the evolution of trust and caring between two very different women— strangers waiting for the late bus to Atlanta. Ava is a self-confident young woman who has chosen this event as an opportunity to start over. The silent young black woman, on the other hand, is fearful, suspicious, and less self-directed than her fellow traveler. In this essentially extended monologue, Ava's prying turns to honest concern. As their unique communication develops, the young woman appears to find a direction in her life and joins Ava for the trip to Atlanta. As in her other plays, Cleage captures characters in small moments of self-definition that give her women strength and direction.

Flyin' West provides a new and unique perspective on the traditional telling of how the West was won. Seen through the eyes of four adventurous African-American women, the play depicts their struggle for land and independence in nineteenth-century Kansas.

SELECTED PRODUCTION HISTORY

The following list does not include Pearl Cleage's performance art pieces. Contact the playwright for information and availability.

The Sale (one-act farce)
   Production, Morehouse/Spelman College Players, Atlanta, 1972

Hymn for the Rebels (one act)
   Production, Sons and Ancestors Players, San Francisco, 1974

puppetplay (full-length piece for two actresses and a marionette)
   Production, New Play Project, Just Us Theater, Atlanta, 1982
   Production, Just Us Theater, Atlanta, 1983
   Production, Negro Ensemble Company, New York, 1983

Hospice
   Production, New Federal Theatre, New York, 1983
   Production, Colonade Theatre, New York, 1984
   Production, Just Us Theater, Atlanta, 1985
   Production, MAMU Players, Johannesburg, South Africa, 1990

Good News
   Production, Just Us Theater, Atlanta, 1984
   Production, Sojourner Truth Theater Company, Ft. Worth, Texas, 1985

Porch Songs
   Production, Phoenix Theater Company, Indianapolis, Indiana, 1985

Banana Bread
   Production, Just Us Theater, Atlanta, 1985

Essentials
   Production, Passage Theater Company, Trenton, New Jersey, 1986

Come and Get These Memories
   Production, Billie Holiday Theater, Brooklyn, New York, 1988

Chain
   Production, Women's Projects and Productions and New Federal Theatre, New York, 1992

Late Bus to Mecca
   Production, Women's Projects and Productions and New Federal Theatre, New York, 1992

Flyin' West
   Production (commission), Alliance Theatre, Atlanta, 1992
   Production, Crossroads Theatre, New Brunswick, New Jersey, 1993
   Production, Long Wharf Theater, New Haven, Connecticut, 1994
   Production, San Diego Repertory Theatre, San Diego, 1994
   Production, Kennedy Center, Washington, D.C., 1994
   Production, Majestic Theatre, Brooklyn, New York, 1994
   Production, Unicorn Theatre, Kansas City, Missouri, 1997

Blues for an Alabama Sky

Production, Alliance Studio Theatre, Atlanta, 1995
Production, Hartford Stage Company, Hartford, Connecticut, 1996
Production, Arena Stage, Washington, D.C., 1996
Production, Olympic Arts Festival, Atlanta, 1996
Production, Huntington Theatre Company, Boston, 1997
Production, Oregon Shakespeare Festival, Ashland, 1997

Bourbon at the Border
Production (commission), Alliance Studio Theatre, Atlanta, 1997

PLAY AVAILABILITY

Chain and *Late Bus to Mecca* are available in Julia Miles, ed., *Playwriting Women: 7 Plays from the Women's Project*. Portsmouth, New Hampshire: Heinemann, 1993.

Flyin' West is published in Kathy A. Perkins and Roberta Uno, eds., *Contemporary Plays by Women of Color: An Anthology*. New York: Routledge, 1996.

Hospice is published in Woodie King, Jr., ed., *New Plays for the Black Theatre*. Chicago: Third World Press, 1989.

AWARDS

AUDELCO Awards, New York, Best Play and Best Playwright, *Hospice*, 1983

National Endowment for the Arts, Residency Grant, Just Us Theater Company, Atlanta, 1983–1987

Susan Smith Blackburn Award, Finalist, *Hospice*, 1984

Grahamstown Festival, South Africa, First Prize, *Hospice*, 1990

Pearl Cleage has won numerous state and local arts council awards in addition to support from the Coca-Cola Foundation and AT&T for her various literary and performance works.

DESCRIPTIVE AND CRITICAL RESPONSES

Churnin, Nancy. "Promising *Flyin' West* at San Diego Rep." Review of *Flyin' West*. *Los Angeles Times*, 27 September 1994, F4.
Gussow, Mel. "*Chain* and *Late Bus to Mecca*." Review of *Chain* and *Late Bus to Mecca*. *New York Times*, 4 March 1992, C19.
Klein, Alvin. "*Flyin' West* on Stage." Review of *Flyin' West*. *New York Times*, 19 June 1994, C19.
Pousner, Howard. " 'I Have Always Known I'm a Writer.' " *Atlanta Journal and Constitution*, 19 March 1995, M4.
Worrell, Kris. "Playwright, Poet, Pundit: Pearl Cleage." *Atlanta Constitutional*, 13 October 1993, E1.

KATHLEEN COLLINS

(1942–1988)

BIOGRAPHY

Born in Jersey City, New Jersey, Kathleen Collins died at the age of forty-six of cancer. Not only was she a filmmaker, translator, fiction writer, playwright, and educator, but she was also a role model for many young black students while she was an associate professor of film at City College of New York.

She received a BA in philosophy and religion from Skidmore College and an MA in French literature and cinema from the Middlebury Graduate School in France, and she did doctoral course work at Union Theological Seminary. From 1965 to 1967, she worked as a translator for *Cahiers du Cinema* in Paris. After returning to the United States, Collins worked on various films and at National Educational Television. In 1973 she was hired by City College where she taught for fifteen years. Her first film, *The Cruz Brothers and Mrs. Malloy*, a comedy featuring two Latino men and a white woman, was criticized for not addressing the black experience. *Losing Ground*, the best known of her films, tells the story of a middle-class, black woman's struggle to find herself within her marriage. It was screened at the Museum of Modern Art and appeared on American Playhouse. In her films, as well as in her plays, she refused to depict blacks in the traditional role of heroic or resigned victim. She believed herself to be more of a writer than a filmmaker, and at the time of her death she was finishing a novel and beginning preproduction work for a feature film. Collins had a daughter and two sons in her first marriage and two stepchildren from her second husband, Alfred Prettyman.

PLAY DESCRIPTIONS

Collins's major plays, *In the Midnight Hour* and *The Brothers*, are both about upper middle-class black families, characters infrequently featured on the stage (or in any media) in the early 1980s, and both are distinguished by an unconventional structure. The plays reflect her background in philosophy and religion for they are concerned with the reflective themes of finding meaning and purpose in life. Collins allows characters to speak their inner thoughts through monologues and reveals character primarily through language rather than action, often through monologues.

In the Midnight Hour takes place in a room in a Harlem apartment that is described as a place where people want to stay and talk. On the evening and morning when the play takes place, Ralph and Lillie Daniels host Ralph's best friend Floyd, their daughter and son, the son's new girlfriend, and a jazz piano player, Chips, who is secretly in love with the daughter. The conversation that extends from late afternoon into the next morning is underscored by music, notably versions of "In the Midnight Hour," pointing up that the play is constructed more like a musical composition than a narrative-driven drama. During a dialogue between the son and his girlfriend, the realistic mode shifts and the mother and father appear in a flash-forward. While, on the surface, the characters seem well-insulated from Harlem street life and the civil rights movement by the style in which they live, fissures appear and the discontent of the son and daughter is revealed. The young people enter from an outside world of political unrest into the protective room, and, by the end of play, we know that the apartment cannot continue to provide a sanctuary.

The Brothers alerts us to the presence of political upheaval but similarly keeps reality distant by using a radio announcement of Gandhi's death and a broadcast of Martin Luther King's assassination to bracket the play. The characters are the wives and sister of the Edwards brothers who come together when Nelson Edwards, a former track star, takes to his bed at the age of thirty-one in mourning over "the Negro void" and refuses to get up again. As the women tend to him and try to persuade him to rise out of bed, the ways in which their lives have been circumscribed by the Edwards brothers become evident. Act I begins with his confinement and Act III, twenty years later, starts with preparations for Nelson's funeral. Although the brothers, who "should have been born white" because they "spend their entire lives trying to jump out of their skins," are seen only through the women on stage, their off-stage characters are revealed as clearly as the characters of those on stage. Collins said in an interview that in her work she takes an audience to the explosive moment, "but that's basically where I leave you" (Hudson, 69). Her plays, full of literate talk and wit, compliment an audience's intelligence by withholding easy resolutions.

SELECTED PRODUCTION HISTORY

In the Midnight Hour
> Reading, Women's Project at the American Place Theatre, New York, 1980
> Production, Richard Allen Center for Culture and Art, International Black Theatre Festival, New York, 1982

The Brothers
   Production, Women's Project at the American Place Theatre, New York, 1982
   Production, Kunta Repertory Theatre, Pittsburgh, 1982

The Reading
   Reading, Women's Project at the American Place Theatre, New York, 1984

When Older Men Speak
   Reading, Women's Project at the American Place Theatre, New York, 1985

Only the Sky Is Free
   Reading, Richard Allen Center for Culture and Art, New York, 1986

PLAY AVAILABILITY

The Brothers is available in Margaret B. Wilkerson, ed., *Playscript: 9 Plays by Black Women*. New York: New American Library, 1986; Julia Miles, ed., *The Women's Project 2*. New York: Performing Arts Journal Publications, 1984.

In the Midnight Hour is published in Julia Miles, ed., *The Women's Project: Seven New Plays*. New York: Performing Arts Journal Publications, 1980.

Other plays and rights: Prettyman Agency, 215 West 98th Street, Suite 12B, New York, New York 10025.

AWARDS

New York State Council on the Arts, Post-Production Grant, 1980

American Film Institute Grant, 1981

Susan Smith Blackburn Award, Finalist, *The Brothers*, 1983

AUDELCO Award, Finalist, *The Brothers*, 1983

DESCRIPTIVE AND CRITICAL RESPONSES

Hudson, William. "Kathleen Collins, 1942–88." *Village Voice*, 11 October 1988, 69.
Mitchell, Loften. Review of *The Brothers*, *N.Y. Amsterdam News*, 17 April 1982, 28.
Nicholson, David. "A Commitment to Writing: A Conversation with Kathleen Collins Prettyman." *Black Film Review* 5, no. 1 (Winter 1988–1989): 6–15.
Rich, Frank. "Theater: Black Anguish in *Brothers*," *New York Times*, 6 April 1982, C13.

KIA CORTHRON

(1961–   )

BIOGRAPHY

Kia Corthron created and acted out stories as a child in her home in Cumberland, Maryland. However, it was her first playwriting class, taken her senior year in college, that convinced her to pursue the art in earnest. She earned a BA in communications at the University of Maryland at College Park, and after graduation she settled in the Washington, D.C., area. Corthron was selected for a year-long workshop at George Washington University under the direction of playwright Lonnie Carter. Four years later, she moved to New York City to study playwriting at Columbia University. She received her MFA in playwriting in 1992 and currently resides in New York City.

Corthron is a member of the Women's Project Playwrights Lab, Playwrights Horizons' African-American Playwrights Project, and the Dramatists Guild.

PLAY DESCRIPTIONS

Kia Corthron combines political and social issues with richly textured characters and original, rhythmic language. Yet, her explorations of private pain are suffused with humor and hope. In *Cage Rhythm*, Corthron delineates the lives of women inside a prison. Through the gritty depictions of Avery, T. J., Montana and other women, she addresses the issues of racial inequality in sentencing (white women go to rehab after being arrested for drug use, black women go to prison) and the dissolution of the family unit when women are incarcerated. However, these issues never overshadow the real lives of these women who are struggling, each in their various ways, to survive. Avery, a drug addict, relies on Narcotics Anonymous and astral projection to keep her going. In her projections she joins her children on idyllic jaunts in the park; in reality, her children have been placed in foster care or adopted, and her actual meeting with her daughter is awkward and unsatisfying. T. J., Avery's cellmate, a lifer who spends most of her time in segregation, is the target of the correctional officers' hatred and fear for her part in the accidental killing of a policeman. As these women struggle to negotiate a life for themselves behind bars, the things we take for granted (combs, hand mirrors, candy bars) take on an importance that resonates throughout Corthron's play. These objects, which become the tokens of love, hate, reconciliation, and bribery, make up the action of the play.

In *Come Down Burning*, a companion piece to *Cage Rhythm*, Kia Corthron explores the issues of poverty and its consequences (children who die of malnutrition and back-alley abortions) through the exquisitely drawn lives of Skoolie, Tee, and Bink. Skoolie, a self-sufficient woman in her early thirties, is forced to move around on a flat cart after a childhood accident left her legs paralyzed and useless. She fixes hair and performs an occasional illegal abortion to support herself. Her younger sister, Tee, and Tee's two children have made their periodic return to the renovated shack that Skoolie calls home. Tee, a slow woman but well-meaning mother, has trouble taking care of herself and the children she cannot seem to stop having. Two babies who have died from malnutrition are buried in the backyard, and another is on the way. Their lives of quiet struggle and endless hope are depicted in the small events of their lives. Tee's inability to confront the teacher who has been abusive to her daughter is painfully rendered while Skoolie's quiet confrontation with the same teacher is a humorous tale of vindication. The pain, both physical and psychological, that women must endure in choosing an abortion is delineated in Bink's vacillation. Considering the limitations imposed on these women's lives, it is shocking, yet not surprising, when Tee's self-induced abortion ends in her bloody death.

Corthron's *Catnap Allegiance* explores the lives of soldiers who find themselves in the middle of the desert during the Persian Gulf War. They are pumped full of medicines without an accompanying explanation and are ordered to "take no prisoners . . . eliminate and go." *Wake Up Lou Riser* features the sisters who confront the Ku Klux Klan member who lynched their brother. In *Life by Asphyxiation*, Corthron depicts death row inmates and the accommodations (bribery, fantasy, and food) that they use to survive the last days and hours of their lives.

SELECTED PRODUCTION HISTORY

Wake Up Lou Riser
  Workshop, Columbia University, New York, 1990
  Workshop, Circle Repertory Company Lab, New York, 1991
  Production, Ramapo College, Mahwah, New Jersey, 1994

Come Down Burning
  Workshop, Voice and Vision, Northampton, Massachusetts, 1991
  Reading, Playwrights Horizons, New York, 1992

Workshop, Long Wharf Theatre, New Haven, Connecticut, 1993
Reading, Philadelphia Theatre Company, Philadelphia, 1993
Production, American Place Theatre, New York, 1993
Reading, Hartford Stage, Hartford, Connecticut, 1994

Cage Rhythm
Workshop, Long Wharf Theatre, New Haven, Connecticut, 1993
Reading, American Place Theatre, New York, 1993
Reading, Philadelphia Theatre Company, Philadelphia, 1993
Reading, Playwrights Horizons, New York, 1994
Reading, New York Theatre Workshop, New York, 1994
Reading, Genesis Festival, Crossroads Theatre, New Brunswick, New Jersey, 1994

Catnap Allegiance
Reading, Manhattan Theatre Club, New York, 1993
Reading, Circle Repertory Company, New York, 1993

Werewolf Sing
Reading, Second Stage Theatre, New York, 1994

Life by Asphyxiation
Production, New Theatre Wing, Playwrights Horizons, New York, 1995

Seeking the Genesis
Production, Goodman Theatre, Chicago, 1996
Production, Manhattan Theatre Club, 1997

PLAY AVAILABILITY

Cage Rhythm is available in Sydné Mahone, ed., *Moon Marked and Touched by Sun: Plays by African-American Women*. New York: Theatre Communications Group, 1994.

Come Down Burning is published in Howard Stein and Glenn Young, eds., *The Best American Short Plays 1993–94*. New York: Applause, 1994; Kathy A. Perkins and Roberta Uno, eds., *Contemporary Plays by Women of Color: An Anthology*. New York: Routledge, 1996.

Kia Corthron's other plays are available through her agent: John Santoianni, Tantleff Office, 375 Greenwich Street, Suite 700, New York, New York 10013; (212) 941–3939.

AWARDS

Van Lier Playwriting Fellowship, New York, 1992

New Professional Theatre Screenplay/Playwriting Festival Award, New York, Winner, *Come Down Burning*, 1993

Schomberg Fellowship, Ramapo College, Mahwah, New Jersey, 1994

Hedgebrook Colony Writing Residency, Langley, Washington, 1996

DESCRIPTIVE AND CRITICAL RESPONSES

Corthron, Kia. ''Introduction to *Cage Rhythm*.'' In *Moon Marked and Touched by Sun*, edited by Sydné Mahone, 35–37. New York: Theatre Communications Group, 1994.

Hannaham, James. "Cameos: Come Down Burning." Review of *Come Down Burning*. *Village Voice*, 23 November 1993, 106.

Perkins, Katy A., and Roberta Uno, eds. "Kia Corthon," 90–92. In *Contemporary Plays by Women of Color: An Anthology*. New York: Routledge, 1996.

Reiter, Amy. "Kia Corthron: Giving the Voiceless a Voice." *American Theatre*, October 1994, 77.

CLARE COSS

(1935–   )

BIOGRAPHY

Clare Coss has a BA in theatre from Louisiana State University and a master's degree in theatre education from New York University and, in the mid-1970s, she completed a master's degree in social work at the State University of New York-Stony Brook and trained as a psychotherapist. She divides her two careers between her psychotherapy practice in New York City and her writing work in her studio on Long Island.

In the late 1960s, when Coss began writing plays, she dealt primarily with two major themes: plays inspired by women breaking down interior and exterior barriers and plays about women who strove to forge their vision of a just society. In 1971 the Berkshire Theatre Festival gave Coss her first full production. From 1977 to 1981, she was a cofounder and co–artistic director of the Women's Experimental Theatre, and producer Margot Lewitin invited the group to be in residence at the Interart Theatre in New York. There, with Sondra Segal and Roberta Sklar, Coss coauthored a trilogy on women in the family. Then, in the early 1980s, Coss left in order to write her own plays. Various readings and workshops led to productions of three of her plays. In 1996 she edited an anthology of lesbian love poems, *Arc of Love*, published by Simon and Schuster.

She and her partner, Blanche Wiesen Cook, celebrated their twenty-fifth year together in 1994. They live in New York City and East Hampton.

PLAY DESCRIPTIONS

Coss utilizes conventions of the theatre of the absurd in *Growing Up Gothic* but employs a more traditional, realistic structure in *Lillian Wald* and *The Blessing*.

Growing Up Gothic comprises three related one acts: *Madame USA, One Drop of a Schizophrenic's Blood Will Kill a Tankful of Tadpoles*, and *The Dutiful Daughter*. The plays center around a daughter who travels through memories of her erotic self, her mother, and her father in order to achieve a clearer understanding of her adult self.

Lillian Wald: At Home on Henry Street is a one-character play about Lillian Wald, who founded the Henry Street Settlement, the Visiting Nurse Service, and the Neighborhood Playhouse. In this drama, Wald risks everything to confront President Wilson in May 1916 in an attempt to lead the world away from war.

The Blessing, a full-length play, tells the story of an elderly woman who, stuck in an adult home and unable to take care of herself, tries to escape with her roommate to live with her lesbian daughter and her partner. The daughter and her lover must deal with the longings of the mother and the realities of their life together.

SELECTED PRODUCTION HISTORY

The Star Strangled Banner
    Production, Berkshire Theatre Festival, Stockbridge, Massachusetts, 1971

The Well of Living Water (coauthored with Mel Spiegel, score by Thiago de Mello)
    Production, Old Testament Story Theatre, Cathedral of St. John the Divine, New York, 1974

Titty Titty Bang Bang (one act)
    Production, Women's Theatre Troupe, Vancouver, British Columbia, 1974

The Daughters Cycle (coauthored with Sondra Segal and Roberta Sklar)—*Daughters* (1977), *Sister/Sister* (1978), and *Electra Speaks* (1979)
    Production, Interart, New York, 1979–1980

Growing Up Gothic (three one acts)
    Production, Theatre for the New City, New York, 1983

Lillian Wald: At Home on Henry Street
    Production, New Federal Theatre, New York, 1986
    (On video at the Film and Video Collection, Lincoln Center Library for the Performing Arts)

The Blessing
    Production, American Place Theatre, New York, 1989

PLAY AVAILABILITY

Daughters is published in *The Massachusetts Review* (Summer) 1983.

The Daughters Cycle is available through the playwright: Clare Coss, 240 West 98th Street, New York, New York 10025.

Growing Up Gothic and *The Blessing* are available through her agent: Helen Merrill
   Agency, 435 West 23rd Street 1A, New York, New York, 10011.

Madame USA is published in *Works* (Summer/Fall) 1971.

Titty Titty Bang Bang is published in *Aphra* (Fall) 1971.

AWARDS

Playwright in Residence, Berkshire Theatre Festival, 1971

National Endowment for the Arts, *The Daughters Cycle*, 1977–1980

New York State Council on the Arts, *The Daughters Cycle*, 1977–1980

The Women's Fund, *The Daughters Cycle*, 1977–1980

DESCRIPTIVE AND CRITICAL RESPONSES

Feral, Josette, and Barbara Kerslake. "Writing and Displacement: Women in Theatre."
   Modern Drama (December 1984): 549–63.
Gussow, Mel. "A Theme and Variations on Mother and Daughter." Review of *The
   Blessing. New York Times*, 22 May 1989, C12.
Sklar, Roberta. " 'Sisters' or Never Trust Anyone outside the Family." *Women and
   Performance: A Journal of Feminist Theory* (Spring-Summer 1983): 58–63.

MIGDALIA CRUZ

(1958–   )

BIOGRAPHY

Migdalia Cruz was raised in the South Bronx by working-class Puerto Rican parents. She attended Stuyvesant High School in New York and went to Lake Erie College in Ohio where she received a BFA, magna cum laude, in 1980. She earned an MFA in playwriting from Columbia University in 1984. From 1984 to 1990, she was nurtured in the International Arts Relations' (INTAR) Hispanic-Playwrights-in-Residence Laboratory, where she worked under **Maria Irene Fornes**. Cruz credits this experience as the time when she "learned to tell the truth" in her writing.

Cruz has taught playwriting at Princeton University and Amherst College and has guest lectured at Yale University, Wesleyan University, Mount Holyoke College, and Columbia University. In 1988 she received a McKnight Fellowship and a National Endowment for the Arts Playwriting Fellowship for 1990–91. She was awarded the Clara Rotter Fellowship for a New Dramatist at the Royal Court Theatre in London, England, in 1994.

Migdalia Cruz recently completed her first teleplay, *How!?*, and is working on commissions from the Arena Stage (Washington, D.C.), the Working Theatre (New York), a play about Lolita Lebron (the Puerto Rican independence movement heroine) for the Latino Chicago Theatre (Chicago), and the film version of her one-act play *Dreams of Home*. She is a member of the New Dramatists and currently resides in New Canaan, Connecticut.

PLAY DESCRIPTIONS

Migdalia Cruz's work is described as startling and uncompromising. Her highly charged images are both theatrically powerful and emotionally compelling. A bleak vision is leavened by her lyrical, poetic quality, which leads to a highly original sense of black comedy. *Miriam's Flowers* exemplifies these distinctive characteristics. Set in the South Bronx in 1975, the episodic play interweaves the past, present, and fantasy into a vivid depiction of a Puerto Rican family's disintegration. The death on the railroad tracks of a seven-year-old boy, Puli, provides the crucible for the family. Delfina denies her son's death, while Nando, Delfina's lover and Puli's father, seeks out his son's grave to express his sorrows and fears. Puli's sixteen-year-old sister, Miriam, turns to religiously inspired masochism ("when saints bleed, they smell like flowers") and obsessive sexual encounters. Consumed by guilt at being alive, Miriam uses a razor to cut flower patterns into her arms. She enacts a ritual of self-inflicted pain and torture, a vivid reminder that she is alive; meanwhile, Delfina descends into an alcoholic haze. Life constantly teeters toward death as each family member grieves in his or her own way and blames the others for Puli's accident.

Another examination of an urban crisis set in the South Bronx is *The Have-little*. The brutal reality in the lives of a Puerto Rican family is juxtaposed against the myths and poetry that sustain their inner lives. The descent of the Rivera family into alcoholism, abuse, teenage pregnancy, and death is offset by poignant scenes of love, caring, and hard-fought joy. During the course of the play, Lillian Rivera is transformed from an innocent thirteen-year-old schoolgirl into a orphaned mother of fifteen, who freezes to death with her baby in their abandoned apartment. Lillian's life devolves around her mother, Carmen, who wants to throw Lillian out of the house after she accuses Lillian of letting her boyfriend touch her; her father, Jose, whom Carmen does not allow into the apartment but who sneaks in when Carmen is not there and enacts a seductive, masochistic ritual with his daughter; Michi, Lillian's best friend, who takes off without a good-bye; and Lillian's boyfriend, who dies of an overdose, leaving a pregnant child behind. Carmen dies at home, and Jose sinks further into alcoholism and denial. The play is a heightened image of the perpetual struggle: cruelty and pain intertwine with fleeting moments of tenderness and compassion.

The subway station at New York's 103rd Street and Lexington Avenue is the setting for *Dreams of Home*, Cruz's bittersweet tale of love and caring among the homeless. The fear and isolation that protect the displaced persons on the street are gradually eroded as Sandra and Pedro begin a friendship that slowly blossoms into love. Aided by Dolores, the angel of death, and her assistant Hobie, the two denizens of the darkened subways share their dreams and memories as well as their food. When Sandra realizes that her gangrenous foot will not allow her to leave the subway platform, Pedro performs the ultimate act of love; he jumps onto the tracks of an oncoming train with Sandra in his arms.

SELECTED PRODUCTION HISTORY

Not Time's Fool
  Production, Theatre for the New City, New York, 1986

Production, INTAR Theatre, New York, 1986
Production, Festival Latino, New York Shakespeare Festival, New York, 1986

Sensible Shoes
Production, Duo Theatre, New York, 1987

Lillian
Staged reading, Main Project Playwright, Sundance Institute, Utah, 1987
Staged reading, New Dramatists and Duo Theatre, New York, 1987

Lucy Loves Me
Staged reading, 92nd Street Y and New Dramatists, New York, 1987
Staged reading, C.E.A.D./Theatre d'Aujourd'hui, Montreal, Quebec, 1988
Production, Frank Theatre, Minneapolis, 1991
Production, Latino Chicago Theater, Chicago, 1992

Loose Lips, Coconuts, She Was Something . . . (one-act plays)
Production, Summer Festival, WOW Cafe, New York, 1987

When Galaxy Six and the Bronx Collide (musical play)
Production, Duo Theatre, New York, 1988
Production, HOLA Festival, New York, 1988

Welcome Back to Salamanca
Production, INTAR Theatre, New York, 1988

The Touch of an Angel
Production, Duo Theatre, New York, 1989

Telling Tales (one-act play)
Production, Home for Contemporary Theatre and Arts, New York, 1990

Miriam's Flowers
Production, Playwrights Horizons, New York, 1990
Production, Old Red Lion, London, 1991
Production, Intersection for the Arts/LATA, Los Angeles, 1992

Occasional Grace (musical composed by Amina Claudine Myers)
Production, En Garde Arts, New York, 1991

Street Sense (play with music composed by Linda Eisenstein)
Production, Cleveland Public Theatre, Cleveland, Ohio, 1991

The Have-little
Production, INTAR Theatre, New York, 1991

Whistle ("Collateral Damage" Gulf War protest)
Production, Shaliko Company at La Mama, ETC, New York, 1991

Fur
Staged reading, INTAR Theatre, New York, 1991
Staged reading, Playwrights' Center, Minneapolis, 1991
Staged reading, Latino Chicago Theater, Chicago, 1992
Production, Steppenwolf Theatre Company, Chicago, 1997 (co-production with Latino
    Chicago Theater)

Frida: The Story of Frida Kahlo (an opera; book by Hilary Blecher, lyrics by Cruz,
composed by Robert X. Rodriguez)
Production, American Music Theatre Festival, Philadelphia, 1991
Production, American Repertory Theatre, Cambridge, Massachusetts, 1992

Production, Brooklyn Academy of Music with the Women's Project, Brooklyn, New York, 1992

Production, Houston Grand Opera, Houston, Texas, 1993

Running for Blood: No. 3 (radio play)
Broadcast, Radio Stage, WNYC/FM, New York, 1992

Rushing Waters (full-length play with songs by Darren Brady, Danny Vincente, and La Rue Marshall)
Staged reading, New Dramatists, New York, 1992
Production, Cornerstone Theatre, Pacoima, California, 1993

Dreams of Home (one-act play)
Production, Latino Chicago Theater, Chicago, 1993

Cigarettes and Moby-Dick
Staged reading, Magic Theatre and Festival Latino, San Francisco, 1993
Staged reading, Royal Court Theatre, London, 1994

Latins in La-La Land
Staged reading, New Dramatists, New York, 1994
Staged reading, Public Theatre, New York, 1994

Another Part of the House (from Garcia Lorca)
Reading, BRAVA! for Women in the Arts, San Francisco, 1995
Production, Classic Stage Company, New York, 1997

PLAY AVAILABILITY

Dreams of Home has been published in Howard Stein and Glenn Young, eds., *The Best American Short Plays 1990–1992*. Garden City, New York: Fireside Theatre, 1991, 1992.

Miriam's Flowers has been published in *Plays in Process*, vol. 11, no. 1. New York: Theatre Communications Group, 1990; Linda Feyder, ed., *Shattering the Myth: Plays by Hispanic Women*. Houston, Texas: Arte Publico Press, 1992.

Telling Tales has been published in Eric Lane, ed., *Telling Tales: New One-Act Plays*. New York: Penguin Books, 1993.

Other scripts are available from her agent: Peregrine Whitlesey, 345 East 80th Street, New York, New York 10021; (212) 737–0153.

AWARDS

Excellence in the Arts Award, Borough of Manhattan, *Not Time's Fool*, 1986

McKnight Fellowship, Playwrights' Center, Minneapolis, 1988–1989

National Endowment for the Arts, Playwriting Fellow, 1990–1991

Susan Smith Blackburn Prize, First Runner-up, *The Have-little*, 1991

Pew Trust/TCG Resident Artist, Classic Stage Company, New York, 1994–1995

Clara Rotter Fellowship for New Dramatist, Royal Court, London, 1994

DESCRIPTIVE AND CRITICAL RESPONSES

Abbe, Elfrieda. "Words and Art from the Soul." *Milwaukee Sentinel*, 27 October 1989.

Cruz, Migdalia. "Fire." *Stageview*, May–June 1993, 7.

———. "What It Means to Be an Hispanic Playwright—or Am I Latina? or What?" *Ollantay Theatre Magazine*, 1, no. 2 (July 1993): 40–42.

———. "Writing Home: Interviews with Suzan-Lori Parks, Christopher Durang, Eduardo Machado, Ping Chong and Migdalia Cruz." By Cathy Madison. *American Theatre*, October 1991, 42, 138, 140.

Greene, Alexis. "South Bronx Memoirs: Migdalia Cruz Explores Her Urban Roots." *American Theatre*, June 1990, 58.

Hampton, Wilborn. "*The Have Little*." Review of *The Have-little*. *New York Times*, 12 June 1991, C14.

Koehler, Robert. "Fantasy at the Fringe." *Los Angeles Times*, 5 February 1993, F3–4.

Steele, Mike. "Hatred, Psychic Abuse Split Veneer of Modern Culture in 'Lucy.' " Review of *Lucy Loves Me*. *Star Tribune* (Minneapolis), 23 February 1991, 2E.

Vaughan, Peter. " 'Miriam's Flowers' Shows Insight to a Family's Pain." Review of *Miriam's Flowers*. *Star Tribune* (Minneapolis), 27 February 1991, 5E.

LINDA FAIGAO-HALL

(1948–   )

BIOGRAPHY

Linda Faigao-Hall received a BA in English literature and theater arts in 1969 from Silliman University in the Philippines. She attended New York University, where she earned an MA in English literature, and studied educational theatre at Bretton Hall College in Wakefield, England. She is currently a doctoral candidate in educational theatre at NYU. In addition to her classwork and playwriting, Faigao-Hall works as an English language instructor at the College of New Rochelle and is director of Management Information Systems at New York's Sheltering Arms Children's Service.

Faigao-Hall has participated in playwriting workshops at the Frederick Douglass Creative Arts Center, the Ensemble Studio Theatre, the Pan-Asian Theatre Company, and the Basement Workshop. She is a member of the Women's Project Playwrights Lab and lives in Brooklyn, New York.

PLAY DESCRIPTIONS

Linda Faigao-Hall draws on both her own Philippine roots and her experiences in America for her work. *State without Grace* is a multigenerational study in family conflict. Although the play is set in the Philippines, the universality of the story transcends ethnic and geographical boundaries. Dominating the home is the tradition-bound matriarch of the family who controls every aspect of her family's lives. Her rebellious granddaughter, Celia, returns home from the United States and sparks a series of confrontations in which the younger characters struggle to assert their individual identities.

In the comedic *Lay of the Land*, a Filipino political émigré searches for an apartment in New York City on the eve of the 1986 Philippine revolution. After answering an advertisement for a sublet in the East Village, she finds herself entangled in strangers' lives when confrontations erupt during an art gallery opening.

Two Women/Two Countries is the collective title for two one-act plays. The first play, *Sparrow*, is set in the Philippines and recounts the experiences of a Filipina who returns to her country of origin after a ten-year absence in the United States. She has come to plead with a childhood friend for the release of her brother who was abducted and is being held hostage by a left-wing assassination squad. *Burning Out*, set in the United States, depicts the violent encounter among a Caucasian social worker, an Asian American computer systems analyst working at a New York City foster-care agency, and an African American who was once a child in foster care and comes to claim his case records after serving ten years in prison.

In *Woman From the Other Side of the World*, a Filipina nanny comes to the United States to take care of a thoroughly assimilated and Americanized Filipino boy. She becomes the catalyst for his mother's painful confrontation with a Philippine past she would much rather forget and the American present to which she has escaped.

A world-weary caucasian Wall Street broker falls in love with a recent Filipina immigrant who is profoundly Catholic and a virgin in Faigao-Hall's recent *God, Sex, and Blue Water.*

SELECTED PRODUCTION HISTORY

State Without Grace
  Production, Pan-Asian Repertory Theatre Company, New York, 1984
  Production, Asian-American Theatre Company, San Francisco, 1985

Requiem
  Production, Henry Street Settlement Arts for Living Center and Alliance for Asian American Arts and Culture, New York, 1986
  Staged reading, Pan-Asian Repertory Theatre, New York, 1989
  Staged reading, East-West Theater Company, Los Angeles, 1990

Men Come and Go (one-act play)
  Production, LAHI, Actor's Institute, New York, 1987

Americans (a performance piece)
  Production, LAHI, Chelsea Theater Arts Center, New York, 1987
  Production, Catskills Reading Society, Ellenville, New York, 1991

Two Women/Two Countries (two one-act plays)
  Staged reading, Women's Performance Theatre Conference, Dramatist's Guild, New York, 1987
  Staged reading, Henry Street Settlement, New York, 1988
  Staged reading, Catskills Reading Society, Ellenville, New York, 1991
  Reading, Philippine Consulate, New York, 1996

Woman From the Other Side of the World
   Production, Ma-Yi Theater Ensemble, New York, 1994
   Production, East West Players, Los Angeles, 1997

Lay of the Land
   Reading, New Georges Theatre, New York, 1996

The Boy Who Wouldn't Read (play for children)
   Production, P. S. 282, Brooklyn, New York, 1996

Pidgin' Hole
   Staged reading, Tandem Acts Festival, Women's Project and Productions, New York,
      1996

PLAY AVAILABILITY

Woman From the Other Side of the World is published by Dramatic Publishing, P.O.
   Box 129, Woodstock, Illinois 60098.

For production information, contact Linda Faigao-Hall's literary representative: Ann Far-
   ber, 99 Park Avenue, New York, New York 10016; (212) 861–7075.

AWARDS

Henry Street Settlement Arts for Living Center and Alliance for Asian American Arts
   and Culture Award, Winner—Best Play, *Requiem*, 1986

Hudson River Classics Playwriting Contest, Hudson, New York, Second Prize, *Lay of
   the Land*, 1994

DESCRIPTIVE AND CRITICAL RESPONSES

Gussow, Mel. "Theater: Pan Asian's *State without Grace*." Review of *State without
      Grace. New York Times*, 28 November 1984, C21.
Thrall, Judy. "*State without Grace*." Review of *State without Grace. Backstage*, 23
      November 1984.

EVELINA FERNANDEZ

(1954–   )

BIOGRAPHY

Evelina Fernandez was born in East Los Angeles, California, the youngest of five children. When she was six months old, her family moved to Phoenix, Arizona, where she lived until 1964 when her parents were divorced. She then returned to East Los Angeles to live with her grandparents, mother, and siblings. Evelina began writing short stories and speeches in elementary school and tried her hand at acting in junior high productions. In high school she admits she attended only drama, choir, and typing classes. She dropped out of school at seventeen and attended beauty school but dropped out when she realized "she was not good at combing hair." At nineteen she was married and celebrated with a big, traditional Mexican wedding, but she was divorced "before her family had paid off the bill."

Fernandez attended East Los Angeles College, California State University, where she became involved in Chicano theatre and the Chicano movement, which was working to defend the rights of undocumented workers. She also made three trips to Cuba with the Venceremos Brigade during the 1970s and 1980s. In 1978 Fernandez began her professional acting career by playing Della in Luis Valdez's *Zoot Suit.*

In 1981 she met Jose Luis Valenzuela and began working with him at El Teatro de La Esperanza, touring nationally and internationally with the troupe during the next four years. It was during this period that Evelina Fernandez resumed her writing while she was learning the collective creation process.

In 1984 she and Jose Luis moved back to East Los Angeles where she continues her work in theatre, film, and television. She starred with Edward James Olmos in the critically acclaimed 1992 film *American Me* and won a Golden

Eagle Award for her performance. She has written a sitcom for Disney (*Marcey, Por Vida*) and a feature screenplay (*Luminarias*), and she is currently working on a feature film for Columbia Pictures (*Our Lady of Tarzana*). Fernandez is also a poet and a motivational speaker.

Evelina Fernandez and her husband, who is a professor at UCLA and artistic director of the Latino Theatre Lab, live in East Los Angeles with their two children.

PLAY DESCRIPTIONS

Evelina Fernandez's plays clearly delineate the Chicano experience, but they successfully transcend cultural exclusiveness by embedding that experience within universal themes: friendship, love, and aging. Her first one-act play, *How Else Am I Supposed to Know I'm Alive?*, is a good example of the playwright's ability to bridge the specific with the universal. The play is set in the kitchen where Nellie, a "well-endowed" Chicana in her early fifties, is preparing to entertain the rotund, middle-aged married man she has been seeing. Nellie is interrupted in her musings and preparations by her best friend Angie, a forty-eight-year-old Chicana. With the familiar tone of their chatter in the opening moments of the encounter, Fernandez establishes a touching and realistic portrait of female friendship. It becomes readily apparent, however, that Angie needs to discuss a serious topic. In a question-answer ritual that must have been enacted numerous times in their relationship, Angie finally reveals that she is pregnant. Nellie learns that the father is the handsome man they had noticed at bingo, and Angie describes the details of their night of passion in which a combination of wine and tenderness allowed Angie to experience her first orgasm. A mother of nine and a grandmother, Angie is considering an abortion, but she decides to have the child and give it to the widowed and childless Nellie. As soon as Nellie allows herself to imagine that her dream may, in fact, be coming true, Angie gets her period. Despite her dashed hopes and dreams for a child, Nellie does not allow her disappointment to dampen her indomitable spirit.

The ease and familiarity that characterize women's intimate conversations and close friendships, which was established in the one-act play, is even more fully realized in Fernandez's more recent play, *Loving Rage*. With the caveat that the "material may be offensive to Anglos, Latinos, Asians, African-Americans, Men, Women, Homosexuals, Jews and Catholics," Fernandez proceeds to examine the issue of racism, particularly racism among Latinos. From the vantage point of four upwardly mobile Latinas, she creates a series of relationships for each. Andrea, a divorce lawyer, develops a relationship with Joseph Levinson, another divorce lawyer, despite Andrea's intense dislike of white men. Sofia, a therapist who prefers rich, white men, is ultimately attracted to a Mexican waiter. Lilly, an elementary schoolteacher, is recovering from a long string of romances with undocumented workers when she meets Lu, a Korean. The various forms of prejudice and bias are explored: internalized racism, overt racism, racism that the women initiate, and racism that is directed at them. Despite the rage that fuels the racism, all learn that the barriers can be dismantled by love and understanding. The friendship among the women provides the foundation for their continuous, and often painful, changes and growth.

SELECTED PRODUCTION HISTORY

How Else Am I Supposed to Know I'm Still Alive? (one-act play)
   Production, Plaza de La Raza, Los Angeles, 1989
   Production, Teatro Latino, Milwaukee, Wisconsin, 1989
   Production, El Centro Su Teatro, Denver, Colorado, 1990
   Production (national tour), El Teatro Campesino, San Juan Bautista, California, 1992–
      1993
   Production, La Compania, Albuquerque, New Mexico, 1994

Los Angeles (one-act play)
   Production, El Centro Su Teatro, Denver, Colorado, 1990

August 29
   Production, Los Angeles Theatre Center, Los Angeles, 1990

Loving Rage
   Staged reading, La Plaza de La Raza, Los Angeles, 1994

PLAY AVAILABILITY

How Else Am I Supposed to Know I'm Still Alive? is published in Kathy A. Perkins and Roberta Uno, eds., *Contemporary Plays by Women of Color*. New York: Routledge Press, 1996.

All other scripts are available through Latino Theatre Lab, 3540 North Mission Road, Los Angeles, California 90033; (213) 223–2475.

AWARDS

Nuevo Chicano Los Angeles Playwriting Contest, First Place, *How Else Am I Supposed to Know I'm Still Alive?*, 1989

CineFestival, San Antonio, Texas, Special Jury Award, *How Else Am I Supposed to Know I'm Still Alive?*, 1993

DESCRIPTIVE AND CRITICAL RESPONSES

Dillard-Rosen, Sandra. "California Author's Plays Have Multicultural Appeal." *Denver Post*, 18 June 1990.
Fernandez, Evelina. "Introduction to . . . *Alive*." In *Contemporary Plays by Women of*

Color, edited by Kathy A. Perkins and Roberta Uno, 158–59. New York: Routledge Press, 1996.

Huerta, Jorge. "Professionalizing Teatro: An Overview of Chicano Theatre during the 'Decade of the Hispanic.' " *Theatre Forum* (Spring 1993): 54–59.

Morales, Ed. "Shadowing Valdez." *American Theatre* 97 (November 1992): 14–19.

FIVE LESBIAN BROTHERS

(fl. 1989–   )

BIOGRAPHY

The brothers, Maureen Angelos, Babs Davy, Dominique Dibbell, Peg Healey, and Lisa Kron, have performed together for years in various combinations working out of the WOW Cafe Theatre. Many early collaborations, such as *Pair of Dykes Lost*, directed by Lisa Kron, were created before all the brothers were present. They became a company in 1989 and, as a group, they write and perform their own material. Three of the group were trained in theatre; Dominique is an art student, and Babs has a degree in museum curating. All of them come from different parts of the country: Angelos from Washington, D.C.; Davy from Minneapolis; Dibbell from Claremont, California; Healey from East Northport, New York; and Kron from Lansing, Michigan. In their years together, they have developed a common language that facilitates their communal writing and researching. They share cultural source material, such as books and videos, and improvise to develop their plays, which explore such dark themes as homophobia and sexism with satire, parody, farce, and an occasional musical number. In an interview with Kate Bornstein, Dibbell stated that their philosophy is ''irreverence . . . for the pre-set rules for what 'lesbian theatre' is supposed to look like or say. And . . . we're all drawn to both the stupid joke and absurd humor.''

The three full-length plays developed by all the Brothers are *Voyage to Lesbos*, *Brave Smiles . . . Another Lesbian Tragedy*, and *The Secretaries*, which premiered at the WOW Cafe Theatre; the latter two plays added the directing perspective of Kate Stafford. In addition to their appearances at WOW, the Brothers have performed in New York at the Downtown Art Company, Dixon Place, La Mama, the New York Theatre Workshop, and Performance Space 122, as well as in cities throughout the United States.

Their characteristic way of working is to conceive, create, and rehearse a piece; try it out in downtown performance spaces; take the play on the road for further trial and rewriting; then return to New York with a well-honed, polished script. For their latest work *Brides of the Moon*, the Brothers performed the work in progress at the WOW Cafe in New York, in September 1996. Using a split stage, the performers counterpointed women astronauts in a spaceship with a skewed family headed by a mother who has been forced to conceal her scientific genius. As farcically comic as their earlier work, *Brides* touches a deeper resonance in its depiction of women's frustrated ambitions. They went on tour with performances culminating at Theatre Rhinoceros in San Francisco in late 1996. A New York production is slated for spring 1997. A lesbian book of humor, authored by the Brothers, will be published by Simon and Schuster, fall 1997.

PLAY DESCRIPTIONS

Brave Smiles . . . Another Lesbian Tragedy is a satire spiced with a camp sensibility. Act I takes place in 1920 at the Tilue-Pussenheimer Academy, an orphanage for girls in Europe. Miss Philips, the girls' favorite teacher, tucks them in at night and gives them all a kiss. At the end of Act I, the head mistress, Frau von Pussenheimer, hangs herself in despair because Miss Philips gets the most attention from the orphans. Act II begins about thirty years later and picks up the lives of the former schoolmates just as tragedies begin to occur. After two of the girls are reunited and confess their undying love for each other, one is hit by a truck. The bereaved hits the bottle and while in the Bowery stumbles upon another classmate who kills a bum in self-defense and is sent to the electric chair (with echoes of Susan Hayward in *I Want to Live*). In the last scene of the play, after the former alcoholic widow has found happiness with another classmate at her home in Southhampton, she is diagnosed with a brain tumor and dies. While *Brave Smiles* satirizes the exclusionary and, often, malicious environment of teenage girls and the expectation of straight society for the inevitable tragic consequences of a lesbian life (as well as the celebrated instinct for ''dyke drama'' among lesbians), it does so with inspired silliness and witty references to popular culture.

When asked about the inspiration for *The Secretaries*, Angelos commented that ''we've all lived under the tyranny of the workplace.'' Functioning as a revenge play in the Grand Guignol tradition, *Secretaries* follows the introduction of Patty into the secretarial pool of women who work for the Cooney Lumber Mill in Big Bone, Oregon, where only the best secretaries work. The women, who work for a despotic employer who demands standards of weight as well as office efficiency, have bonded in strange cultlike ways. They all live off Slimfast shakes and have the same menstrual cycle. More important, they take a chain saw to a lumberjack a month, claiming his jacket (much like appropriating an athlete's letter jacket) because men's clothes are cheaper and better made. Using the frame of the initiation of an innocent into a more knowing society, the play examines contemporary perceptions of women, from the proliferation of body image commercials to the glut of chain saw massacre movies, as well as the painful subjects of internalized oppression and women's cruelty to women.

SELECTED PRODUCTION HISTORY

Voyage to Lesbos
   Production, WOW Theatre Cafe, New York, 1989

Brave Smiles . . . Another Lesbian Tragedy
   Production, WOW Theatre Cafe, New York, 1992
   Production, Theatre Rhinoceros, San Francisco, 1993
   Production, New York Theatre Workshop, New York, 1993

The Secretaries
   Production, WOW Theatre Cafe, New York, 1993
   Production, Theatre Rhinoceros, San Francisco, 1994
   Production, Alice B. Theatre, Seattle, 1994
   Production, New York Theatre Workshop, New York, 1994

Brides of the Moon
   Production, WOW Theatre Cafe, New York, 1996
   Production, Theatre Rhinoceros, San Francisco, 1996

PLAY AVAILABILITY

Brave Smiles . . . Another Lesbian Tragedy is published in Eric Lane and Nina Shengold, eds., *The Actor's Book of Gay and Lesbian Plays*. New York: Penguin, 1995.

Other plays are available from Sami Blackwell, 225 East 25th Street, New York, New York 10010.

AWARDS

Best Performance Group, New York Press, 1991

New York Dance and Performance Award ("Bessie"), 1993

Obie Award, *The Secretaries*, 1995

DESCRIPTIVE AND CRITICAL RESPONSES

Bornstein, Kate. "She Ain't Heavy, She's My Brother." *Theatre Rhinoceros 16th Anniversary Program*, September 1993, 18–20.
Brantley, Ben. "A Secretarial Pool out for Blood." Review of *The Secretaries*. *New York Times*, 22 September 1994, C20.
Curnin, Nancy. "Polished Satire from Five Lesbian Brothers." Review of *Brave Smiles*. *Los Angeles Times*, 21 April 1993, F5.
Harvey, Dennis. "Troupe Pools Satiric Talents in *Secretaries*." Review of *The Secretaries*. *San Francisco Chronicle*, 9 January 1994, 28.
Holden, Stephen. "*Brave Smiles . . . Another Lesbian Tragedy*." Review of *Brave Smiles . . . Another Lesbian Tragedy*. *New York Times*, 19 June 1993, A16.

Hurwitt, Robert. "*The Secretaries* Sharpen Their Nails, Go for the Kill." Review of *The Secretaries*. *San Francisco Examiner*, 19 January 1994, C3.

Kotz, Liz. "The Fraternal Feminine: On the Five Lesbian Brothers." *Artforum*, December 1993, 13.

MARIA IRENE FORNES

(1930–   )

BIOGRAPHY

One of the preeminent playwrights of our time, Maria Irene Fornes was born in Havana, Cuba. After her father's death in 1945, her mother moved the family to New York where Fornes learned to speak English. She left New York in 1954 for a painting career in Europe and, while in Paris, saw Roger Blin's original production of *Waiting for Godot*. "When I left that theatre I felt that my life was changed, that I was seeing everything with a different clarity" (Cummings, 52). She returned to the United States in 1957 to pursue a career as a textile designer until her career took an unexpected turn.

Her playwriting career began with "an obsession that took the form of a play and I felt I had to write it" (Cummings, 51). Although Fornes's play *The Widow* was published in Havana in 1961, her first produced play was *There! You Died* (later produced under the title *Tango Palace*) in 1963, which launched her highly successful career as a serious playwright. Fornes became one of the leaders in the off-Broadway and off-off-Broadway movement of the 1960s and 1970s with such plays as *The Successful Life of 3* and *Dr. Kheal*, as well as the musical *Promenade* written with Al Carmines.

In 1972 Fornes and several other playwrights founded the New York Theatre Strategy to make opportunities available for playwrights whose work would not otherwise be produced. It was during this period that Fornes began her distinguished teaching career at INTAR and numerous other theatres and colleges across the country. Hispanic theatre scholar Jorge Huerta, who recognizes her immense contribution to Latino theatre, claims that Fornes "has touched almost every Latino playwright working today" (Huerta, 57).

Fornes also usually directs and occasionally designs sets for her own work and directs plays by other dramatists as well. She has established a reputation as a translator and adapter, having adapted works by Federico García Lorca, Pedro Calderón de la Barca, Virgilio Pinera, and Anton Chekhov. Despite her many awards, innumerable accolades, and the esteem of fellow playwrights and others in the theatre industry, Fornes's work is, sadly, infrequently performed at major theatres. She received a TCG/Pew Charitable Trust Grant for a residency in 1996–1998 at Women's Project and Productions in New York, where Irene Fornes continues to live.

PLAY DESCRIPTIONS

Maria Irene Fornes's plays encompass several genres while retaining an avant-garde, experimental flavor. Her early plays were often categorized as absurdist, and she was identified with the emerging off-off-Broadway theatre. However, Fornes considers *Fefu and Her Friends* a breakthrough in both style and content. "*Fefu* dealt more with characters as real persons rather than voices that are the expression of the mind of the play." The play focuses on eight women friends who gather at Fefu's New England home in 1935 to discuss a fund-raising program. During the course of the play, their actions and interactions with each other, as well as their relationships with the men in their lives, are examined. Fornes emphasizes these interactions among the women by fragmenting the second act into four areas: the kitchen, the study, a bedroom, and the garden. The audience is divided into four groups, and the four scenes are played simultaneously; the audience moves into the next space at the conclusion of a scene. An unusual sense of intimacy is established as a result of this unique staging which enhances the playwright's exploration of female friendship. (For more detail about *Fefu*, see Tiffany Ana Lopez's chapter in the front of the volume.)

Mud depicts a violent love triangle among three characters who are eking out a drab existence in a rough-hewn, Appalachian-type setting. Mae attempts to keep the home in order: she brings in ironing and tries to get medical help for Lloyd, who is progressively wasting away with a prostate infection. She is also trying to improve her situation, to raise herself above her dirt-poor circumstances by going to elementary school. Lloyd, on the other hand, is content with demeaning and brutalizing Mae. Henry is invited into the relationship when he is asked to read the medical information Mae has picked up from the clinic. Henry provides a higher level of discourse, and Mae asks him to stay as her lover. Henry's usefulness is over when a paralyzing accident prevents him from "talking straight," and Mae realizes she must leave the dysfunctional situation. Both Henry and Lloyd try to talk her out of leaving but are successful only when Lloyd shoots the departing Mae.

Sarita is the story of a thirteen-year-old Hispanic girl from the South Bronx who is obsessively attracted to a habitually unfaithful boyfriend. The twenty short scenes cover a period of eight years (1939–1947).

Fornes's *The Conduct of Life* again explores issues of dominance, cruelty, and sexuality. The play is set in the comfortable Latin American home of Orlando, an ambitious military officer, and Leticia, his wife, who is older by ten years. Orlando, determined to gain power, begins within his own household by withholding love and money from Leticia. He expands his dominance and control over Nena, a destitute girl of twelve, who is kept hidden by Orlando while he tortures and rapes her. With Olimpia, Leticia and Orlando's servant, the pattern of cruelty and domination is complete; the power relationships in the domestic sphere are a microcosm of the political and social tyranny embodied in Orlando's military position. Only when Orlando humiliates Leticia publicly after she has taken a lover and she shoots her husband is it possible to break the vicious cycle of power and domination.

Passion plays a primary role in *Abingdon Square*, Fornes's turn-of-the-century Jamesian-like study of desire and frustration. Set in pre–World War I Greenwich Village, the play traces several years in the relationship of Marion and Juster. Marion is married at the age of fifteen to Juster, a widower three times her age. Little more than a child herself, Marion establishes a close relationship with Michael, Juster's son who is Marion's age. She fantasizes being with a young man who is more suited to her age and temperament; her fantasy materializes into a lover named Frank. After a period of years, Juster finds indisputable proof of her infidelity, banishes her from their house, and withholds their son, Thomas. Driven by passion that conflates hate, revenge, and misplaced affection, both Marion and Juster imagine shooting the other. However, when Juster suffers a stroke after threatening to kill Marion, she forsakes her former life to return to their home at Abingdon Square and nurse her husband back to health.

Whereas passions seethed under the veneer of Edwardian respectability in *Abingdon Square*, in *What of the Night?* Fornes returns to the raw power and violence that characterized such earlier plays as *Mud* and *The Conduct of Life*. Composed of four short plays, the piece follows the life of a "family" and friends from 1938 into the future. *Nadine*, set in the depressed Southwest of 1938, depicts what people will do to get what they want. *Springtime*, set in a small Eastern city in 1958, follows the state of affairs of three people whose relationships become entwined until the two women who loved each other break off their relationship. *Lust*, which covers the period from 1968 to 1983, depicts Ray's rise to corporate power until he is consumed by the imagery of submission and domination. The fourth playlet, *Hunger*, is set at some undisclosed time in the future following an economic disaster. It reintroduces some of the characters from the other plays in the quartet. The power-mad Ray in the third play is now homeless with an equally hopeless assortment of characters. As the play ends, the Angel empties their rations (animal entrails) onto the floor while Ray sobs as he looks to the heavens. The plays may be performed separately, and *Springtime* is frequently anthologized.

SELECTED PRODUCTION HISTORY

There! You Died (also produced under title *Tango Palace*)
  Production, Actor's Workshop, San Francisco, 1963
  Production, Firehouse Theatre, Minneapolis, 1965
  Production, Theatre Genesis, New York, 1973

The Successful Life of 3
  Production, Firehouse Theatre, Minneapolis, 1965
  Production, Sheridan Square Playhouse, New York, 1965

Promenade (musical with Al Carmines)
  Production, Judson Poets' Theatre, New York, 1965
  Production, Promenade Theatre, New York, 1969

The Office
  Production, Henry Miller's Theatre, New York, 1965

A Vietnamese Wedding
  Production, Washington Square Methodist Church, New York, 1967
  Production, La Mama, New York, 1969

The Annunciation
  Production, Judson Poets' Theater, New York, 1967

Dr. Kheal
  Production, Judson Poets' Theater, New York, 1968
  Production, London, 1969

The Red Burning Light: or Mission XQ
  Production, Open Theatre European Tour, Zurich, 1968
  Production, La Mama, New York, 1969

Molly's Dream (music by Cosmos Savage)
  Production, New York Theatre Strategy, New York, 1968

The Curse of the Langston House
  Production, Playhouse in the Park, Cincinnati, Ohio, 1972

Aurora
  Production, New York Theatre Strategy, New York, 1974

Cap-a-Pie (music by José Raul Bernardo)
  Production, INTAR, New York, 1975

Washing
  Production, Theatre for the New City, New York, 1976

Lolita in the Garden
  Production, INTAR, New York, 1977

Fefu and Her Friends
  Production, New York Theatre Strategy, New York, 1977
  Production, American Place Theatre, New York, 1978

In Service
  Production, Padua Hills Festival, Claremont, California, 1978

Eyes on the Harem
Production, INTAR, New York, 1979

Evelyn Brown (A Diary)
Production, Theatre for the New City, New York, 1980

Blood Wedding (adaptation of play by Federico García Lorca)
Production, INTAR, New York, 1980

Life Is Dream (adaptation of play by Pedro Calderón de la Barca)
Production, INTAR, New York, 1981

A Visit
Production, Padua Hills Festival, Claremont, California, 1981
Production, Theatre for the New City, New York, 1981

The Danube
Production, Padua Hills Festival, Claremont, California, 1982
Production, Theatre for the New City, New York, 1983
Production, American Place Theatre, New York, 1984

Mud
Production, Padua Hills Festival, Claremont, California, 1983
Production, Theatre for the New City, New York, 1983

Sarita (music by Leon Odenz)
Production, INTAR, New York, 1984

No Time
Production, Padua Hills Festival, Claremont, California, 1984

The Conduct of Life
Production, Theatre for the New City, New York, 1985

Cold Air (adaptation and translation of Virgilio Pinera)
Production, INTAR, New York, 1985

A Matter of Faith
Production, Theatre for the New City, New York, 1986

Drowning (adaptation of story by Anton Chekhov; produced with six other one-act plays
under the collective title *Orchards*)
Production, Lincoln Center Theatre at the Lucille Lortel, New York, 1986

Art
Production, Theatre for the New City, New York, 1986

The Mothers
Production, Padua Hills Festival, Claremont, California, 1986

Lovers and Keepers (three one-act musicals with music by Tito Puente and Fernando
Rivas)
Production, INTAR, New York, 1987

Abingdon Square
Production, the Women's Project at American Place Theatre, New York, 1987

Uncle Vanya (adaptation of play by Anton Chekhov)
Production, Classic Stage Company, New York, 1987

Hunger (one-act play)
  Production, En Garde Productions, New York, 1987

And What of the Night? (includes four one-act plays: *Hunger, Springtime, Lust,* and *Nadine* [formerly *The Mothers*])
  Production, Milwaukee Repertory Theatre, Milwaukee, Wisconsin, 1989

Oscar and Bertha
  Production, Magic Theatre, San Francisco, 1992

Terra Incognita (music by Roberto Sierra)
  Developmental work begun at Storm King Arts Center, continued at Sienna, Italy, and performed at Yale Cabaret, New Haven, Connecticut, 1992
  Production, INTAR with Women's Project and Productions, New York, 1997

Summer in Gossensass (formerly called *Ibsen and the Actress*)
  Workshop, Women's Project and Productions, 1979
  Workshop, Iowa Playwright's Workshop, Iowa City, Iowa, 1995
  Workshop, Padua Hills Festival, Claremont, California, 1995

PLAY AVAILABILITY

Abingdon Square is published in Julia Miles, ed., *WomensWork: Five Plays from the Women's Project.* New York: Applause, 1989.

Cold Air is published in *Plays in Process*, vol. 6, no. 10. New York: Theatre Communications Group, 1985.

Drowning is published in *Orchards, Orchards, Orchards.* New York: Broadway Play Publishing, 1987.

Fefu and Her Friends is published in *Performing Arts Journal* 11, no. 3 (Winter 1978): 112–40; *Fefu and Her Friends: A Play.* New York: PAJ Publications, 1990.

Lovers and Keepers is published in *Plays in Process*, vol. 7, no. 10. New York: Theatre Communications Group, 1987.

Mud, The Danube, Sarita and *The Conduct of Life* are published in Maria Irene Fornes, *Fornes: Plays.* New York: PAJ Publications, 1986.

Oscar and Bertha is published in Murray Mednick, et al., eds., *Best of the West: An Anthology of Plays from the 1989 & 1990 Padua Hills Playwrights Festivals.* Los Angeles: Padua Hills Press, 1991.

Promenade, The Successful Life of 3, Tango Palace, Molly's Dream, A Vietnamese Wedding, and *Dr. Kheal* are published in Maria Irene Fornes, *Promenade and Other Plays.* New York: PAJ Publications, 1987.

Springtime (from *What of the Night?*) is published in Rosemary Curb, ed., *Amazon All Stars: 13 Lesbian Plays.* New York: Applause, 1996.

Terra Incognita is published in *Theater* 24, no. 2 (1993): 99–111.

What of the Night? is published in Rosette C. Lamont, ed., *Women on the Verge: 7 Avant-garde American Plays.* New York: Applause, 1993.

AWARDS

John Hay Whitney Foundation Fellowship, 1961

Centro Mexicano de Escritores Fellowship, 1962

Obie Award for Distinguished Playwriting, *The Successful Life of 3* and *Promenade*, 1965

Cintas Foundation Fellowship, 1967

Boston University–Tanglewood Fellowship, 1968

Rockefeller Foundation Grant, 1971

Guggenheim Fellowship, 1972

Creative Artist Public Service Grant, 1972

National Endowment for the Arts Grant, 1974

Creative Arts Public Service Grant, 1975

New York State Council on the Arts, 1976

Obie Award for Distinguished Directing, *Eyes on the Harem*, 1979

Obie Award, Sustained Achievement, 1982

Obie Award, *The Danube*, *Mud*, and *Sarita*, 1984

Rockefeller Foundation Grant, 1984

National Endowment for the Arts, 1984

American Academy and Institute of Arts and Letters Award in Literature, 1985

Obie Award for Best New Play, *The Conduct of Life*, 1985

Playwrights U.S.A. Award, Translation of *Cold Air* by Virgilio Pinera, 1986

Susan Smith Blackburn Award, Finalist, *The Conduct of Life*, 1986

Obie Award, *Abingdon Square*, 1987

Susan Smith Blackburn Award, Finalist, *Abingdon Square*, 1988

National Endowment for the Arts Opera-Musical/Meet the Composer/INTAR Commission, 1990

Pew/Theatre Communications Group Charitable Trust Grant, 1996–1998

DESCRIPTIVE AND CRITICAL RESPONSES

Many published responses to Fornes's work are available; a highly selective number are included here.

Austin, Gayle. "The Madwoman in the Spotlight: Plays of Maria Irene Fornes." In *Making a Spectacle: Feminist Essays on Contemporary Women's Theatre*, edited by Lynda Hart, 76–85. Ann Arbor: University of Michigan Press, 1989.

Betsko, Kathleen, and Rachel Koenig. "Maria Irene Fornes." In *Interviews with Contemporary Women Playwrights*, 154–67. New York: Beech Tree Books, 1987.

Cummings, Scott. "Seeing with Clarity: The Visions of Maria Irene Fornes." *Theater* 17, no. 1 (Winter 1985): 51–56.

Fornes, Maria Irene. " 'I Write These Messages That Come.' " *The Drama Review* 21 (December 1977): 25–40.

Geis, Deborah R. "Wordscapes of the Body: Performative Language as *Gestus* in Maria Irene Fornes's Plays." *Theatre Journal* 42 (October 1990): 291–307.

Huerta, Jorge. "Professionalizing Teatro: An Overview of Chicano Theatre during the 'Decade of the Hispanic.' " *Theatre Forum* (Spring 1993): 54–59.

Jacobson, Lynn. "Brawl in the Family." *American Theatre* 9, no. 1 (April 1992): 10–11.

Kent, Assunta. "Introduction." In *Amazon All Stars: 13 Lesbian Plays*, edited by Rosemary Curb, 93–98. New York: Applause, 1996.

Marranca, Bonnie. "The Aging Playwright and the American Theatre." *Village Voice*, 16 June 1992, 94.

———. "The State of Grace." *Performing Arts Journal* 41 (May 1992): 24–31.

O'Malley, Lurana Donnels. "Pressing Clothes/Snapping Beans/Reading Books: Maria Irene Fornes's Women's Work." *Studies in American Drama, 1945 to the Present* 4 (1989): 103–17.

Savran, David. *In Their Own Words: Contemporary American Playwrights*. New York: Theatre Communications Group, 1988.

Telgen, Diane, and Jim Kemp, eds. *Notable Hispanic American Women*, 160–64. Detroit: Gale Research, 1993.

J. e. FRANKLIN

(1937–)

BIOGRAPHY

Born and raised in Houston, Texas, J. e. Franklin graduated from the University of Texas. In addition to her dramatic works, Franklin has written an autobiographical account delineating the transformation of her first major work, *Black Girl*, from video to stage and ultimately to screen in *Black Girl: From Genesis to Revelations*.

Franklin has also taught full-time at the University of Iowa and the City University of New York. Other academic positions include resident director at Skidmore College and playwright in residence at Brown University. She is a resident scholar at the Arthur A. Schomburg Center for Research in Black Culture in New York City.

PLAY DESCRIPTIONS

J. e. Franklin's plays provide penetrating glimpses into a panorama of African American life. *Black Girl* is Franklin's portrayal of an embittered and dysfunctional Texas family. Billie Jean, an aspiring dancer, dreams of escape from her upbringing but is systematically defeated by her nasty mother and wicked stepsisters in this modern update of the Cinderella story.

In *The Prodigal Sister*, Franklin creates a contemporary musical that relies on rhymed dialogue approaching a rap beat and musical numbers using a do-wop group for backup. Drawing on undisguised religious parallels, the plot traces Jackie's physical and spiritual journey. Driven from her home after her mother learns that she is pregnant, the runaway Jackie falls prey to a series of trials and tribulations in the big city. While Jackie seeks a way to return home, her parents begin to regret the harsh treatment of their daughter. Jackie's friends at the casket factory, where she is working, suggest that she ship herself home in one of their products. The young girl's surprise arrival provides a satisfying resolution to this modern morality play.

Franklin's more recent work uses sharply honed language and a gritty realism to depict sides of black life that are not often shown on stage. *Christchild* is the first episode in an octet of plays charting the lives of Katherine and Benjamin Henderson and their children. Set in rural Texas of the 1930s, the play shows the desperate lives of a family living in desperate times. Part of the fallout of Katherine (aged thirty-five) and Benjamin's (sixty-five) intergenerational marriage is Benjamin's abusive treatment of his wife and his hatred for his oldest child, Tom. Blaming Tom's physical deformity (six fingers on one hand) for the cause of all their economic and personal troubles, Benjamin is eager to send the boy away. Only Sister Gertie, the neighborhood crone with mystical powers, can see that Tom is special and shows him his new-found spiritual vision. Desperate to win his father's approval and end the family's financial difficulties, Tom enters a contest to wrestle a bear. The money he wins displaces his father's enmity only temporarily, and Tom is forced to leave the family and strike out on his own. *Where Dewdrops of Mercy Shine Bright* picks up where the previous play ended. It is Christmas morning, and Tom has just run away. Believing that Tom has taken the money, Benjamin, who threatens his family with a gun, takes out his hostility and anger on them. He humiliates Joyce, his oldest daughter, by accusing her of being a chippy, beating her, and forcing her to stand naked in front of him; he torments the younger children by locking away their toys. Joyce is finally compelled to run away, and Katherine takes her youngest son, Benjamin, Jr., with her to her mother's. Addie, the youngest child and her father's favorite, who is left behind, reveals that Tom did not take the money. Benjamin admits that he did not want to drive his wife away and leaves with Addie to try and win her back.

Gray Panthers is a series of four ten-minute plays, each with at least one older character. *Hot Methuselah* depicts Alice, who is angry with her elderly husband, Charles, for having an adulterous relationship with an apparent prostitute. Her resolution to leave her husband begins to slip away when she realizes how pitiful he is. *S'posed-to-be Daddy* concerns a reconciliation between Gideon, who is eighty, and his wayward son, Carey, who has returned home to ask his father's forgiveness. Gussie Lee, Gideon's younger wife, facilitates the father-son resolution. *The Closer the Kin* focuses on Preston, who is seventy-five, who comes to terms with the conflict in his duty to his handicapped sister (whom his wife hates) and his duty to his wife Cora.

SELECTED PRODUCTION HISTORY

Black Girl
    Production, New Federal Theatre, New York, 1971
    Production, New Federal Theatre at Henry Street Settlement, New York, 1995

The Prodigal Sister
  Production, Theater de Lys, New York, 1974

Christchild
  Reading, Church of the Crucifixion, New York, 1979
  Reading, George Street Playhouse, New Brunswick, New Jersey, 1984
  Reading, Second Stage, New York, 1987
  Production, Rites and Reason Theatre, Providence, Rhode Island, 1989
  Production, New Federal Theatre, New York, 1992

Where Dewdrops of Mercy Shine Bright
  Production, Rites and Reason Theatre, Providence, Rhode Island, 1990

Gray Panthers (four ten-minute plays)
  Production, Ensemble Theatre, Houston, Texas, 1994

PLAY AVAILABILITY

Black Girl is available from Dramatists Play Service, 440 Park Avenue South, New York, New York 10016; (212) 683–8960.

Christchild is published in Marisa Smith, ed., *Women Playwrights: The Best Plays of 1993*. Newbury, Vermont: Smith and Kraus, 1994.

The Prodigal Sister is available from Samuel French, Inc., 25 West 45th Street, New York, New York 10036; (212) 206–8990.

AWARDS

Drama Desk Award, Winner, *Black Girl*, 1971

Kennedy Center's New American Play Award, *Christchild*, 1992

Fellow, US/Mexico Artists' Exchange Program, 1994

DESCRIPTIVE AND CRITICAL RESPONSES

Albright, William. "Tender *Gray Panthers* Explores Woes of Old Age." *Houston Post*, 25 October 1994, D5.
Brantley, Ben. "Cinderella as Recast in Black for the 70's." *New York Times*, 14 November 1995, C14.
Evans, Everett. "*Panthers* Filled with Earthy Acting, Truths." *Houston Chronicle*, 25 October 1994, D3.
Holden, Stephen. "*Christchild*." Review of *Christchild*. *New York Times*, 2 December 1992, C18.

TERRY GALLOWAY

(1950–   )

BIOGRAPHY

Born in Germany where her father was stationed in the U.S. Army, Galloway spent her adolescent years in Berlin before the family returned to the United States and settled in Texas. The victim of an experimental drug prescribed for her mother when she was pregnant, Galloway suffered a profound hearing loss that ultimately resulted in deafness in her early twenties. In her autobiographical *Heart of a Dog*, she chronicles growing up in Germany and Texas and learning to understand her deafness. Galloway performs as well as she writes, but, because her hearing declined gradually, her performance is not marked by any vocal "deaf" quality. She is an adept lip reader and does not work with a translator.

While an undergraduate at the University of Texas, Galloway became known for her work at their experimental Shakespearean workshop, Shakespeare at Winedale, and for her role in the Heiner Muller play *Mauser* which he directed. She helped found Esther's Follies, a cabaret theatre in 1977 (which is still operating), and wrote, performed, and directed several hundred comic skits, including the legendary "Jake Ratchett, Short Detective." While a graduate student in playwriting at Columbia University, Galloway wrote her first one-woman performance piece which she performed at the WOW Cafe in 1982. A year later, the Woman's Project and Productions produced her *Heart of a Dog* at the American Place Theatre. She presented her subsequent performance piece, *Out All Night and Lost My Shoes*, largely based on *Dog*, in cities in the United States and England and at the Edinburgh Festival. A popular interpreter of her own work, Galloway, described by Jan Bresauer as "one of the most unrelenting and perceptive female comedic performers" (1991), continues to write and perform at many diverse venues. Irreverent humor, a sense of play, a love of parody, and compassion are characteristics of all of her work.

A collection of her poems, *Buncha Crocs in Surch of Snac*, was published by Curbstone Press in 1980, and "Eat the Rich" is available in Roz Warren's *Women's Glibber* (1993). Terry Galloway was featured in the film *Gay TV: The Movie* as Fishin' Gal Gus. She is a cofounder and codirector of the Mickee Faust Players in Tallahassee, Florida, where she lives and is at work on a full-length six-character play, *In the House of Moles*.

PLAY DESCRIPTIONS

Heart of a Dog (subsequently *Out All Night and Lost My Shoes*) is a collection of stories about Galloway's family and her difficult adolescence combined with her poems, humorous sketches (including "The Etiquette of Suicide"), and an extended "radio show" featuring Jake Ratchett, short detective. A seemingly dissimilar collection of poetry, personal history, and comedy sketches, the piece is held together by vivid, recurring images of the terrors present in our contemporary world and the particular demons that beset an overly sensitive writer who, because of her deafness, lives in a silent world.

Lardo Weeping, an hour-long, one-person performance work, features the character Dinah LaFarge, an agoraphobe of Falstaffian proportions, who eats, dictates letters, and believes in Automatic Mind Command. She is as equally fascinated by tabloids and celebrity gossip as she is by Emily Dickinson and Virginia Woolf. In performance, Galloway wears a fat suit, and in the climax of the piece she does a mock strip, shedding bits of her anatomy—breasts, genitalia, and umbilical cord—and then sticking herself back together as she symbolically picks up the pieces of her life.

SELECTED PRODUCTION HISTORY

Hamlet in Berlin (early draft of *In the House of Moles*)
    Staged reading, Women's Project and Productions at American Place Theatre, New
        York, 1988

Heart of a Dog
    Production, Horace Mann Theatre, Columbia University, New York,
        1983
    Production, Women's Project and Productions at American Place Theatre, New
        York, 1983
    Production, Burbage Theatre Ensemble, Los Angeles, 1984
    Production, Reponde de Capite, Little Rock, Arkansas, 1988

Lardo Weeping
    Production, Capitol City Playhouse, Austin, Texas, 1988
    Production, Chicago House, Austin, Texas, 1991
    Production, P. S. 122, New York, 1992
    Production, Finborough, London, 1993

Production, Alice B. Theatre, Seattle, 1994

Production, Tampa Bay Performing Arts Center, Tampa, Florida, 1994

Production, Y' Teresa Arte Alternativo, Mexico City, 1994

Production, Highways, Santa Monica, California, 1995

Out All Night and Lost My Shoes

Production, First New York International Festival of the Arts, P. S. 122, New York, 1988

Production, Loft Theatre, Tampa, Florida, 1989

Production, Solo Mio Festival, Life on the Water, San Francisco, 1990

Production, LACE, Los Angeles, 1990

Production, Seven Stages, Atlanta, 1990

Production, Mid-Atlantic Arts Festival, Arena Theatre, Washington, D.C., 1990

Production, Manhattan Theatre Club, New York, 1990

Production, Danceworks, Toronto, Canada, 1990

Production, New Orleans Center for Contemporary Arts, New Orleans, 1990

Production, Walker Arts Center, Minneapolis, 1991

Production, Tron Theatre, Glasgow, Scotland, 1991

Production, Zap Club, Brighton, England, 1991

Production, Highways, Santa Monica, California, 1991

Production, Finborough, London, 1992

Production, Edinburgh Festival, Scotland, 1992

Production, Dance Theatre Workshop, New York, 1994

PLAY AVAILABILITY

Heart of a Dog is published in Julia Miles, ed., *Plays from the Women's Project*. New York: Performing Arts Journal Publications, 1984.

Lardo Weeping is published in Kristin Graham, ed., *The Great Monologues from the Women's Project*. Lyme, New Hampshire: Smith and Kraus, 1994.

Out All Night and Lost My Shoes is published by Apalachee Press, Tallahassee, Florida, 1993

AWARDS

Villager Downtown Theatre, Award for Outstanding Solo Performance, New York, *Heart of a Dog*, 1983

Florida Division of Cultural Affairs, Individual Artist Fellowship in Playwriting, 1990

Pew, Development Grant, *Lardo Weeping*, 1991

National Endowment for the Arts, Fellowship in Theatre, 1991–1992

DESCRIPTIVE AND CRITICAL RESPONSES

Breslauer, Jan. ''Performance Pick of the Week.'' Review of *Out All Night. L.A. Weekly*, 19–25 April 1991.

Churnin, Nancy. "Artist Who's Caught between Two Worlds." *Los Angeles Times*, 23 April 1990, F5.

Dworkin, Norine. "Lardo Weeping." Review of *Lardo Weeping*. *Village Voice*, 14 January 1992, 92.

Godfree, Paula. "Life Is Tougher than Art, but Art Is Tough: Interview with Terry Galloway." *Firewood: A Feminist Quarterly* 32 (Spring 1991): 87–97.

Hoffman, Jan. "War Zones." Review of *Heart of a Dog*. *Village Voice*, 14 June 1983, 97–98.

Milvy, Erika. "Lardo Drips with Wit." Review of *Lardo Weeping*. *New York Post*, 15 January 1992.

TERRY GARNER

(1953–)

BIOGRAPHY

Garner, who was born in Knoxville, Tennessee, began writing at an early age and won publication in the National Scholastic Short Story Contest at the age of sixteen. (One of the judges was Joyce Carol Oates.) At the University of Tennessee, Garner majored in English and wrote for the student newspaper, while publishing short stories in small literary magazines. Her first stage production was of two one-acts at the university in 1980. In 1982 she moved to San Francisco where she continued to write plays. Garner has had productions throughout the Bay Area and in Los Angeles. Her most widely known play, *Livin' on Salvation Street*, is distinguished by its idiomatic Southern speech and manners and gently eccentric characters, whose lineage is linked to Carson McCullers and Eudora Welty. Following a successful production at Theatre Rhinoceros in San Francisco in the mid-1980s, the play was produced in Los Angeles where it was directed by Dorothy Lyman. Theatre Rhinoceros revived the play for their eighteenth season. Garner continues to live and work in San Francisco. She is at work on a new play, *Romeo and the Apothecary's Wife*.

PLAY DESCRIPTIONS

Livin' on Salvation Street is a largely realistic, coming-of-age, dark comedy that captures the repressiveness of the 1950s for gay teenagers. The play details one eventful week in the life of three generations of an all-female family. Granny Blue, who lives on the memories of a brief career as a gospel singer, pressures her rebellious granddaughter, Wilma, to carry on her musical aspirations. The mother, a tour guide in Cave City, Kentucky, where they all live, mediates between the irascible matriarch and her daughter, who with her tomboyish, unsociable behavior is a misfit in her high school. The daughter's one friend, Clyde, happily celebrates his sexuality with Billy Bob, who plays the tuba in the school band. When Granny Blue attempts to set up an audition for her granddaughter on the Glory Gospel Hour, Wilma decides to join the army, which she feels is the only way to get out of her house and her town. The play is punctuated with music from the 1950s, particularly that of Elvis Presley, whom the mother adores. In a program note, Garner described *Salvation Street* as having a dreamlike quality where "strange things happen and there is an inter-play between illusion, reality, myth, romance and escape."

SELECTED PRODUCTION HISTORY

Possessions (one act)
  Production, National Women's Theatre Festival, Santa Cruz, California, 1984

Livin' on Salvation Street
  Production, Theatre Rhinoceros, San Francisco, 1985
  Production, Fountain Theatre, Los Angeles, 1986
  Production, Theatre Rhinoceros, San Francisco, 1993 (revival)

Sissy Goes West
  Production, Intersection for the Arts, San Francisco, 1987

PLAY AVAILABILITY

Plays are available from Terry Garner, 2115 Castro Street, San Francisco, California 94117.

AWARD

Artist in Residence, Dorland Arts Colony, 1987

DESCRIPTIVE AND CRITICAL RESPONSES

Goodman, Dean. "*Livin' on Salvation Street*." *Dramalogue*, 15–21 April 1993.
Weiner, Bernard. Review of *Livin' on Salvation Street*. *San Francisco Chronicle*, 30 January 1985, 55.
Winn, Steven. "Gospel and Generational Conflict." *San Francisco Chronicle*, 7 February 1993, 6.

P. J. GIBSON

(1951–   )

BIOGRAPHY

P. (Patricia) J. (Joann) Gibson was born in Pittsburgh, Pennsylvania but raised in Washington, D.C., and Trenton, New Jersey. She holds a BA degree in English and religion from Keuka College, Keuka Park, New York (1973) and an MFA in theatre from Brandeis University (1975) under a Shubert Fellowship. She also studied under J. P. Miller, the author of *Days of Wine and Roses.*

Gibson, who began her writing career at the age of nine, has produced over thirty plays in addition to poetry and prose. She is currently working on two novels (*Neidyana* and *The Cyclic*) and a collection of erotic short stories, portions of which have appeared in the Doubleday anthology *Erotique Noir—Black Erotica.* She has also written a screenplay for Bill Cosby and an episode for the "Edge of Night" daytime drama.

An educator as well as a writer, Gibson is an assistant professor of English at John Jay College of Criminal Justice in New York City, where she teaches literature, English, and creative writing courses. She teaches a course in black theatre at Rutgers University, in New Brunswick, New Jersey, and spends her summers at the University of California-Berkeley, where she teaches theatre, English, and film-related courses. P. J. Gibson has taught playwriting at the Bushfire Theatre in Philadelphia and at Playwrights Horizons in New York, the city she currently calls home.

PLAY DESCRIPTIONS

P. J. Gibson's plays generally explore the psychic scars and personal joys of relationships in their myriad forms. She also chronicles the historical journey of blacks in the American landscape. The historical drama *My Mark, My Name* is based on the first black regiment of Rhode Island, 1776–1783. The play addresses the world's facing the ''freed'' black men and women after the Revolutionary War. It was a time when ''freedom'' did not mean security but was a world where a slave, living in the midst of freed black men, must make a dramatic move to gain his freedom. Set in a secluded mountain lodge, *Konvergence* is a gritty realistic conflict drama. Derek and Nanyel meet after a year's agreed upon separation to see if they can reconstruct their marriage. They are faced with the reality of changes within themselves and in their partners, changes that have made them into different people. The realistic drama *Miss Ann Don't Cry No More* is set in a house divided into four apartments. The play reflects the lives, conflicts, desires, passions, and dreams of those who occupy the house.

Unveilings (previously titled *The Unveiling of Abigail*) is a realistic drama in which a former college professor is given unexpected birthday gifts: revelations of lies, deception, and cheated years with the man she loved. Gospel music provides an important component of *Clean Sheets, Can't Soil* in which a woman, fleeing from her emotions, returns to the source of her fears to find that she is not the only member of her family who is running. The opera *Ain't Love Grand?* uses four couples of varying ages (teens, twenties, thirties, and forties) to explore humorously the permutations of love triangles among themselves.

One of Gibson's most frequently produced plays is the realistic drama *Long Time since Yesterday*. This essentially realistic drama reunites former college roommates and friends at the funeral of another friend who has committed suicide. The emotional circumstances of their reunion provides the impetus for these professional, middle-class black women, now in their thirties, to reveal their fears and deep-seated antagonisms. The overt and long-standing hostility between Laveer and Panzi, who both claim to be the deceased's best friend, erupts in the play's climax. When it is revealed that Panzi's seduction of the emotionally vulnerable Janeen contributed to Janeen's suicide, the resentment-filled air can finally be cleared.

Brown Silk and Magenta Sunsets is a drama of obsessive love and regret. The play is set in a luxurious penthouse where the reclusive, alcoholic Lena relives past memories and tries to make amends in the present. She is aided in her psychic exploration by the figures in three portraits who come to life, haunting her memory and prodding her into action. When the seduction of a young artist, who reminds her of the one true love of her life, does not end the regrets and self-recrimination, Lena makes the ultimate fatal decision.

For her most recent play, P. J. Gibson was commissioned by the Women's Center of John Jay College of Criminal Justice to examine the issues of sexual violence and the healing process. *Masks, Circles: Healing the Pain* is the emotionally powerful result. Based on interviews with survivors, the play explores the relationships between victims and perpetrators.

SELECTED PRODUCTION HISTORY

Shameful in Your Eyes
Production, Keuka College, Keuka Park, New York, 1971

The Black Woman
Production, Keuka College, Keuka Park, New York, 1972
Production, State University of New York–Cortland, Cortland, 1972

The Ninth Story Window
Production, Brandeis University, Waltham, Massachusetts, 1974

Spida Bug (one-act play for children)
Production, Brandeis University, Waltham, Massachusetts, 1975
Production, Boston School System Tour, Boston, 1975

Swing/Slide
Production, Brandeis University, Waltham, Massachusetts, 1975
Production, Cubiculo Theatre, New York, 1975

Void Passage
Production, Rites and Reason Theatre, Providence, Rhode Island, 1977
Production, Players Company Theatre, Trenton, New Jersey, 1978
Production, Kumba Workshop Theatre, Chicago, 1978

My Mark, My Name
Production, Rites and Reason Theatre, Providence, Rhode Island, 1978
Production, Soul Peoples Repertory, Indianapolis, 1981
Production, International Black Arts Festival, New York, 1982
Production, Trenton Theatre Guild, Trenton, New Jersey, 1986
Production, Bushfire Theatre, Philadelphia, 1989
Production, Powerhouse Theatre Company, Richmond, Virginia, 1990

Konvergence
Production, Rites and Reason Theatre, Providence, Rhode Island, 1978
Production, Players Company Theatre, Trenton, New Jersey, 1978
Production, Kumba Workshop Theatre, Chicago, 1978
Production, Oakland Ensemble Theatre, Oakland, California, 1982
Production, B&G Productions, Dramatists Theater, New York, 1994

The Androgyny
Production, Cardboard Clowns Theatre, Frankfurt, Germany, 1979

The Zappers and the Shopping Bag Lady
Production, Tour CETA Arts Program/Black Theatre Alliance, New York, 1979

Miss Ann Don't Cry No More
Production, Frederick Douglass Creative Arts Center, New York, 1980
Production, Bushfire Theatre, Philadelphia, 1988

Angel
Staged reading, Family Theatre, New York, 1981

The Unveiling of Abigail
Production, Arts Festival, Torino, Italy, 1981

Unveilings (two-act play previously titled *The Unveiling of Abigail*)

Production, Eccentric Circles Theatre, New York, 1982
Production, Rainbow Connection Theatre, Los Angeles, 1986
Production, Side Stage Theatre Company, New York, 1991
Production, Bushfire Theatre, Philadelphia, 1992
Production, Place in the Sun Production, New York, 1994

Clean Sheets, Can't Soil
Production, Rites and Reason Theatre, Providence, Rhode Island, 1983
Production, Swinma Productions, 18th Street Playhouse, New York, 1988

Ain't Love Grand? (opera)
Production, Black Spectrum Theatre, New York, 1984

Long Time since Yesterday
Production, New Federal Theatre, New York, 1985
Over forty additional productions throughout the United States to date

Private Hells, Sketches in Reality (three one-act plays)
Production, New York University, New York, 1986

Brown Silk and Magenta Sunsets
Production, Penumbra Theatre Company, St. Paul, Minnesota, 1988
Production, Paul Robeson Theatre, Buffalo, New York, 1988
Production, Paul Robeson Theatre and Richard B. Harrison Players, Greensboro, North
   Carolina, 1990
Production, SsQ Theater and Repertory, Maitland, Florida, 1991

Masks, Circles: Healing the Pain
Staged reading, John Jay College of Criminal Justice, New York, 1994
Workshop, University of Michigan, Ann Arbor, 1995
Production, California State University, Sacramento, 1997

Rotating
Production, Oakland Ensemble Company, California, 1997

Deep Roots
Production, Bushfire Theatre, Philadephia, 1997

PLAY AVAILABILITY

Brown Silk and Magenta Sunsets is published in Margaret B. Wilkerson, ed., *9 Plays by
Black Women.* New York: New American Library, 1986.

Kovergence is published in Woodie King, Jr., ed., *New Plays for the Black Theatre.*
Chicago: Third World Press, 1989.

Long Time since Yesterday is published by Samuel French, 45 West 25th Street, New
York, New York 10010–2751; William B. Branch, ed., *Black Thunder: An Anthology
of Contemporary African American Drama.* New York: Mentor Books, 1992.

P. J. Gibson's other plays are available from the playwright: 400 West 43rd Street #14L,
New York, New York 10036; (212) 736–0644.

AWARDS

Shubert Fellowship, Playwriting Grant, 1974

Grant, Rhode Island Committee for the Humanities, *My Mark, My Name*, 1978–1979

National Endowment for the Arts, Playwriting Grant, 1978

Key to the City, Mayor's Office, Indianapolis, *My Mark, My Name*, 1980

AUDELCO Award, Best Dramatic Play of the Year, Winner, *Long Time since Yesterday*, 1985

U.S. Representative, First International Women Playwrights Conference, Buffalo, New York, 1988

PSC-CUNY Research Grant, 1994

DESCRIPTIVE AND CRITICAL RESPONSES

Gussow, Mel. "The Stage: 'Long Time.' " Review of *Long Time since Yesterday*. *New York Times*, 10 February 1985, 63.

Massa, Robert. "Rued Times." Review of *Long Time since Yesterday*. *Village Voice*, 26 February 1985, 88–89.

GLORIA GONZALEZ

(1940–   )

BIOGRAPHY

Gloria Gonzalez, a native New Yorker, was born to a Cuban mother and a Spanish father. From the age of five, Gonzalez knew she was destined to be a writer, and after high school, she became a professional journalist and freelance writer. In addition to working for various New Jersey papers as an investigative reporter and at the New York *News*, the *Times*, and the *Post*, Gonzalez began to write stories and scripts. A television play, *Gaucho* (1970), which depicts a young boy's longing to return to his native Puerto Rico, was shown on CBS and on ABC's "After School Special." She adapted her television script into a juvenile novel in 1977. She has also written *The Glad Man* (1975) and *A Deadly Rhyme* (1986) for the youth market.

After seeing her first professional theatre production, Gonzalez turned to playwriting. She studied at the New School under Jean-Claude van Itallie and under Lee Strasberg. Her plays were produced off-off-Broadway and in numerous theatres throughout the country. During the 1980s and 1990s, Gonzalez continued her theatrical writing and also wrote for television, including "Kate and Allie," "Comedy Zone," and an NBC movie, *The Day the Women Got Even* (1981).

In 1991, leaving New York for the wide open spaces of the West, Gloria Gonzalez moved to Las Vegas, Nevada. Her disenchantment with opportunities in the theatre is reflected in her recent concentration on writing novels.

PLAY DESCRIPTIONS

Gloria Gonzalez's one-act plays *Moving On!*, *Cuba: Economy Class!*, and *The New America* are published collectively under the title *Moving On!*. The three plays are interconnected in that all three take place in moving vehicles that are traveling on the same stretch of highway at the same time. The action is seen through the eyes of three separate couples, each of whom is near a major decision in their lives. *Moving On!* depicts a middle-aged couple on the way home from Al's high school reunion. Seeing his old friends from the ghetto and their very different lifestyles has triggered all of Al's frustration with his own middle-class existence. Al is willing to give up his cushy middle-class existence (sell the house and take up the criminal law practice that he always wanted) if Carolyn will go along with the plan. Carolyn, who refuses to listen to his dreams and ideas, turns the conversation to redecorating the house and ordering Chinese food. Before they turn off the highway, Al's convictions are dashed and they return home. In *Cuba: Economy Class!*, Jackson, an affable young man of Irish and Cuban descent, befriends the driver, Herbie, of the Greyhound bus on which he and his friend are riding. After Jackson wins Herbie's confidence, he calmly informs the driver that he is hijacking the bus at gun point and is taking the bus to Miami. *The New America* is the story of a young, naive couple: Arnie (age nineteen) and his girlfriend Shirley (age seventeen). The two kids in love are running away from home to start a new life in Canada. Arnie is dodging the Vietnam War, and Shirley is going with him as his child bride. Their innocent dreams of a new life are touching in light of the reality that awaits them.

The popular *Cafe con Leche*, which finds its roots in the playwright's own Latina background, marks a significant transition in her work. The comedy is set in the apartment of the Cabreras family on New York's East Side as the family frantically prepares for the oldest son's return from prison. What follows is a family play that ranges from farcical byplay (mistaken identities) to treating such serious issues as crime and education. Unfortunately, the play is not available in English translation at this time.

SELECTED PRODUCTION HISTORY

Chicken Little's Ass Is Falling
   Production, Playbox Theatre, New York, 1970

Celebrate Me (written with Edna Schappert)
   Production, Playbox Theatre, New York, 1971

Love Is a Tuna Casserole
   Production, New York Theatre Ensemble, New York, 1971

Tidings, Comfort and Joy (with Edna Schappert and Joseph Gath)
   Production, Playbox Theatre, New York, 1971

Moving On! (collective title for the one-act plays *Moving On!*, *Cuba: Economy Class!*, and *The New America*)
   Production, Playbox Theatre, New York, 1971

Waiting Room
   Production, Theatre at Noon, New York, 1974

A Sanctuary in the City
   Production, Theatre Americana, Altadena, California, 1975

Curtains
   Production, Hudson Guild Theatre, New York, 1975

Let's Hear It for Miss America
   Production, Country Dinner Playhouse, St. Petersburg, Florida, 1976

A Former Gotham Gal
   Production, New Playwrights Theatre, Washington, D.C., 1980

Cafe con Leche
   Production, Gramercy Arts Theatre, New York, 1984
   Production (in permanent repertory), Repertorio Espanol, late 1980s–present

Padre Gomez y Santa Cecilia
   Production, Repertorio Español, New York, 1987 and 1989–1990

Honeymoon Serenade
   Production, Teatro Avante, Miami, 1991

PLAY AVAILABILITY

Curtains is available from Dramatists Play Service, 440 Park Avenue South, New York, New York 10016; (212) 683–8960.

Moving On!, the collective title for three one acts (*Moving On!*, *Cuba: Economy Class!*, and *The New America*) is published by Samuel French, Inc., 25 West 45th Street, New York, New York 10036.

AWARDS

Jacksonville University National Playwriting Contest, First Place, *Curtains*, 1975

Webster Groves Russell B. Sharp Annual Playwriting Award, *Lights*, 1976

Stanley Drama Award, *Cafe con Leche*, 1983

DESCRIPTIVE AND CRITICAL RESPONSE

Robertson, Nan. "*Cafe con Leche*: A Bit of Home Brew." Review of *Cafe con Leche*. *New York Times*, 2 November 1984, C3.

SILVIA GONZALEZ S.

(1958–   )

BIOGRAPHY

Silvia Gonzalez S. was born and raised in California's San Fernando Valley. She attended Loyola Marymount University in Los Angeles and was selected to study at the Loyola Rome Center in Italy. While in Italy she met her future husband, Tom Scherer, who was from Chicago. Gonzalez S. completed her undergraduate studies at the Loyola University of Chicago, where she earned a BS in education. Her husband's medical education, however, necessitated that they move frequently in the next several years.

While teaching in Yuma, Arizona, Gonzalez S. wanted to continue her interest in stand-up comedy and ventriloquism. However, after learning about the asphyxiation of undocumented workers in a boxcar in 1987, she was compelled to write her first theatre piece, *Boxcar*. Her first play was immediately followed by a playwriting fellowship at INTAR in New York.

When she returned to Chicago, Silvia Gonzalez S. became a member of the Chicago Dramatists Workshop and a literary manager for Body Politic Theatre, where she has the distinction of being that theatre's first Latina playwright. While at the Body Politic Theatre, she instituted the Unknown Playwrights Staged Readings to ensure that the work and not the playwright was being judged. During this period, she also taught a playwriting workshop to students in inner-city Chicago.

Silvia Gonzalez S. currently resides in central Oregon where she works with the Central Oregon Arts in Education program. She is also working on playwriting, poetry, and video projects with the Museum at Warm Springs Indian Reservation and is finding ways to help Latino students in Madras, Oregon. She is working on projects with the Sundance Film Institute and Walt Disney Studios. Gonzalez is a member of the Dramatists Guild, the New Dramatists, the

Chicago Dramatists Workshop, the Minneapolis Playwrights' Center, and the Northwest Playwrights Guild.

PLAY DESCRIPTIONS

Based on the 1987 tragedy of a group of undocumented workers trapped and asphyxiated in a railroad boxcar, Gonzalez's *Boxcar* blends historical reality with fantasy and mysticism to personalize the dilemma of illegal immigration. As the workers' journey toward the United States is dramatized, we are introduced to them individually as they relate their dreams, hopes, and histories. Juxtaposed against their stories is the spiritual journey of Roberto, an American border patrol officer of Mexican descent. Seeing himself as a murderer for performing his duties as a border patrol officer, he is tormented by guilt. His conflicted spirit is haunted by an Aztec Skull Dancer who also appears to the workers trapped in the boxcar. Finally Roberto is guided by the spirit of his grandmother to find the men, but their rescue comes too late for all but one of them.

Los Matadores blends the fantastic and the real into a poignant story of dreams, longing, and tragedy. In the play, set in Valencia, Spain, in 1931, an aging picador is forced to fulfill his lifelong dream of being a matador by stabbing his mattress which doubles as the bull. After he buys an oil painting of a flamenco dancer and a guitar player, the figures come to life to dance and play for his fantasy. The young housemaid enters into the picador's fantasy world when she torments him with the symbolic suit of lights that he wears in his imagination. The picador kills the bull only to discover that the wounded matador is the maid's husband.

The real and the surreal again collide in *The Migrant Farmworker's Son*, a drama of familial division and reconciliation. Henry's migrant farm–working parents have shielded him from the harsh realities of life and have allowed him to live like an American boy with few worries. After being visited by an apparition of his daughter, however, Henry's father begins to criticize him for "having it all" and being ungrateful. When the father's hostility is transformed into physical abuse, Henry's mother attempts to act as mediator. Henry seeks advice and counsel from Oliverio, an old farmworker who recites poetry in the field under the stars and who attempts to bring the family together with his words of wisdom. Henry learns about his father's guilt and pain over the drowning of his daughter on the same day he had severely punished her. Only after the family is reconciled does Henry learn that Oliverio had been killed in a field accident fifteen years ago. With their mission accomplished, Oliverio, Henry's dead sister, and the Mexican peasants exit in the manner of a Diego Rivera mural.

Alicia in Wonder Tierra (or I Can't Eat Goat Head) is a wild retelling of *Alice in Wonderland* with a touch of *The Wizard of Oz*. Alicia is a thoroughly Anglocized Mexican American young woman who is cut off from and denies her Latina roots. Using Mexican folk imagery, the play takes Alicia on a symbolic journey into her cultural heritage. Alicia's rabbit hole is a Mexican curio shop, and her guides to the famed Pottery Maker are a puppet, a gargantuan Armadilla, and a horny toad. In the topsy-turvy world of this "cultural cuisinart," Alicia faces a tree full of talking heads, the Elvira gang, a Jewish Aztec priest, the Distorted Memory Forest, and the Village of Laughter.

Gonzalez's one-act plays span a wide range of subjects and styles. *Plution* is a Felliniesque play about a dysfunctional family, guns, and Father's Day gifts. *Marionetas* (1991) involves puppets in a Mexican curio shop who come alive at lunch hour and notice they are being ignored by Yuppies. *The Border* is an abstract depiction of border entry from the Hispanic point of view. The two-man play *T* portrays the physical and mental torture inflicted on one man by the other. The torturer dances around his victim with surrealistic representations of various forms of torture; his victim uses fantasy and fond memories to preserve his sanity and endure the torturer's attempts to steal his personality. *La Llorona Llora* draws on Mexican history and myth. In the sixteenth century, the Spanish conquistadors married the indigenous people and created the mestizo. La Llorna, usually known as "the boogie man" in Mexico, is the Mexican Medea.

SELECTED PRODUCTION HISTORY

Boxcar
> Production, Arizona Commission on the Arts Play Fest, Phoenix, 1988
> Development, MultiCultural Playwrights' Festival, Seattle Group Theatre, Seattle, 1989
> Production, Theater Works, Phoenix, Arizona, 1990
> Production, Original Theatre Works, Los Angeles, 1991
> Staged reading, Portland International Performance Festival, Portland, Oregon, 1993
> Staged reading, New Dramatists, New York, 1995

Waiting Women
> Reading, Phoenix Playwrights' Workshop, Phoenix, Arizona, 1988
> Workshop, Chicago Dramatists Workshop, 1993

Rivals
> Reading, Hispanic Playwrights' Lab, INTAR II, New York, 1990

Los Matadores
> Reading, Chicago Dramatists Workshop, Chicago, 1991
> Workshop, Victory Gardens Theatre, Chicago, 1992
> Production, Body Politic Theatre, Chicago, 1994

The Migrant Farmworker's Son
> Staged readings, Victory Gardens Theatre, Chicago, 1991
> Staged reading, 1991 Border Playwrights Project, Borderlands Theatre, Tucson, Arizona, 1991
> Staged reading, Playwrights' Festival, Chicago Dramatists Workshop, Chicago, 1991
> Workshop production, Chicago Dramatists Workshop, Chicago, 1992

Plution (one-act play)
   Staged reading, Chicago Dramatists Workshop, Chicago, 1991

Marionetas (one-act play)
   Staged reading, Chicago Dramatists Workshop, Chicago, 1991

Gang Girl (one-act play)
   Production, American Blues Theatre, Chicago, 1991

Cassandra (renamed *Imaginary Lover*)
   Staged reading, Chicago Dramatists Workshop, Chicago, 1992

Mexican Muse (one-act play)
   Staged reading, Chicago Dramatists Workshop, Chicago, 1991

Don't Promise
   Staged reading, Body Politic Theatre, Chicago, 1992

The Border (one-act play)
   Production, Aguijon II Theatre Company, Chicago, 1992 (bilingual)

T (one-act play)
   Production, Stage of One's Own Theatre Company, Chicago, 1992

La Llorona Llora (one-act play)
   Production, Whole Arts Theatre Company, Kalamazoo, Michigan, 1993
   Production, Blue Rider Theatre (with Whole Arts Theatre Company), Chicago, 1994

Alicia in Wonder Tierra (or I Can't Eat Goat Head)
   Staged reading, New Visions/New Voices, Kennedy Center, Washington, D.C., 1993
   Staged reading, Hispanic Playwright Project, South Coast Repertory Theatre, Costa
      Mesa, California, 1993
   Production, Coterie Theatre, Kansas City, Missouri, 1995

U Got the Look (one-act play)
   Staged reading, New Dramatists, New York, 1994
   Workshop, Original Theatre Works/Cerritos College, Norwalk, California, 1994
   Staged reading, New Dramatists, New York, 1995

Fiesta (play for young audiences)
   Production, Kennedy Center, Washington, D.C., 1995

Squeezed Avocados
   Staged reading, New Dramatists, New York, 1996

The Shrinking Wife
   Staged reading, New Dramatists, New York, 1996

PLAY AVAILABILITY

La Llorona Llora, The Migrant Farmworker's Son, and *Alicia in Wonder Tierra (or I
   Can't Eat Goat Head)* are published by Dramatic Publishing Company, P.O. Box 129,
   Woodstock, Illinois 60098.

Other plays are available through her agent: Helen Merrill, 435 West 23 Street 1A, New
   York, New York 10011; (212) 691–5326.

AWARDS

Third Step Theatre, New York, Annual Spring Fest, Finalist, *Los Matadores*, 1991

Steppenwolf Theatre, Chicago, New Play Program, Finalist, *Waiting Women*, 1991

Mark Taper Forum, Play Development, Finalist, *The Migrant Farmworker's Son*, 1991

Gilmore Creek Playwriting Award, Finalist, *Boxcar*, 1991

Stanley Drama Award, Finalist, *Boxcar*, 1991

Lee Korf Playwright Award, Cerritos College, *Boxcar*, 1991

Stanley Drama Award, Finalist, *The Migrant Farmworker's Son*, 1992

Denver Center Theatre Company, US West Theatrefest, Finalist, *The Migrant Farmworker's Son*, 1992

Jane Chambers Playwriting Competition, Finalist, *Waiting Women*, 1992

Southwest Theatre Association, Finalist, *U Got the Look*, 1994

Oregon Arts Council Fellowship Grant in Theatre, 1995

Lila Wallace/Reader's Digest Grant, *Alicia in Wonder Tierra (or I Can't Eat Goat Head)*, 1995

DESCRIPTIVE AND CRITICAL RESPONSES

Trussell, Robert. "Only Her Subconscious Knows for Sure." *Kansas City Star*, 13 October 1995, 19.
———. "Retelling Rivals Bizarreness of the Original Alice." Review of *Alicia in Wonder Tierra (or I Can't Eat Goat Head). Kansas City Star*, 13 October 1995, 19.

JUDY GRAHN

(1940–   )

BIOGRAPHY

Born in Chicago, Grahn was raised in New Mexico and has lived in northern California since 1968. In 1969 she began publishing her own work and founded the first all-women's press, the Women's Press Collective, where she has worked as editor, printer, bookkeeper, and fund-raiser. In 1984 she received a BA from San Francisco State University.

A poet, novelist, feminist theorist, and playwright, Grahn is best known for her poetry collection, *The Work of a Common Woman*, which celebrates the lives of ordinary women, and the long poem *A Woman Is Talking to Death*. Grahn's introduction to theatre started early in her career when she collaborated with a musician and dancer to create a performance art piece in San Francisco in the late 1960s, and she continues to perform work in collaboration with other artists. Most of her poetry has been staged as drama or mixed with music and dance. The *Common Woman Poems* received many amateur presentations in the 1970s and was performed by a lesbian jazz quartet on the West Coast. One of her short stories, *The Psychoanalysis of Edward the Dyke*, was adapted as part of an off-Broadway production by Jonathan Katz. Portions of *A Woman Is Talking to Death* were incorporated into a Dance Brigade production which toured in the 1970s.

The Queen of Wands, a book-length set of related poems that trace Helen, a goddess of weaving, was adapted and performed by the Golden Gate Players in San Francisco and then toured England and Amsterdam. A full-length verse play, *The Queen of Swords*, was adapted by Grahn, with dramaturgical assistance from director Adele Prandini of Theatre Rhinoceros who produced the play.

Grahn teaches women's writing workshops and classes and has taught courses at Stanford University and New College of California. About herself as a lesbian writer, Grahn says, "I think of myself as a writer who writes *out* from that particular position of being a lesbian and also being a working-class woman from birth, as writing out into the world at large and about lots of women" (Yalom, 90). She lives with poet Paula Gunn in Oakland, California.

PLAY DESCRIPTIONS

In both *The Queen of Wands* and *The Queen of Swords*, Grahn revises well-known myths by endowing goddesses with the power they lost in traditional histories. *Swords* is the most fully realized play since Grahn adapted the book with the director and in collaboration with the composers. The verse play tells the story of Helen Venus who is married to a dull man obsessed with his telescope. To escape she goes exploring and falls down a hole into Underland—a lesbian bar owned by Ereshkigal and patronized by Crow Dykes. There she travels through the Belowworld's seven gates to recover her personal and mythic memory from her polluted consciousness. This leads to her identity as Helen of Troy and on to an older memory of the goddess El-Ana, the Sumerian Inanna and Venus. Nothing, the keeper of the gates of the underworld, inspires many puns, such as "I don't work for Nothing." The stage version deletes several characters and edits the dialogue and, in the Theatre Rhinoceros production, dance made an important contribution.

SELECTED PRODUCTION HISTORY

The many adaptations of Grahn's poetry and prose for the stage are impossible to catalogue. As Grahn says, "Much of my work has been produced . . . 'off the cuff'—in bars, women's centers, churches . . . and sometimes without permission, notification or payment of royalties. This has been because so much of my audience, female, working-class, Gay, has been . . . ignorant of procedures, impelled by emotional motivations."

The Queen of Wands
  Tour to Bath, Edinburgh, London, and Amsterdam, 1986
  Production, Golden Gate Players, San Francisco, 1989

The Queen of Swords
  Production, Theatre Rhinoceros, San Francisco, 1989
  Production, Miami, 1993 (adapted from the book version)
  Production, Hollywood Moguls, Los Angeles, 1994

PLAY AVAILABILITY

The Queen of Swords is published in Judy Grahn, *The Queen of Swords*. Boston: Beacon Press, 1987.

The Queen of Wands is published in Judy Grahn, *The Queen of Wands*. Trumansburg, New York: Crossing Press, 1982.

AWARDS

Poem of the Year Award, *American Poetry Review*, 1979

National Endowment for the Arts, 1980

American Book Award, 1983

Modern Library Association, Gay Book Award, 1985

Women's Foundation of San Francisco, Pioneer Gay Writer Award, 1989

Lambda Book Award, Nonfiction, 1989

DESCRIPTIVE AND CRITICAL RESPONSES

Case, Sue-Ellen. "Judy Grahn's Gynopoetics: *The Queen of Swords.*" *Studies in the Literary Imagination* 21 (Fall 1988): 47–67.

Perry, David. "Fosse-esque Dancing and Surrealistic Sets." *Bay Area Reporter*, 16 March 1989, 30.

Weiner, Bernard. "Matters of the Heart on Stage." *San Francisco Chronicle*, 15 March 1989, E3.

Yalom, Marilyn, ed. *Women Writers of the West Coast: Speaking of Their Lives and Careers.* Santa Barbara, California: Capra, 1983.

JESSICA HAGEDORN

(1949–   )

BIOGRAPHY

Jessica Hagedorn was born and raised in Manila, the Philippines. She immigrated with her family to San Francisco when she was thirteen. Hagedorn attended the American Conservatory Theatre's training program where she honed her performance skills: her goal was to combine the theatre with her other talents, poetry and music.

Jessica Hagedorn's evolution as a poet and a multimedia and performance artist began with the publication of her first book of poetry (*Four Young Women*) in 1972. In San Francisco she was also involved with a collective of women writers and artists of color (including Thulani Davis and **Ntozake Shange**) who worked in a style of performance that merged dance, film, poetry, and music. Hagedorn organized a band called the West Coast Gangster Choir which allowed her to incorporate the imagistic kind of writing she preferred into performance.

Hagedorn moved to New York in 1979 where she continues to create experimental performance art. She has moved into the fields of video and filmmaking, and recently she made her debut as a screenwriter with *Fresh Kill*, a feature film produced and directed by Shu Lea Chang. Her nondramatic writing continues to be widely anthologized. A novella, *Pet Food and Tropical Apparitions* (1981), which won the American Book Award was followed by the highly acclaimed *Dogeaters* (1990), a vivid depiction of Philippine life. *Danger and Beauty* (1993) is a collection of Hagedorn's poetry and fiction.

Jessica Hagedorn resides in New York with her daughter and performs with the group Thought Music (Laurie Carlos, **Robbie McCauley**, and John Woo).

PLAY DESCRIPTIONS

Jessica Hagedorn's works are verbal and visual collages that combine her interests in poetry, music, dance, and visual media. Often drawing on autobiographical material, her pieces meld her Filipino background with an urban New York sensibility. The themes that continue to "obsess" her are "otherness, the idea of revolution on many levels, terrorism, dominant culture vs. so-called minority culture. And the idea of home, what homesickness and home mean" (Champagne, 93).

In the *Tenement Lover*, she juxtaposes images of Filipino immigrants with blonde, California, sunbather-types overlaid with newscasts of the ostentation that typified the Marcos regime. Affluence collides with poverty and power-lessness, and dreams offer the only escape from harsh realities.

Hagedorn's *Last Days . . .* is more traditionally structured but retains many of the poetic images and stream-of-consciousness monologues that characterize her other work. Estrella is the matriarch of a small family (a son and daughter in their thirties) who emigrated from Manila to San Francisco about thirty years ago. Mickey, the son, remains in the shabby apartment with his mother, but Minnie, the daughter, has moved out on her own. Having been left by an un-faithful husband, Estrella has found solace in the physical pleasures of life: nice clothes, rich food, and Rita Hayworth movies. Despite Estrella's attempts to keep her children tied to her, she fails. Christina, Mickey's estranged wife, reclaims her husband, and Minnie retains her separation. In the end, Estrella is left alone with her food and her memories.

Drawing on the form and style of the minstrel show, the collaborators-performers (Hagedorn, Robbie McCauley, and Laurie Carlos) enact a series of musical riffs on racism and popular culture in *Teenytown*. Satiric songs and poetry are interspersed among old familiar tunes like "Dixie" and "Summer-time"; takeoffs on Dorothy Dandridge and Stepin Fetchit are juxtaposed against paeans to Tammy Bakker, Elvis, and nontraditional casting. A send-up of the "Johnny Carson Show" with the racist comedy team of Jones and Bones brings the entire minstrel show motif full circle; it is a powerful comment on the influence and pervasiveness of cultural forms.

SELECTED PRODUCTION HISTORY

Where the Mississippi Meets the Amazon (with Thulani Davis and Ntozake Shange)
    Production, Public Theatre, New York, 1977

Mango Tango
    Production, Public Theatre, New York, 1978

Tenement Lover
    Production, The Kitchen, New York, 1981

Crayon Bondage
    Performance, Real Art Ways, Connecticut, 1982

Peachfish
    Production, Basement Workshop, New York, 1983

The Art of War/Nine Situations (dance/theatre collaboration with Blondell Cummings)
Production, Dance Theatre Workshop, New York, 1984

Ruined (collaboration with Nancy Owens, Colin Lee, and Butch Morris)
Production, Art on the Beach, New York, 1985

Holy Food
Production, Magic Theatre, San Francisco, 1988

Teenytown (with Laurie Carlos and Robbie McCauley)
Production, Franklin Furnace, New York, 1988
Production, Danspace Project (St. Mark's Church), New York, 1988

Airport Music (with Han Ong)
Production, Public Theatre, New York, 1994
Production, Berkeley Repertory Theatre, Berkeley, California, 1994

PLAY AVAILABILITY

Teenytown is published in Lenora Champagne, ed., *Out from Under: Texts by Women Performance Artists*. New York: Theatre Communications Group, 1990.

Tenement Lover is published in Misha Berson, *Between Worlds: Contemporary Asian-American Plays*. New York: Theatre Communications Group, 1990.

AWARDS

New York State Council on the Arts, Writer-in-Residence Grant Basement Workshop, 1982

New York State Council on the Arts, Collaboration Grant, Basement Workshop, *Peachfish*, 1983

National Endowment for the Arts, InterArts Grant, *The Art of War/Nine Situations*, 1984

Macdowell Colony Fellowship, 1985, 1986, 1988

DESCRIPTIVE AND CRITICAL RESPONSES

Champagne, Lenora. "Laurie Carlos, Jessica Hagedorn, Robbie McCauley." In *Out from Under: Texts by Women Performance Artists*, edited by Lenora Champagne, 91–94. New York: Theatre Communications Group, 1990.
Dunning, Jennifer. "Dance: 'The Art of War' by Cummings and Hagedorn." Review of *The Art of War/Nine Situations*. *New York Times*, 15 November 1984, C20.
Eder, Richard. "Stage: 'Mango Tango,' a Poetic Series." Review of *Mango Tango*. *New York Times*, 30 May 1978, C6.
Gelb, Hal. "Airport Music." Review of *Airport Music*. *The Nation* 259 (26 September 1994): 323–24.
Gussow, Mel. "3 'Satin Sisters' Spin a Poetry of Nostalgia at Stage Cabaret." Review of *Where the Mississippi Meets the Amazon*. *New York Times*, 20 December 1977, 44.
Hagedorn, Jessica. "Jessica Hagedorn." In *Between Worlds: Contemporary Asian-*

American Plays, edited by Misha Berson, 76–79. New York: Theatre Communications Group, 1990.

———. "On Theater and Performance." *MELUS* 16, no. 3 (Fall 1989): 13.

"Interview with Jessica Hagedorn." *Dispatch* 6, no. 1 (Fall 1987): 14–16.

WENDY HAMMOND

(1955–   )

BIOGRAPHY

Wendy Hammond was born in Newport, Rhode Island, and, although the family traveled a great deal, she considers Utah her home. She received her MFA from New York University's Dramatic Writing Program where she studied with Tina Howe, Len Jenkin, and Michael Weller. Hammond has taught playwriting courses at several universities and in the prison ward of Bellevue Hospital. Through the Chesterfield Film Project, Hammond spent a year in Hollywood but was glad to return to the East Coast.

Her first play with lesbian characters and themes, *Julie Johnson*, was commissioned by the Actors Theatre of Louisville for their 1994 season. During a panel discussion with audience members, Hammond was asked if she was gay. Although, at the time, she said she preferred not to answer that question, she later wrote a moving preface to her play: "I didn't write *Julie Johnson* because I'm gay. Perhaps the play is partly a response to my own Mormon background, a religion and culture of breathtaking beauty and warmth. . . . Which makes it difficult for Mormons who are . . . gay. . . . I wrote (the play) because I needed to write about someone who isn't living truthfully, who begins to live truthfully, and how wonderful and terrible that is." Hammond regularly performs a one-person play *Wendy in the Wacko Ward*. She is a screenwriter as well as a playwright. She teaches at Vassar College and lives nearby. Wendy Hammond is a member of the New Dramatists.

PLAY DESCRIPTIONS

An early play of Hammond's, *Carl and the Professor*, is about the symbiotic relationship between Freud and Jung, a study of the mentor-mentee relationship.

Later plays explore the immediate world of the psychologically damaged, usually those of the lower economic classes and often the victims of abuse. The protagonist of *The Ghostman* is a fifty-three-year-old miner who goes on a rampage of violence, hitting an old lady in the street, attacking his grandson, and finally chopping off his own leg. He is placed in a hospital where he is diagnosed as a victim of child abuse which he has repressed all his life. The prize-winning *Jersey City* tells in vivid detail about the abuse and molestation of a fifteen-year-old girl by her father. She runs away and is taken in by a young Salvadorian refugee who, because of his youth, has difficulty understanding that her encouragement of sado-masochistic lovemaking could stem from her history as an abused child.

The title character of the play *Julie Johnson* is a poorly educated, battered Jersey housewife who gets the courage to throw her husband out of her house after he violently objects to her secretly attending a computer class. Her best friend, Claire, inspired by Julie's brave efforts to improve herself and her life, leaves her husband and moves in with her and her children. Julie soon realizes that she is attracted to Claire and confesses her attraction to her understanding computer teacher and to a disbelieving Claire. They soon become lovers, which they try to keep secret from Julie's children and the rest of the world they live in. The closeted life, however, becomes too confining and wearing on Claire, and she returns to her husband and the friends whose company she missed. Having passed the GED, Julie continues to study for the SAT exams and makes it clear that she will continue living her life as a lesbian.

SELECTED PRODUCTION HISTORY

The Ghostman
> Workshop, Long Wharf Theatre, New Haven, Connecticut, 1989–1990 (exact date unknown)
> Production, Salt Lake Acting Company, Salt Lake City, Utah, 1990
> Production, Stonehill Project, New York, 1990s (exact date unknown)

Family Life
> Production, Home for Contemporary Theatre and the Stonehill Theatre Project, New York, 1989

Jersey City
> Production, Second Stage, New York, 1989

Julie Johnson
> Workshop, New Play Festival, Philadelphia Theatre Company, Philadelphia, 1991
> Production, Actors Theatre of Louisville, Humana Festival, Louisville, Kentucky, 1994
> Production, Bailiwick Repertory, Chicago, 1995

PLAY AVAILABILITY

Family Life: Three Brutal Comedies is published by Broadway Play Publishing, 56 East 81st Street, New York, New York 10028–0202.

Julie Johnson is published in Marisa Smith, ed., *Humana Festival '94: The Complete Plays*. Lyme, New Hampshire: Smith and Kraus, 1994.

Other plays are available from her agent: Helen Merrill, 425 West 23rd Street, Suite 1A, New York, New York 10011; (212) 691–5326.

AWARDS

New York Foundation Arts, Grant, 1987

Drama League Award, *Jersey City*, 1988

McKnight Fellowship, 1989

National Endowment for the Arts, Playwriting Grant, 1989–1990

Sundance Institute, 1993

Chesterfield Film Project, 1994

DESCRIPTIVE AND CRITICAL RESPONSES

Christiansen, Richard. "Something Old, Something New." Review of *Julie Johnson*. *Chicago Tribune*, 1 April 1994, V1.

Koenenn, Joseph C. "A Play about Jersey City." Review of *Jersey City*. *Newsday*, 24 May 1990, II5.

KIM HINES

(1955–   )

BIOGRAPHY

Kim Hines first set foot on the professional stage at the age of twelve when she became a member of the Children's Theatre Company (CTC) in Minneapolis, Minnesota. She literally grew up there, attending Theatre School and continuing to perform in CTC productions from 1969 to 1973. Hines went to Macalester College in St. Paul, Minnesota, and graduated in 1976 with a BA in speech and theatre and visual art.

Kim Hines began her playwriting career in 1981 with *Just Remember My Name*, a play about women and racism that is frequently used by universities and nonprofit organizations to begin a dialogue on racism.

As an actor, Hines has performed at the Guthrie Theatre, Mixed Blood Theatre, Out and About, Frank Theatre, Illusion Theater, Minneapolis, Minnesota; the Penumbra Theatre, St. Paul, Minnesota; and the Southern Theater, and she has been a resident actor at the Playwrights' Center for many years. Her directing credits include work at At the Foot of the Mountain Theater, the Minnesota High School for the Arts, Spirit of the Horse Theatre, Park Square Theater, and Theater in the Round.

Kim Hines is a mentor for the Intermedia Arts Mentor-Extensions Series, a core member of the Playwrights' Center and the Screenwriter's Workshop, both in Minneapolis, and a member of Actor's Equity Association. She lives and works in Minneapolis.

PLAY DESCRIPTIONS

Kim Hines's honesty as a playwright allows her to create characters who are real, complex reflections of the world we live in. She uses her experiences as an African American and as a lesbian to create plays that weave a variety of themes into one richly constructed cloth. In *Just Remember My Name*, she brings together five women (African American, white, and Jewish) in a women's studies class to study racism. It is through their classroom discussions, confrontations, fantasies, journal entries, memories, and other assignments that each learns the elements in their backgrounds, values, and cultures that feed their prejudices.

Who Was I the Last Time I Saw You? can be performed as a one-woman show or by four separate African American characters. Through monologues we are introduced to Mavis, an eighty-year-old woman who has just been kicked out of the choir for singing too loud. Through song and story she reveals her survival techniques in dealing with her two husbands during the Depression and World War II. Portia is a lesbian in her mid-thirties who sells Mary-Kay cosmetics. A lipstick lesbian, she has a commentary on being self-employed and a minority within a minority within a minority. Beverly is a twenty-five-year-old single mother of three who lives on welfare. She folds clothes in the park while she tells her often humorous and compelling story about becoming a parent at the age of fifteen and again at twenty and about her abandonment by a "Right to Life" group that had convinced her to keep her babies. Christy is a ten-year-old girl on the threshold of puberty in the summer of 1965. As she tries to understand the world around her, especially the civil rights movement, she struggles with the changes going on inside her.

In *Brother, Brother*, a successful African American man lies in a coma after trying to commit suicide. While his younger brother tries to discover the reasons for his older brother's action, the sacrifices that people of color make in order to achieve success are examined. *Do Not Pass Go* explores the emotional trauma of an African American gay man struggling through the last stages of AIDS. His anger and combativeness constantly erupt as the people around him force him to take responsibility for his illness and his relationships with others. Hines makes use of her extensive knowledge of black history in *Slavery to Freedom: Let Gospel Ring!*. The two-character play, backed up by a gospel choir, is a "painless and entertaining" lesson in the history of gospel music in America.

SELECTED PRODUCTION HISTORY

Just Remember My Name (one-act and full-length versions)
   Production, At the Foot of the Mountain, Minneapolis, 1982
   Production, numerous colleges and nonprofit organizations nationally, 1982–1996

Who Was I the Last Time I Saw You?
   Production, Walker Art Center and Southern Theatre, Minneapolis, 1992
   Production, Sisterspace, Philadelphia, 1992
   Production, Randolph Street Gallery, Chicago, 1993

Brother, Brother
   Production, Bushfire Theater, Philadelphia, 1992

Do Not Pass Go

Production, Illusion Theater, Minneapolis, 1992
Production, Illusion Theater, Minneapolis, 1993

Magical Adventures of Pretty Pearl
Production, Oakland Ensemble Theatre, Oakland, California, 1992

From Slavery to Freedom: Let Gospel Ring!
Production, Cricket Theatre, Minneapolis, 1993
Production, Illusion Theatre, Minneapolis, 1993

Cut on the Bias
Production, Illusion Theatre, Minneapolis, 1993

Home on the Morning Train
Production, SteppingStone Theater, Minneapolis, 1993

I Believe I'll Run On . . . and See What the End's Gonna Be . . .
Production, Illusion Theatre, Minneapolis, 1994
Workshop, Kennedy Center, Washington, D.C., 1996

PLAY AVAILABILITY

Information about Kim Hines's plays is available through her agent: John Santianni, Tantleff Office, 375 Greenwich Street, New York, New York 10013; (212) 941–3939.

AWARDS

Sunmasil Foundation Grant, Minneapolis, 1992

McKnight Career Advancement Grant, Playwrights' Center, Minneapolis, 1993

Film in the Cities Screenwriting Fellowship, 1994

DESCRIPTIVE AND CRITICAL RESPONSE

Winn, Steven. "Family Play Built around African-American Folktale." Review of *Magical Adventures of Pretty Pearl*. *San Francisco Chronicle*, 2 June 1992, E3.

ENDESHA IDA MAE HOLLAND

(1944–   )

BIOGRAPHY

Ida Mae Holland was born in Greenwood, Mississippi, where she lived with her mother, who served as the midwife for the rural black community and operated a brothel. At the age of eleven, Holland was raped by the father of a white toddler whom she was baby-sitting. That experience and the need to help support her mother and siblings led the thirteen-year-old Holland into prostitution. Cedric, Holland's son, was born in 1961. Her life was transformed, however, when she walked into the local office of the Student Nonviolent Coordinating Committee (SNCC) in 1962. She worked first as a volunteer at the local level and then traveled around the nation to promote the cause of the civil rights movement. Her support of Martin Luther King, Jr., landed her in jail on numerous occasions. Her activism led to a firebombing that destroyed the Holland home and killed her mother.

Holland headed north, and eventually she enrolled at the University of Minnesota were she earned a BA in African-American studies in 1979, an MA in American studies in 1984, and a Ph.D. in American studies the following year. It was in 1979 that Holland adopted the Swahili name Endesha (*driver*) to celebrate her capacity to drive herself forward. Perhaps the most telling sign of her saga from prostitute to professor came in 1991 when her hometown of Greenwood, Mississippi, declared October 18 to be Dr. Endesha Ida Mae Holland Day. Some of her recollections are included in her *Mississippi Writers: Reflections of Childhood and Youth* (1985).

Her playwriting career was launched by accident. When she found herself four credits short for her undergraduate degree, she was advised to take a course in the theatre department. She enrolled in playwriting and found an artistic outlet for her natural storytelling abilities. While living in Minneapolis, Holland was involved with numerous theatres, including playwright in residence at the Playwrights' Center from 1980 to 1983, and she was the founder and artistic director of the Lorraine Hansberry Writers' Workshop. Since 1986 Holland has taught American studies at the State University of New York (SUNY) at Buffalo, where she continues to write and teach.

PLAY DESCRIPTIONS

Endesha Ida Mae plumbs the depths of her own life and upbringing in the pre–civil rights rural South in her plays. Based on indelible memories and vivid portraits, Holland's plays fill the stage with characters and incidents that many playwrights before her had been reluctant to describe. For example, *Second Doctor Lady*, based on her mother's occupation as the local midwife, was eventually expanded into Holland's well-known work *From the Mississippi Delta*, which has had countless productions all over the United States. In the shorter one-act version, the midwife assists a white woman in the hospital with a difficult birth and then delivers a black baby in a poor, rural home. In *The Reconstruction of Dossie Ree Hemphill*, a rivalry arises between two sisters who are both having an incestuous relationship with the father. The older sister eventually leaves the home situation and the South in an effort to overcome her feelings of worthlessness. The one-woman show *Mrs. Ida B. Wells* highlights the life and contributions of the renowned black lecturer and journalist who wrote for *New York Age*.

Holland's best-known work, however, is *From the Mississippi Delta*. Performed by three actresses, the play is a series of vignettes tracing her life from teenage prostitute to college professor. The poignant tales and searing memories graphically depict the reality of the pre–civil rights South. Holland's painful but triumphant journey is a portrait of an America infrequently seen on stage.

SELECTED PRODUCTION HISTORY

Second Doctor Lady (one-act play expanded into *From the Mississippi Delta*)
    Reading, Mid-West Theatre Conference, Omaha, Nebraska, 1980
    Workshop, University of Minnesota, Minneapolis, 1980
    Production, University of Minnesota, Minneapolis, 1981
    Production, Woman's Theatre, Seattle, 1981
    Reading, Playwrights' Center, Minneapolis, 1982

The Reconstruction of Dossie Ree Hemphill (one-act play)
    Workshop, Experimental Theatre, University of Minnesota, Minneapolis, 1980
    Production, University of Minnesota, Minneapolis, 1981

Requiem for a Snake (stage and television versions)
    Reading, Playwrights' Center, Minneapolis, 1980
    Staged reading, Playwrights' Center, Minneapolis, 1981

Reading, Frank Silvera Writers' Workshop, New York, 1981
Reading, Los Angeles Theatre Workshop, Los Angeles, 1981

Mrs. Ida B. Wells (full-length one-woman play)
Reading, Playwrights' Center, Minneapolis, 1982
Production, American Theatre Association Convention, St. Paul, 1983

From the Mississippi Delta
Production, New Federal Theatre, New York, 1987
Production, Arena Stage, Washington, D.C., 1991
Production, Hartford Stage Company, Hartford, Connecticut, 1991
Production, Circle in the Square, New York, 1991
Numerous productions throughout the United States

The Autobiography of a Parader without a Permit (a dramatic version of her Ph.D. dissertation)
Workshop, Northlight Theatre, Evanston, Illinois, 1992
Reading, Illusion Theatre, Minneapolis, 1993

Homebound
Workshop, Illusion Theatre, Minneapolis, 1993

AWARDS

American College Theatre Festival (Region 5) Playwriting Award, Minneapolis, *Second Doctor Lady* and *The Reconstruction of Dossie Ree Hemphill*, 1981

Lorraine Hansberry Playwriting Award, Second Place, *Second Doctor Lady* and *The Reconstruction of Dossie Ree Hemphill*, 1981

Women Playwrights Festival, Woman's Theatre, Seattle, Finalist, *Second Doctor Lady*, 1981

Helen Hayes Award, Arena Theatre, Washington, D.C., Best Nonresident Play, *From the Mississippi Delta*, 1991

DESCRIPTIVE AND CRITICAL RESPONSES

Collins, Glenn. "Transcending the Past to Master, through Words, the Present." *New York Times*, 5 November 1991, C13.
Evans, Greg. "*From the Mississippi Delta*." Review of *From the Mississippi Delta*. *Variety*, 18 November 1991, 37+.
Hubbard, Kim and Toby Kahn. "Look South, toward Home." *People Weekly*, 2 December 1991, 201–2.
Lederman, Douglas. "A Prize-winning Playwright Seeks to Inspire." *Chronicle of Higher Education*, 27 November 1991, A5.
Whitaker, Charles. "Endesha Ida Mae Holland: From Prostitute to Playwright." *Ebony* 47 (June 1992): 124+.

VELINA HASU HOUSTON

(1957–   )

BIOGRAPHY

Velina Hasu Houston grew up in Junction City, Kansas. Her father, an African American–Native American, was a military man stationed at Fort Riley, Kansas; her mother was a "war bride" who had grown up in Japan. She attended Kansas State University where she earned a BA in journalism, mass communications, and theatre in 1979. Her early success with a play entry in the American College Theatre Festival led her to the playwriting program at the University of California at Los Angeles where she completed her MFA in playwriting in 1981. She is currently enrolled as a doctoral student at the University of Southern California in the School of Cinema-Television.

In addition to her playwriting, Houston has an active career as a teacher, speaker, poet, author of short stories and children's books, screenwriter, editor, and essayist. She is currently head of the playwriting program and resident playwright at the University of Southern California and has also taught at the University of California-Los Angeles. Velina Houston has written screenplays for Columbia Pictures (*Summer Knowledge*), the American Film Institute, Lancit Media Productions, and the Public Broadcasting Service. Her book *The Politics of Life: Four Plays by Asian American Women* (Temple University Press, 1993) was the first anthology to focus on the dramatic literature of Asian American women. She is currently editing a comprehensive anthology of Asian American plays entitled *A Storm Is Blowing from Paradise* for Temple University Press scheduled for publication in 1998. Houston lectures widely on various issues concerning the Japanese experience in America and the phenomenon of the Amerasian legacy.

Houston resides in Santa Monica, California, with her son and daughter.

PLAY DESCRIPTIONS

Velina Hasu Houston, with her stylistic combination of poetry and prose, is intent upon exploring the intersections of things: culture, race, and language. As an Amerasian whose own background reflects three races and four cultures, Houston is in a unique position to conduct this exploration in her plays. She is best known for *Tea*, from her autobiographical trilogy, which delineates the struggles of her multicultural heritage. The first play, *Asa Ga Kimashita (Morning Has Broken)*, describes a young woman's life in Japan during the American occupation immediately following the surrender of her country in 1945. Setsuko watches her father's pride erode as American ways and laws encroach on his way of life. The redistribution of his land through the resettlement acts threaten to turn him from a proud landowner into a tenant farmer. Fumiko, his niece who has enthusiastically embraced the American style of dress and manners, is beginning to influence Setsuko's ideas. This clash of cultures is best exemplified in Setsuko's struggle between following the American soldier she loves and staying with her family for their honor. Her father's suicide and her mother's blessing release her from her family obligations.

American Dreams follows the struggle of Setsuko and Creed, her African American–Native American husband, as they attempt to establish a life in America. The couple is constantly confronted with racism, especially within Creed's own family. Through the course of the play, some of Creed's relatives come to understand that racism is not simply a black-and-white issue.

In *Tea*, Houston's most widely produced play to date, she broadens the autobiographical scope of her trilogy to examine the lives of five Japanese war brides who have made their homes in a Midwestern military town. The play opens with the ritual suicide of one of the brides after she has killed her husband. When the other Japanese women gather in the deceased's home to share ceremonial tea and talk, we are given glimpses into the diversity and commonality of their lives. The fluidity of Houston's nonnaturalistic structure weaves their stories into a tapestry of love, frustration, strength, and loneliness, giving voice to these Asian women who have married American servicemen.

In a departure from the more serious tone of her autobiographical plays, *Christmas Cake* is a farcical satire on ethnic correctness. She has transferred the new Japanese phenomenon of "bachelor schools" (where eligible men are groomed to find a bride in this era of professionally oriented Japanese women) to southern California. An unwed man in his forties is forced by his worried parents into this school in an effort to find a suitable Japanese bride. In this contemporary Japanese twist on an old theme, Houston's comedy reaffirms the centuries-old reality that love wins out despite the parents' best-laid plans.

In *Necessities*, Zelda, a career women in midlife, decides to adopt a child. She advertises in the newspaper for pregnant women who are willing to give up their babies. As the choices (including multiracial adoption) and demands proliferate, Zelda is forced to face a range of emotions she did not know she had.

SELECTED PRODUCTION HISTORY

Asa Ga Kimashita (*Morning Has Broken*)
Production, East West Players, Los Angeles, 1984

American Dreams
Production, Negro Ensemble Company, New York, 1984

Tea
Workshop, Asian American Theater Company, San Francisco, 1985
Staged reading, East West Players, Los Angeles, 1985
Staged reading, Group Theater Company, Seattle, 1986
Production, Manhattan Theatre Club, New York, 1987
Numerous subsequent productions worldwide

Thirst
Production, Asian American Theater Company, San Francisco, 1986

The Legend of Bobbi Chicago (two-act musical; composer/lyricist, Sandy Alpert)
Staged reading, Mark Taper Forum, Los Angeles, 1987

Amerasian Girls (two one acts: *Father I Must Have Rice* and *Petals and Thorns*)
Production, Ensemble Studio Theatre, Los Angeles, 1987

My Life a Loaded Gun
Workshop, Old Globe Theatre, San Diego, 1988
Workshop, Old Globe Theatre, San Diego, 1989

Albatross
Workshop and staged reading, Old Globe Theatre, San Diego, 1990
Workshop and staged reading, Arizona Theatre Company, Tucson, 1991
Staged reading, Theatre/Theatre, Los Angeles, 1992

Necessities
Production, Old Globe Theatre, San Diego, 1991
Production, Purple Rose Theatre, Chelsea, Michigan, 1993

Christmas Cake
Staged reading, East West Players, Los Angeles, 1991
Workshop, Kumu Kahua Theatre, Honolulu, 1992

Broken English
Staged reading, Odyssey Theatre Ensemble, Los Angeles, 1991

The Confusion of Tongues (one act for young audiences)
Production, St. Augustine's By-the-Sea Episcopal Parish, Los Angeles, 1991

Tokyo Valentine
Staged reading, East West Players, Los Angeles, 1992

The Matsuyama Mirror (one act for young audiences)
Production, Kennedy Center for the Performing Arts, Washington, D.C., 1993

Rain
  Staged reading, Women's Project and Productions, New York, 1993

Kumo Kumo (one act for young audiences; sister play to *The Matsuyama Mirror*)
  Staged reading, East West Players, Los Angeles, 1993

Kapi'olani's Faith
  Production, Kumu Kahua Theatre, Honolulu, 1994

Kokoro (*True Heart*)
  Production, Theatre of Yugen, San Francisco, 1994
  Production, Japan Society, New York, 1994

Snowing Fire
  Production, Cornerstone Theatre Company, Los Angeles, 1994

PLAY AVAILABILITY

Asa Ga Kimashita (*Morning Has Broken*) is published in Velina Hasu Houston, *Politics of Life: Four Plays by Asian American Women.* Philadelphia: Temple University Press, 1993.

Tea is published in Roberta Uno, ed., *Unbroken Thread: An Anthology of Plays by Asian American Women.* Amherst: University of Massachusetts Press, 1993; *Plays in Process*, vol. 9, no. 5. New York: Theatre Communications Group, 1989.

Copies of other scripts may be obtained through her agent: Mary Harden, Harden-Curtis Association, 850 7th Avenue, Suite 405, New York, New York 10036; (212) 977–8502.

AWARDS

Lorraine Hansberry Playwriting Award (American College Theatre Festival), National First Prize, 1982

The David Library Playwriting Award for American Freedom (American College Theatre Festival), National First Prize, 1982

Rockefeller Foundation Playwriting Fellow, 1984

DramaLogue Outstanding Achievement in Theatre Award, *Asa Ga Kimashita*, 1985

Los Angeles Weekly Drama Critics' Award, *Asa Ga Kimashita*, 1985

Susan Smith Blackburn Prize, Finalist, *Tea*, 1986

American Multicultural Playwrights' Festival, National First Prize, *Tea*, 1986

Rockefeller Foundation Playwriting Fellow, 1987

San Diego Drama Critics Circle Award, *Tea*, 1988

DramaLogue Outstanding Achievement in Theatre Award, *Tea*, 1989

McKnight Foundation Fellow, 1989

Los Angeles Endowment of the Arts Fellow, *Broken English*, 1991

DramaLogue Critic's Choice, *Tea*, 1991

Los Angeles Times, Critic's Choice, *Tea*, 1991

Vesta Award for Positive Female Images in the Arts, 1991

Jane Chambers Playwriting Award, Finalist, *Necessities*, 1993

Julie Harris Playwriting Competition, Finalist, *Kokoro*, 1993

DESCRIPTIVE AND CRITICAL RESPONSES

Arkatov, Janice. "Playwright Draws on Experience of Growing Up in an Interracial Household." *Los Angeles Times*, 27 January 1991, 3.

Arnold, Stephanie. "Dissolving the Half-Shadows: Japanese American Playwrights." In *Making a Spectacle: Feminist Essays on Contemporary Women's Theatre*, edited by Lynda Hart, 181–94. Ann Arbor: University of Michigan Press, 1989.

Breslauer, Jan. "Hues and Cries." *Los Angeles Times*, 7 July 1991, 3, 66, 70.

Drake, Sylvie. "Two Blistering Commentaries on Brutalization." *Los Angeles Times*, 24 April 1988, 47–48.

Houston, Velina Hasu. "Velina Hasu Houston." In *The Politics of Life: Four Plays by Asian American Women*, edited by Velina Hasu Houston, 205–17. Philadelphia: Temple University Press, 1993.

Oliver, Edith. "Explosive Mixture." Review of *American Dreams. New Yorker*, 20 February 1984, 104.

"Playwright Velina Houston Reaps Sweet Dramatic Fruit from a Complicated Family Tree." *People Weekly* 23 (June 10, 1985): 168.

Shirley, Don. " 'Tea' and Empathy." Review of *Tea. Los Angeles Times*, 29 January 1991, F1, F12.

Uno, Roberta. "Velina Hasu Houston." In *Unbroken Thread: An Anthology of Plays by Asian American Women*, edited by Roberta Uno, 155–60. Amherst: University of Massachusetts Press, 1993.

HOLLY HUGHES

(1955–   )

BIOGRAPHY

Holly Hughes was born in Saginaw, Michigan, where she attended high school. She received a BA in painting from Kalamazoo College and moved to New York to continue visual art studies at the Feminist Art Institute in 1979. After moving to the East Village in 1981, Hughes happened upon the WOW Festival of Feminist Theatre and, moved by its spirit of experimentation and humor, volunteered at the WOW Cafe. Soon she began organizing performance events and became an integral part of the structure of the theatre. Playwriting followed a series of loosely scripted performances, and *The Well of Horniness*, faintly inspired by Radclyffe Hall's *The Well of Loneliness*, was presented at WOW in 1983. Her most notable early work, done in collaboration with Peggy Shaw and Lois Weaver, culminated in *Dress Suits to Hire* which was performed at WOW in 1985 and, in an effort to reach a larger audience, at P. S. 122 and Interart. As one of four artists "defunded" by the National Endowment for the Arts in 1990 for the overt lesbian and sexual content of her work, Hughes was catapulted to national notoriety and fringe-theatre fame. The resulting media attention and governmental scrutiny, depressing and distracting for her, halted any serious writing until 1992 and *No Trace of a Blond*. Following the development of that work, she has written and performed several one-person performance pieces about her mother, her father, and her relationship with them. Hughes is known as a preeminent voice of lesbian sexuality, and her concern with family occupies a central part of her work: "I think family is for me at the heart of every thing. I guess I don't know what other issues there are. I find myself recreating my role within my family in other situations all the time" (Carr, 73). The cover of her recent collected work, *Clit Notes: A Sapphic Sampler*, is done in characteristically iconoclastic style. Hughes poses nearly nude, covered only with a few bits of greenery and dangling apples—a paradisiacal Eve as the tree of temptation displaying her apples, her eyes wide and her mouth open with a "look at this!" expression.

PLAY DESCRIPTIONS

The title of Hughes's first scripted play, *The Well of Horniness*, announces the sexually playful spirit of her writing. Irreverently suggesting that icons will be toppled, it proclaims that lesbians will not be seen as victims. *Well* reads like an extended satiric sketch (and did, in fact, become popular fare on alternative radio WBAI in New York) with its outrageous puns, skewed literalism, and inflated metaphor serving a smorgasbord of lesbian sexual innuendo. Described as "dyke noir" by C. Carr of the *Village Voice*, Hughes's parody of film noir, lesbian culture, and theatre conventions gives the play its distinctive performance style. The story that drives the work (sectioned into Part One, Two, and Three) is intentionally muddled. In the play, set in a peaceful New England town, the heroine, Vicki, formerly a member of the Tridelta Tribads, is trying to forget her past and marry Rod, a discount carpet vice president. Her plan is foiled when he introduces her to his irresistible sister, Georgette (whose "thighs feel like butter left out on a hot stove"), also a former Tribad. Georgette is murdered and Vicki flees. In Part Two, Vicki is pursued by Garnet McClit, lady dick, and Al Dente, police chief. The fun heats up as the story melts in Part Three, "In the Realm of the Senseless," when villainess Babs, a hatcheck girl scorned by Georgette, pulls a gun on McClit and Vicki. When she shoots, Vicki wakes up to find she has been dreaming and that she is safe with Rod. *Well* is often performed as a live radio show with sound effects substituting for visual action.

The Lady Dick, set in a New York clothing rental shop, featured Peggy Shaw and Lois Weaver of **Split Britches** as Deeluxe and Michigan, two lesbians who live a hermetic existence, reliving the past and changing clothing as easily as they shed and add new personas. At the opening, Deeluxe is killed by her own right hand, "Little Peter," while Michigan, with her mechanical dog, Linda, in her lap, watches. In the final moments of the play, Deeluxe overcomes Little Peter by strangling her right hand with her left. A letter appears, as a deus ex machina device, and speaks of males using the tears of women. The piece is filled with pop culture references, many of which call for specific music effects such as Frank Sinatra or the theme song from "A Man and a Woman." Time is fluid and the present flows seamlessly into the past. The ritualized actions of the characters underscore that the text is an exploration of lesbian mores, and the presence of Little Peter alerts us to the difficulty and dangers of hermetic, self-referential relationships.

For a daughter to depict her mother as a sexual being is unusual, particularly when the daughter performs that interpretation on stage. In the one-person play *World without End*, an unorthodox eulogy to her mother, Hughes examines the way in which her mother's sexuality affected her own sexuality as well as the powerlessness and oppression of women's desires. She imagines herself as Eve having hot sex with a man named Adam, admitting that she may be wrong— that "Maybe Mr. Adam is no Dumbo after all." She sees in her mother's dying moments her parents kissing passionately and, as her mother pulls her father on top of her and touches him, Hughes lyricizes, "I see him shimmy. I see him change. I see him, oh I see him. He is an apple in her hands." Sex has become a vehicle that carries her through her mourning to a transcendence. With an unswerving emotional honesty, Hughes explores provocative subjects in an unorthodox and often surprising way.

SELECTED PRODUCTION HISTORY

The Well of Horniness
Production, WOW Cafe, New York, 1983
Production, Source Theatre, Washington, D.C., 1990
Production, Curtains Theatre, Houston, Texas, 1992
Production, Paramount Penthouse, Boston, 1994

The Lady Dick
Production, WOW Cafe, New York, 1985

Dress Suits to Hire (in collaboration with Peggy Shaw and Lois Weaver)
Production, P. S. 122, New York, 1987
Production, Split Britches at Women's Interart, New York City, 1988
Production, University of Michigan, Ann Arbor, 1988

World without End
Production, Life on the Water, San Francisco, 1989
Production, P. S. 122, New York, 1990
Production, Dance Place, Washington, D.C., 1990
Productions in Los Angeles, Boston, and Seattle

No Trace of a Blond
Production, Theatre Artaud, San Francisco, 1992

Snatches
Production, St. Marcus Theatre, St. Louis, Missouri, 1993

Sins of Omission
Production, Beacon Street Gallery, Chicago, 1993

Clit Notes
Production, Highways, Santa Monica, California, 1993
Production, P. S. 122, New York, 1994
Production, Yale Repertory Theatre, New Haven, Connecticut, 1994
Production, Josie's Cabaret, San Francisco, 1995

Cat o'Nine Tales
Production, P. S. 122, New York, 1996

PLAY AVAILABILITY

Dress Suits for Hire is published in *The Drama Review* 33, no. 1 (Spring 1989): 132–52.

The Lady Dick is published in *The Drama Review* 35, no. 3 (Fall 1991): 199–215.

The Well of Horniness is published in Don Shewy, ed. *Out Front.* New York: Grove, 1988.

The Well of Horniness, The Lady Dick, Dress Suits to Hire, World without End, and *Clit Notes* are published in Holly Hughes. *Clit Notes: A Sapphic Sampler.* New York: Grove, 1996.

World without End is published Lenora Champagne, ed., *Out from Under: Texts by Women Performance Artists.* New York: Theatre Communications Group, 1992.

AWARD

National Endowment for the Arts, 1991, revoked 1991, reawarded 1992

DESCRIPTIVE AND CRITICAL RESPONSES

Carr, C. " No Trace of the Bland: An Interview with Holly Hughes." Yale/Theatre. 24, no. 2 (1993): 67–75.

Davy, Kate. "Constructing the Spectator: Reception, Context, and Address in Lesbian Performance." *Performing Arts Journal* 10, no. 2 (1986): 43–52.

———. "From *Lady Dick* to Ladylike: The Work of Holly Hughes." In *Acting Out: Feminist Performance,* edited by Lynda Hart and Peggy Phelen. Ann Arbor: University of Michigan Press, 1993.

———. "Reading Past the Heterosexual Imperative: *Dress Suits to Hire.*" *Drama Review* (Spring 1989): 155–70.

Gelb, Hal. "*The Well of Horniness* and *Clit Notes.*" *Nation,* 20 September 1993, 293.

Harvey, Dennis. "Interview with a Pussy Pusher: 'Queer' Playwright Holly Hughes Redefines the Ambitions of Gay Theatre." *San Francisco Sentinel,* 7 October 1988, 22–24.

Massa, Robert. "We Invented Irony." *Village Voice,* 28 June 1988, 22, 38.

Miller, Lynn C. " 'Polymorphus Perversity' in Women's Performance Art: The Case of Holly Hughes." *Text and Performance Quarterly* 2 (January 1995): 44–58.

Schneider, Rebecca. "Holly Hughes: Polymorphous Perversity and the Lesbian Scientist." *Drama Review* 33, no. 1 (Spring 1989): 171–83.

Solomon, Alisa. "It's Never Too Late to Switch." In *Crossing the Stage: Controversies on Cross-Dressing,* edited by Leslie Ferris. London: Routledge, 1993.

Stone, Laurie. "Her Heart Belongs to Daddy." *Ms. Magazine,* September-October 1994, 88.

NAOMI IIZUKA

(1956–   )

BIOGRAPHY

Naomi Iizuka was born in Tokyo, Japan. She graduated from Yale with a BA summa cum laude in literature in 1987 and followed that with an MFA in playwriting from the University of California-San Diego in 1992. She was commissioned by En Garde Arts of New York to write a site-specific piece, and her short play *Scheherezade* was part of "Pieces of the Quilt," an AIDS benefit theatre event produced by the Magic Theatre in San Francisco in Spring 1996. She is a member of the Playwrights Center in Minneapolis and currently resides in that city.

PLAY DESCRIPTIONS

Iizuka works outside the conventions of traditionally structured, linear theatre, and her work is a fluid exploration of issues without regard to the constraints of time or space. In her surreal drama *Marlowe's Eye*, the historical figures of Christopher Marlowe, Pier Paolo Pasolini, and Ruth Riddle are melded into an investigation of the problematic relationships among religion, sex, obsession, and political power. Marlowe, the English poet and playwright, and Ruth Riddle, a survivor of the conflagration at the Branch Davidian compound in Waco, Texas, move in and out of the same netherworld that is part sterile hospital, part prison, part ambiguous hell. They are joined at times by their accusers, principally the figure of Queen Elizabeth I and two Puritans, who function as guards and as a chorus. The charges of blasphemy leveled against Marlowe are superimposed over his glorification of homosexual desire and his ultimate assassination, conflating sex and politics into a nightmare vision of the uses and abuses of power. Iizuka's fracturing of time and space allows her to juxtapose Marlowe's history with images of Pasolini's brutal death and Riddle's self-mutilation. (See Chiori Miyagawa's chapter in this volume for a further discussion of Iizuka's plays.)

SELECTED PRODUCTION HISTORY

And Then She Was Screaming
  Production, Source Theatre, Washington, D.C., 1990

Lizzie Vinyl
  Production, Fringe Festival, Edinburgh, Scotland, 1990

Portrait of Bianca
  Production, Alice's Fourth Floor, New York, 1992

Crazy Jane
  Production, Hudson Theatre, Los Angeles, 1992

Greenland
  Reading, Audrey Skirball-Kenis, Los Angeles, 1992

Coxinga
  Production, New York University, New York, 1994

Carthage
  Reading, Public Theatre, New York, 1994
  Reading, New York Theatre Workshop, New York, 1994
  Production, Theatre E, San Diego, 1994

Tattoo Girl
  Production, Nada, New York, 1994
  Production, Annex Theatre, Seattle, 1994
  Production, Off Center Theatre, Tampa, Florida, 1995
  Production, Sledgehammer, San Diego, 1995

Skin
  Reading, BRAVA! for Women in the Arts, San Francisco, 1995
  Production, Dallas Theatre Center, Dallas, 1995
  Production, Soho Rep, New York, 1995

Ikeniye
  Production, Nada, New York, 1995
  Production, Telluride Theatre Festival, Telluride, Colorado, 1996

Marlowe's Eye
  Reading, PlayLabs, Minneapolis, 1995
  Production, Tectonic Theatre, New York, 1996

Scheherezade
  Reading, Actor's Gang, Los Angeles, 1996

PLAY AVAILABILITY

Marlowe's Eye is planned for publication in the American Theatre in Literature Series by Sun and Moon Press in 1997.

Skin is published in *TheatreForum*, Winter 1996.

Tattoo Girl is published in Douglas Messerli and Mac Wellman, eds., *From the Other Side of the Century*. Los Angeles: Sun and Moon Press, 1995.

"What Mary Says After" is in Tori Haring-Smith, ed., *More Monologues for Women by Women*. Portsmouth, New Hampshire: Heinemann, 1996.

AWARDS

Japanese American Citizens' League Fellowship, 1989

Selected as participant, Mark Taper Forum Mentor Playwrights' Program, 1990–1992

Dallas Observer's Best Play Award, *Skin*, 1995

Dallas Theater Critics Forum Award, *Skin*, 1995

San Diego *Union-Tribune*'s Top Ten Production Award, *Skin*, 1995

Jerome Playwriting Fellowship, 1995–1996

Many Voices Multicultural Collaboration Grant, 1996

McKnight Advancement Grant, 1996–1997

MARSHA A. JACKSON

(n.d.–)

BIOGRAPHY

Marsha A. Jackson began her study of theatre at Houston's High School for the Performing and Visual Arts, where she earned numerous academic awards, including Outstanding Drama Student. She continued her theatrical training at Smith College, where she was an honors graduate in theatre. Jackson studied under several teachers in her professional training as a performing artist, including Tina Packer at the London Academy of the Dramatic Arts. She credits her playwriting development to her mentor Sonia Sanchez.

Marsha Jackson's talent is multifaceted, with acting and directing included in her list of theatre work. Her Broadway acting debut took place in the 1988 production of *Checkmates*, where she played opposite Denzel Washington. She was a cofounder of Jomandi Productions in Atlanta, which was Georgia's oldest and largest black professional theatre company. Under Jomandi's banner, Jackson has written plays, directed her own work and the work of others, and performed in numerous productions. Jackson has also taught at Spelman College in Atlanta.

PLAY DESCRIPTIONS

Marsha Jackson's plays are noted for portraying a wide range of female experience and for exemplifying a strong political consciousness without veering off into didacticism. Jackson's most successful play, *Sisters*, is a humorous and poignant tale of two very different women stranded on New Year's Eve in an Atlanta office building during a freak blizzard. Olivia, the stylish business woman who was her nouveau riche parents' "little princess," has been pampered and sheltered all her life. Cassie, on the other hand, is the tough survivor;

she has had to fight for everything that she can call her own. Olivia is an executive in an advertising agency who is running into the harsh realities of the business world. When she bumps her head on the glass ceiling and collides with the color barrier, she is willing to throw it all away and quit her job. That prospect is terrifying, however, because she has sacrificed a normal life to give her all to the company. Cassie, who is on the janitorial staff, cleans Olivia's office. Without benefit of school and degrees, she accurately analyzes Olivia and contrasts their two lives. Cassie's lack of material wealth is compensated by her personal and spiritual life; her loving relationship with her young son and her ongoing dialogue with the memory of M'dear (her deceased grandmother) provide emotional sustenance. As the evening progresses, the facades are stripped away and the characters recognize and embrace their similarities rather than focus on their differences.

SELECTED PRODUCTION HISTORY

Witchbird (adapted from the Toni C. Bambara story)
  Production, Jomandi, Atlanta, 1981

Josephine Live! (musical portrait of Josephine Baker)
  Production, Jomandi, Atlanta, 1983
  Production, 14th Street Playhouse, Atlanta, 1990

Savannah (a musical)
  Production, Jomandi, Atlanta, 1984

Dunbar Fantasy (play for young audiences)
  Production, Jomandi, Atlanta, 1987

Sisters
  Production, Jomandi, Atlanta, 1987 and 1995
  Production, Joyce Theatre, New York, 1990

PLAY AVAILABILITY

Sisters is available in Woodie King, Jr., ed., *The National Black Drama Anthology: Eleven Plays from America's Leading African-American Theatres.* New York: Applause, 1995.

AWARDS

Entertainer of the Year Award, Atlanta Business League/Black Women Entrepreneur, 1986

Fulton County Arts Council Individual Artist Award, 1988

DESCRIPTIVE AND CRITICAL RESPONSES

Albright, William. "Playwright Spreads Some Sisterly Love." *Houston Post*, 28 October 1990, G12.

Gussow, Mel. "Two Disparate Women Who Find a Sisterly Tie." Review of *Sisters*. *New York Times*, 7 June 1990, C19.

Hagans, Gail. "Jomandi Co-Founder Has Numerous Roles to Play." *Atlanta Constitution*, 31 May 1990, XE6.

Hulbert, Dan. "All the Faces of a Legend Recaptured in *Josephine*." *Atlanta Constitution*, 16 February 1990, D7.

———. "Anita and Me." *Atlanta Constitutional*, 22 September 1993, B1.

Klein, Alvin. "Odd Couples in 'Daisy' and 'Sisters.' " Review of *Sisters*. *New York Times*, 11 November 1990, XII 15.

MERCILEE M. (LEE) JENKINS

(1946–)

BIOGRAPHY

Jenkins was born in Detroit where she attended school. Perhaps growing up in Detroit in the 1950s encouraged a sense of humor because Jenkins turned to stand-up comedy, one of her many performance activities, on the way to becoming a playwright and professor. She began her professional life as a writer-performer on KPFA radio in Oakland, California, in the 1970s after completing a master's degree in speech communication at San Francisco State University. At the University of Illinois, Champaign-Urbana, where she received her Ph.D., she developed an interest in oral history. After she returned to the Bay Area and completed her dissertation on women's storytelling, Jenkins became involved with the Antenna Theatre where she worked as an interviewer and audio artist. She received a California Humanities Grant for "Liberty," a taped tour of the S.S. *Jeremiah O'Brien*, based on the histories of the women who built Liberty ships and the men who sailed them. In the mid-1980s Jenkins began working with the Tale Spinners Theatre writing plays based on oral histories. Three of those plays have been produced. The second play of the three, *Dangerous Beauty: Love in the Age of Earthquakes and AIDS*, is based on her own experiences as a bisexual woman becoming content with her sexuality and friendships. Her solo performance work continues through such pieces as the comedic *Feminist and Fit* and the serious *You Made Me Love You* based on the death of a friend from AIDS. Jenkins's most recent plays are *She Rises Like a Building to the Sky*, based on the history of the Women's Building in San Francisco, and *The Two-Bit Tango*, adapted from the novel by Elizabeth Pincus.

PLAY DESCRIPTIONS

The genesis of Jenkins's plays is based in oral histories; however, they are not delineated solely by historical event or the words of the interviewees. She combines the actual with the fictionalized, to greater or lesser extent, depending on the subject matter. *Dangerous Beauty*, resurrected from journal and notebook and shaped for the stage, is autobiographical. In the play, a chance encounter on a Berkeley street following the Loma Prieta earthquake reunites Annie and Tom nearly twenty years after they had had a romance but not a sexual relationship. Since that time, Annie has alternated boy/girl/boy/girl believing that "somebody has to be living proof that bisexuality is not just a phase." Tom has had a long-term on-off involvement with a lover who is now dying of AIDS. They are both willing to resume a friendship but first must deal with old resentments. Two flashback scenes, "her version" and "his version," use identical dialogue but end with Annie running off crying in "hers" and Tom in "his." Scenes alternating between monologue and dialogue sequence recall a way of life in the 1970s that cannot work for these old friends in the 1990s.

A Credit to Her Country, which incorporates more of the oral history methodology, uses actual interviews with lesbian and bisexual women in the military as the primary source. From over two dozen interviews, Jenkins crafted monologues and invented scenes. Much of the text uses the actual language of the women, thus, the nuances of conversational speech are preserved. One male character plays a variety of military men, including a recruiter, a harassing officer, and a gay male. While the majority of characters describe mistreatment, assault, painful interrogations, and dishonorable discharge, some fondly remember friends, falling in love, and manipulating a male system. Most express sadness at being unable to have open relationships with the women they loved while they received recognition for performing their jobs in an exemplary fashion.

SELECTED PRODUCTION HISTORY

Presenting Mrs. Latamore
   Workshop, Tale Spinners Theatre at Julian Theatre, San Francisco, 1988

Dangerous Beauty: Love in the Age of Earthquakes and AIDS
   Production, Tale Spinners Theatre at Climate Theatre, San Francisco, 1991
   Production, Tale Spinners Theatre at The Marsh, San Francisco, 1992

The Fan's Tale (from *The Candlestick Tales*)
   Production, Tale Spinners Theatre at The Marsh, San Francisco, 1993 and 1994

A Credit to Her Country
   Workshop, Tale Spinners Theatre and Theatre Rhinoceros, San Francisco, 1994
   Production, Tale Spinners Theatre, San Francisco, 1995

The Two-Bit Tango (adapted from the novel by Elizabeth Pincus)
   Production, Josie's Cabaret and Juice Joint, San Francisco, 1996

PLAY AVAILABILITY

You Made Me Love You is published in Frederick Corey, ed., *HIV Education: Performing Personal Narratives*. Tempe: Arizona State University Press, 1993.

Other plays are available through the author: Lee Jenkins, Speech and Communication Studies, San Francisco State University, San Francisco, California 94132.

AWARDS

California Council for the Humanities Grant, "Liberty," 1985

Horizon Foundation, Grant, *A Credit to Her Country*, 1994

Midwest Radio Theatre Contest, *A Credit to Her Country*, 1995 (second place)

DESCRIPTIVE AND CRITICAL RESPONSES

Mackey, Heather. "The Love Bug." *San Francisco Bay Guardian*, 11 March 1992, 40.
Pierce, Liz. "History and Beyond." *San Francisco Bay Times*, 24 February 1994.
Winn, Steven. "Gritty Accounts of Sex in the '90s." *San Francisco Chronicle*, 8 April 1991, F2.

JULIE JENSEN

(1942–   )

BIOGRAPHY

Jensen, who was raised in Beaver, Utah, has lived in New York City, California, Detroit, Georgia, Virginia, New Hampshire, Ohio, and, currently, Nevada. She holds a BA and MA from Utah State University and a Ph.D. in theatre from Wayne State University in Detroit. In the 1970s she began writing plays, and between 1974 and 1977, with her partner Mary Roberts, she explored improvisational methods of composition and performance. They performed their own material at the Grand Circus Exchange, Detroit, Michigan a theatre they managed for three years, at the Attic Theatre in Detroit, and in a showcase in New York. A teacher of playwriting, Jensen has taught at a number of colleges and universities and now heads the graduate program in playwriting at the University of Nevada–Las Vegas. Prior to that position, she lived in Los Angeles and wrote for film and television. She wrote episodes for a Norman Lear pilot, worked in comedy development for Columbia Pictures Television, and cowrote a half-hour film for the American Film Institute. Because of her varied geographical past, Jensen said in correspondence about herself that "she thinks she knows a lot about America."

PLAY DESCRIPTIONS

Jensen's plays often deal with troubled, working-class families who are held together by the resources of the wife and mother. The perspective is quirky and off-center, and a character's damaged psyche is manifested as a darkly humorous eccentricity. In *Stray Dogs*, Nyda, the mother, is married to Myers, an alcoholic, and has two young boys: one hyperactive and mean-spirited and the other well-behaved but judgmental because of his adherence to the Mormon religion. The family is sustained by Wells, Myers's brother. On the day the play takes place, the town is shooting dogs to protect their sheep. When Nyda's drunken husband comes home to shoot their dog, he shoots his brother instead because he is jealous of the attention Wells pays to his family. Myers runs away and Nyda is left with the dead body of the man who has cared the most for her and her boys. Because the mother "is capable of seeing both herself and her chaotic life as something of a joke," as the playwright says, the play has a comic tone despite the tragic outcome of the action.

White Money uses humor, as well, to tell the story of a young woman, Ella, and her journey through the heartland of America. Everyone in her life is addicted to watching television; the women follow a televangelist and the men are glued to television wrestlers. Because they will not listen to Ella when she warns of the danger of television, she speaks directly to the audience. Her travels include stops at her mother's trailer in Panaca, Nevada, a truck stop near Las Vegas where she waitresses in proximity of an atomic test site and ends in Oklahoma City. The metaphors, drawn from popular culture, reinforce the satiric commentary on television, politics, and religion.

How Not to Get Fucked in Less than 40 Lessons, a two-character one-act play, is part of the "Lost Vegas Series," which features a spunky young woman who hitchhikes a ride with a truck driver she recognizes as a fifth-grade classmate. The man tries various seductive ploys that fail before he attempts to rape the woman at a roadside graveyard. She evades his attempts by belittling his masculinity. Angered, he leaves her by the side of the desert road. The woman concludes, "They ain't no such thing as a free ride if you're gonna tell the truth."

SELECTED PRODUCTION HISTORY

Cisterns
  Production, Attic Theatre, Detroit, 1982
  Production, Back Alley Theatre, Los Angeles, 1983

Day of the Races (one-act play)
  Production, Quaigh Theatre, New York, 1983 and 1985
  Production, Performers Forum, Colorado Springs, 1986

Night Line (one-act play)
  Production, Negro Ensemble Company, New York, 1983

Old Wives Tale (one-act play)
  Production, Women's Project and Productions at American Place Theatre, New
    York, 1984
  Production, Theatre of NOTE, Los Angeles, 1986

Stray Dogs
  Production, Arena Stage, Washington, D.C., 1986
  Production, Acting Ensemble, South Bend, Indiana, 1988

A Little Less than Kin (two one-act plays)
  Production, Acting Ensemble, South Bend, Indiana, 1987

Thursday's Child
  Production, Capital Repertory Company, Albany, New York, 1988
  Production, Attic Theatre, Detroit, 1991

White Money
  Production, Salt Lake Acting Company, Salt Lake City, Utah, 1991
  Production, Mill Mountain Theatre, Roanoke, Virginia, 1992
  Production, Source Theatre, Washington, D.C., 1992
  Production, Powerhouse Theatre, Los Angeles, 1993

How Not to Get Fucked in Less than 40 Minutes (one-act play)
  Production, Los Angeles Theatre Center, Los Angeles, 1993
  Production, The Complex, Los Angeles, 1994

The Total Meaning of Real Life (one-act play)
  Production, Rubie Theatre, Los Angeles, 1993

The Greatest Love (one-act play)
  Production, The Complex, Los Angeles, 1993

The Liberace Museum (one-act play)
  Production, Friends and Artists Theatre, Los Angeles, 1993

Last Lists of My Mad Mother
  Reading, Audrey Skirball–Kennis Theatre, Los Angeles, 1996

PLAY AVAILABILITY

How Not to Get Fucked in Less than 40 Minutes is published in *The Literary Review: An International Journal of Contemporary Writing* 35, no. 3 (Fall 1992).

The Liberace Museum is published in *Alaska Quarterly* (Spring 1994).

Old Wives Tale is excerpted in *Georgia Review* 37, no. 1 (Spring 1983).

Stray Dogs is published by Dramatists Play Service, 440 Park Avenue, New York, New York 10016.

White Money is published in *Plays in Process*, vol. 12, no. 5. New York: Theatre Communications Group, 1991; also excerpted in *Kenyon Review* 16, no. 2 (Spring 1993).

Other plays are available from Karin Wakefield, Epstein-Wyckoff and Associates, 280 South Beverly Drive, Suite 400, Beverly Hills, California 90212; (310) 278–7222.

AWARDS

Dramatists Guild Award, *Stray Dogs*, 1986

Kentucky Foundation for Women, Grant, *White Money*, 1989

Award for New American Plays, *White Money*, 1990

James Thurber Playwright-in-Residence, 1994

DESCRIPTIVE AND CRITICAL RESPONSES

Demaline, Jackie. "Woman Playwrights Still Fight Stereotype." *Times Union* (Albany, New York), 12 February 1988, C5.

Kakutani, Michiko. "Stage: Women's Project Presents Three Works." Review of *Old Wives Tale. New York Times*, 28 March 1984, C23.

Melich, Nancy. " 'White Money' Talks in Stellar Premiere." Review of *White Money. Salt Lake Tribune*, 24 March 1991, E7.

Solomon, Alisa. "Genderfication." *Village Voice*, 26 March 1984.

MICHAEL ANGEL JOHNSON

(1947–   )

BIOGRAPHY

Born in Boston, Johnson spent summers visiting her Methodist minister uncle in different parts of the United States. She believes that watching him "perform in the pulpit" was her first exposure to drama and to the power of language. After graduating from high school in Brookline, Massachusetts, Johnson went to Sweden for a year then attended Boston University where she took courses in painting, literature, and philosophy and worked part-time as a psychiatric aid in a mental hospital. She interrupted her studies for another sojourn in Europe and spent a year in Naples, Italy. After returning to the United States and the university, she gave up school to work full-time as an accountant. Three years later, she went to France in order to write. Teaching English as a second language supported her work on a novel, short stories, and poetry for four years before she returned to the United States to finish an undergraduate degree at Goddard College. In 1987 Johnson received an MFA in playwriting from the Yale School of Drama.

Johnson lives in New York City where she writes, teaches at New York University and the Borough of Manhattan Community College, and is a writer, dramaturg, and director for the 52nd Street Project and dramaturg with the Young Playwrights Festival. Johnson is a member of the Playwrights Lab at the Women's Project and Productions.

PLAY DESCRIPTIONS

Johnson's plays often deal with the debilitating effects of prejudice on both black and white characters. Well-rounded, complex characters and understated, at times lyrical, dialogue are features of her work. The story of a Vietnamese family struggling with the challenges of life in a strange country is the framework of the realistic play *Ancient Echoes*. At the opening, the mother has been hospitalized after an attempted suicide, following a rape by American soldiers. The difficulties the family has in adjusting to life in the United States are underscored by the family's American tutor, Liz, a graduate student, who in misunderstanding the Vietnamese culture, advises the teenage daughter to defy her parents. The conflicts between Dr. Cho, Liz's advisor, and Liz, and among the family point up the complexities of assisting in assimilation, even by the most well intentioned.

The more lyrical *Eden* is a memory play that tells the story from the perspective of Simone, the daughter of a black preacher in the South. Events occurring from the 1960s to the 1980s begin when the girl is eleven and befriends Mrs. Donaghue, a woman who has recently lost her daughter but who is criticized by neighbors because she will not attend church. Through the friendship of Simone, she begins attending church. Years later, when Simone returns to attend her funeral, she finds that Mrs. Donaghue willed her house to the church. In seamlessly conceived flashbacks, we learn that the two had become close and had helped each other understand some racially motivated crimes in the neighborhood, including Simone's father's defense of a white man who had raped and murdered a black woman. At the end, when the Rev. James agrees to paint Mrs. ''D's'' house her favorite pink color, the daughter lets go of the bitterness she felt toward her father.

SELECTED PRODUCTION HISTORY

The Portrait
    Production, Yale School of Drama, New Haven, Connecticut, 1984
    Reading, Women's Project and Productions, New York, 1994

The Girls
    Production, Yale School of Drama, New Haven, Connecticut, 1985

The Apartment
    Production, Afro Cultural Centre, New Haven, Connecticut, 1986
    Reading, Double Image Theatre, New York, 1988

Shadows
    Production, Theatre in the Works, New York, 1987

No Dessert for You, My Friend?
    Reading, Women's Project and Production, New York, 1989

Ancient Echoes
    Reading, East West Players, Los Angeles, 1993
    Reading, Tandem Act Festival, La Mama La Galleria, New York, 1995

The Dream
    Reading, Women's Project and Production, New York, 1993

Eden
    Production, Theatre Row Theatre, 42nd Street Collective and Evening Shades, New York, 1996

The Visitor
  Reading, Theatre 603, New York, 1996

Waves
  Workshop, Ensemble Studio Theatre Octorberfest, 1996

PLAY AVAILABILITY

Plays are available from the Women's Project and Productions, 55 West End Avenue, New York, New York 10023 and from the author at 224 West 10th Street, Apt. 6, New York, New York 10014.

AWARDS

MacDowell Fellow, 1988

Yaddo Fellow, 1988

Blue Mountain Fellow, 1988

Theodore Ward Playwriting Prize, Finalist, 1996

KAREN JONES-MEADOWS

(1953–)

BIOGRAPHY

Karen Jones-Meadows was born in 1953 and attended Wheelock College. In addition to her playwriting, Jones-Meadows works as a screenwriter, producer, and educator. She writes for adult and young audiences and gives workshops and develops curricula for both adults and children. She has worked with the Negro Ensemble Company, the Hudson Guild Theatre, the Women's Project, the Frederick Douglass Creative Arts Center, and the Creative Arts Team, New York City; the Houston Ensemble Theatre, Texas; the Penumbra Theatre, St. Paul, Minnesota; and the Luna Stage Company, Montclair, New Jersey.

Jones-Meadows is the author of several screenplays including *Yes Moments* for Fox Television; *Eclipse*, a dramatic teleplay for young adults; and *Hip Hop in the Promised Land*, a short film series for Comedy Central/Broadway Video.

Jones-Meadows was appointed McGee Professor of Writing at Davidson College in Davidson, North Carolina, in spring 1995. In 1996 Jones-Meadows was selected Keynote Speaker and workshop leader for the Association of International Schools of Africa where she visited and presented workshops in five countries. She has one son and has recently moved to Albuquerque, New Mexico.

PLAY DESCRIPTIONS

Karen Jones-Meadows's work excels in the characterization of volatile and intricate relationships. *Henrietta* traces the evolution of a relationship between Henrietta, a fiftyish derelict, and Sheleeah, a successful, young, working woman in her late twenties. Henrietta sits on a crate outside a New York brownstone and hurls insults at passers-by. Adept at sensing the vulnerabilities and weaknesses of those who pass her on the street, Henrietta knows who to curse and who to avoid. When Sheleeah confronts the older woman for yelling at her, their odd relationship is launched. From this tentative beginning, a friendship emerges in small increments: Sheleeah agrees to chat with Henrietta on the street during a quiet Sunday morning; later she goes to Henrietta's home for a modest dinner. As they share a bottle of sherry and the stories of their lives, each realizes the parallels in their seemingly disparate and unrelated lives. A dysfunctional dynamic gradually evolves in which each fulfills the fantasies of the other: Sheleeah becomes a stand-in for Henrietta's dead daughter, and Sheleeah tries to transform Henrietta's modest fruit salad–making business into the entrepreneurial success story that the young woman yearns to accomplish herself.

In *Tapman*, Jones-Meadows explores the volatile relationship between a father and daughter. The Tapman is an old blues musician who has lost his nerve to perform and finds solace at the bottom of a scotch bottle. His band, frustrated at missing gigs because of his failure to show up, wants to set off on their own, using his name and reputation. Despite his critical and financial success, the love of a good woman, and the caring concern of his daughter, the Tapman is tapped out. Coming near the end of his life, the old man realizes that without a record he has no legacy unless he can get his daughter to carry on the tradition. The sparring between father and daughter is tied into Sherry's love-hate relationship with her own musical talents. Thanks to her father's wrangling and her young son's insistence, however, Sherry joins her father on stage.

SELECTED PRODUCTION HISTORY

Henrietta
> Production, Atlanta New Play Project, Atlanta, 1984
> Production, Negro Ensemble Company, New York, 1985
> Production, New Black American Play Project, North Carolina, 1986
> Production, Ensemble Theatre Company, Houston, Texas, 1986
> Production, Encore Theatre Company, Washington, D.C., 1991

Tapman
> Reading, Women's Project and Productions, New York, 1986
> Production, Hudson Guild Theatre, New York, 1988

Major Changes
> Production, Penumbra Theatre Company, St. Paul, Minnesota, 1989
> Workshop, New Federal Theater, New York, 1990

Harriet's Return (play in young adult and adult versions)
> Production, Michigan Theatre Center, Ann Arbor, 1992 (young adult version)
> Production, Crossroads Theatre, New Brunswick, New Jersey, 1994 (adult version)

In the Name of the Woman (contributing writer)
> Production, Luna Stage Company, Montclair, New Jersey, 1993

Everybody's Secret (young adult play)
> Production, Creative Arts Team, New York, 1994

Brandon's Bounty
Production, Bushfire Theatre, Philadelphia, 1997

Sala Cinderella
Production, St. Louis Black Repertory Company, Missouri, 1997

PLAY AVAILABILITY

Jones-Meadows's plays can be obtained through her agent: Joyce Ketay Agency, 1501 Broadway Suite 1910, New York, New York 10036; (212) 354–6825.

AWARDS

Atlanta New Play Project Award, *Henrietta*, 1984

Drama League of New York Play Writing Award, *Henrietta*, 1985

AUDELCO Awards, Six Nominations, *Tapman*, 1988

Cornerstone Competition, Penumbra Theatre Company, St. Paul, Minnesota, First Prize Award, *Major Changes*, 1989

McGee Professor of Writing Award, Davidson College, 1995

International Independent Film and Video Award for Comedy, Black Filmmakers Hall of Fame, 1995

DESCRIPTIVE AND CRITICAL RESPONSES

Beaufort, John. "Gusto and Unpretentiousness from the Negro Ensemble Company." Review of *Henrietta. Christian Science Monitor*, 4 February 1985, 32.
———. " 'Tapman': Blues Singer with a Big Ego." Review of *Tapman. Christian Science Monitor*, 3 March 1988, 22.
Gussow, Mel. "Lonesome Blues." Review of *Tapman. New York Times*, 1 March 1988, C17.
Hurley, Joseph. "Moses Gunn on Tap as a Blues Singer." *Newsday*, 4 March 1988, Weekend sec. 14.
Rich, Frank. "Star Turn in Harlem." Review of *Henrietta. New York Times*, 29 January 1985, C13.

JUNE JORDAN

(1936–   )

BIOGRAPHY

Poet, essayist, political activist, teacher and playwright, Jordan was born in Harlem to Jamaican parents and grew up in Bedford Stuyvesant, Brooklyn. Her father, who believed strongly in a good education, read Shakespeare to her and required her to memorize poetry as a child and sent her to the Northfield School for Girls. She attended Barnard College but left early to marry, have a child, and participate in civil rights work. After her divorce, Jordan wrote and taught at the City University of New York, Sarah Lawrence, Yale, and, for many years, State University of New York-Stony Brook. Known as an impassioned and rigorous teacher of writing and literature, as a mesmerizing speaker and reader of her own poetry, and as a tireless campaigner for peoples' rights, Jordan frequently speaks and reads at colleges and universities across the United States.

Jordan is a regular columnist for the *Progressive*, and her essays, poems, and articles appear in a wide range of publications from the *New York Times* to *Essence*. In 1995 Routledge published *June Jordan's Poetry for the People: A Revolutionary Blueprint*, which describes her extremely successful method of teaching poetry as well as the Poetry for the People Collective she founded in the Bay Area of California. Jordan has published over twenty-one books, primarily poetry and essays, and is published in more than thirty collections, including the *Norton Anthology of Modern Poetry* (1990). June Jordan is a professor of African-American studies at the University of California-Berkeley, where she lives.

PLAY DESCRIPTIONS

Jordan's plays contain much of what works so well in her poetry: a complicated moral and ethical stance; pared down dialogue that operates, like a poem, on many levels; a strong rhythmic sense and a clear voice. Characters in her plays are most often twenty-year-olds whose energy and fervor for justice is equaled or perhaps surpassed by their belief in love. *All My Blessings*, her most autobiographical play, follows a young child growing up in Bedford Stuyvesant, Brooklyn, dominated by a strong father with decisive ideas about education, through the death of her mother and her embrace of political activism, to her reconciliation with her father.

The musical *Bang Bang Uber Alles* tells the story of a group of young activists who decide to hold a benefit concert in Ku Klux Klan territory to protest racial violence. The play is distinguished by powerful lyrics and an eclectic score that features jazz, Latin, folk, gospel, and ballad rhythms.

Jordan's most produced dramatic work, *I was looking at the ceiling and then I saw the sky*, is the result of a collaboration among director Peter Sellars, composer John Adams, and Jordan. In the piece subtitled "earthquake/romance," a diverse group of young people are thrown together following the Los Angeles earthquake. The characters, black, white, Latina, and Vietnamese, reflect the racial mix of so many big cities, and their stories originate from their racial and cultural identities. For them, the playwright says, life in the nineties is "earthquake/romance."

SELECTED PRODUCTION HISTORY

For the Arrow That Flies by Day (also titled, *The Issue*)
    Reading, Public Theatre, New York, 1981

Bang Bang Uber Alles (with composer Adrienne B. Torf)
    Reading, Women's Project and Productions at the American Place Theatre, 1985
    Production, Seven Stages Theater, Atlanta, 1986

All My Blessings
    Reading, New Dramatists, New York, 1988
    Reading, Eureka Theatre, San Francisco, 1990

I was looking at the ceiling and then I saw the sky: earthquake/romance
    Performance, Cal Performances, University of California-Berkeley, 1995
    Performance, Lincoln Center, Serious Fun Festival at John Jay Theater, New York, 1995
    Productions in many European theatres, including MC 93 Bobigny, Paris, France; and the Thalia Theater, Hamburg, Germany, in 1995

PLAY AVAILABILITY

I was looking at the ceiling and then I saw the sky is published by Scribner (New York), 1995.

Other plays available from June Jordan, Department of African American Studies, University of California-Berkeley, Berkeley, California 94720.

AWARDS

National Association of Black Journalists Achievement Award for International Reporting on the Black Condition, 1984

Playwright in Residence, New Dramatists, 1987–1988

Lila Wallace-Reader's Digest Writer's Award, 1995

Numerous other awards including a McDowell Fellow, Rockefeller Foundation Grant, National Endowment for the Arts Fellowship, and Prix de Rome

DESCRIPTIVE AND CRITICAL RESPONSES

Davis, Reid. "Alive from Berkeley: Peter Sellars and June Jordan Collaborate on a New Opera." *Theater/Week*, 10–16 July 1995, 18–22.

Erickson, Peter. "After Identity: A Conversation with June Jordan." *Transition: An International Review* 63 (1994): 132–49.

Greene, Cheryll Y., and Marie D. Brown. "Woman Talk." *Essence*, May 1990: 92–96, 190–97.

Griffiths, Paul. "Earthquake Weather." *New Yorker*, 29 May 1995, 94–95.

Jefferson, Margo. "A Utopia at Serious Fun, Plus a Quake." *New York Times*, 16 July 1995, C5, 22.

Littlejohn, David. "Onstage: The United Colors of Los Angeles." *Wall Street Journal*, 25 May 1995, A12.

Pollon, Zelie. "Naming Her Destiny: June Jordan Speaks on Bisexuality." *Deneauve* 47 (February 1994): 27–28.

Schwarz, Robert K. "In a Tough Neighborhood on the Border of Opera." *New York Times*, 9 July 1995, 25.

HONOUR KANE

(1961–   )

BIOGRAPHY

Born in Dublin, Ireland, Kane (formerly Molloy) grew up watching her father perform in all kinds of theatre: from pantomimes, to *Waiting for Godot*, to his weekly television show. At night she went to sleep listening to family tales (including stories about her grandfather, a clown who wrote his own material), myths, and histories. In 1969 her American-born mother, with her six children, returned to Pennsylvania which she had left in the 1950s to write her dissertation at Trinity College. Kane attended Allentown College and toured as a member of Bethlehem's Touchstone Theatre with ensemble-created work in the 1970s. She received a BFA from New York University in 1983 and, disgruntled with the straight-girl roles available for women, began writing and performing her own work. Rejecting her Meisner training, Kane immersed herself in Eastern-movement theatre and finally went to Asia where she continued her movement studies. Her Artformance Productions, an ensemble of women writers, chore-ographers and performers, led to her writing short plays and to the playwriting program at Brown University where she graduated with an MFA in 1991. During that time, she received a New York Foundation for the Arts fellowship which she used to travel to London to study with Caryl Churchill. Kane says that she is intrigued "with the relationship between the construction of gender and con-scription to a preferred sexuality as well as the relationships between the con-struction of theatre, of family and the constrictions of society." She lives and works in New York City.

PLAY DESCRIPTIONS

Kane's work is characterized by a density of language, lyricism, and theat-ricality. *Maiden Voyages*, written with Bronagh Murphy, chronicles the stories of five women who are brought together in an Irish maternity ward. One character, a midwife, serves as the connection among the women who include a teenager raped and impregnated by her father, a working-class woman giving birth to her seventh child, an upper-class housewife ambivalent about motherhood, and an artist whose pregnancy is part personal and part social statement. Scenes are tied together with haunting Irish chanteys that also open and close the play.

Tongues of Stone, with research and counsel by Diana Arecco, is a historical allegory about the censorious Puritan Anthony Comstock and the women he pursued because they attempted to take control of their bodies and reproductive lives. The play moves fluidly back and forth in time between the office and women's clinic of Madame Restell in 1877 and the art studio of Salmon Case in 1906, where Nuala Fury, a young Irish woman models partially nude. Restell and her assistant and lover, the African American Sarah Washington, provide abortion assistance and a variety of gynecological services to women in New York City. The central event that brings together characters from the 1800s and the 1900s is Restell and Washington's efforts to secure an unwanted baby for a woman whose husband insists on an heir from his wife who cannot give birth. The young model, who aspires to a career as a painter, steps through the frame into Restell's office where she gives birth to a pair of boots which the barren woman embraces as her new baby boy. Comstock, pretending to be a distraught husband seeking abortion-producing powders for his sick wife, arrests the Madame. Out on bail, she is silenced by one of her clients who makes her murder look like a suicide. Stage directions instruct that Comstock and Case are to be played by women. At the beginning and the close of the play, the actors form a chorus that eulogizes the place "where our house is."

SELECTED PRODUCTION HISTORY

Fishes Bliss
    Production, Women's Interart, New York, 1987
    Reading, INTAR II, New York, 1988

Hard Times/Love You Down (with Tamal Amal Jamal Jordan and Deonna Brown)
    Production, Henry Street Settlement, New York, 1989

No Special Bed (one act)
    Production, BACA Downtown, Brooklyn, 1990
    Production, St. Peter's Church, New York, 1991

Justa Babe (one act)
    Reading, Working Theatre, New York, 1990
    Workshop, New Plays Festival, Brown University, Providence, Rhode Island, 1991

Maiden Voyages (written with Bronagh Murphy)
    Workshop, Women in Theatre Festival, Boston, 1990
    Workshop, Royal Court Theatre Upstairs, London, 1990
    Production, New Georges, New York, 1993

Sticky 'n Juicy on da Senate Floor
    Production, AS 220, Providence, Rhode Island, 1991
    Production, Home for Contemporary Theatre, New York, 1991
    Production, Knitting Factory, New York, 1992

Me the Howlin: Ballad for My Dublin Family
    Production, New Works Project, Public Theatre, 1992
    Production, Nada, New York, 1993

Tongues of Stone (with Diana Kane [formerly Arecco])
    Workshop, Royal Court Theatre Upstairs, London, 1993
    Workshop, Flesh and Blood Ensemble, Sydney, Australia, 1994
    Workshop, New Georges, New York, 1994
    Production, Bellvoire Street Theatre, Sydney, Australia, 1995

Into the Sky (written with Diana Kane [formerly Arecco])
    Reading, Ma-Yi Theatre Ensemble, New York, 1994
    Staged reading, L.E.N.D. Festival of New Plays, New York, 1995

Kane's performance work has been seen at HERE, $3 Bill, WOW Cafe, Knitting Factory, Home, Working Theatre, Theatre Outlet (Allentown, Pennsylvania), Westbeth, and Irish Arts Centre, among others. Dance texts with choreography by Susan Hefner have been performed at the Ohio Theatre, One Dream Theatre, Dixon Place, Dia Center for the Arts, Henry Street Settlement and RAPP Arts Center, all in New York.

PLAY AVAILABILITY

Kane's plays are available from James Flynn, Berman, Boals and Flynn, 225 Lafayette Street, No. 1207, New York, New York 10012; (212) 699–0339.

AWARDS

Lotta Crabtree Grant to Women in Theatre, 1989

New York Foundation for the Arts Playwriting Fellow, 1990

Edward Albee Foundation Residency, 1992

Pew Fellowship in the Arts Scriptworks, 1992–1993

Linder Fellow at Millay Colony for the Arts Playwriting Fellow, 1993

Audrey Skirball-Kenis Playwright Exchange at Royal Court, 1993

Pennsylvania Council on the Arts Playwriting Fellow, 1993

National Endowment for the Arts, 1993

Flesh and Blood Theatre Playwriting Residency, Sydney, Australia, 1994

DESCRIPTIVE AND CRITICAL RESPONSES

Dunning, Jennifer. "Dance in Review: Susan Hefner and Dancers." *New York Times*, 18 October 1993, C15.

Gehman, Geoff. " 'Molloy' Follows in Father's Acting, Writing Footsteps." *Morning Call*, Allentown, Pennsylvania, 6 March 1993.

O'Kelly, Eamon. "Voyage of the Maidens." *Irish Voice*, New York, 6 July 1993, 33.

Solomon, Alisa. "Back to the Future." Review of *Maiden Voyages*. *Village Voice*, 27 April 1993, 110.

ADRIENNE KENNEDY

(1931–)

BIOGRAPHY

Born Adrienne Hawkins in Pittsburgh, Pennsylvania, Kennedy grew up in a comfortable, middle-class suburb of Cleveland, Ohio. Her parents, both educated professionals, encouraged their imaginative daughter to attend the predominantly white Ohio State University. The easy mixing of ethnic cultures in her hometown did not prepare her for the hostility and racism she encountered at the university. She graduated in 1953 with a BA in education, and two weeks later she married Joseph Kennedy. Although she had always been a voracious reader, it was not until she awaited the return of her husband serving in Korea that Kennedy began to write plays.

When her husband returned from the service, the couple moved to New York City where she studied creative writing at Columbia University from 1954 to 1956 and at the American Theatre Wing in 1958. It was as a student at the Circle in the Square School in 1962 that Kennedy submitted her first play, *Funnyhouse of a Negro*, to Edward Albee's workshop. Fearful of revealing too much of herself in her plays, it was through Albee's encouragement that Kennedy continued writing. He later produced the play off-Broadway, and Kennedy won an Obie for Distinguished Play. What followed was a rich period of creativity. Kennedy divorced her husband in 1966 and moved to London for the next three years. Her travels to England and Africa have had a profound influence on her work.

In addition to plays, Kennedy has written short stories, a mystery novel (*Deadly Triplets*, 1990), and nonfiction, including a series of personality sketches and reminiscences collected under the title *People Who Led to My Plays* (1988). She has taught creative writing at Yale University, Princeton University, the University of California-Berkeley (Chancellor's Distinguished Lecturer), and the University of California-Davis. During the 1995–1996 season, the Signature Theatre Company of New York, in residence at the Public Theatre, honored Adrienne Kennedy by producing an entire season of her works. She considers her two sons her main achievement in life.

PLAY DESCRIPTIONS

Adrienne Kennedy's plays defy traditional dramatic structure. Her early works are poetic landscapes which explore a fragmented, nightmarish world where character is fractured and multiplied. These expressionistic journeys are part autobiography and part hallucination. Symbols and images replace realism; brutality and violence are juxtaposed against the imagistic, lyrical beauty of her language. Meaning emerges, not from traditional plot and character development, but from an accumulation and collision of images. These characteristics are evident in Kennedy's first play, *Funnyhouse of a Negro*. Sarah, a young black woman living in an apartment in New York, is visited by Queen Victoria, the Duchess of Hapsburg, Patrice Lumumba, and Jesus, who is a hunched-back yellow-skinned dwarf. Verbal images of rape, murder, and suicide are interspersed with visual images of characters losing their hair in this psychic struggle of ethnic identity. *A Rat's Mass* depicts a brother and sister rat whose blackness is juxtaposed against Rosemary's white Catholicism. Images of Nazis, Catholic communion, blood, Easter, and incest, along with a procession of Biblical figures (Jesus, Joseph, Mary, Wise Men, and a Shepherd), fill the stage in this exorcism of oppression. *The Owl Answers* is dominated by characters who multiply and divide in this imagistic search for identity. She Who is Clara Passmore Who is the Virgin Mary Who is the Bastard Who is the Owl is trying to reconcile her black heritage with her white ancestry. *A Movie Star Has to Star in Black and White* features Clara, a new mother who is recently separated from her husband. In slipping between the reality of a shattered relationship and the fantasy world of film, Clara's world is examined in all of its multilayered complexity.

Although she has not abandoned the fluid style and melding of fantasy and reality that characterize her early work, Kennedy's more recent plays have stabilized the fractured characters to a degree and utilize a "plot" more traditionally situational than image oriented. She has, however, retained the psychic searching that pervades the earlier work, and the violence is more verbal than overt. Representative of this newer style are a series of one-act plays collectively titled *The Alexander Plays*. In *She Talks to Beethoven*, set in Ghana in 1961, the established writer Suzanne Alexander is awaiting the return of her husband, David. The radio announces that David may have been arrested for his political connections to Frantz Fanon. When Suzanne begins to read from published diaries that detail Beethoven's life, the composer and his room suddenly appear in the midst of Suzanne's world. The historical is made tangible, if not real, as the two converse, occasionally interrupted by radio updates of David's situation. Kennedy melds past and present in *The Ohio State Murders*. Suzanne Alexander returns to her alma mater to give a talk on the violent imagery in her work. Her explanation in the present becomes the story from the past in which the young Suzanne is a student at Ohio State University in 1949. The plot revolves around her affair with a white English professor, her unexpected pregnancy, the murder of her two children, and her meeting David Alexander, her future husband. The mystery is also a vivid depiction of the racism that pervaded the predominantly white campus in the late 1940s. The extended monologue *The Film Club* describes Suzanne's ordeal in London awaiting the release of David from the African jail and her relationship with her sister-in-law, Alice, an erstwhile filmmaker. The dramatized version of the monologue is *The Dramatic Circle*.

June and Jean in Concert is the dramatized version of Kennedy's memoir *People Who Led to My Plays*. The playwright's evocation of the divided self is physically manifested on stage through twin sisters, June and Jean, who represent the narrative "I" of the autobiographical work. Their simultaneous existence in both past (1940s) and present (1974) provides a double-edged take on the events of a life.

Kennedy's most recent *Sleep Deprivation Chamber* brings the more abstract horror of the earlier nightmare visions into concrete reality. Utilizing her unique ability to blend fact and fantasy, past and present, Kennedy and her coauthor, her son Adam, have written a contemporary drama of racism and police brutality. Based on the real-life arrest and beating of Adam Kennedy, the play traces the effects of that incident on the family.

SELECTED PRODUCTION HISTORY

Funnyhouse of a Negro
  Workshop, Circle in the Square, New York, 1963
  Production, East End Theatre, New York, 1964
  Production, Signature Theatre Company, New York, 1995

The Owl Answers
  Production, White Barn Theatre, Westport, Connecticut, 1965
  Production, New York Shakespeare Festival, 1969 (produced with *A Beast's Story* under the collective title *Cities in Bezique*)

A Rat's Mass
  Production, Theatre Company of Boston, Boston, 1966
  Production, La Mama, New York, 1969

The Lennon Play: In His Own Write (full-length adaptation of John Lennon's stories and poems with Victor Spinette)
  Production, National Theatre Company, London, 1967
  Production, Summer Theatre Festival, Kingston, Rhode Island, 1968

A Beast's Story
  Production, New York Shakespeare Festival, 1969 (produced with *The Owl Answers* under the collective title *Cities in Bezique*)

Sun (monologue)
Production, Royal Court Theatre, London, 1969

A Lesson in Dead Language
Production, Theatre Genesis at St. Mark's Church, New York, 1971

An Evening with Dead Essex (one-act documentary drama)
Production, American Place Theatre, New York, 1973

A Rat's Mass/Procession in Shout (full-length improvisational jazz opera)
Production, La Mama E.T.C., New York, 1976

A Movie Star Has to Star in Black and White
Production, New York Shakespeare Festival, New York, 1976
Production, Signature Theatre Company, New York, 1995

A Lancashire Lad (children's musical)
Production, Empire State Plaza Performing Arts Center, Albany, New York, 1980

Black Children's Day (children's play)
Production, Rites and Reasons, Providence, Rhode Island, 1980

Electra and *Orestes* (adaptations of Euripides's plays)
Production, Julliard, New York, 1981

Diary of Lights ("A Musical without Songs")
Production, City College of New York, New York, 1987

She Talks to Beethoven (one-act play collectively titled *The Alexander Plays*)
Production, River Arts, Woodstock, New York, 1989

The Ohio State Murders (one-act play collectively titled *The Alexander Plays*)
Production, Great Lakes Theater Festival, Cleveland, Ohio, 1992

June and Jean in Concert (play version of *People Who Led to My Plays*)
Production, Signature Theatre Company, New York, 1995

Sleep Deprivation Chamber (coauthored with her son, Adam Kennedy)
Production, Signature Theatre Company, New York, 1996

The Alexander Plays
Production, Signature Theatre Company, New York, 1996

PLAY AVAILABILITY

Adrienne Kennedy's work has been frequently anthologized during her thirty-year career. No attempt will be made to include every possible citation; rather a single source for each play will be identified.

A Beast's Story is published in Adrienne Kennedy, *Cities in Bezique: Two One-Act Plays.* New York: Samuel French, 1969.

Funnyhouse of a Negro, The Owl Answers, A Lesson in Dead Language, A Rat's Mass, Sun, A Movie Star Has to Star in Black and White, and adaptations of the Greek plays *Electra* and *Orestes* are published in Adrienne Kennedy, *Adrienne Kennedy in One Act.* Minneapolis: University of Minnesota Press, 1988.

The Lennon Play: In His Own Write is available in Stanley Richards, ed., *The Best Short Plays of the World Theatre, 1968–73.* New York: Crown Publishers, 1973.

She Talks to Beethoven, The Ohio State Murders, The Film Club, and *The Dramatic Circle* are published in Adrienne Kennedy. *The Alexander Plays.* Minneapolis: University of Minnesota Press, 1992.

AWARDS

Stanley Award, Wagner College, Staten Island, New York, *Funnyhouse of a Negro,* 1963

Obie Award, Distinguished Play, *Funnyhouse of a Negro,* 1964

Guggenheim Fellowship for Creative Writing, 1967

Rockefeller Foundation Grant, 1967–1969

Rockefeller Foundation Grant, 1970

National Endowment for the Arts Fellowship, 1972

Lila Wallace–Reader's Digest Writers' Award, 1994

American Academy of Arts and Letters in Literature Award, 1994

Obie Award, Best New American Play, *June and Jean in Concert* and *Sleep Deprivation Chamber* (with Adam Kennedy), 1996

DESCRIPTIVE AND CRITICAL RESPONSES

Barnett, Claudia. "This Fundamental Challenge to Identity: Reproduction and Representation in the Drama of Adrienne Kennedy." *Theatre Journal* 37, no. 2 (1993): 141–55.

Brantley, Ben. "Glimpsing Solitude in Worlds Black and White." Review of *Funnyhouse of a Negro* and *A Movie Star Has to Star in Black and White. New York Times,* 25 September 1995, C11, 13.

———. "Restless Voices of a Writer's Past." Review of *June and Jean in Concert. New York Times,* 13 November 1995, 21, 24.

———. "Righting a Wrong in a World out of Joint." Review of *Sleep Deprivation Chamber. New York Times,* 27 February 1996, 11.

Bryant-Jackson, Paul K., and Lois More Overbeck, eds. *Intersecting Boundaries: The Theatre of Adrienne Kennedy.* Minneapolis: University of Minnesota Press, 1992.

Diamond, Elin. "An Interview with Adrienne Kennedy." *Studies in American Drama, 1945–Present* 4 (1989): 143–57.

Jefferson, Margo. "A Family's Story Merges with the Nation's." Review of *Funnyhouse of a Negro* and *A Movie Star Has to Star in Black and White. New York Times,* 8 October 1995, 4, 43.

Robinson, Marc. *The Other American Drama,* 115–49. Cambridge, England: Cambridge University Press, 1994.

SUSAN KIM

(1958–)

BIOGRAPHY

Susan Kim was born in New York City and continues to live there. She received her BA cum laude in English and theatre from Wesleyan University in 1980. Since graduation she has worked primarily in television as a producer and writer. Some of her television writing projects include the Nickelodeon series "Gullah Gullah Island," "Allegra's Window," and "Are You Afraid of the Dark?". Kim has written for Public Broadcasting Service's series "Reading Rainbow," and recently she produced the children's special "Totally Tropical Rain Forest," hosted by Dudley Moore, for National Geographic, for which she received an Emmy nomination in 1995. She coproduced the eight-part WNET/KCET series, "Television," which aired nationwide on PBS in 1989. In 1993 Kim received a Writers Guild of America (WGA) nomination for her coauthored episode "The Case of the Calpurnian Kugel Caper" for the Children's Television Workshop's "Square One TV."

Susan Kim is a member of the Dramatists Guild and the Writers Guild of America, and she is a member of the Ensemble Studio Theatre in New York. Her play *Where It Came From* was commissioned by Second Stage in New York.

PLAY DESCRIPTIONS

Susan Kim's work is marked by a strong dramatic sense. Although her adaptation of Amy Tan's novel *The Joy Luck Club* demonstrates the playwright's sensitivity in investigating her Asian roots, most of Kim's work explores the dangers of contemporary urban life. *Rapid Eye Movement* is a one-act play that critic Mel Gussow described as a "delusionary comedy" that takes place in a "toxic domestic environment" (1992, C2). In the play, a woman imagines being besieged by mad dogs. While a dog barks and howls outside her apartment door, the woman fantasizes that her husband has been transformed into a snarling beast. Her pragmatic solution to this psychic fear is to "be careful who you let in, and take lots of pills."

The full-length play *The Arrangement* is a study in obsessive behavior. Jack, a young professional, becomes fixated on Annie, a woman who lives in the building across the street from where Jack works. Although Jack has never met the object of his desire, he has found her name and telephone number. As he begins to succumb to the darker, more obsessive side of his personality, Jack takes up with Kara, a woman he met in a bar and who also lives across the street from Annie. Jack asks Kara to wear a blonde wig that makes her look more like Annie. Kara complies with Jack's wishes, all the while hoping to fill the void left by the death of her previous boyfriend in a motorcycle accident. When their relationship deteriorates, Kara attempts suicide. The play ends with Kara and Jack huddled on the hospital bed, realizing that their arrangement has, in fact, brought each other the intimacy, maybe even love, they had been seeking.

Kim's full-length adaptation of Amy Tan's novel *The Joy Luck Club* adheres closely to the original book by fluidly juxtaposing past and present on stage. The play, which focuses on mother-daughter relationships, details the conflicts and struggles of four Chinese-born women and their American-born daughters. The older generation is determined to pass on the traditions that had culturally defined their roles and identities. The younger women, on the other hand, alternately rebel against and acquiesce to their cultural legacy. They struggle to reconcile their Chinese heritage with their American independence. Each begins to realize that they cannot escape the indelible mark that mothers leave on their daughters.

SELECTED PRODUCTION HISTORY

Open Spaces
  Production, Ensemble Studio Theatre, New York, 1988

Death and the Maiden (one-act play)
  Production, Ensemble Studio Theatre, New York, 1990
  Production, Westbeth Theatre, New York, 1991

Swimming out to Sea
  Production, Home for Contemporary Theatre, New York, 1991

Rapid Eye Movement (one-act play)
  Production, Ensemble Studio Theatre, New York, 1991
  Production, John Houseman Theatre, New York, 1992
  Production, Home Box Office New Writers Project, Los Angeles, 1994

Guts
  Production, Raft Theatre, New York, 1991

Seventh Word, Four Syllables (one-act play)
   Production, Ensemble Studio Theatre, New York, 1993

The Arrangement
   Production, Watermark Theatre at the Ohio Theatre, New York, 1993

The Joy Luck Club (based on Amy Tan's novel)
   Production, Long Wharf Theatre and Shanghai People's Arts Theatre, Beijing, China, 1993

PLAY AVAILABILITY

Susan Kim's plays may be obtained through her agent: Greg Wagner, c/o Writers and
   Artists, 19 West 44th Street, Suite 1000, New York, New York 10036; (212) 391–
   1112.

AWARD

Drama League Award, Outstanding New Play, *Open Spaces*, 1988

DESCRIPTIVE AND CRITICAL RESPONSES

Gussow, Mel. "Psychological Warfare Claims Two." Review of *The Arrangement. New
   York Times*, 22 March 1993, C14.
———. "Women Taking Their Places, Rightful or Not." Review of *Rapid Eye Move-
   ment. New York Times*, 25 September 1992, C2.
McGinnis, John. "Amy Tan Bestseller Premieres on Chinese Stage." Review of *The Joy
   Luck Club. Wall Street Journal*, 19 August 1993, A8.
Tyler, Patrick E. "Joint Production Takes 'The Joy Luck Club' to China's Stages." *New
   York Times*, 27 November 1993, 11.

TINA LANDAU

(1963–)

BIOGRAPHY

Born to film producer parents, Landau lived in Riverdale, a New York City suburb, until she was fourteen. Her family then moved to Beverly Hills, California, where she completed high school at Beverly Hills High. Landau returned east to attend Yale University and, after she graduated, she moved to New York City where she worked at the usual variety of rent-paying jobs (waitressing and telephone sales) and some not so usual (screen writing: authoring the script for *Friday the 13th, Part Five*). She returned to school for graduate work at the Institute for Advanced Theatre Training at Harvard University where she was the first student to direct a professional production. Noted more as a director than as a writer, Landau most often does both: writing or adapting and directing, usually in collaboration with a composer. Inspired by Anne Bogart as a student, Landau has developed a unique style of ensemble-created texts with herself as primary writer. She and Bogart have worked together, as well, on such pieces as *American Music* for the Actors Theatre of Louisville (ATL) in Louisville, Kentucky, and *American Vaudeville* for the Alley Theatre, in Houston, Texas. While Landau's choice of subjects is eclectic, ranging from the American Revolution to adaptations of Dickens's *A Christmas Carol* and the plays of Anton Chekhov, several of her works that she has written and directed have had homosexual themes, notably *1969*, a commissioned piece for ATL, and *Stonewall: Night Variations* for En Garde Arts to commemorate the twenty-fifth anniversary of the Stonewall riots.

PLAY DESCRIPTIONS

Landau credits everyone from the actors to the production assistants for their contributions of ''ideas, images, staging'' to the production of *1969*, created in four weeks of rehearsal at ATL. She feels that the published text of the play is merely a blueprint without the addition of the gestures, movements, and sound that accompanied the original production. Specific descriptions of scenery, movement, and sound accompany the relatively simple story line of a young gay man's tormented final weeks of his senior year in high school. Scenes of Howie's ostracism, after a classmate calls him a faggot, are interwoven with familiar images and sounds of the 1960s drug culture, political assassinations, and rock music. The play is bookended with clips from the well-known (to rock fans) Dick Cavett television interview with Janis Joplin prior to her triumphant return to her high school reunion in Port Arthur, Texas, where she had been shunned by classmates. The play creates a portrait of a seminal era in American history and tells the coming-of-age and coming-out story of a young person growing up in a conservative, suburban environment who longs for a kinder world: "There's a place called Washington Square Park, in a place called Greenwich Village . . . a huge place, where you can get lost—where people talk fast, walk fast, act cool," he tells a confidant. In the last scenes Howie arrives in New York during the Gay Pride March and is befriended by a Drag Queen calling herself Glinda the Good Witch, echoing the Oz motif that runs through the play.

Appropriately, Landau's next work was *Stonewall: Night Variations*, in which the character of Howie reappears. The play was inspired by Pride Day, 1993, when she and Gregory Gunther admired the diverse groups of people celebrating their freedom. They agreed to work together on a theatre piece and, according to Gunther's program notes that were written by him as dramaturg for the production, divided the research of the events leading up to Stonewall, the participants, and the riots that occurred on the night of 27 June 1969. They realized that without film and television coverage of the riots, there was little consensus among the witnesses; therefore, the play is conceived as an invocation of the spirit of the event rather than as a work of documentary theatre. An epic performance piece with more than fifty actors, dancers, and singers, with music by Ricky Ian Gordon and film segments by Jennie Livingston, *Stonewall* was presented on Pier 25 on the Hudson River while ships, cruise tour boats, and gulls drifted by in the background.

SELECTED PRODUCTION HISTORY

A Christmas Carol (adapted from the novel by Charles Dickens; music by Adam Guettel)
    Production, Trinity Repertory Theatre, Providence, Rhode Island, 1989

Rebecca (adapted from the novel by Daphne Du Maurier)
    Production, Trinity Repertory Theatre, Providence, Rhode Island, 1990

American Vaudeville (with Anne Bogart)
    Production, Alley Theatre, Houston, Texas, 1992

States of Independence (with composer Ricky Ian Gordon)
  Production, American Music Theatre Festival, Philadelphia, 1993

1969
  Production, Actors Theatre of Louisville, Louisville, Kentucky, 1994

Stonewall: Night Variations (music by Ricky Ian Gordon)
  Production, En Garde Arts at Pier 25, New York, 1994

Floyd Collins (with composer Adam Guettel)
  Production, American Music Theatre Festival, Philadelphia, 1994
  Production, Playwrights Horizons, New York, 1996

PLAY AVAILABILITY

1969 is published in Marisa Smith, ed., *Humana Festival '94: The Complete Plays.*
Lyme, New Hampshire: Smith and Kraus, 1994.

Unpublished plays are available from the Helen Merrill Agency, 435 West 23rd Street,
Suite 1A, New York, New York 10011; (212) 691–5326.

AWARDS

Louis Sudler Prize, Yale University, 1985

Dorothy Stickney Award, 1990

Princess Grace Foundation Grant, 1991

Theatre Communications Group/National Endowment for the Arts Director Fellow, 1992

National Endowment for the Arts, Artistic Associate at the American Music Theater
Festival, 1993

Commissions from the Actors Theatre of Louisville, American Music Theater Festival,
and Houston Grand Opera, 1993 and 1994

Janus Award from the Actors Theatre of Louisville, 1994

Rockefeller Foundation Grant, 1994

W. Alton Jones Grant, 1995

DESCRIPTIVE AND CRITICAL RESPONSES

Brantley, Ben. "Carnival above Ground, Tragedy Below." Review of *Floyd Collins.*
    New York Times, 4 March 1996, C14.
————. "Stonewall Liberation: Who and How." *New York Times*, 25 June 1994, A13.
Kelly, Kevin. "A Murky, Unintentionally Silly *Rebecca.*" *Boston Globe*, 25 January
    1990, 38.
Pareles, Jon. "Dreams and Exploiters in a Slice of Americana." *New York Times*, 18
    April 1994, C11.
Stearns, David Patrick. "Ambitious Show of Independence." *USA Today*, 7 May 1993,
    D4.

CHERYLENE LEE

(1953–   )

BIOGRAPHY

Cherylene Lee was born in Los Angeles where her career in the theatre started at an early age, when she and her sister had a singing and dancing act and performed in musical revues in Las Vegas. These appearances led to work in film, television, and the theatre. Her most notable stage performance was in *A Chorus Line* in New York and on tour. To her mother's disappointment, her performing career ended abruptly when she grew out of juvenile roles.

A summer volunteer job at the La Brea tar pits in Los Angeles cultivated Lee's intense interest in paleontology, and she majored in the field at the University of California-Berkeley where she received her BA in 1975. She continued in the sciences and earned her master's degree in geology at UCLA in 1979.

Cherylene Lee's career as a playwright emerged in the period from 1981 to 1984. She was living in Seattle and could not find work as a scientist, performer, or dancer. She started writing poetry and short fiction and won a creative poetry prize, but since her fiction seemed a form of dialogue, she naturally gravitated to writing plays. Some of her short stories and poetry have been anthologized in *American Dragons* (HarperCollins, 1993) and *Charlie Chan Is Dead* (Viking/Penguin, 1994). She lives in San Francisco and is a member of the New Dramatists.

PLAY DESCRIPTIONS

As a second-generation Chinese American, Cherylene Lee is, not surprisingly, interested in the issues of assimilation as well as the differences in American and Chinese values. In *Arthur and Leila*, a second-generation Chinese American brother and sister work out their rivalry and hostilities. This two-hander two-act play is set in contemporary Los Angeles. Fifty-seven-year-old Leila Chin-Abernathy is married to a successful Caucasian doctor and is president of the prestigious Asian Cultural Exchange Society. Her older brother, Arthur, who is sixty-four, has had a very different life. Having failed at a variety of jobs and having lost money by gambling, he is reduced to an impoverished state. Still resourceful, however, he sells family heirlooms he inherited as the first-born son of a Chinese shopkeeper. The buyer is his sister, who is eager to own some of the artifacts of her past. Arthur uses the items to barter for the money he desperately needs and as revenge for his sister's good fortune which he believes he deserves. Although the heirlooms turn out to be bogus, cheap imitations, Arthur is an entertaining storyteller. He is capable of improvising persuasive tales while at the same time conveying complex insights about the impact of their heritage. As brother and sister move through these trading sessions, they discover what they mean to each other and begin to work out a tenuous peace. The transactions reveal conflicts between traditional Chinese values and American society, expectations about gender, class differences, and what it means to allow another person the dignity of saving face on her or his terms.

Conflict develops in *Knock Off Balance* when Dorris Ango from Hong Kong visits Doris Eng, the owner of a celebrity look-alike agency in Los Angeles, claiming to be her cousin. They are cousins by concubine, Dorris claims, as their grandfather had two families unknown to each other: one in China and one in the United States. Dorris Ango persuades Doris Eng to take over her prosperous business in Hong Kong in exchange for Ango's taking over Eng's failing agency in Hollywood. Her scheme seemingly involves a picture groom transaction that will import American males for marriage to Hong Kong Chinese women anxious to escape when the Chinese take over Hong Kong in 1997. In reality, Ango wishes to make epic films that will celebrate the promise of a new China to which foreigners will want to immigrate. This play uses flashbacks, disguises, and other stylized devices to address the differences between the Hong Kong Chinese, mainland Chinese, and Chinese Americans and to discuss the larger questions of cultural identity.

SELECTED PRODUCTION HISTORY

Pyros (one-act play)
    Production (video), American Folk Theatre, Seattle, 1983

Aesop's Fantastic Fables (young audiences; coauthor)
    Production, Seattle Repertory Theatre, Seattle, 1984

Yin Chin Bow
    Staged reading, Pan Asian Repertory Theatre, New York, 1986
    Workshop, Asian American Theatre Company, San Francisco, 1987
    Staged reading (and tour to borough libraries), Urban Stages, New York, 1994

Ballad of Doc Hay
    Production, Marin Playhouse Theatre, San Anselmo, California, 1987

Wong Bow Rides Again
Production, East West Players, Los Angeles, 1987

Overtones
Production, Kumu Kahua Theatre, Honolulu, 1988

Bitter Melon
Reading, New Traditions Theater Company at the American Conservatory Theatre, San Francisco, 1991

Memory Square (with Cynthia Leung)
Staged reading, P. F. Flyer Productions, Asian American Theater Company, San Francisco, 1991

Arthur and Leila
Reading, Mark Taper Forum, Los Angeles, 1991
Workshop, Group Theater, Seattle, 1992
Reading, Theatre Exchange, San Francisco, 1992
Reading, O'Neill National Playwrights' Conference, Waterford, Connecticut, 1992
Reading, Women's Project and Productions, New York, 1993
Production, BRAVA! for Women in the Arts, San Francisco, 1993
Production, East West Players, Los Angeles, 1993
Production, Pan Asian Repertory Company, New York, 1994

In the Spirit . . . (text for dancers; collaboration with the Abhinaya Dance Troupe)
Production, Louis B. Mayer Theatre, San Jose, California, 1993

Knock Off Balance
Workshop, New Dramatists, New York, 1994
Workshop, Sundance, Utah, 1995
Reading, Audrey Skirball–Kenis Theatre, Los Angeles, 1996

PLAY AVAILABILITY

Arthur and Leila is published in Marisa Smith, *Women Playwrights: The Best Plays of 1993*. Newbury, Vermont: Smith and Kraus, 1994.

Several of Lee's plays can be found in the Special Collections Library, University of Massachusetts in Amherst; New Dramatists in New York; and the Audrey Skirball-Kenis Theater Library in Los Angeles.

Several plays are available through her agent: Bruce Ostler, Bret Adams, 448 West 44th Street, New York, New York 10036; (212) 765–5630.

AWARDS

Third Step Theater's 3rd Annual Spring Play Reading Festival, New York, Best of Festival, Cowinner, *Yin Chin Bow*, 1990

Mark Taper Forum's Mentor Playwrights Lab, Los Angeles, 1991

Mixed Blood Theater's Playwriting Contest, Minneapolis, Cowinner, *Arthur and Leila*, 1992

South Coast Repertory Theatre Playwriting Contest, Costa Mesa, California, Honorable Mention, *Arthur and Leila*, 1992

Rockefeller MAP Grant, *Arthur and Leila*, 1992

Eugene O'Neill National Playwrights Conference, Waterford, Connecticut, *Arthur and Leila*, 1992

Fund for New American Plays Grant, *Arthur and Leila*, 1993

Residencies at Ucross Foundation, Wyoming; Djerassi Foundation, Woodside, California; Centrum Foundation for the Arts, Port Townsend, Washington

DESCRIPTIVE AND CRITICAL RESPONSES

Bruckner, D.J.R. "Telling Precious Secrets Just as Children Do." *New York Times*, 18 October 1994, C16.

Hurtes, Hettie Lynne. "Serendipity at East West Players *Arthur and Leila*." *Backstage*, 17 December 1993, 4W.

Isaac, Dan. "*Arthur and Leila*." *Backstage*, 21 October 1994, 48.

LISA LOOMER

(n.d.–   )

BIOGRAPHY

A native of Manhattan, Lisa Loomer studied theatre at Brandeis University and New York University's Tisch School of the Arts. She soon began performing off-Broadway as an actress and working with a political comedy group at the West Bank Cafe. Tired of performing other people's monologues, Loomer began writing her own material under the pseudonym Jane da Vinci. Her first work for the theatre was the collaboration titled *A Crowd of Two*, which was produced at New York's American Place Theatre. Her one-woman show *All by Herselves* was performed at the Westside Arts Theatre, New York. In 1985 she served as writer in residence at INTAR in New York. She was a contributor to *A . . . My Name is Still Alice*, which premiered at Second Stage in New York City and has played at numerous locations around the country.

Due to the critical and popular success of *The Waiting Room*, Loomer has been besieged with offers to write sitcoms, screenplays, and articles on health and beauty. She has hopes of writing a Latino sitcom and has made two attempts: "Gloria," about a Puerto Rican talk show host, and "East L.A.," set in an unemployment office. Her film *Looking for Angels* was developed by Sundance in Cuba, where she worked with Gabriel Garcia-Marquez. She adapted Susanna Kaysen's memoir of her two years in a mental institution, *Girl Interrupted*, for Columbia Pictures and is writing a screenplay for Winona Ryder and Fox 2000 based on *Dreaming*. Her recent play *Maria! Maria, Maria, Maria* was commissioned by the Mark Taper Forum in Los Angeles.

Loomer is an alumnus of the New Dramatists. She currently resides with her husband in Sherman Oaks, California.

PLAY DESCRIPTIONS

Lisa Loomer's plays are an exciting melange of styles and forms; she depicts serious topics with bold dashes of humor. Her realistic situations are blended with theatricalism and fantasy to create a poignant vision of contemporary life. For example, in her *Birds*, Loomer creates the portrait of a quirky family trying to accommodate their Mexican roots with their American lifestyles. Although the action takes place during four days in Mexico in 1982, the liberal use of flashbacks to their lives in Los Angeles in the 1960s provides the necessary motivation and development of the vividly drawn characters. The true meaning of family is examined while each member of the Vasquez family resolves his or her dual Mexican/American identities and tests the bonds that tie them together. The familial relationships from the 1960s have been disrupted and altered through adultery, death, marriage, and career. Gloria has returned to Mexico, content to drink herself to death and raise exotic birds instead of children. Jasmine, who has remained in the United States, puts her operatic career above all else. Although Manuel's marriage brings the family together physically, it does not bridge the gaps that keep them apart.

Lisa Loomer's *Chain of Life* is a comic send-up of media-driven contemporary society. No one escapes Loomer's satiric barbs—from television writers trying to cash in on the latest cultural craze, to the pimping of one's artistic integrity in the endless effort to pitch creative ideas to network executives; to the working-class family whose very existence is dictated by the "reality" of the programs.

While fantasy continues to play a major role in Loomer's later plays, the boldly drawn satire of *Chain of Life* is replaced with more muted seriocomic tones. In *Bocon!* (big mouth!), Loomer uses comic elements to underscore the serious topics of "disappearance," one of the life-and-death consequences of political resistance in Latin America. The play delineates the arduous spiritual journey twelve-year-old Miguel follows after his parents are captured by the military in his native Latin America. On his escape to the American border, Miguel encounters the spirits who people the Latin American folklore: La Llorona, the Boogie Woman who drowned her own children; Duende, the leprechaun-like trickster; and Kiki, the old wizard of dance. Miguel goes in search of freedom and of his voice so that he can relate the tragedies in his homeland. Subtitled *A Central American Fable for Young Audiences, Bocon!* is a touching tale of youthful courage and political reality.

Accelerando is a imaginative fable of contemporary life and love. He and She meet at a party and go home together. After sex, they each contemplate life, love, and the possibility of a relationship. In a whirl of quick-changing scenes that reflect the tempo of today, they contemplate these issues together, separately, to the audience, and with their mothers and fathers. Their mothers are characters who emerge from their respective dreams, while their two-dimensional fathers appear only as larger-than-life slide projections. Unwilling to give up their images of themselves, they part only to meet a year later at another party. Their inflexibility has been replaced with compromise, and they are now open to the possibility of a relationship.

Lisa Loomer's best-known play to date is *The Waiting Room*, in which the imaginative blending of the serious and the comic, the past and the present, create a masterful critique of male-defined beauty and male-dominated medicine. The stories of three women from three different historical eras converge (reminiscent of Caryl Churchill's *Top Girls*) when the women meet in a doctor's waiting room. Wanda, a modern woman from New Jersey, has had every type of plastic surgery in an effort to win a bet with her mother: attract a man and get married before reaching the age of forty. Her breast implants, however, now endanger her life. Forgiveness from Heaven is the First Wife (of five) of an eighteenth-century wealthy Chinese man. Her bound feet are beginning to rot. Victoria, an English Victorian woman, is diagnosed as suffering from "hysteria" because of her desire to read books and have sex. She has been subjected to a series of degrading "treatments" in the doctors' efforts to cure her disorders. The insensitive men who control their lives and their images of themselves also intersect throughout the play. Despite the veneer of zany humor, Loomer fearlessly delves into timely issues: body image, breast cancer, and alternative medicine.

SELECTED PRODUCTION HISTORY

Birds
    Production, South Coast Repertory, Costa Mesa, California, 1980s (exact date of production is not available)

Accelerando
    Production, GALA Hispanic Theatre, Washington, D.C., 1993
    Production, Actors Express, Atlanta, 1995

Waiting Room
    Production, Williamstown Theatre Festival, Williamstown, Massachusetts, 1993
    Workshop, New Works Festival, Mark Taper Forum, Los Angeles, 1993
    Production, Mark Taper Forum, Los Angeles, 1994
    Production, Trinity Repertory Company, Providence, Rhode Island, 1994
    Production, Arena Stage, Washington, D.C., 1996
    Production, Vineyard Theatre, New York, 1996

Chain of Life
    Production, Playwright's Arena, Los Angeles, 1994

PLAY AVAILABILITY

Accelerando is published in *Plays in Process*, vol. 12, no. 12. New York: Theatre Communications Group, 1991.

Bocon! is published in *Plays for Young Audiences IV (Plays in Process)*, vol. 10, no. 12. New York: Theatre Communications Group, 1990.

The Waiting Room is published in *American Theatre*, December 1994, 29–51.

Information on Lisa Loomer's plays is available through her agent: Peter Hagan, Writers and Artists Agency, 19 West 44th Street, New York, New York 10036; (212) 391–1112.

AWARDS

American Theater Critics Association Award

Susan Smith Blackburn Prize, Runner-up, *The Waiting Room*, 1993

Jane Chambers Award, Winner, *The Waiting Room*, 1994

DESCRIPTIVE AND CRITICAL RESPONSES

Brantley, Ben. "2 Plays Linked by Oppression." *New York Times*, 1 February 1996, C13.

Breslauer, Jan. "As Her Many Worlds Turn." *Los Angeles Times*, 7 August 1994, CAL 8.

Gussow, Mel. "Playwright's Tough Subject Draws Funny Offers." *New York Times*, 2 November 1994, C13.

King, Robert L. "Performance: *The Waiting Room*." *North American Review* 280 (March 1995): 48.

Sommers, Pamela. "For a Night, He & She Are a 'We.' " Review of *Accelerando*. *Washington Post*, 10 March 1993, C2.

Winer, Laurie. "Beauty and Culture: A Beast Declawed by Female Writers." *Los Angeles Times*, 1 September 1994, F1.

———. "A Search for Truth in Beauty." Review of *The Waiting Room*. *Los Angeles Times*, 12 August 1994, F1.

JOSEFINA LÓPEZ

(1969–   )

BIOGRAPHY

Josefina López was born in Cerritos in the Mexican state of San Luis Potosi. At the age of six, she moved with her parents and seven brothers and sisters to Los Angeles in search of a better life. Although her parents had green cards, the young Josefina lived in fear of being sent back to Mexico since she did not have the appropriate papers. In order to work, the undocumented teenager had to lie about having a social security number. After she graduated from the Los Angeles High School for the Arts, López studied at New York University and the University of California-San Diego before she completed her BA in film and screenwriting at Columbia College in Chicago in 1993.

López's undefined and ambiguous residency status left her feeling excluded from American society, but she was inspired to write about her experiences after seeing a production of Luis Valdez's *I Don't Have to Show You No Stinking Badges. Simply Maria or the American Dream* was written when López was seventeen years old. She has worked with the Los Angeles Theatre Center's Young Playwrights Lab and trained under **Maria Irene Fornes** at INTAR's Hispanic Playwrights Workshop. She continues to write plays and is under contract with Warner Brothers to adapt her first play to the screen.

Her best-known work, *Real Women Have Curves*, has had numerous productions at theatres all over the United States. She has worked as a playwright with several theatres, including San Diego's Playwrights Project, El Teatro Campesino, and El Teatro de al Esperanza; Chicago's Victory Gardens; and the Seattle Group Theatre; and she has worked as a segment producer for the performing artists, Culture Clash.

Josefina López, who continues to live and work in Los Angeles, was awarded a playwriting fellowship by the Mark Taper Forum for 1995–1996.

PLAY DESCRIPTIONS

Josefina López's work balances a comic, sometimes playful, sense of life with an exploration of significant issues in the lives of Latinas. In *Simply Maria or the American Dream*, she splices dreams (or nightmares) with reality to create a comically surreal coming-of-age play that chronicles Maria's growth from birth to womanhood. From her mother Carmen's elopement and wedding to Maria's decision to leave home, the play illuminates the struggles of a Mexican American woman in contemporary society. Maria is caught between the traditional values of her parents' culture and the more Americanized, less patriarchal values of independence and self-determination. When she fails to convince her parents to allow her to attend college, she enters into a dream. Three female figures who metamorphose with each situation function as a chorus in the Brechtian-like episodes. Maria's dream contrasts the Mexican cultural myths (marriage, motherhood, and subservience) with the myth of the American dream, which demands assimilation and conformity. In the end, she seeks her own destiny with "Mexico . . . in my blood . . . And America . . . in my heart."

In *Real Woman Have Curves*, López provides a warm and humorous look at female bonding among Mexican immigrant women. Estela is struggling to maintain a dress shop where she employs her mother, her sister, and two friends. Each of the women has her own burdens and concerns under which she labors. Carmen, who is fifty years old, is afraid she is pregnant with her ninth child; Rosali faints from taking too many diet pills; Pancha walks out after not being paid; and Estela is trying to repay a large debt for her sewing equipment. They all pull together, however, by working through the night to finish a big order and help Estela. Along the way, they discuss important issues: abuse, financial independence, citizenship, and the power that comes from working together. An especially illuminating and comic moment occurs when Ana, hot from the work, takes off her clothes, unashamed of her heavy body. The others soon follow suit and then compare stretch marks, blemishes, and other bodily "flaws." When they recognize their ridiculous obsession with body image, they laugh and cement their new relationship.

SELECTED PRODUCTION HISTORY

Simply Maria or the American Dream
  Production, Playwrights Project, San Diego, 1988

Real Women Have Curves
  Production, Guadalupe Cultural Arts Center, San Antonio, Texas, 1990
  Production, El Teatro Bilingue de Houston, Houston, Texas, 1991
  Production, Seattle Group Theatre, Seattle, 1992
  Production, Victory Gardens Theatre, Chicago, 1993
  Production, Repertorio Español, New York, 1994

PLAY AVAILABILITY

Real Women Have Curves is published by Rain City Project, Seattle, 1988.

Simply Maria or the American Dream is published in Linda Feyder, ed., *Shattering the Myth: Plays by Hispanic Women*. Houston, Texas: Arte Publico, 1992.

AWARDS

Young Playwrights Festival, New York, Semifinalist, *Simply Maria or the American Dream*, 1987

California Young Playwrights Contest, Gaslamp Quarter Theatre, San Diego, Finalist, *Simply Maria or the American Dream*, 1988

U.S. Representative, International Young Playwrights Festival, Australia, 1988

Media Award, National Organization of Christians and Jews, *Simply Maria or the American Dream*, 1988

Gold Award, Corporation for Public Broadcasting, *Simply Maria or the American Dream*, 1988

USA Today All Star Academic National Team, 1993

Playwright Fellow, Latino Theatre Initiative, Mark Taper Forum, Los Angeles, 1995–1996

DESCRIPTIVE AND CRITICAL RESPONSES

Bruckner, D.J.R. "In a Los Angeles Sweatshop, Five Women Find Themselves." Review of *Real Women Have Curves*. *New York Times*, 10 October 1994, C18.

Churnin, Nancy. "Simply Josefina López." *Los Angeles Times*, 29 July 1990, CAL 48+.

Cole, Melanie. "30 under Thirty." *Hispanic* 8, no. 7 (August 1995): 22–32+.

Cruz, Migdalia, Josefina López, and Luis Santeiro. "The Playwrights Speak." *Ollantay Theatre Magazine* 1, no. 2 (July 1993): 40–49.

Huerta, Jorge. "Professionalizing Teatro: An Overview of Chicano Theatre during the Decade of the Hispanic." *TheatreForum*, Spring 1993, 54–59.

Launer, Pat. "*Real Women* a Loving Memory Play." Review of *Real Women Have Curves*. *Los Angeles Times*, 2 April 1994, F14.

Morales, Ed. "Shadowing Valdez." *American Theatre*, November 1992, 14–19.

Smith, Sid. "A Curvy Comedy." Review of *Real Women Have Curves*. *Chicago Tribune*, 24 October 1993, V5.

NIKKI NOJIMA LOUIS

(1937–   )

BIOGRAPHY

Nikki Nojima Louis, a Japanese American playwright, was born in Seattle. At the age of four, Nikki and her mother were placed in an internment camp in Minidoka, Idaho. After the war, she was raised in Chicago where she performed as a teenage professional dancer.

Louis began working in theatre in the mid-1980s and has been active writing, adapting, performing, and producing political works, especially oral histories that have uncovered an array of new and eloquent voices in the Northwest. Louis's emphasis has been on the educational outreach of theatre. Her approach to education is multicultural, multidisciplinary, and experiential. She is a member of Local Access, a Seattle arts-in-education collective. In 1987 she founded Playwrights-in-Progress, an activity of the Northwest Playwrights Guild, and organized a performing writers' group, Women Who Write Too Much, in 1992. Louis also teaches playwriting at Seattle Children's Theatre. She is currently pursuing an MFA in creative writing and is writing fiction and literary performance pieces.

PLAY DESCRIPTIONS

Nikki Nojima Louis's plays to date reflect her several passions and occupations, while combining a poetic, fluid quality with a strong sense of narrative. Her first outing as a playwright, *Word of Mouth*, was a collaborative women's peace show. *Made in America* and *Breaking the Silence* explore the world of Japanese Americans. *Changing Faces* is a choreopoem on female Asian American identity, and *I Dream a World*, songs and stories by "Black Women Who Changed America," is an adaptation of the book by the same name.

Her one-act play *Our Mother's Stories*, subtitled *A Musical and Mythical Story of Early Washington Women*, was written in celebration of Washington state's centennial. The play blends many of Louis's interests: oral history, women's issues, and a structural mutability that allows her to cover the history of the Northwest from the Earth Woman creation myth to the present. Through music, poetry, and dialogue, Louis introduces the women (both factual and mythic) who helped forge the history of the Northwest. Women of all ethnic origins (Asian, African, European, and Native) are united in their common cause.

Louis's longer *Issei, the First Generation* is stylistically related to *Our Mother's Stories*. In her notes on the style of the play, Louis describes it as a "tone poem, a memory play, a play about dreams lost and found." Told from the point of view of an elderly woman, Sachiko, the play recounts the story of her life. Beginning in 1908 with her father's bankruptcy and suicide, the spunky and precocious young Sachiko learns the harsh lessons of perseverance, endurance, and courage which will be the source of her strength for the rest of her life. Her dream is to go to America, and she gets her chance when she sails for the United States in search of her brother who had gone to America ten years earlier. During the odyssey in search of her brother, Sachiko guards cuttings from the family's cherry orchards in Japan. Marriage, miscarriages, and many years intervene before she finds a home (on Bainbridge Island) to plant the trees. The play traces how Sachiko takes root, blossoms, and bears fruit just as her beloved trees thrive in their new home.

SELECTED PRODUCTION HISTORY

Word of Mouth: Women Singing and Speaking for Peace
Production, Langston Hughes Theatre, Seattle, 1984

Japanese Voices in America
Staged reading, University of Washington, Seattle, 1985

Made in America
Production, Pioneer Square Theatre, Seattle, 1985

Breaking the Silence
Production, Northwest Asian American Theatre, Seattle, 1987

Changing Faces
Production, Seattle Group Theatre, Seattle, 1988

Our Mother's Stories (one-act play)
Production, Seattle Group Theatre, Seattle, 1989

Gold! Gold! Gold: Living the Turn of the Century
Production, 1880's Gallery, Seattle, 1990

Most Dangerous Women (cowritten with Jan Maher)
Production, Women's International League for Peace and Freedom, Seattle, 1990

I Dream a World: The Play
  Production, Museum of History and Industry, Seattle, 1991

Issei, the First Generation
  Production, Bainbridge Island Performing Arts, Bainbridge Island, Washington, 1993

Shirley Temple at the Alamo (with Laura Esparaza)
  Production, Seattle Fringe Theatre Festival, 1995

PLAY AVAILABILITY

Nikki Nojima Louis's scripts may be obtained directly from the playwright: Nikki Nojima Louis, 5048 44th N.E., Seattle, Washington 98105; (206) 525–9828.

AWARDS

Artist Trust Fellowship in Theatre, 1988

Washington State Arts Commission, *Our Mother's Stories*, 1988–1989

DESCRIPTIVE AND CRITICAL RESPONSES

Adcock, Joe. "*Changing Faces* Evolves from Actresses' Real-life Stories." Review of *Changing Faces. Seattle Post-Intelligencer*, 15 January 1988.

Johnson, Wayne. "From under the Stereotypes, a Pride and Grace Emerge." Review of *Changing Faces. Seattle Times*, 22 January 1988.

Liebman, Larry. "*Changing Faces*: Women Dissect Identity Crises." Review of *Changing Faces. Puget Sound Business Journal*, 1 February 1988, 23.

LYNN MARTIN

(1965–)

BIOGRAPHY

Lynn Martin is a native Washingtonian and die-hard Redskins fan. She attended Georgetown University from 1983 to 1987 when she received her AB in English. During her college tenure, she became co–artistic director of Georgetown's Black Theatre Ensemble and served as a literary intern at Arena Stage. Martin was then accepted into Columbia University's Oscar Hammerstein II Center for Theatre Arts. While she was a graduate student she had a play produced off-off-Broadway and a workshop production at Columbia. In mid-1989 she began working with Amiri Baraka on his "bopera" *The Life of Bumpy Johnson*. During this period she also worked as a researcher and assistant to George Ferencz and Max Roach and ultimately served as assistant producer on two albums for Max Roach. After a residency at Case Western Reserve University, where her play *The Problem of God* received its world premiere, Martin returned to Columbia to complete her MFA in playwriting in 1990.

The following year, Lynn Martin taught playwriting in a south Bronx high school under the auspices of the Foundation for the Dramatists Guild. She was also a communications and literary intern at the Circle Repertory Company where she worked with playwrights Lanford Wilson and Craig Lucas, among others. In 1992 Martin served on the faculty of Shepherd College in West Virginia as their first playwright in residence. After seeing one of Martin's productions, John Guare invited her participation in a reading series at the Library for the Performing Arts at Lincoln Center. In 1993 Martin was one of five playwrights accepted by the Juilliard School to participate in its inaugural year of playwriting.

Lynn Martin is a member of the Playwrights Horizons' Black Playwrights

Unit in New York City where she lives and works. She is a member of the Dramatists Guild.

PLAY DESCRIPTIONS

Lynn Martin's plays are diverse in their subject, style, and cultural experience. In *Summer Feet Hearts*, she creates a touching tale of personal metamorphosis. The play is set in the backyard of a home occupied by Alice (a woman in her early forties), Jonell (Alice's daughter in her early twenties), and Jewell (Jonell's precocious nine-year-old daughter), where the three are anticipating the arrival of Jonell's father (B. L.) who left before she was born. Each responds to his approaching visit in very different terms: Jonell is eager to meet this man about whom she knows nothing but who has, nevertheless, profoundly affected her life; Jewell has yet to learn the role her absent grandfather has in her life; and Alice's bitterness and rage at the father of her child is manifest in her escapist tactics and sarcastic tongue. Jonell is also developing a relationship with Tanner, their next-door neighbor, but as the youngest in a long line of women who have been abandoned by their men, she is reluctant to allow her callused heart to warm to this new man in her life. It is through B. L.'s determination and Tanner's sincerity that both Alice and Jonell are willing to love again.

Babes in Boyland, a surreal fantasy, is firmly embedded in the harsh reality of New York City. The play depicts the relationships among three men and three women. The women congregate on the rooftop of Elaine's building where the other two women are posing for Elaine's children's book illustrations. The men work and gather in Alice's Aftershock, the bar owned by Elaine's husband Charlie, to exchange exotic drink recipes and get drunk. Various attempts are made to bridge the gap between the men and women, but the results are less than satisfying: Elaine and Charlie's marriage is falling apart, and Llew's attempts to attract Gigi are met with indifference. The brutality of the city, complete with sirens, screams, and reports of savage deaths, provides the perfect backdrop to their disconnected and alienated lives. A mysterious presence rapes two of the women and they begin their transformation into reptilian creatures with hardened skins and even harder hearts. Salvation is sought from a female figure in Riverside Park who provides the antidote to their condition. Martin has created a modern fairytale complete with monsters, princesses, and the possibility of happiness.

Martin's most recent one-act, *The Bodhisattva Locksmith*, is a contemporary urban romance about love and loss.

SELECTED PRODUCTION HISTORY

The Wait (one-act play)
   Production, Samuel French/Double Image Off-Off-Broadway Short Play Festival, New
      York, 1988

The Problem of God
Workshop, Horace Mann Theatre, Columbia University, New York, 1989
Production, Case Western Reserve University, Cleveland, Ohio, 1990

Still Waters
Production, Contemporary American Theatre Festival, Shepherd College, Shepherdstown, West Virginia, 1992
Production, Zebra Crossing Theatre, Chicago, 1993

Summer Feet Hearts
Production, George Street Playhouse, New Brunswick, New Jersey, 1993

Babes in Boyland
Workshop, Arena Stage, Washington, D.C., 1994
Workshop, Lincoln Center Theatre, New York, 1994

Waltzing de Niro
Workshop, Act One/Showtime One-Act Competition, Hollywood, California, 1994

The Bodhisattva Locksmith
Production, New Theatre Wing, Playwrights Horizons, New York, 1995

Pinto and Bone
Production, New Georges Theatre and Here, New York, 1995

Psyche Was Here
Production, Contemporary American Theatre Festival, Shepherd College, Shepherdstown, West Virginia, 1995

The Misanthrope (adaptation of the play by Molière)
Production, Classic Stage Company, New York, 1995

PLAY AVAILABILITY

The Bodhisattva Locksmith is published in *Conjunctions Magazine*, Spring 1996.

Waltzing de Niro is published in Marisa Smith, ed., *Showtime's Act One Festival.* Lyme, New Hampshire: Smith and Kraus, 1994.

Lynn Martin's other plays are available from her agent: Beth Blickers, William Morris, 1350 Avenue of the Americas, New York, New York 10019; (212) 586–5100.

They are also available through New Dramatists, 424 West 44th Street, New York, New York 10019; (212) 757–6960.

AWARDS

Drama League of New York Playwriting Award, Finalist, *Still Waters*, 1988

Mark A. Klein Award for Playwriting, 1990

New York Foundation for the Arts Playwriting Fellowship, *Still Waters*, 1991

Van Lier Fellowship, New Dramatists, New York, 1993–1995

Julliard School Fellowship in Playwriting, 1993

Act One/Showtime One-Act Festival, Hollywood, California, Winner, *Waltzing de Niro*, 1994

W. Alton Jones Foundation Grant, *Psyche Was Here*, 1994

DESCRIPTIVE AND CRITICAL RESPONSES

Bruckner, D.J.R. ''Black Ink: 3 Comedies and Death.'' Review of *The Bodhisattva Locksmith*. *New York Times*, 7 December 1995, C18.
Weber, Bruce. ''The New Renaissance in American Theatre.'' *Interview Magazine*, February 1994, 44–45.

ROBBIE MCCAULEY

(1942–   )

BIOGRAPHY

Robbie McCauley, born in Norfolk, Virginia, in 1942, spent most of her child-hood in Columbus, Georgia, and Washington, D.C. She became involved with experimental and black theatre after moving to New York in the mid-1960s. As an actress, she has performed in Ed Bullins's *The Taking of Miss Janie*, **Ntozake Shange**'s *For Colored Girls . . .* and **Adrienne Kennedy**'s *A Movie Star Has to Star in Black and White* and *Cities in Bezique*. She studied playwriting at the Playwrights' Workshop of the Negro Ensemble Company in New York.

McCauley and Ed Montgomery met in 1979 and they formed the Sedition Ensemble which performed political jazz works, a melange of improvised text and music. She and Montgomery were married, and although he continues to write music for some of McCauley's productions, their working relationship changed. She began an association with Laurie Carlos and **Jessica Hagedorn**, which collaborated under the name Thought Music. McCauley also began her "personal biographical work," in which she explores her personal past within the larger historical context.

McCauley continues to write and perform her own work and is expanding her career as a director. Her most recent directing project was the 1996 Signature Theatre production of Adrienne Kennedy's *The Alexander Plays*.

PLAY DESCRIPTIONS

Although Robbie McCauley's work has metamorphosed into various forms and shapes throughout her almost twenty-year playwriting career, "the issues are the same: Bearing witness to racism" (Patraka, 44). Despite the diversity, the works can be characterized by McCauley's interest in poetry, music, and mixed media. In her works, structured as interconnected scenes, McCauley is more interested in the accumulation of powerful images than in the coherent through line of traditional drama.

In the pieces created for Thought Music, McCauley, Carlos, and Hagedorn explore shared interests not only in poetry and music, but in their common concerns as women of color in a dominant white society. In *Teenytown*, for example, they deconstruct many of the stereotypes and myths that perpetuate racism and sexism. The prologue is an ironic send-up of the minstrel show followed by an Oprah Winfrey–type interview of black entertainers Dorothy Dandridge and Hazel Scott. These scenes are followed in rapid succession with a torch-song eulogy to a friendship, a musical genealogy of black music and its influence on white icons, imagistic reminiscences of their childhood homes, and a send-up of Johnny Carson and "The Tonight Show," among others.

Robbie McCauley's personal family stories include *My Father and the Wars* and *Indian Blood*. The political is inevitably entwined with the personal in these explorations of black manhood in white America; they are also tributes to her own father and grandfather. The plays are critiques of a society in which black men serve in the armed forces, fighting in the name of freedom while their own freedom and liberties are denied; on the personal level, however, the plays bear witness to the smaller, daily wars of survival encountered by black men in an oppressive, racist society.

McCauley turns to the testimony of the women in her family in *Sally's Rape*, which draws on the account of her grandmother's rape by the white plantation owner to personalize American racial and sexual oppression. She divides the audience into three groups and asks them to respond at designated points in the play to employ the audience's verbal participation as a strategy to elicit a greater understanding of their complicity in contemporary racism and sexism.

With *The Buffalo Project* McCauley began a series of site-specific community collaborations that historicize the racial history of a particular geographical area through the stories gathered from those people who lived through the incidents. *The Buffalo Project* explores the 1967 riots in Buffalo, New York. This was followed by *The Mississippi Project*, which delineates the voting rights and civil rights struggles of African Americans in Mississippi during the 1960s. *The Boston Project* explores the 1993 busing issues in that city.

SELECTED PRODUCTION HISTORY

The History of the Universe according to Those Who've Had to Live It (a Sedition Ensemble piece written by McCauley and Ed Montgomery)
  Production, La Mama, New York, 1980

Calling Out! (a Sedition Ensemble piece written by McCauley and Ed Montgomery)
  Production, La Mama, New York, 1983

Loisaida War Party (a Sedition Ensemble piece written by McCauley and Ed Montgom-

ery)
   Production, Charas, New York, 1983

San Juan Hill (also grouped under the collective title *Confessions of a Working-Class Black Woman*)
   Production, Brecht Auditorium, New York, 1983

Nicaragua in Perspective (a Sedition Ensemble piece written by McCauley and Ed Montgomery)
   Production, Off Center Theatre and Taller Latino Americano, New York, 1984

My Father and the Wars (also grouped under the collective title *Confessions of a Working-Class Black Woman*)
   Production, Franklin Furnace, New York, 1985

Indian Blood (also grouped under the collective title *Confessions of a Working-Class Black Woman*)
   Production, The Kitchen, New York, 1987

Congo New York (cowritten with Ed Montgomery)
   Production, New Museum of Contemporary Art, New York, 1988

Part Two: Thinking Out Loud (collaboration with Thought Music)
   Production, Danspace Project, St. Mark's Church, New York, 1988

Teenytown (collaboration with Thought Music)
   Production, Franklin Furnace, New York, 1988

Heat (collaboration between Thought Music and the Urban Bush Women)
   Production, The Kitchen, New York, 1988

Sally's Rape (collaboration with Jeannie Hutchins)
   Production, New York University, New York, 1989
   Production, P. S. 122, New York, 1989 (work in progress)
   Production, BACA Downtown, Brooklyn, New York, 1989
   Production, Studio Museum of Harlem, New York, 1989
   Production, The Kitchen, New York, 1990

The Buffalo Project (site-specific community collaboration)
   Production, Hallwalls Contemporary Art Center, Buffalo, New York, 1990
   Production, Langston Hughes Institute, Buffalo, New York, 1990
   Production, Polish Community Center, Buffalo, New York, 1990
   Production, Diverse Works, Houston, Texas, 1993

Persimmon Peel (collaboration with Thought Music)
   Production, La Mama, New York, 1990
   Production, Working Theatre, New York, 1992

The Food Show (collaboration with Thought Music)
   Production, Nuyorican Poet's Cafe, New York, 1992

The Mississippi Project (site-specific community collaboration)
   Production, Smith Robertson Museum, Jackson, Mississippi, 1992
   Production, Rural Organizing & Cultural Center, Lexington, Mississippi, 1992

The Other Weapon
   Production, Hollywood Moguls Theatre, Los Angeles, 1994

PLAY AVAILABILITY

Sally's Rape is published in Sydné Mahone, ed., *Moon Marked and Touched by Sun*. New York: Theatre Communications Group, 1994.

Teenytown is published in Lenora Champagne, ed., *Out from Under: Texts by Women Performance Artists*. New York: Theatre Communications Group, 1990.

AWARDS

Obie Award, Best Play, Cowinner, *Sally's Rape*, 1992

AUDELCO Award, 1992

DESCRIPTIVE AND CRITICAL RESPONSES

Breslauer, Jan. "An Amateurish *Other Weapon*." Review of *The Other Weapon*. *Los Angeles Times*, 11 March 1994, F18.

Dworkin, Norine. "Sally's Rape." Review of *Sally's Rape*. *High Performance* 15 (Spring 1992): 51.

Howell, John. "Robbie McCauley, *Indian Blood*." Review of *Indian Blood*. *Artforum* 26 (January 1988): 120–21.

McCauley, Robbie. "Introduction to *Sally's Rape*." In *Moon Marked and Touched by Sun*, edited by Sydné Mahone, 213–17. New York: Theatre Communications Group, 1994.

———. "Mississippi Freedom: South and North." *Theatre* 24. 2 (1993): 88–98.

Patraka, Vivian. "Obsessing in Public." Interview with Robbie McCauley. *The Drama Review* 37, no. 2 (Summer 1993): 25–55.

Rosenfeld, Megan. "Spectators at Stage Center: Robbie McCauley Makes Audience Part of Her Performance." *Washington Post*, 5 May 1994, D2.

Sandford, Mariellen R. "Performing Performance Art." *High Performance* 9, no. 2 (1986): 46–49.

Thompson, Deborah. "Blackface, Rape and Beyond: Rehearsing Interracial Dialogue in *Sally's Rape*." *Theatre Journal* 48, no. 2 (May 1996): 123–39.

Whyte, Raewyn. "Robbie McCauley: Speaking History Other-Wise." In *Acting Out: Feminist Performances*, edited by Lynda Hart and Peggy Phelan, 277–93. Ann Arbor: University of Michigan Press, 1993.

CASSANDRA MEDLEY

(1949–)

BIOGRAPHY

Cassandra Medley, who is from Detroit, Michigan, attended the University of Michigan. She served as the literary manager for the American Place Theatre in New York City for five years. Medley taught a playwriting workshop for the Women's Studies Program at Barnard College and for the Montefiore Medical Center Residency Program. She initiated the Playwrights-in-Residence Program, a summer-long dramaturg intensive for individual playwrights at the Ensemble Studio Theatre National Theatre Conference and served as director for the program. Medley's continued association with the Ensemble Studio Theatre of New York includes teaching the Advanced Playwriting Laboratory during the year and an Advanced Playwriting Workshop for the Ensemble Theatre Conference every summer.

Cassandra Medley also teaches playwriting at Sarah Lawrence College and Columbia University. She has served as resident guest faculty with the University of Iowa Playwrights Workshop and is currently writing for television.

PLAY DESCRIPTIONS

Cassandra Medley's plays explore the nuances of human relationships with both humor and compassion. Her vibrant and colorful language contributes to the creation of compelling characters who successfully convey a type while retaining their distinct individuality. The monologue *Ms. Mae* features a seventy-two-year-old black woman at the beauty parlor who chats up the beautician. Ms. Mae relates the story of an attractive young woman on the subway who had her wig stolen right off her head during rush hour. The monologue is a unique mixture of comic image and humiliating pathos as the fashion plate is reduced to a "nappy-headed pickaninny" in front of a trainful of white passengers. Her one-act monologue *Waking Women* evokes Ms. Edie, a working-class black woman in her mid-fifties, who arrives at her neighbor Lucille's house with a potted plant and consolation for Lucille, who has just lost her husband. Ms. Edie's one-sided conversation gradually reveals a caring but somewhat meddlesome woman. The focus of the conversation changes from the deceased Coleman to Ms. Edie's niece and sister-in-law when her obsessive need to gossip overwhelms her sympathy. In relating the story of her niece's pregnancy, despite all her mother's attempts to insulate her daughter from the ways of the world, Medley weaves a poignant and yet humorous tale of kinship, friendship, love, and caring.

By also setting *Ma Rose* at a time of personal crisis, Medley is able to plumb the depths of familial responsibility and love. A Midwestern black family has gathered to determine what course of action to take for the care of the aging matriarch whose "mind ain't right." Vera-Rose, Ma Rose's daughter in her late fifties, is joined by her daughter, Rosa, a successful businesswomen in her mid-thirties, her brother, Wayman, and his wife, Ethel. The issue of Ma Rose's care becomes a family battleground when various family members recommend different solutions. By pitting Rosa against her mother and uncle, Medley has painted a timely portrait of generational conflict centered on elder care. By using flashbacks in Rosa's mind, Medley enables us to see not only the aging Ma Rose but also the strong family leader of the past whose legacy to her granddaughter is the soul-saving value of "having a reunion with yourself."

The one-act play *Dearborn Heights* provides Medley the opportunity to examine the larger sociological issue of segregation and prejudice through an intimate luncheon of two women in suburban Detroit in 1952. Clare, an older woman, is trying to persuade Grace, a young woman who has recently arrived from Knoxville, to join a local ladies club. The class discrimination so prevalent among blacks at the time is just as destructive to their relationship as the more blatant segregation in the diner when the women gradually realize that they are in a "whites only" eating establishment that will not serve them.

SELECTED PRODUCTION HISTORY

Ms. Mae (monologue produced as portion of *A . . . My Name Is Alice*)
  Production, Top of the Village Gate, New York, 1984
  Subsequent extensive production history

terrain
  Staged reading, New Voices Series, Ensemble Studio Theatre, New York, 1984
  Staged reading, Women's Project and Productions, New York, 1984
  Staged reading, Group Theatre, Seattle, 1984
  Staged reading, McCarter Theatre Center, Princeton, New Jersey, 1986

Pay Our Respects
  Production, 52nd Street Project, New York, 1986

Ma Rose (one-act version)
   Production, Marathon, Ensemble Studio Theatre, New York, 1986
Waking Women
   Production, Marathon, Ensemble Studio Theatre, New York, 1987
   Production, Blackberries Productions, Women's Shelters, New York, 1991
Ma Rose (full-length version)
   Production, Women's Project and Productions, New York, 1988
   Production, Eureka Theatre, San Francisco, 1990
   Production, Indiana Repertory Company, Indianapolis, 1996
New Kid
   Production, 52nd Street Project, New York, 1992
Coming in for a Landing
   Production, Women's Project and Productions, New York, 1993
The Senator (one-act children's play)
   Production, 52nd Street Project, New York, 1993
Noon Day Sun
   Production, Ensemble Studio Theatre Octoberfest, New York, 1994
Dearborn Heights
   Production, Marathon, Ensemble Studio Theatre, New York, 1995

PLAY AVAILABILITY

Dearborn Heights is published in Marisa Smith, ed., *EST Marathon '95: The Complete One-Act Plays*. Lyme, New Hampshire: Smith and Kraus, 1995.

Ma Rose is published by Samuel French, 45 West 25th Street, New York, New York 10010–2751; and in Julia Miles, ed., *WomensWork: Five New Plays from the Women's Project*. New York: Applause, 1989.

Mildred (one act) is published in *Muleteeth Magazine* (August 1993) and in *13th Moon Magazine* (December 1991).

Ms. Mae is published in *A . . . My Name Is Alice* available through Samuel French, 45 West 25th Street, New York, New York 10010–2751.

Waking Women is published in Daniel Halpern, ed., *Plays in One Act*. New York: Ecco Press, 1991; Sven Birkerts, ed., *Literature and the Evolving Canon*. Boston: Allyn and Bacon, 1993.

Waking Women, Coming in for a Landing, and *By the Still Waters* are available through her agent: Greg Wagoner, Writers and Artists Agency, 19 West 44th Street, Suite 100, New York, New York 10036; (212) 391–1112.

AWARDS

Minority Playwright's Festival, Seattle, Finalist, *terrain*, 1984

New York Foundation for the Arts Grant, 1987

Susan Smith Blackburn Award in Playwriting, Finalist, *Ma Rose*, 1989

National Endowment for the Arts Grant in Playwriting, 1990

Marilyn Simpson Award, 1994

Professional Theatre Playwrights Award, 1994

Artistic Fellowships with the Albee Foundation, the Blue Mountain Center, the Mac-Dowell Colony, and Yaddo

DESCRIPTIVE AND CRITICAL RESPONSES

Brantley, Ben. "A Mamet Scorcher in a One-Act Series." Review of *Dearborn Heights*. *New York Times*, 3 June 1995, A13, 16.

Gussow, Mel. "Theatre: Four One-Acts in Ensemble Studio Series." Review of *Waking Women. New York Times*, 3 June 1987, C18.

———. "Waging War on Family and Time." Review of *Ma Rose. New York Times*, 22 October 1988, 14.

Rosenberg, Scott. "*Ma Rose*: Anatomy of a Family Crisis." Review of *Ma Rose. San Francisco Examiner*, 22 March 1990, C3.

MARLANE MEYER

(n.d.–   )

BIOGRAPHY

Born in San Francisco and raised in San Pedro, California, Marlane Meyer is of Polynesian and Native American (Cherokee) ancestry on her father's side and German and Swedish on her mother's side. She attended California State University-Long Beach where she studied under Murray Mednick, one of the founders of the Padua Hills Festival. She was the dramaturg for the Latino Actor's Workshop at the Los Angeles Theatre Center in 1986.

Meyer has a bicoastal career; she has worked in both Los Angeles and New York. In addition to a successful television writing career, including episodes of ''Sirens'' (ABC), the teleplay of ''Better Off Dead'' (Lifetime), ''Life Stories'' for NBC, and ''Out of the Sixties'' for HBO, she teaches playwriting at the Yale School of Drama. Meyer is a member of the New York Playwrights Lab, the Dramatists Guild, the Women's Project, PEN Center West, and the Polynesian Society, and she is an alumna of New Dramatists.

PLAY DESCRIPTIONS

Marlane Meyer writes in a style that she describes as ''extended realism''; it is a gritty, evocative melding of poetry with the underbelly of popular culture. *Etta Jenks*, for example, employs twenty-one scenes and fourteen characters to depict one woman's journey through the Los Angeles pornography business. Meyer gives the cliched tale of small-town-girl-arriving-in-the-big-city-to-pursue-her-dream-of-a-film-career a contemporary, ironic twist. Frustrated by her lack of success in the legitimate film industry, Etta falls prey to the money and success promised by the porno business. Through her intelligence, cynicism, and energy, Etta successfully wends her way around or over the pimps, hustlers, and hitmen who populate her world. While working her way up the porno ladder, Etta becomes one of the vendors in the Hollywood meat market by scouting talent and eventually calling the shots. The world of skin and sin is vividly fleshed out with sleezeball characters and philosophical musings. A touch of the spiritual—the out-of-body experience of one of Etta's private "girls"—alters Etta, adding surprise and depth.

In *The Geography of Luck*, Meyer explores the seamier side of Las Vegas in dreamlike and mythic terms. A released convict and former hot singer falls for the stepdaughter of his jailmate. While Vegas lowlifes wheel and deal, the play inquires into the commitments and betrayals of love by evoking haunting imagery and using striking language.

Moe's Lucky Seven is a modern retelling of the Adam, Eve, and snake tale. The contemporary Eden is a dockside bar, Moe's Lucky Seven. Two denizens of the bar, Tiny and Knuckles, tell the story which then unfolds between their scenes. Initially attracted to the snake but frightened of his concept of sex for pleasure, Eve leaves the snake for Adam. The snake's modern manifestation is Drake, the wise and psychic bartender at Moe's. Patsy (Eve's modern equivalent) returns after a long absence in search of Drew (Moe's son and Adam's contemporary counterpart). Drew and Patsy's on-again-off-again relationship is strained when he discovers that she is pregnant and wants to get married, but Drew is finally convinced to do the right thing. On her wedding day, however, Patsy disappears. Meyer's bar world is peopled with colorful characters who explore the transformative power of love and the animalistic nature of human beings.

SELECTED PRODUCTION HISTORY

Starfish and *Strays*
   Production, Uprising Theatre, Long Beach, California, 1986

The Kingfish
   Workshop, Padua Hills Festival, Claremont, California, 1986
   Production, Los Angeles Theatre Center, Los Angeles, 1988
   Production, Public Theatre, New York, 1989
   Production, Magic Theatre, San Francisco, 1995

Etta Jenks
   Production, Los Angeles Theater Center, Los Angeles, 1988
   Production, Women's Project, New York, 1988

The Geography of Luck
   Production, South Coast Repertory, Costa Mesa, California, 1989
   Production, Los Angeles Theater Center, Los Angeles, 1989
   Production, Steppenwolf, Chicago, 1990
   Production, Gilgamesh Theatre, New York, 1995

Relativity (one-act play)
   Production, Women's Project at the Judith Anderson Theatre, New York, 1991

Lon Shaw (later *Why Things Burn*)
  Reading, Public Theatre, New York, 1992

Moe's Lucky Seven
  Reading, New Works Festival, Mark Taper Forum, Los Angeles, 1993
  Production, Playwrights Horizons, New York, 1994

Why Things Burn
  Production, Magic Theatre, San Francisco, 1994

PLAY AVAILABILITY

Etta Jenks is published in Julia Miles, ed., *WomensWork: Five New Plays from the Women's Project.* New York: Applause, 1989; *Plays in Process*, vol. 9, no. 7. New York: Theatre Communications Group, 1988.

The Geography of Luck is published in *Plays in Process*, vol. 11, no. 9. New York: Theate Communications Group, 1991.

Moe's Lucky Seven is published in Marisa Smith, ed., *Women Playwrights: The Best Plays of 1994.* Lyme, New Hampshire: Smith and Kraus, 1995.

AWARDS

Kesselring Award for New Play, *Etta Jenks*, 1987

Dramalogue Award, *Etta Jenks*, 1987

Susan Smith Blackburn Prize, Finalist, *Etta Jenks*, 1987

Brody Foundation Grant for Literature, 1987

Dramalogue Award, *Kingfish*, 1988

Susan Smith Blackburn Prize, Finalist, *Kingfish*, 1989

Dramalogue Award, *Geography of Luck*, 1989

PEN Center West Award, *Kingfish*, 1989

Susan Smith Blackburn Prize, Finalist, *Geography of Luck*, 1990

National Endowment for the Arts Playwriting Fellowship, 1990

Susan Smith Blackburn Prize, Winner, *Moe's Lucky Seven*, 1993

DESCRIPTIVE AND CRITICAL RESPONSES

Arkatov, Janice. "A Think Piece on the Pornography Industry." *Los Angeles Times*, 15 January 1988, VI, 8.
Dolan, Jill. "Gender, Sexuality and 'My Life' in the (University)." *Kenyon Review* 15 (Spring 1993): 185–200.
Gussow, Mel. "Hollywood Ambitions, Cold Realities." Review of *Etta Jenks*. *New York Times*, 14 April 1988, C26.

———. "Kingfish, an Exercise in Absurdism." *New York Times*, 22 December 1989, C5.

Herman, Jan. "The Tough, Tender World of Playwright Meyer." *Los Angeles Times*, 26 August 1989, V1.

SUSAN MILLER

(1944–   )

BIOGRAPHY

Miller grew up in Hazelton, Pennsylvania, received her BA from Penn State University, and earned an MA in English literature from Bucknell University. She has sustained a career writing for stage, television, and film since the early 1970s, first on the West Coast and then in New York City. Theatres that have produced her work include the Mark Taper Forum in Los Angeles, the New York Public Theatre, and the Actors Theatre of Louisville in Louisville, Kentucky. She has written for the television shows "thirtysomething," "L.A. Law," and "The Trials of Rosie O'Neill." In her autobiographical one-person play, *My Left Breast*, Miller says, "I am a one-breasted, menopausal, Jewish, bisexual, lesbian Mom and I am the topic of our times." Miller's life experiences, chronicled in her largely autobiographical plays, range from an examination of the ending of a marriage in *Cross Country* to her bout with breast cancer. Miller admits: "In *My Left Breast*, like in *Cross Country*, I've become a character, and what has happened in my life seems to resonate with broader implications" (Scasserra, 81). Miller teaches dramatic writing at New York University and directs the Legacy Project at the Public Theater, a writing project for people with life-threatening illnesses.

PLAY DESCRIPTIONS

Miller's central character in her plays is a contemporary woman who, informed by a 1970s feminist outlook, struggles with her sense of identity and sexuality. Frankly confessional in tone, the plays use distortions in time and devices such as a chorus of voices in an otherwise realistic style. In *Confessions of a Female Disorder* her protagonist, Ronnie, is confused by her feelings for a girlfriend and her desire to "get laid." Ronnie's history is charted from her enthusiastic embrace of heterosexuality to her marriage and then her questioning of her sexuality when her former college girlfriend comes to visit. The play uses a chorus of cheerleaders and lettermen who, in the style of early feminist-inspired plays, clinically discuss her first menstrual period and her sexual experiences with men. The play moves back and forth in time with appearances from David, her husband, and a psychiatrist in the first-act college scenes. Ronnie becomes Perry in *Cross Country* (continuing Miller's preference for women characters with male names) and David, the patient husband of *Confessions*, is Dan, whom Perry leaves after their child dies at birth. This is followed by an affair with a woman, the adoption of a baby boy, and a move to the West Coast to write. *My Left Breast*, Miller's first openly autobiographical play, uses her own name to tell about her mastectomy, the breakup of an eight-year relationship with a woman, and her love for her adopted son. She performs this one-woman play herself.

SELECTED PRODUCTION HISTORY

Confessions of a Female Disorder
Production, Mark Taper Forum, Los Angeles, 1973

Flux
Production, Public Theatre, New York, 1976
Production, American Repertory Company, London, 1976
Production, Second Stage, New York, 1982

Cross Country
Production, Mark Taper Forum, Los Angeles, 1976
Production, Interart Theatre, New York, 1977

Nasty Rumors and Final Remarks
Production, Public Theatre, New York, 1979
Production, St. Nicholas Theatre, Chicago, 1980

Arts and Leisure
Production, CAST Theatre, Los Angeles, 1985

For Dear Life
Production, Public Theatre, New York, 1989

Repairs
Production, HOME for Contemporary Theatre and Art, New York, 1989

It's Our Town, Too
Production, Fountainhead Theatre, Los Angeles, 1992

My Left Breast
Production, Actors Theatre of Louisville, Louisville, Kentucky, 1994
Production, Watermark Theatre, New York, 1995 and 1996
Production, Trinity Repertory Company, Boston, 1996
Production, New Heights Theatre, Houston, Texas, 1996

PLAY AVAILABILITY

Confessions of a Female Disorder is published in William Hoffman, ed., *Gay Plays.* New York: Avon, 1979.

Cross Country is published in *West Coast Plays: Outstanding New Plays from the Coast.* Berkeley: West Coast Plays, 1977.

It's Our Town, Too is anthologized in Howard Stein and Glenn Young, eds., *The Best American Short Plays of 1992–93.* New York: Applause, 1994; and Eric Lane and Nina Shengold, eds. *The Actor's Book of Gay and Lesbian Plays.* New York: Penguin Books, 1995.

My Left Breast is published in Marisa Smith, ed., *Humana Festival '94: The Complete Plays.* Lyme, New Hampshire: Smith and Kraus, 1994.

Nasty Rumors is published in Rosemary Curb, ed., *Amazon All Stars: Thirteen Lesbian Plays.* New York: Applause, 1996.

Repairs is published in Leah Frank, ed., *Facing Forward.* New York: Broadway Play Publishing, 1994.

Unpublished plays may be obtained from the Joyce Ketay Agency, 1501 Broadway, Suite 1910, New York, New York 10036; (212) 354–6825.

AWARDS

O'Neill National Playwriting Conference, 1973

Rockefeller Foundation Grant in Playwriting, 1975

National Endowment for the Arts, 1976 and 1983

Obie Award, *Nasty Rumors and Final Remarks*, 1979

Susan Smith Blackburn, Finalist, *Nasty Rumors and Final Remarks*, 1980

Yaddo Fellow, 1984

Susan Smith Blackburn, Finalist, *For Dear Life*, 1989

Susan Smith Blackburn, Winner, *My Left Breast*, 1995

Robert Chesley Playwriting Award for Lifetime Achievement, 1996

DESCRIPTIVE AND CRITICAL RESPONSES

Benzel, Jan. "They Talk a Lot, but at Least They're Trying." *New York Times*, 8 January 1989, II5.
Dace, Tish. "Inner Truths of Feminine Psyche Brought to Life by Playwright Susan Miller." *Advocate*, Los Angeles, 21 January 1989.
Drake, Sylvie. "The Inward Journey of a Playwright." *Los Angeles Times*, 18 March 1976, 4, 21.
———. "Stage Watch." *Los Angeles Times*, 11 July 1985.
Feeny, Sheila. "Greater than the Sum of Her Parts." *Daily News*, New York, 1 February 1995, 40.

Gussow, Mel. "Stage: Public's *Nasty Rumors*." Review of *Nasty Rumors*. *New York Times*, 13 April 1979, C3.

Pearce, Michele. "Louisville Sizzles." *American Theatre*, July/August 1991, 54.

Rich, Frank. "Hanging on to All the Right Attitudes Articulately." *New York Times*, 11 January 1989, C17.

Scasserra, Michael. "Self-Examination." *Village Voice*, 7 February 1995, 81–82.

CHIORI MIYAGAWA

(1961–)

BIOGRAPHY

Chiori Miyagawa is a playwright, dramaturg, poet, and fiction writer. She was dramaturg at the Berkeley Repertory Theatre, artistic associate at New York's Public Theatre under JoAnne Akalaitis, literary manager at the Arena Stage, Washington, D.C., and assistant literary manager at Actors Theater of Louisville in Louisville, Kentucky. She has also worked with New York University Tisch School of the Arts Graduate Program, the American Conservatory Theater, and the Young Playwrights Festival. She designed and led the Asian American Playwrights Lab at the Public Theatre and curated and coproduced "Out of the Shadows," a festival of plays and performances that opened the Dance Theater Workshop's thirtieth anniversary season. In the fall of 1996, she curated "Out of the Shadows II: A Celebration of Women" for Dance Theater Workshop.

She is currently artistic associate of the New York Theatre Workshop where she served as dramaturg for Joanne Akalaitis's adaptation and the New York Theatre Workshop production of Jean Genet's *Prisoner of Love*. Under the auspices of the New York Theatre Workshop, she runs a playwriting fellowship for emerging playwrights of color. A short fiction version of *Nothing Forever* was published in 1995. Her chapter on Asian American women playwrights appears in this volume. Miyagawa teaches playwriting at New York University and at The Writers' Voice in New York.

PLAY DESCRIPTIONS

Miyagawa's plays are imagistic, nonlinear explorations of character which combine text and music. *Nothing Forever* is a poetic collage of unresolved memories, alienation, and uncertain hope. A Japanese woman struggles to come to terms with her past and make a decision on the new life she carries inside her. The story is told by a Japanese woman and a non-Asian woman who play characters from the Japanese woman's memory. There is also a man at a piano who sings as the main character's inner voice. The epilogue to *Nothing Forever* is the short play *Yesterday's Window* which depicts a conversation between the main character and her daughter, who may be imaginary. The conversation is constantly being interrupted by a man who delivers memories.

In *America Dreaming*, an Asian American woman's journey through distorted history and false memories ends up with her self-knowledge. Within a series of surreal reveries, the play enacts the poetic love story between the woman, Yuki, and a young Caucasian man, Robert. Within her evocative dreamscape, Yuki explores the attraction/repulsion dynamic of Eastern and Western, past and present.

Firedance explores the question of what will happen if the moment-to-moment reality that we create and desperately hold onto in life is suddenly confirmed. The story follows a woman who gets caught in a false reality that becomes true. *The Huntsville Project: Death Row Factory* is based on the stories of death row inmates incarcerated in the Huntsville, Texas, prison and was commissioned by the Dallas Theatre Center.

SELECTED PRODUCTION HISTORY

America Dreaming (music by Tan Dun)
Staged reading, New York Theatre Workshop, New York, 1993
Production, Vineyard Theatre, New York, 1994

Nothing Forever (play with music; piano score by Fabian Obispo, lyrics by Mark and Campbell)
Workshop, New York Theatre Workshop, 1996

Yesterday's Window
Workshop, Just Add Water Festival, New York Theatre Workshop, New York, 1994
Production, New York Theatre Workshop, New York, 1996

Firedance
Reading, American Conservatory Theatre, San Francisco, 1996
Workshop, Just Add Water Festival, New York Theatre Workshop, New York, 1996

The Huntsville Project: Death Row Factory
Production, Dallas Theatre Center, Texas, 1997

PLAY AVAILABILITY

Plays are available through the playwright: Chiori Miyagawa, 125 Christopher Street, Apt. 2G, New York, New York 10014.

AWARDS

Van Lier Playwriting Fellowship, 1990
Drama Desk Award, nomination, *America Dreaming*, 1994

New York Foundation for the Arts Playwriting Fellowship, 1994

Rockefeller Multi-Arts Foundation Grant, 1994

DESCRIPTIVE AND CRITICAL RESPONSES

Backalenick, Irene. Review of *America Dreaming*. *Back Stage*, 30 December 1994, 29.
Holden, Stephen. "The Melting Pot Myth Unmasked." *New York Times*, 21 December 1994, C19.
Sales, Cristina C. "Chiori Miyagawa: Bridging the Gap." *American Theatre*, October 1994, 74–75.

CHERRÍE MORAGA

(1952–)

BIOGRAPHY

Cherríe Moraga, who was born in Whittier, California, earned a BA in English from Immaculate Heart College of Los Angeles in 1974. She taught English in Providence High School in Burbank, California, before she received a master's degree in feminist studies from San Francisco State University in 1980.

Moraga is a writer whose career defies easy categorization or discernible boundaries. As a playwright, poet, and storyteller, she gives voice to her own Chicana lesbian feminist activist history; as an editor and publisher, she gives voice to other people's histories. In 1981 Moraga and Gloria Anzaldua edited the groundbreaking anthology *This Bridge Called My Back: Writings by Radical Women of Color*; the collection was published by the Kitchen Table: Women of Color Press, a press she help cofound to ensure that women of color would have an outlet for their writing. She served as an editor with the press until 1985. Moraga was coeditor and contributor to *Cuentos: Stories by Latinas*, an anthology of fiction published in 1983, and *Third Woman: The Sexuality of Latinas* in 1989. These were followed by two books of poetry and essays: *Loving in the War Years* in 1983 and *The Last Generation* in 1993. She also served as editorial consultant and business manager for *Conditions Magazine* (Brooklyn, New York) from 1982 to 1983.

Morraga's teaching career also reflects the diversity of her writing and editorial works. She has been an instructor of women's studies at the University of Massachusetts and San Francisco State University. As an instructor in literature, she taught at Stanford University and California State University at Hayward. She was an instructor in writing for Chicano studies at the University of California-Berkeley from 1986 to 1991 and an instructor for writing for performance at Stanford University in 1994 and 1995. Since 1991 Moraga has been an artist in residence and instructor in creative writing at BRAVA! for Women in the Arts in San Francisco, where the majority of her plays are developed and premiered.

Cherríe Moraga continues to live and work in the Bay Area of San Francisco.

PLAY DESCRIPTIONS

Cherríe Moraga's first play, *Giving Up the Ghost*, is a poetic exploration of the life-cycle of a relationship. We are introduced to three characters whose lives and memories fluidly intertwine and frequently occupy the same space emotionally if not physically. Marisa, a Chicana in her late twenties, is the emotional center of this memory play. Through her we are introduced to Amelia, a Mexican-born woman in her fifties, and Corky, Marisa's younger, tougher self at the ages of twelve and seventeen. Amelia, a heterosexual woman who is disgusted (at least temporarily) with men, gradually enters into an emotional and physical relationship with the lesbian Marisa as their shared interest in art evolves. Yet the renewed passion and sense of freedom that Amelia finds in this relationship is unable to fill the longing she feels. Her inherent heterosexuality and her desire to return to her homeland prevent Amelia from fully committing to a lasting relationship with Marisa. Corky, who is woven into the relationship enacted on stage, is the physical manifestation of Marisa's various selves. From an anger-driven young girl, who emulates the macho *cholo* style and denies her own femininity, Corky has become the more mature Marisa, who seeks the softness of Amelia. Corky's brutally vivid monologue about how she was raped in grade school is in sharp contrast to the tenderness that characterizes Marisa's relationship with Amelia.

Shadow of a Man (directed by **Maria Irene Fornes** at its San Francisco premiere), a family drama, blends the stories of a love triangle with a young Chicana's coming-of-age. The Rodriguez family is dominated by females, but it cannot escape the shadows of the men in their lives. Twelve-year-old Lupe, her aunt, Rosario; her sister, Leticia; and her mother, Hortensia form the emotional and physical support system for Manuel, Lupe's father. Manuel, a beer-and-tequila-sodden middle-aged husband, is suffering from a heart pain intensified by his anger and resentment at his wife and his compadre, Conrado, his wife's former lover. Manuel, burdened with suspicions and resentments, has created an atmosphere of sexual and emotional estrangement from his wife, who suffers silently yet loyally. Juxtaposed against the jaded, stultifying atmosphere of the Rodriguez home is Lupe's budding sexual and spiritual awareness. With awe and fear Lupe begins to construct her identity from hard-won wisdom and the lurking shadows that impact her young life.

Moraga's dramatic vision expands well beyond the family to address communal social issues in *Heroes and Saints*. In the play, based on the actual case of environmental degradation in McFarland, California, in the San Joaquin Valley, Moraga creates a miniature community struggling with the health hazards (increased incidence of cancer, birth defects, and miscarriages) of agricultural pesticides. She has peopled her drama with families who are leading the protest against the growers and those who chose to ignore the reality. Despite their political differences, however, the townspeople's bonds of community are strengthened during the course of the play. The dissolution of Dolores's family provides the focal point of the drama. Cerezita, her eighteen-year-old, grotesquely deformed daughter (born with no body, only a head) functions as the objective observer, commentator, and center of this emotionally charged drama. Although she is initially reluctant to hold the government responsible for their communal ills, Dolores comes to understand the necessity for political action when her family dies or disappears around her. It is from these farmworkers and innocent children that the contemporary heroes and saints are wrought.

SELECTED PRODUCTION HISTORY

Giving Up the Ghost
   Staged reading, At the Foot of the Mountain, Minneapolis, 1984
   Production, Front Room Theatre, Seattle, 1987
   Production, Theatre Rhinoceros, San Francisco, 1989

Shadow of a Man
   Development, Hispanic Playwrights-in-Residence Lab, INTAR, New York, 1985
   Staged reading, New Works Festival, Los Angeles Theatre Center, Los Angeles, 1989
   Production, American Conservatory Theatre Playroom, San Francisco, 1989
   Staged reading, Hispanic Playwrights' Festival, South Coast Repertory Theatre, Costa Mesa, CA, 1989
   Production, Eureka Theatre with BRAVA! for Women in the Arts, San Francisco, 1990
   Production, Latino Chicago Theatre, Chicago, 1992

Heroes and Saints
   Staged reading, Latino Lab, Los Angeles Theatre Center, Los Angeles, 1989
   Production, BRAVA! for Women in the Arts, San Francisco, 1992
   Production, Guadalupe Cultural Arts Center, San Antonio, Texas, 1992
   Production, Working Theatre, New York, 1995

Heart of the Earth (with music by Glen Valez)
   Production, INTAR, New York, 1995

Watsonville: Some Place Not Here
   Production, BRAVA! for Women in the Arts, San Francisco, 1996

PLAY AVAILABILITY

Giving Up the Ghost has been published in Cherríe Moraga, *Giving Up the Ghost.* Albuquerque, New Mexico: West End Press, 1986; Cherríe Moraga, *Heroes and Saints & Other Plays.* Albuquerque, New Mexico: West End Press, 1994.

Heroes and Saints has been published in Cherríe Moraga, *Heroes and Saints & Other*

Plays. Albuquerque, New Mexico: West End Press, 1994; Kathy A. Perkins and Roberta Uno, ed., *Contemporary Plays by Women of Color: An Anthology*. New York: Routledge, 1996.

Shadow of a Man has been published in Cherríe Moraga, *Heroes and Saints & Other Plays*. Albuquerque, New Mexico: West End Press, 1994; Linda Feyder, ed., *Shattering the Myth: Plays by Hispanic Women*. Houston, Texas: Arte Publico Press, 1992.

AWARDS

MacDowell Colony Fellowship (for poetry), 1982

Creative Arts Public Service (CAPS) Grant (for poetry), 1983

The American Book Award, 1986

California Arts Council Artists in Community Residency Award, 1991–1992

Kennedy Center Fund for New American Plays Award, *Shadow of a Man*, 1991

Southern California Women for Understanding Lesbian Rights Writers Award, 1991

The Outlook Foundation Literary Award, 1991

The Dramalogue Award for Playwriting, *Heroes and Saints*, 1992

The Will Glickman Playwriting Award, *Heroes and Saints*, 1992

The Critics' Circle Award for Best Original Script, *Heroes and Saints*, 1992

The Pen West Literary Award for Drama, *Heroes and Saints*, 1993

National Endowment for the Arts Theatre Playwrights' Fellowship, 1993

Kennedy Center Fund for New American Plays, *Watsonville*, 1995

DESCRIPTIVE AND CRITICAL RESPONSES

Alarcon, Norma. "Interview with Cherríe Moraga." *Third Woman* 3, no. 1–2 (1986): 124–34.

Berson, Misha. "*Shadow of Man* Brings to Light Machismo's Frailties." *San Francisco Chronicle*, 4 November 1990, DAT, 37.

DeRose, David J. "Cherríe Moraga." *American Theatre* 13, no. 8 (October 1996): 76–78.

Gelb, Hal. "Theater." Review of *Heroes and Saints*. *Nation* 255 (2 November 1992): 518–20.

Harvey, Dennis. "Reviews: *Heroes and Saints*." *Variety*, 27 April 1992, 101.

Huerta, Jorge. "Professionalizing Teatro: An Overview of Chicano Theatre during the 'Decade of the Hispanic.' " *Theatre Forum*. Spring 1993, 54–59.

Moraga, Cherríe. "Introduction to *Heroes and Saints*." In *Contemporary Plays by Women of Color*, edited by Kathy A. Perkins and Roberta Uno, 230–32. New York: Routledge, 1996.

Morales, Ed. "Shadowing Valdez." *American Theatre* 9, no. 7 (November 1992): 14–19.

Noyes, Katia. "The Dream Images of Cherríe Moraga." *San Francisco Sentinel*, 8 November 1990, 18.

Rosenberg, Lou. "The House of Difference: Gender, Culture and the Subject-in-Process on the American Stage." *Journal of Homosexuality*, 26, nos. 2–3 (1993): 97–110.

Umpierre, Luz Marie. "With Cherríe Moraga." *America's Review* 14, no. 2 (Summer 1986): 54–67.

Winn, Steven. "Macho Drives Drama of Latino Family." Review of *Shadow of a Man*. *San Francisco Chronicle*, 14 November 1990, E3.

———. "Protest Theatre Alive in the Mission." Review of *Heroes and Saints*. *San Francisco Chronicle*, 21 April 1992, E1.

Yarbro-Bejarano, Yvonne. "Cherríe Moraga's *Giving Up the Ghost*: The Representation of Female Desire." *Third Woman* 3, nos. 1–2 (1986): 113–20.

———. "The Female Subject in Chicano Theatre: Sexuality, 'Race,' and Class." *Theatre Journal* 38 (1986): 389–407.

———. "Cherríe Moraga's *Shadow of a Man*: Touching the Wounds in Order to Heal." In *Acting Out: Feminist Performance*, edited by Lynda Hart and Peggy Phelan, 85–104. Ann Arbor: University of Michigan Press, 1993.

LESLI-JO MORIZONO

(1957–)

BIOGRAPHY

Lesli-Jo Morizono's hometown is Berkeley, California, where she received a BA in psychology from the University of California. As a young girl, she dreamed of being an actress, and at the age of fifteen, she won an acting scholarship to the American Conservatory Theatre's Summer Congress Training Program. Morizono says, "Luckily, I learned in time that I didn't have the talent or a strong stomach for acting. Now I write plays and screenplays, something I enjoy enormously." In 1992 she graduated with an MFA in dramatic writing from New York University's Tisch School of the Arts. She lives with her husband, Toshio, and her dog, Washington (a.k.a. "mongrel from hell"), in New York City.

PLAY DESCRIPTIONS

Lesli-Jo Morizono's plays have a fantastical quality that transcends the realistic situations motivating the drama. In her short play *Fried Rice*, she depicts a humorous spiritual encounter between Mary, an Asian American, and Willie Wing, the African American proprietor of a Chinese restaurant located in the desert near the California-Nevada border. Mary stops into the restaurant on her way through the desert. After she sees God's face in a plate of deluxe fried rice, Willie begins to believe in and see the apparition. They both see what they want to see: Mary's God has Chinese features and will reveal the whereabouts of her muderous mother; Willie's God, complete with jerri curls, is his ticket to fame and franchises. As they argue over the validity of their own vision, their prejudices and racism erupt. Epithets and racial slurs are hurled at each other in rapid-fire manner, culminating only when the plate of fried rice is scattered on the floor. Blaming themselves for God's death, they are united in the end as they begin chopping vegetables for another plate of fried rice.

Morizono's full-length play *In the Valley of the Human Spirit* explores the reconciliation that Cory, a Japanese American woman in her thirties, ultimately achieves with her recently deceased father, Sam. Cory has returned to her California home to attend her father's funeral and to oversee the sale of his house. When the real estate agent leaves Cory alone to say her good-byes to her childhood home, Cory encounters her father's spirit in the house. The play interweaves the reality of Cory's final visit to her house with incarnations of her father at different times in his life. The flashbacks force Cory to understand her own shame in being Japanese and rejecting her father. As her past is revealed to her, Cory is able to accept her father and his cultural legacy. In the end, she decides to keep the house that bore the scars and joys of her family.

SELECTED PRODUCTION HISTORY

Dirty Business (10-minute play)
Staged reading, Public Theatre, New York, 1991

Fried Rice
Staged reading, Public Theatre, New York, 1993

In the Valley of the Human Spirit
Staged reading, National Playwrights Conference, Eugene O'Neill Theater Center, Waterford, Connecticut, 1993

The Nap
Staged reading, New York Theatre Workshop, New York, 1995

Now I Lie
Staged Reading, New York Theatre Workshop, New York, 1996

PLAY AVAILABILITY

Copies of scripts may by obtained through Morizono's agent: Helen Merrill, Ltd., 435 West 23rd Street, 1A, New York, New York 10011; (212) 691–5326.

AWARDS

Joe Callaway Award, New York University, Second Place, *In the Valley of the Human Spirit*, 1992

Eugene O'Neill National Playwrights Conference, 1993

PHYLLIS NAGY

(1960–   )

BIOGRAPHY

Born in New York City, Phyllis attended New York University Tisch School of the Arts in Dramatic Writing where she received her BFA with honors. She studied primarily with Len Jenkins. Nagy also minored in music theory and composition. In 1992 she moved to London where she now makes her home and writes for film, television, and radio as well as the theatre. Phyllis completed a feature-length film script, *The Night They Buried Judy Garland*, for BBC television and a one-hour teleplay, *Bait and Switch*, under commission. She has been playwright in residence at the Royal Court Theatre since 1974.

PLAY DESCRIPTIONS

Nagy's plays, often set in exotic environments, are highly atmospheric and theatrical and deal with characters who live at the fringes of society and whose behavior is frequently violent. The lyrical, at times ambiguous, language in the early plays has given way to a more direct dialogue in her current work. Sound plays an important role in the production of her plays. *Plaza Delores*, a surreal play that begins in the late 1980s, is set in a hotel in an indeterminate location, where three women and a young Marine live. Bright Eyes, a middle-aged poet, drifter, and ex-con, enters and marries the older Cibella while trying to seduce her daughter, Lola. He kills Lola while hitting her; however, her boyfriend, the Marine, is framed for the murder and subsequently hangs himself. The play closes with Lola singing triumphantly about being taken where she belongs, to the "valley of tears." The play, told in a series of nonchronological short scenes, is characterized by the mysterious behavior of its characters and rich symbolism.

In *Butterfly Kiss*, also from the 1980s, Lily murders her mother, and Martha,

Lily's lover, tries to discover the motive after Lily is imprisoned. Flashbacks, sparked by Lily's memories, are set in various locations: Jones Beach, a woman's bar, Queens, a high rise in Manhattan, and a patio in Fort Lauderdale. From these the story emerges of a grandmother and mother living off alcohol and dreams and an academic father isolated in his butterfly collection.

Awake takes place in a Brooklyn Heights alleyway positioned between two apartment buildings and the Jehovah's Witnesses Watchtower complex. Yvonne, a black Jehovah's Witness, is trying to escape by standing at the wire fence and calling for help. Living in apartments surrounding the complex are Ginger; her mama's-boy son, Clifford; and Jessie, a lesbian who is having relationship problems with her lover, Isabelle. By the end, a flood is on its way, Yvonne escapes, Clifford shoots his mother, and Jessie and Isabelle are reunited. The desperation of urban life is depicted, and concomitant themes of racism, prejudice, homelessness, and sexism are explored.

Weldon Rising, set during a brutally hot summer in the meat-packing district of New York, uses a gritty urban setting to convey a sense of apocalyptic happenings. The characters (two gay men, Natty and Marcus, a transvestite prostitute, and two lesbians) are traumatized by the fatal stabbing, shown in flashback, of Natty's lover, Jimmy. When the killing occurred, Natty ran away, Marcus froze in horror, and the two women called the police. None have been the same since. Marcus cannot get a customer, the two women steal useless items and drink beer, and Natty is unbalanced. The heat rises to 120 degrees, and the world begins to melt down. Characters combust when Jimmy's ghost gives a knife to Natty who rips up a map of the meat-packing district.

Seemingly disparate characters connect in *The Strip*, which premiered in 1995 in London. Ava Coo, an aspiring lounge singer described as a female impersonator, is instructed by the mysterious Otto Mink to find his Tumblewood Junction club where a singing gig may await her. She is accompanied on her journey from New Jersey to Las Vegas by Calvin Higgins, who came to repossess her car but fell for Ava instead, and Kate Buck, a down-and-out-journalist in search of a mass murderer, who also falls for Ava. Paralleling Ava's journey are the adventures of Ku Klux Klanner Lester Marquette and his wife and baby who have been escorted to London by Otto. Lester is abducted by Martin after he mistakenly wanders into a gay bar. Meanwhile, his wife, Loretta, persuades Martin's oppressed partner Tom to accompany her to Liverpool where they find justice and make plans to travel to Roanoke, Virginia. By the end, all the characters appear in Las Vegas and, as an earthquake rumbles, Otto emerges from the Sphinx replica at the Luxor Hotel to tell the assembly that he has what they want: booze, car stereos, and fax modems. In the final moment, a character tells the baby, ''We got possibilities, little fella, endless possibilities,'' and the baby lets out an ''unsettling cry.'' Astrology, extrasensory communication, and circumstance bring characters together in their pursuit of unrealistic dreams. Humor and theatricality help make this epic indictment of contemporary values engaging.

SELECTED PRODUCTION HISTORY

Plaza Delores
Production, Covered Bridges Theatre Company, Vermont, 1989

Butterfly Kiss
Workshop, New Works Festival, Los Angeles Theatre Centre, Los Angeles, 1990
Production, Almeida Theatre Company, London, 1994

Girl Bar
Workshop, Midwest PlayLabs, Minneapolis, 1990
Production, Loft Theatre, Tampa, Florida, 1992 and 1993
Production, Celebration Theatre, Los Angeles, 1994

Weldon Rising
Production, Royal Court Theatre (in association with the Liverpool Playhouse), London, 1992
Production, Lubeck Buhnen Hansestadt, Lubeck, Germany, 1994
Production, Beersheva Municipal Theatre, Israel, 1994

Entering Queens
Tour, Gay Sweatshop Theatre Company, United Kingdom, 1993

The Scarlet Letter (adapted from the novel by Nathaniel Hawthorne)
Production, Denver Centre Theatre, Denver, Colorado, 1994
Production, Classic Stage Company Repertory, New York, 1994
Production, New Repertory Theatre, Newton, Massachusetts, 1996

Trip's Cinch
Production, Humana Festival, Actors Theatre of Louisville, Louisville, Kentucky, 1994

Disappeared
Production, Leicester Haymarket Theatre/Midnight Theatre Company, England, 1995

The Strip
Production, Royal Court Theatre, London, 1995

PLAY AVAILABILITY

Butterfly Kiss is published by Nick Hern Books, London, 1994 (distributed through Theatre Communications Group).

Disappeared is published by Samuel French, 45 West 25th Street, New York, New York 10010–2751.

Girl Bar is available through Rain City Projects, Seattle, Washington, 1991.

The Scarlet Letter is published in *American Theatre*, February 1995.

The Strip is available from Nick Hern Books, London, 1995.

Trip's Cinch is published by Dramatic Publishing, P.O. Box 129, Woodstock, IL 60098; and in Marisa Smith, ed., *Humana Festival '95: The Complete Plays*. Lyme, New Hampshire: Smith and Kraus, 1994.

Weldon Rising is published in Annie Castledine, ed., *Plays by Women 10*. London: Methuen, 1994.

Weldon Rising and *Disappeared* are published together by Methuen, London, 1996, 1992.

Unpublished plays may be obtained from her agent: Mel Kenyon, Casarotto Ramsay Ltd., 60–66 Wardour Street, London W1V 3HP; 071–287–4450.

AWARDS

National Endowment for the Arts Playwriting Fellowship, Residency at the Mark Taper Forum, Los Angeles, 1989–1990

New York Foundation for the Arts Playwriting Fellowship, 1989–1990

McKnight Foundation Playwriting Fellowship, Residency at the Playwrights Center, Minneapolis, 1991

Runner-Up, Mobil International Playwriting Competition, 1992

National Endowment for the Arts Playwriting Fellowship, 1993–1994

Arts Council Playwright in Residence, Royal Court Theatre, London, 1994

Susan Smith Blackburn, Second Prize, *Disappeared*, 1995

DESCRIPTIVE AND CRITICAL RESPONSES

Armistead, Claire. "*Weldon Rising*." *Guardian*, Manchester, 14 December 1992, II 8.
Billington, Michael. "*Butterfly Kiss*." *Guardian*, Manchester, 18 April 1994, II 6.
Bradley, Jeff. "Scarlet Prophet of Feminism." *Denver Post*, 17 March 1994, E8.
Brantley, Ben. "Magnifying Metaphors in a Work Rich in Them." Review of *The Scarlet Letter*. *New York Times*, 20 October 1994, C18.
Canby, Vincent. "Dissecting Hawthorne." *New York Times*, 30 October 1994, II 36.
Stayton, Richard. "*Girl Bar*: Call it a Little-Seen Classic." *Los Angeles Times*, 18 March 1994, F25.

LYNN NOTTAGE

(1964–   )

BIOGRAPHY

Lynn Nottage is from Brooklyn, New York, where her interest in playwriting began in high school. Nottage attended Brown University, majored in American literature and creative writing, and earned a BA (with honors) in 1986. Although two of her plays were produced for the new play festival at Brown, Nottage considered playwriting a hobby until she was encouraged by her professor, **Paula Vogel**. Nottage attended Yale School of Drama where she got an MFA in playwriting in 1989.

After graduation from Yale, Lynn Nottage returned to New York and began working for Amnesty International where she served as interim communications director and press representative. The Amnesty experience influenced her playwriting in ways that were unexpected. A program note for *Poof!* stated:

Rather than discovering through her work material for her writing, Lynn found it difficult to deal with the issues that she confronted daily. Thus Lynn places her work into two categories: 'pre-Amnesty' and 'post-Amnesty.' Before her affiliation with AI her style was what she describes as "heavy and dramatic." Since then, though her plays deal with the same basic issues, she treats them "lighter and with more humor." This shift in perspective occurred through her need to divorce herself in some way from the emotional drain of other people's suffering which she experienced at work.

In addition to commissions received from the Actors Theatre of Louisville in Louisville, Kentucky, and the Dance Theatre Workshop and Second Stage, both in New York, Lynn Nottage was a resident artist with Mabou Mines in New York in 1992 and 1993. She has participated in a number of awareness-raising theatre projects including *Shelter*, a collection of short works by women drawing attention to the plight of homeless women, and she was a producer of *Naked*

Rights, a celebration of the Universal Declaration of Human Rights. She was a member of the New Works Project (1989–1992), the Playwrights Horizons Writer's Unit, and the Next Step (African American Writers Initiative). Lynn Nottage has written a film script, *Table Stakes*, for Silver Productions and has commissions from the Manhattan Theatre Club and Playwrights Horizons.

PLAY DESCRIPTIONS

Lynn Nottage addresses serious social issues through the voices of complex, lively, and often eccentric characters. In *Rhinestones and Paste*, Bobby Saint Marie, an African American transvestite, celebrates her third birthday as a woman. Bobby's lover, a street poet, converts to Islam, and her mentor, the glamorous would-be soul singer Ladybug, is on the verge of murder. The delicate balance of this Brooklyn ecosystem is thrown off kilter by an epidemic no one discusses.

Why'd Furgie Kill His Inlaws? examines a father-son relationship pulled apart by violence. After a twelve-year absence, a man returns home on Christmas Day. Accompanied by his fiery-tongued girlfriend, who is nine months pregnant, and a pocketful of boastful tales, he is not welcomed by his father, a drunken civil servant who has long since adjusted to life without his son.

In *Las Meninas*, Nottage explores the historical possibility that Queen Maria Teresa, wife of Louis XIV of France, gave birth to an illegitimate daughter, Louise Marie Therese. Told from the daughter's point of view, the play looks back as the girl tries to piece together her heritage from her confinement in a convent where she has been raised since she was an infant. Her dark skin, kinky hair, and strong jaw suggest that she is the progeny of the queen and her African attendant, Nabo. Moving back in time, the play depicts the growing relationship and love between these two outcasts lost amid the glittering court of the seventeenth century.

Nottage's *Brooklyn after the Glow* follows two homeless men who discover a glowing, phosphorescent orb in the midst of a Brooklyn junkyard. They believe they have finally found their fortune only to discover later that their treasure is radioactive waste.

Poof! again shows Nottage's ability to meld serious topics with comic form. Loureen, a battered housewife, is released from her struggle when her husband spontaneously combusts. This short play follows Loureen after she leaves a pile of smoking ash and a pair of cheap glasses as the only evidence of his demise and moves swiftly from fear and guilt to relief and even pleasure.

The Por' Knockers is an explosive drama about direct political action in contemporary America. The play is set in a Brooklyn safehouse where four African Americans and a Jewish compatriot gather after setting fire to a government office building. Their triumph is a short-lived one, however, when they learn that the flames ignited an adjacent building, resulting in the deaths of several black children. The situation provides a powerful psychic crucible; their own fears, hatreds, dreams, and frustrations are exposed while they explore their personal and political options in the wake of the catastrophe.

SELECTED PRODUCTION HISTORY

Rhinestones and Paste
    Production, Yale Cabaret, New Haven, Connecticut, 1987

Parenthetical Glance at the Dialectical Nature of the African American's Quest for Autonomy
    Production, Yale Cabaret, New Haven, Connecticut, 1988
    Production, Rites and Reasons, Providence, Rhode Island, 1989
    Production, Black Theatre Festival, University of New Haven, New Haven, Connecticut, 1990

Ida Mae Cole
    Production, Yale Cabaret, New Haven, Connecticut, 1989
    Production, Knitting Factory, New York, 1990
    Production, Shelter Project at St. Peter's Church, New York, 1991

Inspite of the Revolution
    Production, BACA Downtown, Brooklyn, New York, 1990

Otis' Option
    Production, Knitting Factory, New York, 1992

Las Meninas
    Workshop, New York Shakespeare Festival, New York, 1992
    Workshop, Voice and Vision, Smith College, Northampton, Massachusetts, 1992
    Workshop, Mabou Mines/Suite, New York, 1993

Ida Mae Cole Takes a Stance in *A . . . My Name Is Still Alice* (monologue)
    Production, Second Stage, New York, 1992–1993
    Production, Seattle Group Theatre, Seattle, 1993
    Production, Mixed Blood Theatre, Minneapolis, 1993

Poof! (fifteen-minute comedy)
    Production, Humana Festival, Actors Theatre of Louisville, Louisville, Kentucky, 1993
    Production, Action Theatre, Singapore, 1993
    Production, City Stage Ensemble, Denver, Colorado, 1993

The Por' Knockers
    Production, Dance Theatre Workshop, New York, 1994
    Production, Vineyard Theatre, New York, 1995

Crumbs from the Table of Joy
    Production, Second Stage, New York, 1995
    Production, South Coast Repertory, Costa Mesa, California, 1996
    Production, Detroit Repertory Company, Michigan, 1997

Mud, River, Stone
    Production, Studio Arena Theatre, Buffalo, New York, 1996 (co-production with The Acting Company, New York)

PLAY AVAILABILITY

Brooklyn after the Glow, *Why'd Furgie Kill His Inlaws?*, *Rhinestones and Paste*, and *Las Meninas* are available at New Dramatists, 424 West 44th Street, New York, New York 10036; (212) 757–6960.

Ida Cole Takes a Stance is included in *A . . . My Name Is Still Alice*, published by Samuel French, 45 West 25th Street, New York, New York 10010–2751; (212) 206–8990.

Poof! is published in Marisa Smith, ed., *Humana Festival '93: The Complete Plays*. Newbury, Vermont: Smith and Kraus, 1993; Leah D. Frank, ed., *Facing Forward*. New York: Broadway Play Publishing, 1995.

All other plays are available through Nottage's agent: Peter Hagan, Writers and Artists, 19 West 44th Street, Suite 1000, New York, New York 10036; (212) 391–1112.

AWARDS

Heideman Award, Winner, *Poof!*, 1992

White Bird Playwriting Contest, Winner, *Brooklyn after the Glow*, 1993

Van Lier Playwriting Fellow, New Dramatists, New York, 1993–1995

Playwriting Fellowship, New York Foundation for the Arts, 1994

DESCRIPTIVE AND CRITICAL RESPONSES

Barnwell, Michael. "Fire and Water." Review of *The Por' Knockers*. *American Theatre*, November 1995, 10.
Brantley, Ben. "Though a Melodrama, Life Is Not a Movie." Review of *Crumbs from the Table of Joy*. *New York Times*, 22 June 1995, C18.
Evans, Greg. "Legit Reviews: *Crumbs from the Table of Joy*." Review of *Crumbs from the Table of Joy*. *Variety*, 26 June 1995, 92.
Yang, Jeff. " 'Cameos' Out of the Shadows." Review of *The Por' Knockers*. *Village Voice*, 18 October 1994, 98.

MADELEINE OLNEK

(1965–   )

BIOGRAPHY

Olnek, who was raised in Connecticut, made her stage debut as Toto in *The Wizard of Oz* at the age of nine. She received a BFA in drama from New York University's Tisch School of the Arts where she studied at the Stella Adler studio. Olnek was part of a group of students who, as protégés of David Mamet, formed the Practical Aesthetics Workshop, which became the Atlantic Theatre Company. During this time she coauthored *A Practical Handbook for the Actor*, published by Vintage, with other students of Mamet's and W. H. Macy's. In her final year at NYU's Experimental Theater Wing, she decided that she wanted to pursue playwriting as a career. Olnek was introduced to the WOW Cafe and began working with the Bad Neighbors Theater Company; she returned to WOW where she knew she could work in a supportive environment and "write without consequences." Most of her plays have been performed at WOW.

While maintaining a New York base, Olnek attended Brown University on a fellowship to their MFA Creative Writing Program and received her degree in the spring of 1996.

PLAY DESCRIPTIONS

Olnek's plays carry the irreverent spirit of the iconoclastic theatre venues in which they were bred and produced. The comedic, satiric tone, however, comes within a postmodern, absurdist style and sensibility that creates ever-shifting worlds, attached to the familiar but on the verge of becoming unanchored. Olnek says that the ludicrousness of popular culture "feeds into an examination of the absurd in society" (Eigo, 7) that is compelling, particularly as a lesbian excluded, in a sense, from that culture. In the one-act *Co-Dependent Lesbian Space*

Alien Seeks Same, aliens from the planet Zots who experience the "big love" emotion, thought to cause holes in the Ozone, are sentenced to a stay on Earth. The rulers believe that contact with earthlings will lead to a broken heart and cure the superior Zots of the damaging effects of love. A banished alien, Zoinx, meets Jane who, diagnosed by her therapist with low self-esteem, readily falls for someone she believes is companionably alienated. Lesbian mating behavior is shrewdly and sympathetically sent up through the difficulties in cross-planetary relationships.

Double Awareness Double Awareness explores the nature of normalcy and insanity through the perspective of Samantha, a lesbian who is trying to cope with the mental breakdown of her seemingly perfect brother Scott. The play divides between scenes in the mental hospital (and childhood flashbacks) to scenes aboard a commuter train where Samantha meets a mysterious Beautiful Woman and has a series of unfulfilling sexual encounters.

A recent work, *Spookyworld*, takes place in an amusement park, where a woman has a low-paying job as a ghost, and at lesbian parties in a woman's bedroom. The playwright describes the play as morphing "between haunted house and party, looking at the crossover, the ways that someone's bed is a haunted house and a haunted house is like a party" (Eigo, 21). The play aspires to her goal of writing unsettling subject matter with "a childlike fun" (Eigo, 21).

SELECTED PRODUCTION HISTORY

Room and Board
    Production, Dixon Place, New York, 1989
    Production, National Women's Theatre Festival, New York, 1989
    Production, Theatre Club Funambules, New York, 1989

Bad Neighbors: The Lower East Side Soap Opera (Episode one)
    Production, Dixon Place (produced by the Bad Neighbors Theater Company), 1990

It's Not the Shoes That Dance Themselves to Pieces (written for Alternate Visions Theatre Company)
    Production, WOW Cafe, New York, 1992
    Production, La Mama, New York, 1992
    Production, Gay and Lesbian Center, New York, 1992

A Bird in the Hand
    Production, Atlantic Theatre Company, New York, 1992
    Production, CuCuRacha, New York, 1992
    Broadcast, WBAI, New York, 1992

Co-Dependent Lesbian Space Alien Seeks Same and *The Jewish Nun*
    Production, Dixon Place, New York, 1992
    Production, WOW Cafe, New York, 1992
    Production, One Dream Theatre, New York, 1993
    Production, "No Shame Festival," Public Theatre, New York, 1993

The Destiny of Mimi
  Production, WOW Cafe, New York, 1993

Double Awareness Double Awareness
  Production, Dixon Place, New York, 1994
  Production, WOW Cafe, New York, 1994
  Production, Brown University, Providence, Rhode Island, 1996

Spookyworld
  Production, WOW Cafe, New York, 1995
  Production, Brown University New Play Festival, Providence, Rhode Island, 1995

How To Write While You Sleep
  Reading, Bay Area Playwrights Festival, San Francisco, 1996

PLAY AVAILABILITY

A Bird in the Hand is published in *The Argonaut* (Spring 1993).

The Jewish Nun is published in Eileen Myles and Liz Kotz, eds., *The New Fuck You: Adventures in Lesbian Reading*. New York: Semiotext(E), 1995.

For other scripts, contact the playwright: 55 West 14th Street, 18b, New York, New York 10011.

DESCRIPTIVE AND CRITICAL RESPONSE

Eigo, Jim. "Madeleine Olnek and the Women of WOW (& Me)." *Movement Research: Performance Journal* 11 (Fall 1995): 7, 21.

MONICA PALACIOS

(1959–   )

BIOGRAPHY

Comic writer and performer Monica Palacios was born and raised in San Jose, California, where she started by writing funny short stories. She attended an all-girls' Catholic high school ("great preparation for lesbianism and the theatre" [Smith]) before sampling a smorgasbord of colleges, including New York University. She graduated from San Francisco State University in 1984 with a BA in film studies and screenwriting.

In 1982 Palacios began performing comedy routines in San Francisco's mainstream as well as alternative venues. As her lesbian identity emerged more clearly in her comedy, Palacios chose not to be involved in "that very negative, racist, sexist, homophobic environment" (Leader, 18) of the straight clubs. She teamed up with Marga Gomez, and the women billed themselves as "the only Latin female comedy duo in the universe" (Arrizon, 25). She was also instrumental in developing an all-Latino comedy troupe, Culture Clash.

In 1987 Monica Palacios located in Los Angeles where she currently maintains her writing, performing, and producing career. Palacios continues to tour her bold autobiographical piece *Latin Lezbo Comic*, which was recently seen off-Broadway and was featured on the Public Broadcasting Service. She tours colleges with her lecture/performance show *Greetings from a Queer Senorita*. Palacios has also collaborated with performance artists Luis Alfaro and Beto Araiza to create solo and collective works called *Deep in the Crotch of My Latino Psyche*. The most recent manifestation of her act, which she calls "part stand-up, part performance, part Chihuahua," is a spoken word/slide show titled *Confessions . . . A Sexplosion of Tantalizing Tales*.

In addition to performing her own work, Palacios is active as a producer. She recently produced "Fierce Tongues/Women of Fire," a three-day festival of

Latina artists funded in part by the city of Santa Monica, California, where she unveiled new short works titled *Que Queer!*. Palacios is also cochair of VIVA, Lesbian and Gay Latino Artists, which produces performance and art shows, and she is the project director of VIVA's HIV/AIDS outreach project, Teatro VIVA.

Monica Palacios's writing has appeared in several forums including Simon and Schuster's anthology *Latinas* (1995), *Consuming Passions: Lesbians Celebrate Food* (1994), *Chicana Lesbians: The Girls Our Mothers Warned Us About* (1991), *Lesbian Bedtime Stories 2* (1991) and in the *Literary Art Journal, Ten Percent*, and *Outlook* magazines.

PLAY DESCRIPTIONS

Described as a latter-day Lenny Bruce, comic writer and performer Monica Palacios delights in pushing the boundaries of both form and content in her work. She uses the stage as a powerful educational weapon to face the taboos of sexism, racism, and homophobia head-on. Although her art is forged from a distinctive life experience as a lesbian Chicana, Palacios's work explores broad, universal themes: relationships, love, and family. By showing the similarities, rather than the differences, among people, Palacios's work promotes positive images of lesbians, gays, Latinos, people of color, and women. It is this agenda, combined with a zany sense of humor, that characterizes Palacios's multicharacter plays to date. In *Seagullita* (1994), a young woman who has been jilted by her lover gets advice from a flamboyant, Sapphic gull. In *La Llorona Loca* (1994), Palacios transforms an old Mexican myth. The revisionist version of the legend of the Mexican Medea who drowns her own children is given a lesbian twist replete with hip anachronisms and ribald humor.

SELECTED PRODUCTION HISTORY

Seagullita (one-act play)
   Production, Celebration Theatre, Los Angeles, 1994

La Llorona Loca (one-act play)
   Production, Celebration Theatre, Los Angeles, 1994

PLAY AVAILABILITY

Monica Palacios's plays are available from the playwright: 2118 Wilshire Blvd., Suite 374, Santa Monica, California 90403; (310) 827–4793.

AWARDS

Artistic Excellence, Writer/Performer, VIVA, Lesbian and Gay Latino Artists, Los Angeles, 1990

Playwright Fellow, Latino Theatre Initiative, Mark Taper Forum, Los Angeles, 1995–1996

DESCRIPTIVE AND CRITICAL RESPONSES

Arrizon, Alicia. "Monica Palacios: Latina Lezbo Comic." *Crossroads*, Los Angeles (May 1993): 25.

Breslauer, Jan. "Heard the One about Lesbian Comics?" *Los Angeles Times*, 18 July 1993, CAL5.

———. "The Serious Side of a Latina Comic with a Cause." *Los Angeles Times*, 7 December 1994, F4.

———. "Unfinished Plays, Provocative Voices." Review of *La Llorona Loca. Los Angeles Times*, 4 February 1994, F25.

Johnson, Wayne. "Gay, Lesbian Actors Hit It Big at Alice B." Review of *Latin Lezbo Comic. Seattle Times*, 27 September 1991.

Leader, Jory. "Working on a New Routine: Gay Comedians Performing in L.A.'s Mainstream Clubs." *Daily News*, 3 August 1992: 18–19.

Martinez, Al. "Always Leave 'em Thinking." *Los Angeles Times*, 26 February 1991, B2.

Smith, Bruce G. "Attacking Racism, Homophobia—Playfully." *L.A. Times*, 11 September 1994.

SUZAN-LORI PARKS

(1964–   )

BIOGRAPHY

Born in Fort Knox, Kentucky, the daughter of an Army man, Parks traveled across the United States, from Texas to Vermont, until the family was transferred to Germany where she attended junior high school and quickly learned to speak German. She remembers her childhood fondly because of the way her parents experienced the places they lived. After graduating from Mt. Holyoke with a BA in English and German literature and thinking that she wanted to become an actress, Parks studied at the Drama Studio, London, where she received a postgraduate degree in 1986.

Her interest in playwriting was piqued earlier through a writing class she took with James Baldwin, who suggested that she try plays because of her fondness for writing dialogue. Parks's emergence into theatre-world visibility was explosive. Productions of parts of *Imperceptible Mutabilities in the Third Kingdom* at BACA Downtown, Fringe Series, in Brooklyn, New York, beginning in 1986, attracted such attention that the theatre opened its 1989 season with all four parts of Parks's play, the first time the theatre had brought back any work for a second showing. The play was well received, and the Manhattan Theatre Club presented Part 4 in 1990, the year it won an Obie for Best Play. *The Death of the Last Black Man in the Whole Entire World* followed with presentations at BACA and a production at Yale Repertory's 1992 Winterfest, where she shared a bill with veteran playwrights Colette Brooks and **Maria Irene Fornes**. Parks was interviewed, and her works were heralded by serious critics, analyzed in theatre journals, and widely published.

Her work has found a home at several major nonprofit theatres, including the Public Theatre in New York, as well as Yale Rep and the Actors Theatre of Louisville in Louisville, Kentucky, and a major interpreter in director Liz Diamond, whose visually dynamic productions of the plays have provided theatrical correlatives for the enigmatic, dense language of this playwright. Not surprisingly, Parks cites Gertrude Stein, **Adrienne Kennedy**, Zora Neal Hurston, James Joyce, and William Faulkner as influences. She, however, also acknowledges the importance of jazz, blues, and the pop music of James Brown. What she consistently resists are two-sentence summaries of her work and a categorizing of the plays as tracts about race: "I really get a little ill when people use only my African-Americanness to talk about my plays . . . they [the plays] go beyond subject matter, beyond the characters, beyond the plot, to a kind of world view made up of a cultural history" (Madison, 37). Parks has taught at various institutions, including the New School and Yale School of Drama, where she is an associate artist, and her film script for Spike Lee's film company 40 Acres and a Mule, *Girl 6*, was released in the spring of 1996. She is a student of Seido karate and a member of the New Dramatists.

PLAY DESCRIPTIONS

In her collection of plays, *The America Play and Other Works*, Parks includes three essays that describe her interest in history, provide ways to understand her nontraditional stylistic features (such as her lack of stage directions), and offer a glossary of the phonetically spelled words in her plays. Her emphasis on historical events and characters she attributes to an attempt to make a version of history through theatre because so much of "African-American history has been unrecorded, dismembered, washed out" (Parks, 4). Repetition and revision, so central to jazz, is Parks's way of subverting a linear narrative and creating "a drama of accumulation" (Parks, 9). The physicality of her language has inherent movement, and her idiosyncratic spellings and the spatial appearance of the text give clues to action. Meaning is embedded in the sound of the words, and reading the plays aloud is crucial to penetrating their mysteries.

In *Imperceptible Mutabilities*, written in four parts and a reprise, Part 1 *Snails* shows three black women as they are observed by a white naturalist through a camera hidden in a replica of a giant cockroach in their living room. He later poses as an exterminator, and the detached scientific observer becomes the eliminator of his own investigation. As the women begin talking about themselves in the third person, they become objects for scientific study. Part 3 features an old black woman, an ex-slave, who remembers her life as resembling the painful extraction of teeth. Two white children (black actors in white face) stand at her bed for pictures, echoing the image that runs throughout the play of photography as a process that selects and embalms. The most accessible narrative, which occurs in Part 4, tells of a Sergeant Smith who, separated from his wife and children, remembers, "Wavin. Wavin at my uther me who I could barely see." Later he instructs his daughter to "look very far out over the water and give me a wave" although he realizes that to her (and presumably to the country he is serving) "I'll look like just a speck." When he finally returns home to children who barely know him, he has lost his legs while saving a boy described as an Icarus figure. Now crippled, he will earn the "distinction" that will merit a photograph to record the moment and that will increase the gap between reality and image.

The stylization of a gesture, as described in the dialogue and symbolized by photographed images in *Mutabilities*, is echoed in the penny show performed by the Foundling Father who reenacts the assassination of Abraham Lincoln in *The America Play*. Historic events are further filtered and poignantly recreated as a black man impersonates the white man who freed the slaves but whose ambivalence toward the Civil War is a matter of record. Analogies to an absent African American colonial past are present in the vocation of the black man as a grave digger who "sees" historical recreations in a vast hole containing a theme park of early American history (all white). When the Foundling Father (also punningly referred to as a Foe Father and faux-father) disappears in the second act, his wife, with the aid of an ear trumpet, listens through her tunnel for sounds of her husband while her young son digs for artifacts of his missing father. As in Part 4 of *Mutabilities*, a faithful wife and progeny wait for the head of the family (and imitative head of country in *America*) and create their own history.

Venus, Parks's most linear play to date, uses a woman protagonist to examine historical gaps in an African American past. Like the Foundling Father, the Venus Hottentot finds her recognition in a side show. The notoriety of the character, who is based on an actual person and incidents, comes from her odd-shaped, large buttocks. Brought from Africa, she is exhibited in England and then becomes the mistress of a doctor who submits her to examination by his fellow anatomists. As in *America*, a play within a play contrasts one theatricalized version of reality with another. *Venus* is more accessible because the narrative follows a chronological journey from Miss Sartje Baartman's decision to leave Africa to make her fortune in England, to her indenture in the freak show, to her rescue and betrayal by the anatomist. With characteristic humor, Parks puns on the posterior as a literal past and revisits (and revises) the imagery of the white male scientist observing a black female (as in *Mutabilities*). The world of *Venus* is less hermetic than Parks's earlier plays but certainly no less richly textured. Again, she creates a many-layered portrait of a victimized protagonist who escapes victimization by resourcefulness, humor, and intelligence. The play, according to Parks in a publicity brochure from The Public Theatre, "looks through the characters, at the three faces of God or the three faces of Love—one is the face of the loved, one is the face of the unloved and the third is the face of the lover and that face has two aspects, the rememberer and the dismemberer."

SELECTED PRODUCTION HISTORY

Imperceptible Mutabilities in the Third Kingdom
Production, BACA Downtown, Brooklyn, New York, 1986–1990

Production (Part 4 only), Manhattan Theatre Club, New York, 1990
Production, New City Theatre, Seattle, 1991

Betting on the Dust Commander
Production, Gas Station, New York, 1987
Production, Company One Theater at Cathedral Theater, Hartford, Connecticut, 1990
Production, Working Theatre, New York, 1991

Pickling
Production, BACA Downtown, Brooklyn, 1988
Broadcast, New American Radio, New York, 1990

The Death of the Last Black Man in the Whole Entire World
Production, St. Mark's Poets Theatre, New York, 1988
Production, BACA Downtown, New York, 1989, 1990
Production, Yale Repertory Theater, New Haven, Connecticut, 1992

The Third Kingdom
Broadcast, SoundPlay Series, 1991

Devotees in the Garden of Love
Production, Humana Festival, Actors Theatre of Louisville, Louisville, Kentucky, 1992

The America Play (commissioned by Theater for a New Audience)
Production, Yale Repertory Theater, New Haven, Connecticut, 1994
Production, Public Theater, New York, 1994

Venus (commissioned by the Women's Project and Productions)
Production, Yale Repertory Theater, New Haven, Connecticut, 1996
Production, Public Theater, New York, 1996

PLAY AVAILABILITY

The America Play is also available in *American Theatre*, March 1994, and through the Dramatists Play Service.

The America Play and Other Works, published by the Theatre Communications Group, 1995, contains the following plays: *Betting on the Dust Commander, Imperceptible Mutabilities in the Third Kingdom, The Death of the Last Black Man in the Whole Entire World, The America Play, Pickling*, and *Devotees in the Garden of Love*.

Betting on the Dust Commander is also available through Playwrights' Press, New York, 1987.

The Death of the Last Black Man in the Whole Entire World is also published in Sydné Mahone, ed., *Moon Marked and Touched by Sun*. New York: Theatre Communications Group, 1994; Rosette C. Lamont, ed., *Women on the Verge: 7 Avant-Garde American Plays*. New York, Applause, 1993.

Imperceptible Mutabilities in the Third Kingdom is also published in Ross Wetzsteon, ed., *The Best of Off-Broadway: Eight Contemporary Obie-Winning Plays*. New York: Mentor, 1994.

Snails is published in Howard Stein and Glenn Young, eds., *Best Short Plays of 1991–92*. New York: Applause, 1992.

Direct inquiries can be made to her agent: Brad Kalos, ICM, 40 West 57th Street, New
   York, New York 10019; (212) 556–5600.

AWARDS

MacDowell Colony Fellow, 1989

Rockefeller Multi-Cultural Arts Grant, *The Last Black Man*, 1990

Obie Award, Best New American Play, *Imperceptible Mutabilities*, 1990

National Endowment for the Arts Playwriting Award, 1991

Ford Foundation Grant, 1992

Whiting Foundation Writers Award, 1992

New Foundation for the Arts

Kennedy Center Fund for New American Plays, 1995

W. Alton Jones Foundation, 1995

Lila Wallace–Reader's Digest Fellow, 1995–1996

Obie Award for Playwriting, *Venus*, 1996

DESCRIPTIVE AND CRITICAL RESPONSES

Brantley, Ben. "Of an Erotic Freak Show and the Lesson Therein." Review of *Venus*.
   New York Times, 3 May 1996, C3.
Chaudhuri, Una. "Posterior's Sake." *Stage Bill: Public Access*, March 1996, 8–12.
Drukman, Steven. "Suzan-Lori Parks and Liz Diamond: Doo-a-diddly-dit-dot." *Drama
   Review* 39, no. 3 (Fall 1995): 56–75.
Feingold, Michael. "Carnival Knowledge." Review of *Venus*. *Village Voice*, 14 May
   1996, 81.
Gussow, Mel. "Dangers of Becoming Lost in a Culture." Review of *The Last Black
   Man. New York Times*, 25 September 1990, C15.
———. "Identity Loss in *Imperceptible Mutabilities*." *New York Times*, 20 September
   1989, III 24.
Hartigan, Patti. "Theater's Vibrant New Voice." *Boston Globe*, 14 February 1992, 37.
Holden, Stephen. "Working One-Acts '91." Review of *Dust Commander. New York
   Times*, 26 June 1991, C12.
Madison, Cathy. "Writing Home." Interview. *American Theatre*, October 1991, 36–38.
Munk, Erika. "The Next Stage: Is Playwright Suzan-Lori Parks the Voice of the Future."
   Washington Post, 28 February 1993, G3.
Parks, Suzan-Lori. "Essays: Possession, from Elements of Style, An Equation for Black
   People On Stage." *The America Play and Other Works*. Theatre Communications
   Group. New York, 1995: 3–22.
Richards, David. "Seeking Bits of Identity in History's Vast Abyss." Review of *The
   America Play. New York Times*, 11 March 1994, C3.

Soloman, Alisa. ''Signifying on the Signifyin': The Plays of Suzan-Lori Parks.'' *Theatre* (Yale University) 21, no. 3 (Summer-Fall 1990): 73–80.

Williams, Monte. ''From a Planet Closer to the Sun.'' *New York Times*, 17 April 1996, C1, 8.

ESTELA PORTILLO-TRAMBLEY

(1936–)

BIOGRAPHY

Estela Portillo, who was born in El Paso, Texas, has spent most of her life working in that Texas city. She received a BA and an MA in English from the University of Texas–El Paso. From 1957 to 1964, Portillo-Trambley taught high school English in El Paso and was chair of the English Department at El Paso Technical Institute. Since 1979 she has been affiliated with the Department of Special Services in the El Paso public schools.

In addition to her career in education, Portillo-Trambley has actively promoted Chicano culture in El Paso. She hosted a radio talk show, "Estela Sez " (1969–1970), and wrote as well as hosted the cultural program "Cumbres" for an El Paso television station from 1971 to 1972. Her television experience led her toward a full-time writing career, including the position of resident dramatist at the El Paso Community College from 1970 to 1975, where she also produced and directed the college productions and taught classes. Portillo-Trambley holds the distinction of being the first Chicana to write a musical comedy.

Portillo-Trambley's *Rain of Scorpions and Other Writings* (1975) is the first collection of short stories published by a Chicana writer. *Impressions* (1971) is a collection of her haiku poetry, and *Trini* (1986) is a novel. She edited *Chicanas en literatura y arte* for *Il Grito* in 1973, the first all-women's issue of a major Chicano journal.

Portillo-Trambley married Robert Trambley in 1953 and has five children. She continues to make her home in El Paso, Texas.

PLAY DESCRIPTIONS

While Portillo-Trambley's work is firmly rooted in realistic situations and believable characters, a mystical quality, often originating in Chicano traditions, pervades the plays. She develops strong female characters who frequently defy convention. Their struggles complement the political dimension that underlies all her work. In *The Day of the Swallows*, Portillo-Trambley evokes the world of Dona Josefa, the powerful woman who dispenses her care and largess in the barrio surrounding the hacienda. Among the priest and villagers her reputation verges on sainthood. She, however, prefers to live in a house separated from the others, where she creates a sanctuary of peace and perfection. No matter how much she tries to control her world, the tranquillity she has sought to create is being shattered by events over which she has no control. Don Esquinas, the owner of the hacienda, blames Dona Josefa for his wife's alcoholism and banishes her from his home. Alysea, the young woman who has shared Dona Josefa's home, is preparing to leave and join her young Indian lover in the mountains. As Josefa's world crumbles and the guilt mounts, she confesses to the priest that she is responsible for David's tragic "accident" the night before. He had caught Josefa and Alysea making love, and, to prevent the truth of her life being revealed to the people, she cut out his tongue. Unable to accept her lesbianism, Dona Josefa commits suicide.

Morality Play uses techniques from the medieval morality plays to depict the 5,000-year-old struggle between Power and Humanism. Man, the Superhuman, rescues faith, hope, and charity during the course of the play while escaping the dehumanizing effects of manmade institutions and their value systems.

Autumn Gold is unique among Portillo-Trambley's published plays in that the story takes place in a typical middle-class American home. Esther Forbes's daughter, Helen, is concerned about her mother's recent erratic behavior. Esther, who is eager to enjoy her golden years to their fullest, reawakens to sexual desire, even in the wake of her dear friend's death. Portillo-Trambley's play is a paean to life and love.

Sor Juana is a dramatization of events in the life of Sor Juana Inez de la Cruz, a seventeenth-century Mexican nun and playwright. Portillo-Trambley's telling of the story, which focuses on the last few years of Sor Juana's life, uses flashbacks to reconstruct the earlier events that shaped her career. The powerful character who emerges from the play is a passionate, intelligent woman whose choices and decisions have largely been manipulated by those around her: her patrons, the Church hierarchy, and a lost lover. As Sor Juana approaches the end of her life, she learns to make choices based on her own needs and feelings.

SELECTED PRODUCTION HISTORY

The Day of the Swallows
   Production, El Espejo Quinto Sol, San Francisco, 1971
   Production, Nosotros, Los Angeles, 1979

Morality Play (musical)
   Production, Chamizal National Theatre, El Paso, Texas, 1974

Black Light

Production, Chamizal National Theatre, El Paso, Texas, 1975
Reading, South Coast Repertory Theatre, Costa Mesa, California, 1987

Sun Images (musical)
Production, Chamizal National Theatre, El Paso, Texas, 1976

Isabel and the Dancing Bear
Production, Chamizal National Theatre, El Paso, Texas, 1977

The Burning (radio play)
Production, Western Public Radio Workshop, 1983

PLAY AVAILABILITY

The Day of the Swallows is published in several journals and anthologies including
Roberto J. Garza, *Contemporary Chicano Theatre*. Notre Dame, Indiana: University
of Notre Dame, 1976.

Puente Negro, Autumn Gold, Blacklight, and *Sor Juana* are published in Estela Portillo-
Trambley, *Sor Juana and Other Plays*. Tempe, Arizona: Bilingual Press, 1983.

Sun Images is published in *Revista Chicano-Riquena* 7 (Winter 1979): 19–42; and in
Nicolas Kanellos and Jorge A. Huerta, eds., *Nuevos Pasos: Chicano and Puerto Rican
Drama*. Houston: Arte Publico Press, 1989.

AWARDS

Quinto Sol Award for Literature, San Francisco, 1972

Texas Writers Recognition Award, 1982

Women's Play Competition, St. Edward's University, Austin, Texas, Winner, *Puente
Negro*, 1984

Hispanic Playwriting Competition, New York Shakespeare Festival, Second Place, *Blacklight*, 1985

DESCRIPTIVE AND CRITICAL RESPONSES

Dewey, Janice. "Dona Josefa: Bloodpulse of Transition and Change." In *Breaking
    Boundaries: Latina Writing and Critical Readings*, edited by Asuncio Delgado,
    39–47. Amherst: University of Massachusetts Press, 1989.
Novoa, Bruce. "Estela Portillo [Trambley]." In *Chicano Authors: Inquiry by Interview*,
    edited by Bruce Novoa, 163–81. Austin: University of Texas Press, 1980.
Parr, Carmen Salazar. "Surrealism in the Work of Estela Portillo." *MELUS* 7, no. 4
    (Winter 1980): 85–92.
Vowell, Faye Nell. "A MELUS Interview: Estela Portillo-Trambley." *MELUS* 9, no. 3
    (Winter 1982): 19–28.

DOLORES PRIDA

(1943–)

BIOGRAPHY

Dolores Prida was born in Caibarien, Cuba. Not long after the revolution in 1959, her father fled to Miami in a boat; the rest of the family followed in 1961. Since Prida arrived in this country with nothing, she had to borrow money from her uncle to get to New York. The oldest of three children, Prida went to work in a bakery to earn money for the family. She advanced to office work within six months, and eventually she honed her journalism skills by editing the employee newsletter. Prida earned a degree in Latin American Literature from Hunter College in New York in 1969.

Although theatre was not a part of Dolores Prida's life in Cuba, she was exposed to the art in Manhattan where she saw her first play. In 1976 she had her first experience working in the theatre with the collective Teatro de Orilla in the Lower East Side and afterward wrote her first play. She honed her dramaturgical skills at DUO, an experimental theatre on East 4th Street. From DUO she moved on to INTAR, the Puerto Rican Traveling Theatre, and Repertorio Español where she writes scripts in English, Spanish, and a bilingual combination.

In addition to her theatre work, Prida has written for television and film. For the past ten years, Dolores Prida has been the editor of the newsletter for the Association of Hispanic Arts. She is a frequent lecturer and has taught playwriting at several colleges and universities. In 1989 she was awarded a Doctor of Humane Letters honorary degree by Mount Holyoke College for her contributions to the American theatre. Prida is single and lives in East Harlem, New York City.

PLAY DESCRIPTIONS

Dolores Prida's English or bilingual scripts include *Beautiful Señoritas*. In this early work, the playwright establishes her primary themes (feminism and biculturalism) which are treated in a style that juxtaposes broad humor with serious, thought-provoking issues. This play with music is a send-up of traditional feminine roles (beauty queens, cabaret performers, martyrs) as Girl receives a revue-like education in what it is to be a "real woman." In a series of musical numbers, Girl is instructed about how to catch a man and make him happy. The Girl emerges as an amalgam of her Latin heritage, but by the end she has been stripped of the stereotypical trappings to reveal a fresh face, a new woman alive with possibilities.

Although Prida's indebtedness to Bertolt Brecht was evident in the previous play, *The Beggar's Soap Opera* (1979) is a full-fledged musical comedy tribute to Brecht's *The Three Penny Opera* set among South Bronx "poverticians."

The bilingual play *Coser y Cantar* (1981) is an exploration of a woman's identity. The woman's alter egos are depicted as two separate characters: She, the liberal, Americanized self; and Ella, the traditional Hispanic self. Their cultural divergence is accented by the fact that She speaks English and Ella speaks Spanish. The comedy of the warring selves gradually grows more serious in tone when the real world encroaches on their dreams and plans: first She's lover phones to break up with her, and then the chaos (shooting and sirens) outside begins to invade their space. The play ends with both egos seeking a way out but unable to find the actual and metaphorical map for escape.

Prida returns to the musical comedy form with *Savings*, a modern morality play about the gentrification of a multiethnic neighborhood. Italian, Asian, Cuban, Puerto Rican, African American, and Jewish neighbors will face displacement. Only when they unite as a community with threats to sue and picket and march do they stand a chance to retain their neighborhood.

Prida's other plays include *La Era Latina*, a bilingual musical comedy, and *Crisp!*, a commedia dell'arte musical comedy based on Jacinot Benavente's *Los intereses creados* (the bonds of interest). *Juan Bobo*, a bilingual play with music for children, is based on the Puerto Rican folk character. *Pantallas* is a black comedy in Spanish on the subjects of Spanish soap operas and nuclear disaster. Her popular play in Spanish *Botanica* delineates three generations of Puerto Rican women who must grapple with generational and cultural gaps while managing a botanica (a religious and medicinal herb shop).

SELECTED PRODUCTION HISTORY

Beautiful Señoritas (with music by Tania Leon and Victoria Ruiz)
    Production, Duo Theater, New York, 1977
    Production, Inner City Cultural Center, Los Angeles, 1980
    Production, Teatro Repertorio Español, New York, 1995

The Beggar's Soap Opera (musical with music by Paul Radelat)
Production, INTAR with Duo, New York, 1979

La Era Latina (musical comedy cowritten with Victor Fragoso and music by Paul Radelat)
Production, Puerto Rican Traveling Company, New York, 1980
Production, Teatro Latino de Minnesota, Minneapolis, 1981

Coser y Cantar (one-act bilingual play)
Production, Duo Theater, New York, 1981 and 1982
Production, Women One World Festival, New York, 1981
Production, Actores Unidos, Teatro Bellas Artes, San Juan, Puerto Rico, 1985
Production, Teatro Repertorio Español, New York, 1995

Crisp! (musical comedy with music by Galt MacDermot)
Production, INTAR, New York, 1981

Juan Bobo (bilingual play for children with music by Eddie Ruperto)
Production, Duo Theater, Art Connection Program, New York, 1982

Savings (musical comedy with music by Leon Odenz)
Production, INTAR, New York, 1985

Pantallas (one-act play in Spanish)
Production, Duo Theater, New York, 1986

Botanica (in Spanish)
Production, Teatro Repertorio Español, New York, 1991 (continues to date in the repertory)

PLAY AVAILABILITY

Beautiful Señoritas, Coser y Cantar, Savings, Pantallas, and *Botanica* are published in Dolores Prida, *Beautiful Señoritas and Other Plays*. Houston: Arte Publico Press, 1991.

Pantallas is published in Luis F. Gonzalez-Cruz and Francesca M. Colecchia, eds., *Cuban Theater in the United States: A Critical Anthology*. Tempe, Arizona: Bilingual Press, 1992.

Savings is published in Denis Lynn Daly Heyck, ed., *Barrios and Borderlands: Culture of Latinos and Latinas in the US*. London: Routledge, 1994.

Screens is published in Luis F. Gonzalez-Cruz and Francesca M. Colecchia, eds., *Cuban Theater in the United States: A Critical Anthology*. Tempe, Arizona: Bilingual Press, 1992.

AWARDS

Cintas Literature Fellowship, 1976

Creative Arts Public Service Playwriting Fellowship, 1979–1980

International Third World Competition, Caracas, Venezuela, Special Award, *La Era Latina*, 1981

INTAR/Ford Foundation Playwright in Residence, 1982–1983

Manhattan Borough President's Excellence in the Arts Award, 1987

Doctor of Humane Letters, *Honoris Causa*, Mount Holyoke College, 1989

Manhattan Borough President's Excellence in the Arts Award, 1990

Lila Wallace–Reader's Digest Foundation Grant, *Botanica*, 1991

DESCRIPTIVE AND CRITICAL RESPONSES

Prida, Dolores. "The Show Does Go On: Testimonio." In *Breaking Boundaries: Latina Writing and Critical Readings*, edited by Asuncion Horno-Delgado et al., 181–88. Amherst: University of Massachusetts Press, 1989.

Sandoval, Alberto. "Dolores Prida's *Coser y Cantar*: Mapping the Dialectics of Ethnic Identity and Assimilation." In *Breaking Boundaries: Latina Writing and Critical Readings*, edited by Asuncion Horno-Delgado et al., 201–20. Amherst: University of Massachusetts Press, 1989.

Umpierre, Luz Maria. "Interview with Dolores Prida." *Latin American Theatre Review* 22, no. 1 (Fall 1988): 81–85.

Waldman, Gloria F. "Hispanic Theatre in New York." *Journal of Popular Culture* 19, no. 3 (Winter 1985): 139–47.

Watson, Maida. "The Search for Identity in the Theater of Three Cuban American Female Dramatists." *Bilingual Review* 16, nos. 2–3 (May-December 1991): 188–96.

Weiss, Judith. "The Theaterworks of Dolores Prida." In *Beautiful Señoritas and Other Plays*, by Dolores Prida. Houston: Arte Publico Press, 1991.

AISHAH RAHMAN

(1937–   )

BIOGRAPHY

Aishah Rahman, born Virginia Hughes, was raised as a foster child in New York's Harlem by a "straight-laced religious family." After high school graduation in 1954, Rahman sought the freedom that New York's Greenwich Village offered. In the 1960s, however, she attended Howard University where she earned a BA in political science. She returned to New York City to begin her teaching career at Queens College and her political activism with Congress of Racial Equality (CORE) and other groups. It was during this period that Virginia Hughes converted to Islam and took the name Aishah Rahman.

Rahman's writing career was inspired by the 1971 production of LeRoi Jones's (Amiri Baraka's) play *Slave Ship*, and she felt compelled to pen *Lady Day: A Musical Tragedy*, an exploration of the "interior landscape" of singer Billy Holiday. Rahman's daughter, Yoruba, was born while her first play was receiving a 1972 production at the Brooklyn Academy of Music. Wanting to devote more attention to her writing and her new daughter, Rahman left the city to teach at Amherst College in Massachusetts. She returned within a few years to continue writing and to begin a ten-year teaching stint at Nassau Community College on Long Island. In 1985 she formed Blackberry Productions with actor and dancer Stephanie Berry.

In 1990 Rahman was invited to lecture at Brown University. While there she met **Paula Vogel**, the director of the creative writing program, who offered her a visiting professorship. That one year turned into a permanent position at Brown. Rahman's most recent projects include the play *Only in America*, which emerged from the Clarence Thomas–Anita Hill hearing, and *Anybody Seen Marie Laveau?*, an opera based on the nineteenth-century New Orleans voodoo practitioner. Aishah Rahman currently lives in Providence, Rhode Island, where she continues to teach and write.

PLAY DESCRIPTIONS

Aishah Rahman writes in a tradition she calls "the 'jazz aesthetic' which acknowledges the characters' various levels of reality." This multiplicity of ideas and experiences is evident in *Unfinished Women Cry in No Man's Land while a Bird Dies in a Gilded Cage*, a musical collage in twelve scenes. In this play, set in 1955, Rahman juxtaposes scenes of the utilitarian Hide-a-Wee Home for Unwed Mothers against the plush boudoir where black saxophonist Charlie Parker (the Bird) spends the last hours of his life. Rahman explores the young women's dreams and passions, their circumstances and choices, by using the emotion-laden day when the young girls must decide whether to give up their unborn babies for adoption. Mattie, who was gang raped, resents having to make this choice since she has never even had a boyfriend; Consuelo deludes herself by believing that her boyfriend will arrive to take her and her baby away; Paulette, a middle-class college graduate, was "caught"; and the streetwise Wilma let Charlie Parker's music make love to her while she was having sex with her boyfriend. In counterpart to these scenes of new life (both wanted and unwanted) is the long riff on Parker's death by drugs. Through his narcotic-induced haze, the Bird laments his frustration at being unable to produce the one perfect sound that would give his life meaning. As the reality of Parker's death affects each of the women in her own way, the enormity of their choices descends upon the Hide-a-Wee Home.

The Mojo and the Sayso, a haunting tale of personal and familial reconciliation, is set in the living room of the Benjamin home, where the expected reality of the situation is undercut by the play's quasi-absurdist quality. Acts and Awilda Benjamin are absorbed by their disparate activities: Acts is assembling an automobile in the living room while Awilda searches for her white gloves so that she can go to church. Their son, Linus, was killed three years ago that day, and a check as payment for wrongful death has recently arrived. Although Awilda begs Acts to tell her what really happened on that fateful morning, Acts continues working on the car, ignoring her pleas. Blood, their other son, arrives to terrorize the house in his new persona of a gun-wielding street punk. Awilda returns from church with the pastor in tow to announce that the money from the check will be donated to the church. Blood holds the pastor hostage and forces the man of the cloth to reveal his true colors: he is a deceptive con artist who bilks money from vulnerable people. After the pastor has been exorcised from the house, Acts is able to tell the story of his son's death. While he explores his own complicity in the event, he tears the check up into tiny pieces. After the three have rid themselves of the guilt, resentment, and anger surrounding Linus's death, they set off together for Mexico in Acts's rebuilt car.

SELECTED PRODUCTION HISTORY

Lady Day: A Musical Tragedy (full-length musical)
    Production, Brooklyn Academy of Music, New York, 1972

Transcendental Blues
    Production, Frederick Douglass Creative Arts Center, New York, 1976
    Production, Manhattan Theater Club, New York, 1977

Unfinished Women Cry in No Man's Land while a Bird Dies in a Gilded Cage (full-length play with music)
    Production, Public Theatre, New York, 1977
    Production, St. Louis Black Repertory Company, St. Louis, Missouri, 1987–1988
    Production, Penumbra Theatre Company, Minneapolis, Minnesota, 1989

The Tale of Madame Zora
    Production, Ensemble Studio Theatre, New York, 1986

Lady and the Tramp
    Production, Westbank Theatre Cafe, New York, 1987

The Mojo and the Sayso
    Production, Crossroads Theatre, New Brunswick, New Jersey, 1988
    Production, Judith Anderson Theatre, New York, 1993

PLAY AVAILABILITY

The Mojo and the Sayso is published by Sydné Mahone, ed., *Moon Marked and Touched by Sun: Plays by African-American Women*. New York: Theatre Communications Group, 1994; and by Broadway Play Publishing, 1989; and *Plays in Process*, vol. 10, no. 5. New York: Theatre Communications Group, 1988.

Unfinished Women Cry in No Man's Land while a Bird Dies in a Gilded Cage is published in Margaret B. Wilkerson, ed., *Nine Plays by Black Women*. New York: New American Library, 1986.

AWARDS

AUDELCO Award Nomination, *Transcendental Blues*, 1976

Susan Smith Blackburn Award, Finalist, *Windhawk!*, 1986

Doris Abramson Playwriting Award, Winner, *The Mojo and the Sayso*, 1988

Rockefeller Foundation Fellowship, 1988

New York Foundation for the Arts Fellowship, 1988

DESCRIPTIVE AND CRITICAL RESPONSES

Barnes, Clive. "Stage: Chelsea Players' Tragedy of Billie Holiday." Review of *Lady Day: A Musical Tragedy. New York Times*, 26 October 1972, 39.

Gussow, Mel. "Stage: 'Madame Zora' A Biographical Musical." Review of *The Tale of Madame Zora. New York Times*, 2 March 1986, 64.

Hawkins, Yvette. "Aishah Rahman: A Life-long Passion for Words and Music." *Black Masks* 11, no. 2 (April-May 1995): 5–6, 8.

Koger, Alicia Kae. "Jazz Form and Jazz Function: An Analysis of *Unfinished Women Cry in No Man's Land while a Bird Dies in a Gilded Cage.*" *MELUS* 16, no. 3 (Fall 1989): 99–111.

Rahman, Aishah. "Introduction to *The Mojo and the Sayso.*" *Moon Marked and Touched by Sun: Plays by African-American Women*, edited by Sydné Mahone, 283–85. New York: Theatre Communications Group, 1994.

———. "Tradition and a New Aesthetic." *MELUS* 16, no. 3 (Fall 1989): 23–26.

Sinclair, Aboila. "*Mojo and the Sayso* Dramatic Probing of Truth." *Amsterdam News*, New York (28 August 1993): 25.

SANDRA RODGERS

(1956–)

BIOGRAPHY

Sandra Rodgers is an East Indian whose great-grandfather, a Scotsman, married an Indian woman when he was stationed in India. Rodgers, who grew up in England, arrived in Los Angeles in 1986 only to "flee" in 1989 to the Bay Area, where she currently resides. In 1993, while she was laying the groundwork for a novel loosely based on her family's move from India to England in the 1950s, Rodgers spent three months in India and England. Her experience in India motivated her to return to work on a more "Indian" enterprise. She will return to India in 1996 to initiate an in-country project based on the communities of street children in Bombay. In the meantime, Rodgers is completing an MFA in creative writing at San Francisco State University.

PLAY DESCRIPTIONS

Sandra Rodgers's dramas encompass a diversity of styles. Her play *Owning Half the Dog* is a poetic, imagistic narrative of forgiveness and acceptance. Nella, an Asian American woman in her forties, gymnastically employs a balancing beam to physicalize her struggle to free herself from her family. Nella is poised between an emerging relationship with Samuel, an American, and her Asian family's stifling codependency. Her father, Manirung, her mother, Sarasvati, and her brother, Massulah, are emotionally bound to each other through dependence and guilt, a concept Rodgers concretizes by showing them entangled in a knitted web that keeps growing as Sarasvati endlessly knits. Nella's intimacy with Samuel is challenged as she attempts to work through some childhood "sexual transgression with the father that crossed the line where love becomes too much" and which still scars her sexual psyche. Although Massulah is hopelessly encased in the familial dysfunction, the play suggests a hopeful resolution of Nella's dilemma. She proclaims her willingness to return to Samuel after undergoing a journey of self-discovery: a visit to islands around the world.

The soaring poetic images of *Owning Half the Dog* are more grounded in the realistically rendered full-length play *Ram Ram*. *Ram Ram* depicts the evolving relationship between Lourdes Mary, an East Indian women in her thirties, and her American roommate, Kay. As the play opens, Kay solicits Dr. Samson, an American psychiatrist, to help Lourdes Mary. Kay is convinced that Lourdes Mary, Kay's houseguest for the past three months, needs to exorcise some of the demons from her past in India. While their friendship blossoms, Lourdes Mary begins to reveal the past which she has managed, up until now, to run away from or at least hold at bay. She tells of the political repression and imprisonment that she and her pediatrician husband endured. The assassination of her husband forced her to leave India and abandon her children to the care of her aunt. As Lourdes Mary begins to open up and heal her emotional scars, she assumes American dress and her friendship with Kay is transformed into a full-blown love affair. However, a spectral figure, Sunil, which stills haunts her, forces her to choose between returning to her children in India or staying with Kay. (See Chiori Miyagawa's chapter in this volume for more information about Rodgers.)

SELECTED PRODUCTION HISTORY

Solomon Mukand
Staged reading, Bay Area Playwrights Festival, Magic Theatre, San Francisco, 1992

Texic Shock Syndrome (one-act play)
Staged reading, Upstart Stage, Berkeley, California, 1993
Workshop, BRAVA! for Women in the Arts, San Francisco, 1993

Pitted Date (one-act play)
Staged reading, Upstart Stage, Berkeley, California, 1993

Owning Half the Dog
Staged reading, Bay Area Playwrights Festival, Magic Theatre, San Francisco, 1994

Ram Ram
Staged reading, New Georges, New York, 1995

Long Division (one-act play)
Staged reading, Studio Theatre, San Francisco State University, 1995

Elefan (one-act play)
Staged reading, Project Artaud, San Francisco, 1996

Perks
Staged reading, Studio Theatre, San Francisco State University, 1996

PLAY AVAILABILITY

Scripts are available from the playwright: Sandra Rodgers, 1035 Underhills Road, Oakland, California 94610; (510) 452–0934.

AWARDS

Writer's Digest Writing Competition—Play Category, Second Place, *Ram Ram*, 1994
Highsmith Award, *Ram Ram*, 1995

DESCRIPTIVE AND CRITICAL RESPONSE

Stein, Ruthe. "Playwrights on Edge of Discovery." *San Francisco Chronicle*, 2 August 1994, E1–2.

KATE MOIRA RYAN

(1966–   )

BIOGRAPHY

Born in Yonkers, New York, to second-generation Irish parents, Ryan attended Catholic elementary and high schools. She received a BA from Trinity College in Washington, D.C., where she majored in English. Selected as a participant in the Young Playwrights Festival at Playwrights Horizon, in New York, Ryan began her public playwriting career at the age of nineteen. Encouraged by that recognition, and following a year at Oxford and graduation from Trinity, Ryan enrolled in the graduate playwriting program at Columbia University where she completed an MFA under the tutelage of Howard Stein. While there, Ryan wrote *Rescuing Marilyn*, a satiric farce that skewers the conservative Right, which received a production at the Loft Theatre in Tampa, Florida. While at Columbia, she completed a literary internship at the Women's Project and Productions which began an association that developed into an artistic home for Ryan. In a cooperative production with New Georges, the Women's Project produced *The Autobiography of Aiken Fiction* in New York and has continued to develop her plays through readings and dramaturgical support. She is also a member of the New Dramatists. With composer Kim Sherman, she is developing a musical, *Leaving Queens*, which was commissioned by the Women's Project.

PLAY DESCRIPTIONS

Ryan's plays are characterized by an iconoclastic, quirky humor that is evident in the witty dialogue and often absurdly comic situations. *The Autobiography of Aiken Fiction* explores violence and the persecution of lesbians from a family perspective. The playwright was motivated by her investigations into teen suicide and her discovery that from 30 to 40 percent of those suicides are committed by gay youth. In this darkly comic play, two teenagers forbidden to see each other execute a daring escape. The bizarre getaway features an Alzheimers-striken grandmother who, disguised as a nun and programmed through a tape recorder and headphones, rescues her granddaughter's girlfriend. The two girls take off on a road trip through America during which protagonist Aiken is accompanied by her re-creations of famous dead literary figures: Mary McCarthy, Djuna Barnes, and others. The play ends with Aiken's finding her own biography.

Ryan's more recent works, *Hadley's Mistake* and *Damage and Desire*, although still distinguished by witty language, are less maniacally farcical. Biography as a resource and subject of drama continues to interest Ryan. *Hadley* parallels the disintegration of Ernest Hemingway's first marriage to Hadley with the doomed relationship between a Hemingway scholar and her young protégé. Structurally, the play moves back and forth in time and fancifully juxtaposes scenes in the past with events in the present. A bittersweet romance, *Hadley* examines the consequences of accident and age difference in a straight relationship and in a lesbian one.

The most realistic of Ryan's plays to date, the one-set three-character *Damage and Desire*, chronicles the attempts of a poet to come to terms with her sister's cancer, her best friend's betrayal, and her own addiction to alcohol. Wit and erudition characterize the protagonist's monologues, such as the one that eulogizes the "extinction of the last 5 and Dime." The conflict between the lesbian poet and the gay playwright exposes some controversial issues besetting the gay and lesbian community.

SELECTED PRODUCTION HISTORY

Rescuing Marilyn
  Production, Loft Theatre, Tampa, Florida, 1992

Hadley's Mistake
  Workshop, Taper Lab 1993–1994 New Work Festival, Mark Taper Forum, Los Angeles, 1993

The Autobiography of Aiken Fiction
  Production, Women's Project and New Georges at the Samuel Beckett Theatre, New York, April 1994

Castro Convertible Girl
  Production, TWEED Festival, Vineyard Theatre, New York, 1994

Leaving Queens
  Workshop, Women's Project at the Theatre Row Theatre, New York, 1996

Readings of these and other plays have been held at New Dramatists, Women's Project, Dixon Place, Manhattan Theatre Club, Primary Stages, BRAVA! for Women in the Arts, Eureka Theatre, Intersection for the Arts, MidWest Playwrights Lab, and Williamstown Theatre Festival among others.

PLAY AVAILABILITY

"Free Ride on the Queen Mary" is published in Jocelyn A. Beard, *The Best Women's Stage Monologues of 1992*. Newbury, Vermont: Smith and Kraus, 1992.

Other plays and information are available through Ryan's agent: Beth Blickens at William Morris, 1350 Avenue of the Americas, New York, New York 10019; (212) 586–5100.

AWARDS

Edward Albee Fellowship, 1990

MacDowell Fellowship, 1992

Yaddo Fellowship, 1993

Van Lier Fellowship at the Women's Project, 1993

Sumner Locke Elliot Fellowship to the Australian National Playwrights Conference, 1994

New York Foundation for the Arts Playwriting Fellowship, 1994

Helene Wurlitzer Foundations Fellowship, 1995

New Dramatist Playwright-in-Residence at the Royal National Theatre, 1996

Susan Smith Blackburn Award, Finalist, *Hadley's Mistake*, 1997

DESCRIPTIVE AND CRITICAL RESPONSES

Bougetz, Susan. "The Autobiography of Aiken Fiction." An interview with Kate Ryan in Women's Project. *Dialogues* Women's Project, New York, 10, no. 3: 1, 5.

Hurley, Joseph. "Probing the Past." *Irish Echo*, New York, 3–9 April 1996, 4.

Van Gelder, Lawrence. "The Autobiography of Aiken Fiction." Review of *The Autobiography of Aiken Fiction. New York Times*, 5 May 1994, C20.

MILCHA SANCHEZ-SCOTT

(1953–   )

BIOGRAPHY

Milcha Sanchez-Scott was born on the island of Bali, and her heritage reflects a diversity of ethnic and cultural influences. Her mother is of Indonesian, Chinese, and Dutch ancestry; her father was born in Colombia and raised in Mexico. She attended a Catholic girls' school near London, while her father was working in Europe. However, she also spent time in Colombia and Mexico before the family moved to La Jolla, California, when Sanchez-Scott was fourteen years old. She attended the University of San Diego, where she earned a degree in literature, philosophy, and theatre.

After graduation she worked at the San Diego Zoo and later in an employment agency for maids in Beverly Hills. She began collecting the stories of the immigrant women who were applying for work, and it was from this experience that Sanchez-Scott's first play, *Latina*, evolved. It was also around that time that she was hired by the L.A. Theatre Works to act in a project at the women's prison in Chino. "I'd found a channel to get all sorts of things flowing out. I liked controlling my own time, and *making* things" (Osborn, 246).

Sanchez-Scott was invited to join **Maria Irene Fornes**'s playwriting workshop at INTAR in New York City in 1984–1985. Her family drama, *Roosters*, was released on video in 1995. She was a member of the New Dramatists. Sanchez-Scott lives in Los Angeles where she has worked with the group Artists in Prison and Other Places. She is an alumna of the New Dramatists and has been commissioned to write *La Carmen*, a contemporary adaptation of Georges Bizet's opera, for the Mark Taper Forum.

PLAY DESCRIPTIONS

Milcha Sanchez-Scott's work frequently explores women's experiences in an Hispanic American bicultural context. Her plays are a combination of gritty realism with flights of surrealistic fantasy. In *Latina* she delineates the lives of the Latin American immigrant women who work in and for an employment agency that specializes in domestic help. The characters run the gamut from Sarita, the fully assimilated Latina who speaks perfect English and wants to be an actress, to the New Girl, an illegal immigrant who has just arrived from a mountain village in Peru. The women wear their various cultures and backgrounds as badges of honor which often conflict with one another, yet they are all united in their struggle against the economic oppression and sexism that pervade their lives.

In two highly imaginative one-act plays, the playwright employs athletic prowess as a means of gaining Anglo success for a young Latina. In the *Dog Lady*, Rosalinda is training for an all-California Catholic girls' marathon. The romantic young woman sees winning this race and its free trip to Rome as a way of escaping the Los Angeles barrio; she motivates herself by traversing the world in her imagination. She is ultimately aided in her success by Luisa Ruiz, the Dog Lady, whose magic potions give Rosalinda the swiftness and agility of a dog. Whether Rosalinda's success can be attributed to hard work, Mexican mojo, or divine guidance, it is apparent that the entire neighborhood is transformed by Rosalinda's winning the race. In the companion one-act play, *The Cuban Swimmer*, a long-distance swimmer is aided by a magical intervention while she races from San Pedro to Catalina Island. Her family follows her in a leaky boat but provides little guidance for her endeavors.

Roosters is the story of the Morales family's struggle to reconcile Old World Mexican values, such as honor and machismo, with more nurturing, life-affirming values. This conflict is symbolically waged between Gallo, the head of the family who has just been released from prison for manslaughter, and his son, Hector, who has been doing menial labor in order to support the family. The center of their personal battle is the rooster, Zapata, that Hector has inherited from his grandfather but Gallo has trained as a killer. Gallo hopes to breed the bird into a new strain of fighting cocks and thereby regain his prestige in the community; Hector plans to trade the rooster to their primary cockfighting competitors in exchange for calling off the vendetta against Gallo. The conflict between these two ways of life is exotically enacted in a lethal dance, a symbolic counterpoint to the overt naturalism of the play. The real victims in this battle, however, are the women of the family. Juana, the loyal and trusting wife, is powerless over her husband's comings and goings; she must be content with brief moments and hollow promises. A comic and touching antidote to Juana's gullibility is Chata's (her sister) cynicism about men. As the partially retired whore-with-a-heart-of-gold, she is not so quick to trust in men's promises or to rely on them for her survival. It is Gallo's daughter (Angela), however, who is both the most damaged and transformed by her familial situation. The precocious teenager has retreated into a world of spiritual fantasy: she dons wings and serves tea to saint dolls. When Hector refuses to continue fighting his father and throws down his knife, Angela's spiritual transcendence, the quality she has been seeking throughout the play, is manifested in her unearthly, magical levitation. A new familial relationship, if not a new world, appears imminent when Gallo's violence is replaced with Hector and Angela's life-affirming values.

SELECTED PRODUCTION HISTORY

Latina
Production, L.A. Theatre Works, Los Angeles, 1980

Dog Lady (one-act play)
Production, INTAR, New York, 1984

The Cuban Swimmer (one-act play)
Production, INTAR, New York, 1984

Roosters
Development, Hispanic Playwrights-in-Residence Laboratory, INTAR, New York, 1985
Development, Playwrights Laboratory, Sundance Institute, Utah, 1986
Production, INTAR, coproduced by the New York Shakespeare Festival, New York, 1987
Production, Eureka Theatre, San Francisco, 1987
Television production for "American Playhouse," Los Angeles, 1988
Video, 1993

Stone Wedding
Production, Los Angeles, 1988

Evening Star (one-act play)
Production, Theatre for a New Audience, New York, 1988

Carmen (adaptation of Georges Bizet's opera)
Production, Los Angeles Theatre Center, 1988

El Dorado
Production, South Coast Repertory, Costa Mesa, California, 1991

The Old Matador
Production, Arizona Theatre Company, Phoenix, 1995

PLAY AVAILABILITY

The Cuban Swimmer is published by the Dramatists Play Service. New York, 1988; and in Daniel Halpern, ed., *Plays in One Act*. New York: Ecco Press, 1991.

Dog Lady is published in Ramon Delgado, ed., *The Best Short Plays of 1986*. New York: Applause Books, 1986; and by the Dramatists Play Service. New York, 1988.

Evening Star is published by Dramatists Play Service, New York, 1989.

Latina is published in Jorge A. Huerta, ed., *Necessary Theatre: Six Plays about the Chicano Experience*. Houston: Arte Publico Press, 1989.

Roosters is published in Elizabeth Osborn, *On New Ground: Contemporary Hispanic-*

American Plays. New York: Theatre Communications Group, 1987; *American Theatre*, September 1987; and by the Dramatists Play Service, New York, 1988.

AWARDS

Dramalogue Awards, *Latina*, 1980

Vesta Award, *Dog Lady* and *The Cuban Swimmer*, 1983

Le Compte du Nouy Prize, 1985

Rockefeller Foundation, First Level Award for American Playwriting, 1987

Playwright Fellow, Latino Theatre Initiative, Mark Taper Forum, Los Angeles, 1995–1996

DESCRIPTIVE AND CRITICAL RESPONSES

Arkatov, Janice. "Playwright Enters World of Cockfighting in *Roosters*." *Los Angeles Times*, 15 June 1988, VI, 3.

Bouknight, Jon. "Language as a Cure: An Interview with Milcha Sanchez-Scott." *Latin American Theatre Review* 23, no. 2 (Spring 1990): 63–74.

Gussow, Mel. "Stage: 'Roosters' at INTAR." Review of *Roosters*. *New York Times*, 24 March 1987, C15.

Henry, William A. "Visions from the Past: Emerging Playwrights Trade Anger for Dialogue." *Time* 132 (11 July 1988): 82–83.

Huerta, Jorge. "*Latina*." In *Necessary Theatre: Six Plays about the Chicano Experience*, edited by Jorge Huerta. 76–81. Houston: Arte Publico Press, 1989.

———. "Professionalizing Teatro: An Overview of Chicano Theatre during the 'Decade of the Hispanic.' " *TheatreForum* (Spring 1993): 54–59.

JOAN SCHENKAR

(1946–   )

BIOGRAPHY

Schenkar was born and raised in Seattle, Washington, in the 1940s in a comfortable Jewish household but attended Episcopalian preparatory schools. She left the West Coast for Bennington College, where she planned to major in archaeology but graduated in literature. Although she continued her studies for a time at the University of California at Berkeley, she returned to the East for a doctoral program at the State University of New York at Stony Brook, but left the program when the university refused to accept a play as her dissertation. Her plays reflect her academic training in the way she draws on history and literature. Schenkar's distorted treatment of facts is, however, unique. "I go to the ends of my nerves and bring back the news. . . . I get up out of my dreams and write. I allow myself to dream things I cannot live through" (Zimmer, 96). Her playwriting began on a farm in Vermont, and she continues to alternate living in the country with living in New York City. In the city, she has worked with Joseph Chaikin's Winter Project and the Polish Laboratory Theatre as a playwright in residence and has taught creative writing at the School for the Visual Arts. Schenkar has studied ballet, painting, and music, and she plays several instruments. She sees the composition of her plays as similar to musical composition and feels her plays should be played like Noel Coward without the subtext. Her plays are widely produced by experimental theatres and colleges and universities in North America, Great Britain, and Europe, and her work is the subject of a number of analyses in academic journals. Schenkar is a member of P.E.N., the Brontë Society, the League of Professional Theatre Women, the Women's Project, and the Dramatists Guild.

PLAY DESCRIPTIONS

Schenkar appropriately subtitles many of her plays, "A Comedy of Menace." Her work, characterized by a visceral and musical language, challenges audience expectations with their nightmarish, comedic representations. *Cabin Fever* features three characters, a woman and two men, who sit on a porch and lament the winter weather which apparantly is so severe that unusual methods of survival prevail. The two men speak in hard New England accents and the woman in an unidentifiable country dialect about the perverse behavior of their neighbors, including blatant instances of cannibalism. As the play winds down, the men threaten to kill and eat their companion but fate intervenes. When the men suffer a kind of paralysis, the woman draws a knife and the stage direction reads, "the stage appears to be running in blood."

In *Signs of Life*, the story of Jane Merritt, a P. T. Barnum freak called the "Elephant Woman" parallels the story of Alice James, Henry's invalid sister, whose diaries he plumbed for his fiction and then burned at her death. Jane's consolation for her limited, isolated life is reading Jane Austen, Emily Dickinson, and the Brontës; Alice's consolation is the aggravation she causes Henry and the comfort she receives from her nurse and lover, Katherine Loring. Other characters include an alcoholic and mercenary Barnum; Dr. Sloper, a knife-collecting gynecologist whose favorite instrument is the "uterine guillotine"; and a narcoleptic, self-serving Henry James. Both women die premature deaths, frustrating the male keepers who draw creative (and monetary) sustenance from them. Alice dies of breast cancer and Jane of a broken neck when she deliberately lets her heavy head snap. Alice speaks for both these courageous and tenacious women when she says, "Life is such a tragedy, that it *requires* a happy end."

The Universal Wolf, subtitled "a vicious new version of 'Little Red Riding Hood,' " deconstructs the patriarchal underpinnings of the fairy tale and, in a challenging reversal, portrays the grandmother as a wolf in sheep's clothing. In this version, Little Red beats the wolf, a French structuralist, to her grandmother's house. She hides in the closet and, when he finds her, chops him up with an axe. Grandmother, however, is a butcher by trade, and the play ends with her butchering her granddaughter. The appearance throughout of projected images of Claude Lévi-Strauss, Roland Barthes, Alain Robbe-Grillet, and Teresa de Lauretis emphasizes the intellectual influences and helps to underscore that in this play women are not to be regarded as caretakers or victims.

Burning Desires, another "comedy of menace," finds Schenkar returning to a favorite subject, Joan of Arc, whom she featured in an earlier musical, *Fire in the Future*. The play, epic in scope, includes a battle between Joan's supporters (the Bonfire Girls) and her enemies (the Boy Scouts). It is also personal in its references to Schenkar's adolescence during the 1950s. In this unique rendering of the saint's story, it is 1957, Joan smokes Gauloises, and she drives a white Triumph convertible in Seattle where it always rains, where "*This* time, she might not burn." Her miraculous birth, signaled by an uncharacteristic shining sun, results in an unorthodox religious interest: Emily Dickinson, the Brontës, Gertrude Stein, and Diana of the Ephesians are revered as saints while the icons of the baby Jesus and Mary and the star of David are honored. In the climactic moment, Joan's evil scientist/doctor father pleads to a council of surgeons that, because of her insanity, he must perform a lobotomy. Joan's saints send a bolt of lightning just in time, burning down the hospital and saving her from her father. At the end of the play she is standing triumphantly by her Triumph convertible against a skyline of Seattle admitting that "my mission, my *real* mission, was to be put here, in this time and place, and to be made uncomfortable enough to tell my story." It is a fitting coda for the play and for the mission of the playwright.

SELECTED PRODUCTION HISTORY

The Next Thing and *Cabin Fever*
  Production, La Mama Hollywood, Los Angeles, 1976

Cabin Fever
  Production, St. Clements, New York City, 1977
  Production, WPA Theatre, New York, 1978
  Production, Public Theatre, New York, 1978
  Production, Florida Studio Theatre, Sarasota, 1979
  Production, Theatre for the New City, New York, 1983
  Production, Gate Theatre, London, 1986

Signs of Life
  Production, Women's Project at the American Place Theatre, New York, 1979
  Production, King's Head Theatre, London, 1983
  Production, Horizons Theatre, Washington, D.C., 1984

The Lodger
  Production, Theatre of the Open Eye, New York, 1979
  Production, Theatre for the New City, New York, 1988

Mr. Monster
  Production, Florida Studio Theatre, Sarasota, 1980

The Last of Hitler
  Production, Changing Scene Theatre, Denver, Colorado, 1982
  Production, Theatre for the New City, New York, 1984

Fulfilling Koch's Postulate
  Production, Theatre for a New City, New York, 1986
  Production, Gate Theatre, London, 1986

Joan of Arc (musical)
  Production, New Music Theatre Ensemble of the Minnesota Opera, Minneapolis, 1986

Fire in the Future (musical)

Production, New Music Theatre Ensemble of the Minnesota Opera, Minneapolis, 1987

Family Pride in the 50's
Production, Theatre for the New City, New York, 1987
Production, Omaha Magic Theatre, Omaha, Nebraska, 1987

Bucks and Does
Production, Williams Art Center, Williamstown, Massachusetts, 1987

Hunting Down the Sexes
Production, Home Theatre, New York, 1987

Between the Acts
Production, Theatre for the New City, New York, 1989

The Universal Wolf
Production, Ubu Repertory, New York, 1990

Burning Desires
Reading, New Dramatists, New York, 1995

PLAY AVAILABILITY

Cabin Fever and *Signs of Life* are published by Samuel French, 45 West 25th Street, New York, New York 10010.

The Universal Wolf is anthologized in Rosette C. Lamont, *Women on the Verge: 7 Avant-Garde Plays*. New York: Applause, 1993.

Others plays are available from Joan Schenkar, Box 814, North Bennington, Vermont 05257.

AWARDS (SELECTED)

New York State Creative Arts Public Service Playwriting Grant, 1979

Visiting Fellow, Ragdale Foundation, 1979

New Dramatists Member, 1980

Visiting Fellow, MacDowell, 1980

National Endowment for the Arts Playwriting Fellow, 1981–1982

Arthur Foundation Grant, 1983, 1984, 1988, and 1989

Joe and Emily Lowe Foundation Grant, 1983

Obie, Nomination, 1983

New York State Council on the Arts Grant, 1986 and 1989

Kertu Schubert Travel Grant to Belgium, 1988

New York State Creative Arts Public Service Production Grant, 1988

Numerous playwright-in-residence grants

DESCRIPTIVE AND CRITICAL RESPONSES

Diamond, Elin. ''Crossing the *corpus callosum*: An Interview with Joan Schenkar.''
   Drama Review 35 (Summer 1991): 99–101.
Munk, Erica. ''On the Woman Question.'' *Village Voice*, 18 June 1979, 100.
Patraka, Vivian M. ''An Interview with Joan Schenkar.'' *Studies in American Drama* 4
   (1989): 187–202.
———. ''Mass Culture and Metaphors of Menace in Joan Schenkar's Plays.'' In *Making
   a Spectacle: Critical Studies in Contemporary Women Playwrights*, edited by
   Lynda Hart, 25–40. Ann Arbor: Univeristy of Michigan Press, 1989.
Rosenfeld, Megan. ''Dream Weaver.'' *Washington Post*, 25 October 1984, D7.
Stasio, Marilyn. ''Signs of Life at APT.'' *New York Post*, June 1979, 44.
Wilson, Ann. ''History and Hysteria: Writing the Body in Portrait of Dora and Signs of
   Life.'' *Modern Drama* 32 (March 1989): 73–88.
Zimmer, Elizabeth. ''Joan Schenkar: 'I Get Up out of My Dreams and Write.' '' *Village
   Voice*, 6 March 1984, 96.

NTOZAKE SHANGE

(1948–   )

BIOGRAPHY

Born Paulette Williams in Trenton, New Jersey, Ntozake Shange moved with her family to St. Louis, Missouri, at the age of eight. When she was thirteen, she returned with her family to complete high school in New Jersey, where her surgeon father and educator mother entertained black musicians, writers, and political leaders in their home. In 1970 she graduated with a BA in American studies from Barnard College, and she completed an MA in American studies at the University of Southern California in 1973. Following a difficult separation from her first husband and frustrated at the limited career options for women, Williams chose to take the African name of Ntozake Shange (meaning "she who comes with her own things" and one "who walks like a lion") in 1971.

During Shange's multifaceted career, she has been a poet, author, dancer, actress, director, educator, installation artist, and musician. (Her band was Zaki and the Palm Wine Drunkards.) She has held several academic posts at California State College, City College of New York, and Rutgers University, and she was the Mellon Distinguished Professor of Literature at Rice University and a professor of drama at the University of Houston, among others. She has directed plays for the New York Shakespeare Festival and other theatres and has performed in several jazz/dance/poetry ensembles on both coasts. In addition to her theatre pieces, she has written several volumes of poetry and fiction. Her poetry includes *Nappy Edges* (1978), *A Daughter's Geography: Poetry* (1983), and *Matrilineal Poems* (1983); her fiction includes *Sassafrass, Cypress & Indigo: A Novel* (1982), *Betsy Brown* (1985), *The Love Space Demands*, and her recent book *Liliane: Resurrection of the Daughter* (1995).

Shange resides in Philadelphia with her daughter where she writes and teaches; she has recently directed several plays for the Ensemble Theatre in Houston, Texas.

PLAY DESCRIPTIONS

Ntozake Shange's plays consistently challenge the traditional forms of dramaturgy. Her "choreopoem" style is a mélange of storytelling, poetry, street vernacular, and dance. Her exploration of language is an essential part of her redefinition of what it is to be black and a woman. Shange's trademark dramaturgy was evident in her first, and perhaps best-known, play, *for colored girls who have considered suicide/ when the rainbow is enuf.* By blending dance, color, and poetry, Shange plumbs the personal experiences and psyches of a number of black women to create a celebration of life and survival. Known only as Lady in Brown, Lady in Green, and so forth, the seven women embody the pain and joy of a spectrum of the female experience. (See Sydné Mahone's chapter in this volume for a further discussion of the play.)

In *A Photograph: Lovers-in-Motion*, Shange turns her unique style to an examination of the painful evolution of a love relationship. By focusing on Sean, an ambitious but struggling photographer, she gives us snapshots of his involvement with the three women who are in love with him. Claire, a model and cocaine addict, is primarily concerned with maintaining a highly charged sexual relationship with Sean. The wealthy attorney Nevada seeks to mold Sean into her own buppiefied image, exchanging her values for his. Sean, however, stays with Michael, a dancer, whose firm belief in herself is eventually transferred to him; Sean begins to understand that a belief in oneself outweighs sex and money.

Shange's *Spell #7*, framed by suggestions of a minstrel show, is a fluid, shifting examination of racism. Set in a lower Manhattan bar where a group of African American artists (actors, poets, chorus gypsies) meet and commiserate, the play consists of a series of vignettes tied together by a narrator, a character based on the interlocutor of the minstrel show. Through soliloquy and improvised scenes, the characters reveal the enormous price that racism exacts on them as artists in America: the paucity of jobs, the necessity of embodying white-generated stereotypes, and other humiliations. As in *for colored girls*, the growing sense of self-worth and community are necessary for the characters' survival.

The experimental piece *Boogie Woogie Landscapes* is a blend of surrealism and expressionism that gives voice to the thoughts, dreams, and memories of Layla, a young African American woman. This stream-of-consciousness piece is another in Shange's explorations of what it is to be female in America.

Nomathemba is a modern parable of love in postapartheid South Africa. It chronicles the story of an independent young woman, Nomathemba, who is thrilled with the prospects of freedom that the new South Africa affords and leaves her boyfriend whose mind is set on love and marriage. Their separate quests force them to confront the realities of poverty and desperation in their homeland.

SELECTED PRODUCTION HISTORY

Ntozake Shange's plays have had extensive productions since the beginning of her career. Only the first and significant regional productions or important revivals have been listed.

for colored girls who have considered suicide/ when the rainbow is enuf (full-length choreopoem)
(Workshopped and performed in stages of development in California and New York)
Production, New Federal Theatre, New York, 1976
Production, Public Theatre, New York, 1976
Production, Booth Theatre, Broadway, New York, 1978
Production, New Federal Theatre, New York, 1995

A Photograph: Lovers-in-Motion (two-act poem play originally titled *A Photograph: A Still Life in Shadow* and subsequently produced as *A Photograph: A Study of Cruelty*)
Production, Public Theatre, 1977
Production, Equinox Theatre, Houston, Texas, 1979

Where the Mississippi Meets the Amazon (full-length cabaret in collaboration with Jessica Hagedorn and Thulani Davis)
Production, Public Theatre, 1977

From Okra to Greens (full-length theatre piece)
Production, Barnard College, New York, 1978

Black & White Two-Dimensional Planes (full-length theatre piece)
Production, Sounds in Motion Studio Works, New York, 1979

Spell #7 (two-act choreopoem)
Production, Public Theatre, New York, 1979
Production, Studio Theatre, Washington, D.C., 1991

Boogie Woogie Landscapes (full-length experimental theatre piece)
Production, Frank Silvera Writer's Workshop, New York, 1979

Mother Courage and Her Children (adaptation of the Bertolt Brecht play)
Production, Public Theatre, New York, 1980

It Has Not Always Been This Way (full-length choreopoem in collaboration with Sounds-in-Motion Dance Company)
Production, Symphony Space, New York, 1981

A Daughter's Geography (full-length choreopoem originally titled *Mouths: A Daughter's Geography* and produced as *Triptych & Bocas*)
Production, The Kitchen, New York, 1981
Workshop, Mark Taper Theatre Lab, Los Angeles, 1982
Production, Mark Taper Forum, Los Angeles, 1983

Betsy Brown (a rhythm and blues musical with Emily Mann; music by Bakida Carroll)

Staged reading, Public Theatre, New York, 1981
Workshop, Public Theatre, New York, 1983
Production, American Music Theatre, Philadelphia, 1989
Production, McCarter Theatre, Princeton, New Jersey, 1991
Production, Crossroads Theatre Company, New Brunswick, New Jersey, 1992

The Dancin' Novel: Sassafrass, Cypress & Indigo (full-length play with Dianne McIntyre and Rod Rogers, based on Shange's novella *Sassafrass, Cypress & Indigo*)
Production, Public Theatre, New York, 1982

The Love Space Demands
Production, Crossroads Theatre Company, New Brunswick, New Jersey, 1992
Production, Lorraine Hansberry Theatre, San Francisco, 1992

Nomathemba (musical with Eric Simonson and Joseph Shabalala of Ladysmith Black Mambazo)
Production, Steppenwolf Theater, Chicago, 1995
Production, Kennedy Center, Washington, D.C., 1996

PLAY AVAILABILITY

Betsy Brown is available as a novel published by St. Martin's Press, 1985.

The Dancin' Novel: Sassafrass, Cypress & Indigo is published as a novel by St. Martin's Press, 1982.

for colored girls who have considered suicide/ when the rainbow is enuf is available from several publishers, including Macmillan, 1975; Bantam, 1977, 1985, 1986; and Methuen, 1990, and is frequently anthologized.

From Okra to Greens: A Different Kinda Love Story is published by Samuel French, 1985.

The Resurrection of the Daughter: Liliane (title was later changed to read *Liliane: The Resurrection of the Daughter*) is excerpted in Sydné Mahone, ed., *Moon Marked and Touched by Sun*. New York: Theatre Communications Group, 1994.

Spell #7, A Photograph: Lovers-in-Motion, and *Boogie Woogie Landscapes* are available in Ntozake Shange, *Three Pieces*. New York: St. Martin's Press, 1981.

AWARDS

Outer Critics' Circle Award, *for colored girls who have considered suicide/ when the rainbow is enuf*, 1977

Obie Award, Best Playwright, *for colored girls*, 1977

Tony Award Nomination, *for colored girls*, 1977

Grammy Award Nomination, *for colored girls*, 1977

AUDELCO Award, Best Playwright, *for colored girls*, 1977

Mademoiselle Award, 1977

Obie Award, Outstanding Adaptation, *Mother Courage and Her Children*, 1981

Guggenheim Fellowship, 1981

Medal of Excellence, Columbia University, 1981

Paul Robeson Achievement Award, 1992

Lila Wallace–Reader's Digest Writers Award, 1992

Living Legend Award, National Black Theatre Festival, 1993

DESCRIPTIVE AND CRITICAL RESPONSES

Due to the extensive critical work on Shange, only a few recent articles are listed.

Betsko, Kathleen, and Rachel Koenig. "Interview." In *Interviews with Contemporary Women Playwrights*, edited by Kathleen Betsko and Rachel Koenig. 365–76. New York: Beech Tree Books, 1987.

Brantley, Ben. "7 Sisters Still Reflect Rainbow's Colors." Review of *for colored girls*. *New York Times*, 26 June 1995, C11.

Carroll, Rebecca. "Back at You: Ntozake Shange." *Mother Jones* 20 (January–February 1995): 69.

Cronacher, Karen. "Unmasking the Minstrel Mask's Black Magic in Ntozake Shange's *Spell #7*." *Theatre Journal* 44, no. 2 (May 1992): 177–93.

Deshazer, Mary K. "Rejecting Necrophilia: Ntozake Shange and the Warrior Re-Visioned." In *Making a Spectacle: Feminist Essays on Contemporary Women's Theatre*, edited by Lynda Hart, 86–100. Ann Arbor: University of Michigan Press, 1989.

Lester, Neal A. "At the Heart of Shange's Feminism: An Interview." *Black American Literature Forum* 24 (Winter 1990): 717–30.

———. *Ntozake Shange: A Critical Study of the Plays*. New York: Garland, 1995.

Lewis, Barbara. "Back Over the Rainbow." *American Theatre* (September 1995): 6.

McLarin, Kimberly J. "Native Daughter." *New York Times*, 24 November 1994, C1, 8.

Stevens, Andrea. " 'for colored girls' May Be for the Ages." *New York Times*, 3 September 1995, C5.

ANNA DEAVERE SMITH

(1951–   )

BIOGRAPHY

Born in Baltimore, Maryland, Smith grew up in a predominantly Jewish neighborhood. She briefly pursued linguistics at a small women's school, Beaver College (now coed), before heading to San Francisco in search of Angela Davis and Jane Fonda: "I was looking for the revolution" (Mason, 50), she explains. Acting classes at the American Conservatory Theatre in San Francisco intervened, and by 1976 she had completed an MFA degree and obtained her Equity card. Smith moved to New York, taught acting at Carnegie Mellon, and acted in New York and San Francisco.

Her first professionally produced play, *Aye Aye I'm Integrated*, a monodrama, was produced by the Women's Project where Anna was a member of the Directors Forum, an arena in which she tried out her performances of interviews which catapulted her to national visibility. Her method of interviewing and then performing verbatim the words of the people interviewed started as a teaching device to help student actors get the words off the page. Intrigued with her findings, Smith began taping and performing her interviews under the umbrella title *On the Road* (to which she added *A Search for American Character* several years later) for specific groups, such as women in law for whom she presented her first public performance at their conference in 1985. Other early notable performances included two presentations at the Women in Theatre conferences, which sparked considerable debate and, subsequently, publication and scholarly analyses. Frequent invitations to colleges followed, where Smith typically interviewed a cross section of people around some social issue. The interviews on sexism led to the performance at Princeton University of *Gender Bending: On the Road/Princeton*.

An interview with composer and conductor Tania Leon led to a full-length play, *Piano*, produced by the Los Angeles Theatre Center in 1990. Smith continued to intersperse acting and teaching. She was commissioned to present a portrait of San Francisco by the Eureka Theatre Company, which was performed as *From the Outside Looking In: On the Road San Francisco, 1990.*

In 1991 she was invited to participate in the Festival of New Voices at the Joseph Papp Public Theatre in New York and spent four days conducting several interviews in Crown Heights, the site of a recent conflict between Jews and blacks. The work was well received and led to the longer, much acclaimed *Fires in the Mirror*, a finalist for the Pulitzer Prize. Smith's solo performances have won lavish praise for the originality of her technique and her courage in tackling controversial issues. "Smith is the ideal theatre artist for the '90s, as America attempts to synthesize an increasingly diverse culture," Jack Kroll claimed in *Newsweek* in 1992.

Smith's work is a combination of journalism, linguistics, sociology, and drama. She interviews a very carefully selected group of people who will represent diverse points of view on a topic and then chooses a portion of the interview that can be presented intact. Through her replication of the interviewee's speech behavior, Smith reveals the character of the person. As she repeats the recording of her subject, memorizing the words and manner of speech, she feels she "becomes" the character in a more organic way than would be permitted by the traditional Stanislavski method of character development. Her scrupulously prepared performance texts are an unusual combination of instinctual selection and academic thoroughness, as her titles suggest. Because her primary subject is race, Smith is all the more careful to present viewpoints as accurately as possible. In creating *Twilight*, Smith insisted on four dramaturgs: Asian, Hispanic, African American, and white; two women and two men.

She has also participated in the more commercial entertainment world, appearing in the films *Philadelphia* and *American President* and on the Arsenio Hall television show. However, Smith maintains her position as the Ann O'Day Maples Professor of the Arts at Stanford University and continues to develop *On the Road* performances with nonprofit theatres. Smith's largest project to date, a performance exploring the relationship between the press and the president, takes her "on the road" following the 1996 presidential campaign, then to the Arena Stage in Washington, D.C., the Goodman in Chicago, and the Mark Taper Forum in Los Angeles to present her findings, this time with other actors on stage.

PLAY DESCRIPTIONS

Smith's playwriting has explored distinctly different forms: from the realistic, social issue one-act *Aye Aye I'm Integrated* and *Piano*, a lyrical full-length play set in Cuba in the 1800s on the eve of the revolution, to her journalistically based, one-person performances. The work she is best known for, the solo texts she compiles and performs, chart unexplored territory in the theatre. Because of the uniqueness of her methodology, both in the journalistic composition and the verbatim rendering, the way in which the texts are constructed is as much discussed as their content. The two best-known one-person performances, *Fires in the Mirror* and *Twilight*, are centered on headline events that Smith chooses because they powerfully embody the racial problems in the United States, the issue she believes is *the* issue of our time. *Fires* interviews twenty-six people involved in, or who have opinions about, race and the confrontation between Jews and blacks following the accidental death of Gavin Cato in Crown Heights and the retaliatory murder of an innocent bystander, Yankel Rosenbaum. Racial tension on a larger scale, the riots in South Central Los Angeles that occurred after the acquittal of the officers accused of beating a black man, Rodney King, is the subject of *Twilight*. By presenting forty-six interviewees in this play, including one of the jurors in the King trial, Smith tries to provide an overview of the tragedies by including a large diversity of voices broadly inclusive of race, age, gender, the disenfranchised, and the powerful. By presenting collectively, side by side, Koreans and blacks, scholars and politicians, police chief and gang leader, Smith brings together a company of people who, by their unlikely juxtaposition, help give a broader perspective to our "American Character."

SELECTED PRODUCTION HISTORY

Only performances in theatres are included; the performances are solo unless otherwise noted.

Aye Aye I'm Integrated (one-act play)
  Production, Women's Project and Productions at American Place Theatre, New York, 1984

Chlorophyll Post-Modernism and the Mother Goddess: A Convers/Ation
  Production, Hahn Cosmopolitan Theatre, San Diego, 1988

On Black Identity and Black Theatre
  Production, Crossroads Theatre Company, New Brunswick, New Jersey, 1989

Piano (full-length play)
  Production, Los Angeles Theatre Center, Los Angeles, 1990

From the Outside Looking In: On the Road San Francisco, 1990
  Production, Eureka Theatre, San Francisco, 1990

Identities: Mirrors and Distortions IV
  Production, Festival of New Voices, Public Theatre, New York, 1991

Dream (a workshop)
  Workshop, Crossroads Theatre Company, New Brunswick, New Jersey, 1992

Fires in the Mirror: Crown Heights Brooklyn and Other Identities
  Production, Public Theatre, New York, 1992

Production, Royal Court Theatre, London, 1993
Production (video), "American Playhouse," Public Broadcasting Service, 1993

Twilight: Los Angeles, 1992
Production, Mark Taper Forum, Los Angeles, 1993
Work in progress, McCarter Theatre Center, Princeton, New Jersey, 1993
Production, Public Theatre, New York, 1994
Cort Theatre, Broadway, New York, 1994

Hymn (with Judith Jamison)
Production, Alvin Ailey American Dance Theatre, City Center, New York, 1993

PLAY AVAILABILITY

Ballerinas and Ball Passing is published in *Women in Performance Journal* 3, no. 1 (1987–1988): 7–31.

Fires in the Mirror is published by Anchor Books (1993); also in Sydné Mahone, ed., *Moon Marked and Touched by Sun*. New York: Theatre Communications Group, 1994. The audiotape version is available from Anchor Books Audio Publishing and the videocassette, from PBS Video.

Introduction to Chlorophyll: Postmodernism and the Mother Goddess: A Convers/Ation is published in *Women in Performance Journal* 4, no. 2 (1989): 27–49.

Piano is published in *Plays in Progress* 9, no. 10 (1989).

Twilight: Los Angeles, 1992: A Search for American Character is published by Anchor Books (1994).

AWARDS

Drama-Logue Award, *Piano*, 1991

Fellow, Bunting Institute, Radcliffe College, 1991–1992

Obie Award, *Fires in the Mirror*, 1992

Drama Desk Award, *Fires in the Mirror*, 1992

Lucille Lortel Award, *Fires in the Mirror*, 1992

Joseph Kesselring Prize, *Fires in the Mirror*, 1992

George and Elizabeth Marton Award, *Fires in the Mirror*, 1992

Pulitzer Prize, Runner-up, *Fires in the Mirror*, 1992

Glamour Magazine, Women of the Year, 1993

Rockefeller Grant for Residency at Bellagio, Italy, 1993

Obie Award, *Twilight*, 1994

Tony Award Nomination, *Twilight*, 1994

Commission from Arena Stage, the Goodman Theatre and Mark Taper Forum, 1996

MacArthur Foundation Grant, 1996

Pew/Theatre Communications Group National Theatre Artist Residency Program, 1996

DESCRIPTIVE AND CRITICAL RESPONSES

Ahlgren, Calvin. "Authors 'Journey' Back to Human Nature." *San Francisco Chronicle*, 17 June 1990, D35–36.

Church, Michael. "Voices from Feel-bad Brooklyn." *London Observer*, 21 March 1993, 57.

Clines, Frances X. "The 29 Voices of One Woman in Search of Crown Heights." *New York Times*, 10 June 1992, C1.

Kaufman, Joanne. "Passion Plays: The Actress Forges Art from the Ashes of Racial Conflict." *Washington Post*, 25 April 1993, G1.

Kroll, Jack. "A Woman for All Seasons." *Newsweek*, 26 June 1992: 74.

———. "Fire in the City of Angels." *Newsweek*, 28 June 1993, 62–63.

Lahr, John. "Under the Skin." *New Yorker*, 28 June 1993, 91–94.

Lewis, Barbara. "The Circle of Confusion: A Conversation with Anna Deavere Smith." *Kenyon Review* 15 (Fall 1993): 54–64.

Lyons, Charles R. "Anna Deavere Smith: Perspectives on Her Performance within the Context of Critical Theory. *Journal of Dramatic Theory and Criticism* 9, no. 1 (Fall 1994): 43–66.

Martin, Carol. "Anna Deavere Smith: The Word Becomes You." *Drama Review* 37 (Winter 1993): 45–62.

Mason, Susan. "Smith's Specialty Is Enacting Real People." *American Theatre*, September 1989, 50–51.

Masullo, Robert. "Acts That Are Tough to Beat." *Sacramento Bee*, 24 June 1990, C5.

O'Quinn, Jim. "Getting Closer to America." *American Theatre* 13, no. 8 (October 1996): 18–20.

Richards, Sandra L. "Caught in the Act of Social Definition: *On the Road* with Anna Deavere Smith." In *Acting Out: Feminist Performances*, edited by Lynda Hart and Peggy Phelan. Ann Arbor: University of Michigan Press, 1993, 35–53.

Rugoff, Ralph. "One-Woman Chorus." *Vogue*, April 1993, 238, 242.

Schechner, Richard. "Anna Deavere Smith: Acting as Incorporation." *Drama Review* 37 (Winter 1993): 63–64.

Smith, Chris. "Crown Heights Witness." *New York Magazine*, 29 August 1994, 35–39.

Tate, Greg. "Bewitching the Other." *Village Voice*, 21 July 1992, 98–99.

BEVERLY SMITH-DAWSON

(1955–   )

BIOGRAPHY

Beverly Smith-Dawson was born and raised in Phoenix, Arizona. She attended Arizona State University where she earned a BS in zoology in 1976 and a master's degree in health services administration in 1979. After experiencing what Smith-Dawson refers to as an early "mid-life career crisis," she left hospital administration for theatre. Although her initial interest was playwriting, Smith-Dawson entered the MFA directing program at the Yale School of Drama in order to learn all aspects of theatre. She now divides her time between playwriting and her directing career.

Smith-Dawson's diverse theatre work has taken her to San Francisco, New Haven, Minneapolis, and Washington, D.C. She has been an associate member of the Playwrights' Center in Minneapolis where she was a Jerome Fellow from 1988 to 1989; she also worked with the Children's Theatre of Minneapolis which commissioned her to write *On the Wings of the Hummingbird*. She was the A. L. Hughes Fellow in Directing at the Arena Stage in Washington, D.C., in 1990. The many productions for which she served as assistant director include Des McAnuff's production of *A Walk in the Woods* on Broadway and Lloyd Richards's production of *Joe Turner's Come and Gone* for the Yale Repertory Theatre. Smith-Dawson currently resides in New York City where she is founder and artistic producer of Stormy Weather Productions (SWP). She is a member of the Dramatists Guild.

PLAY DESCRIPTIONS

In her plays, Beverly Dawson-Smith often explores the tenuous bonds of love and familial duty by focusing on the dysfunctional family unit. Her *Medea* is an amalgam of classical myth and contemporary culture. Smith-Dawson uses the classical legend of the princess who murders her own children in retaliation for Jason's rejection in a modernized telling of the tale that creates a drama of racial tension and revenge. Casting Medea as an African and Jason as a white man heightens the tension of their disintegrating relationship, particularly when Jason chooses to marry Creusa, the very blond daughter of Creon. Not even Aegeus Polo, a successful Athenian businessman who can walk on water and who is Medea's old friend, is able to assuage Medea's passion for revenge.

In *Family Portrait*, Smith-Dawson employs the visual tableaux of portrait photographs interspersed with isolated monologues and some dialogue to render a portrait of a dysfunctional family. Although the characters appear normal and healthy at first viewing, their terrible accommodations are revealed as the play progresses. Tandy is Francine's thirty-one-year-old husband; Francine, who is five years older than Tandy, is the mother of twenty-year-old Caryl. Tandy, who has lost his job and his self-esteem, has reverted to snorting cocaine and hanging around the house. Francine becomes consumed with resentment; she is angry with Caryl whose father left Francine when he found out she was pregnant. Her youth has been lost to the responsibility of raising a daughter she did not want. As age creeps up on her, she is desperate to hang on to her man. Caryl is seeking some answers about her real father, knowing that his abandonment has filled her mother with bitterness. Desperate for genuine affection, she begins to enjoy sex with Tandy, and they begin to take risks in their relationship. When Francine catches them in the act, she beats Caryl, but, fearful that she will lose Tandy, she begs him to stay. Tandy, afraid to leave Caryl to her mother's abuse, reaches an agreement with the two women: he sleeps with Caryl in the day while Francine is at work and sleeps with Francine at night. The ostensibly normal portrait is revealed for the fear, abuse, hatred, and sick love that infests the family.

SELECTED PRODUCTION HISTORY

Man with the Blue Guitar
  Production, Black Repertory Group, Berkeley, California, 1984

Atomic Dog Catcher
  Production, Black Repertory Group, Berkeley, California, 1984

Slow Dancin'
  Production, Black Repertory Group, Berkeley, California, 1984
  Production, Theatre Alliance, New Haven, Connecticut, 1985

Family Portrait
  Production, Lorraine Hansberry Theatre, San Francisco, 1984
  Production, San Francisco State University, San Francisco, 1984
  Production, Yale Afro-American Cultural Center, New Haven, Connecticut, 1986
  Production, West Coast Ensemble, Los Angeles, 1990
  Showcase Production, Public Theatre, New York, 1993
  Production, Tribeca Performing Arts Center, New York, 1994

Medea
  Reading, Staged Reading Series, Rutgers University, Newark, New Jersey, 1989
  Reading, McCarter Theatre, Princeton, New Jersey, 1989
  Production, Frank Theatre, Minneapolis, Minnesota, 1991

Water Torture
  Production, One-Act Festival, Actors Theatre of St. Paul, Minnesota, 1989
  Production, Yale Alumni Association, Westbank Cafe/Theatre, New York, 1990
  Showcase Production, Public Theatre, New York, 1993

Composition
  Production, Red Eye Collaborations, Minneapolis, Minnesota, 1989

The Women (play with music)
  Workshop, Illusion Theatre, Minneapolis, Minnesota, 1989

5 Days . . . And Before
  Reading, Hudson Guild Theatre, New York, 1990

On the Wings of the Hummingbird
  Production, Children's Theatre, Minneapolis, Minnesota, 1991

Cover
  Production, Black Ink, Playwrights Horizons, New York, 1995

House of Mirrors
  Reading, Playwrights Horizons, New York, 1996

PLAY AVAILABILITY

Family Portrait is published in *West Coast Plays*, vol. 17/18. Berkeley: California Theatre Council, 1985.

Beverly Smith-Dawson's other scripts are available from the playwright: P.O. Box 1449, Grand Central Station, New York, New York 10163; or call (212) 969–0748.

AWARDS

Cornerstone Playwriting Competition, Penumbra Theatre, St. Paul, Minnesota, First Runner-up, *Medea*, 1988

McDonald Literary Contest, Finalist, *Medea*, 1988

Midwest PlayLabs, Minneapolis, Minnesota, Finalist, *The Surrogate*, 1989

Midwest PlayLabs, Minneapolis, Minnesota, Finalist, *5 Days . . . And Before*, 1990

Sundance Screenwriters Lab, Utah, Finalist, *Heat*, 1990–1991

Midwest PlayLabs, Minneapolis, Minnesota, Finalist, *Composition*, 1991

Midwest PlayLabs, Minneapolis, Minnesota, Finalist, *A Mother's Love*, 1992

O'Neill Center, Waterford, Connecticut, Finalist, *Heat*, 1992

DESCRIPTIVE AND CRITICAL RESPONSES

Bruckner, D.J.R. "Black Ink: 3 Comedies and Death." Review of *Cover*. *New York Times*, 7 December 1995, C18.
Reiter, Amy. "Black Ink." Review of *Cover*. *Back Stage*, 5 January 1996, 44.

DIANA SON

(1965–   )

BIOGRAPHY

Diana Son, who was born in Philadelphia, grew up in Dover, Delaware. She attended New York University and received a BA in dramatic literature in 1987. In 1993 she attended the Iowa Playwrights Workshop at the University of Iowa. Diana Son is currently a member of the Emerging Playwright's Unit in residence at New York's Public Theatre. In addition to having her plays produced at various venues in New York, Son's short stories have been read at colleges, high schools, and museums in the city. Her fiction has been published by the *Asian Pacific American Journal,* and her short story "Fireflies to Bittersweet" appears in *Voices Stirring,* an anthology of Korean American literature. Son is a member of the New Dramatists.

PLAY DESCRIPTIONS

Diana Son has been described as "one of the few Asian American women writers dealing head on with issues of sexuality." In her bold comedy *Boy,* Son confronts the issues of gender discrimination in the raising of children. An exaggerated, parodic style permeates the narrative of birth and maturation. Mama and Dr. Papa Uber Alles eagerly await the birth of their fourth child. Both parents and their three daughters (Hymen, Labia, and Vulva) are convinced that the baby will be a boy. Unwilling to suffer the humiliation when the child is, in fact, born a girl, the parents raise the baby as a boy. Although Boy, as she is called, excels at the masculine skill of carpentry, her sensitivity and kindness set her apart from the other boys her age. Boy uses her carpentry skills to build homes for the squirrels and other animals. Eventually Boy is asked to refurbish a house for Jesse and her daughter, Charlotte. Not until Boy begins to fall in love with Charlotte does the elaborate charade crumble, and Boy is made to realize that she is a young woman. Boy marries Shermie, her childhood buddy, and fails miserably as a wife. When Charlotte returns, Boy leaves Shermie. It is through Charlotte that Boy is able to learn how to fit into the world. (For more on Son's plays, see Chiori Miyagawa's chapter on Asian Americans in this volume.)

SELECTED PRODUCTION HISTORY

Wrecked on Brecht (one act)
  Production, La Mama, New York, 1987

Stealing Fire
  Production, Soho Rep, New York, 1992

R.A.W. ('Cause I'm a Woman) (one act)
  Workshop, Public Theatre, New York, 1993
  Production, TWEED New Works Festival, New York, 1993

The R.A.W. Plays: Short Plays for Raunchy Asian Women
  Production, Home for Contemporary Theatre, New York, 1993

2000 Miles (one act)
  Production, No Pants Theatre Company, New York, 1993
  Production, Ensemble Studio Theatre, New York, 1993
  Production, Under One Roof, New York, 1993
  Production, New Georges, New York, 1995

Fishes
  Reading, Public Theatre, New York, 1995
  Workshop, Mark Taper Forum, Los Angeles, 1995

Boy
  Production, La Jolla Playhouse, La Jolla, California, 1996

PLAY AVAILABILITY

R.A.W. ('Cause I'm a Woman) is published in Kathy A. Perkins and Roberta Uno, eds., *Contemporary Plays by Women of Color.* New York: Routledge, 1996; Eric Lane and Nina Shengold, eds., *Take 10: New 10–Minute Plays.* New York: Vintage, 1997.

Diana Son's unpublished plays are available from Sarah Jane Leigh, ICM, 40 West 57th Street, New York, New York 10019.

AWARD

Van Lier Playwriting Fellowship, New Dramatists, New York, 1993

DESCRIPTIVE AND CRITICAL RESPONSES

Hong, Terry. "Sixth Row Center." *A. Magazine*, Winter 1994, 74.
Yang, Jeff. "Critical Mass." *Village Voice*, 16 March 1993, 92.

SPLIT BRITCHES

(fl. 1980–   )

BIOGRAPHY

The Split Britches company (Lois Weaver, Peggy Shaw, and Deborah Margolin) began in 1980 with a play by that name. Original members Weaver and Shaw founded the WOW (Women's One World) Cafe in 1982, and Split Britches has originated most of their work from this theatre. Weaver began her feminist theatre work with Spiderwoman and stayed with that collective for over seven years. While she was on a European tour, she met Peggy Shaw who was touring with a gay cabaret, Hot Peaches. Shaw was invited to help Spiderwoman, and when Lois Weaver began work on a play based on her three aunts in the Blue Ridge Mountains entitled *Split Britches*, the break from Spiderwoman occurred. Deborah Margolin was invited to script the play in 1981 and later joined as a performer when someone else dropped out. Thus began an enduring historic collaboration in feminist theatre that has provided inspiration for a distinguished group of feminist theatre theoreticians and scholars as well as actors, writers, and directors. In an introduction to her anthology of their work, Sue-Ellen Case summarizes, "They have lived their lives and their relationship on the stage, improvising it into episodes and schtick for almost twenty years. They are the lesbian actors of their time" (Case, 34).

The background of each individual informs the themes and preoccupations of their group work: Margolin as a heterosexual Jewish woman; Shaw as a working-class "butch" lesbian mother; and Weaver as a Southern, working-class "femme" lesbian. Each makes a unique contribution: Shaw in design and visual detail, Margolin as a writer, and Weaver as a director and acting coach. In an interview, Weaver disclaimed a theoretical or political basis for their work: "We talked about our own experiences most all the time. We rarely ever talked about technique or theory or certainly politics."

They are committed to working within and for a community; and the success of WOW, which continues to exist in an upstairs performance space in the East Village, is due, in large part, to their original vision of a place where women could work collaboratively without censure and give back to the organization the time and skills to keep it running. WOW was the original home for **Holly Hughes**, **Carmelita Tropicana**, the **Five Lesbian Brothers**, and **Madeleine Olnek**.

As of this writing, the three members of Split Britches are working separately; Weaver is the co–artistic director of Gay Sweatshop in London; Shaw appeared as an actress off-Broadway at the American Place Theatre in 1996; and Margolin continues to teach, direct, and perform solo pieces, recently at Women's Interart, in New York City.

Acquaintance with the work of Split Britches outside of New York has been enhanced by their extensive touring in the United States, particularly to colleges and universities, and throughout Great Britain and Europe. Now that their plays are readily available in the anthology edited by Sue-Ellen Case, scripts that long have been the object of so much analysis and discussion but unavailable in print will no doubt find a wider appreciation.

PLAY DESCRIPTIONS

Printed versions of the texts of Split Britches provide merely a blueprint for the performed play. Since the three performers are themselves subjects of their work, and frequently disrupt the story to let the audience in on their process of creating, seeing their work is the best way to experience their unique creations. Because of the number of articles and essays describing their productions, fortunately, it is possible to get a sense of their performance style by reading the plays accompanied by descriptions of the productions.

The first piece the group created is in some respects their most traditional. The play *Split Britches* is about three of Weaver's aunts (Cora, Jane, and Emma Gay) and Della Mae, the caretaker of the family. It presents these farm women as they take care of each other in the humblest of circumstances in the 1930s and 1940s in a shack in Virginia. A narrator intercedes to explain the relationships among the women. In viewing the past of one of the performers (Lois Weaver), a perspective on the legacy of women largely forgotten by history emerges.

In *Upwardly Mobile Home*, Weaver plays the role of a country-western singer, Shaw is a lesbian mother, and Margolin is the manager of their act. The three, who live in a van below the Brooklyn Bridge, are waiting for their friend to win a mobile home which she will share. In this piece there are more pointed interruptions of the story line: Margolin, as manager, arranges an audition for which the trio sings "I Want to Be in America" in Yiddish. A hilarious set piece, the song points up the idealization of the immigrants' fantasies of the American dream.

Beauty and the Beast uses the fairy tale to point up the very real history of the butch-femme relationship in lesbian life. Shaw as the beast-butch actively pursues Weaver, the beauty-femme. The fairy-tale narrative is disrupted with vaudeville-style acts, such as an impersonation of Tony Bennett, a portion of a classical ballet featuring the beast and a Jewish rabbi (Margolin), and a dialogue between Shaw and Weaver about their personal fantasies: imagining themselves as James Dean and Katharine Hepburn.

Again using a preexisting text, Split Britches deconstructs *Little Women* by using dialogue from Louisa May Alcott's novel and interspersing it with demonstrations of Italian Renaissance stagecraft and revelations of their own process of creating and rehearsing the piece. Typically, the traditional demarcations between actor and audience, stage and house, and character and actor are subverted. By letting the audience in on their methods of composition and their personal lives as they intersect with creating a fiction, they remind and celebrate the craft of the stage by their willingness to show the scaffolding behind the creation.

SELECTED PRODUCTION HISTORY

Split Britches
Production, WOW Cafe, New York, 1980 and 1981
Production, Nat Horne Theater, New York, 1983
Production, WGBH/WNET "Artists New Works Program," 1988
Extensive European tour

Beauty and the Beast
Production, University of the Streets, New York, 1982

Patience and Sarah (based on the novel by Isabel Miller)
Production, WOW Cafe, New York, 1984

Upwardly Mobile Home
Production, WOW Cafe, New York, 1984

Dress Suits to Hire (a collaboration among Holly Hughes, Peggy Shaw, and Lois Weaver; written by Holly Hughes)
Production, P.S. 122, New York, 1987
Production, Women's Interart, New York, 1988

Little Women: The Tragedy
Production, WOW Cafe and Women's Interart, New York, 1988

Anniversary Waltz
Production, La Mama, New York, 1989
Production, Walker Point Art Center, Milwaukee, Wisconsin, 1990

Belle Reprieve (with Bloolips)
Production, The Orill Arts Center, London, England, 1991
Production, La Mama, New York, 1991 (moved to One Dream Theatre, New York, 1991)

Lesbians Who Kill (written but not performed by Margolin)
Production, La Mama, New York, 1992

Lust and Comfort
Production, La Mama, New York, 1995

PLAY AVAILABILITY

Belle Reprieve is published in Terry Heibing, *Gay and Lesbian Plays Today*. Portsmouth, New Hampshire: Heinemann, 1993.

Split Britches, Beauty and the Beast, Upwardly Mobile Home, Little Women, Belle Reprieve, Lesbians Who Kill, and *Lust and Comfort* are published in Sue-Ellen Case, *Split Britches*. London and New York: Routeledge, 1996.

AWARDS

Villager Award for Best Ensemble, 1985

Obie, company cash award, 1986

Obie, Peggy Shaw for *Dress Suits to Hire*, 1988

Obie, Lois Weaver for *Belle Reprieve*, 1991

CalArts Alpert Award in Theater, Nominees, Peggy Shaw and Lois Weaver, 1995

DESCRIPTIVE AND CRITICAL RESPONSES

Brantley, Ben. "An Old-fashioned Couple, Except Both Are Women." Review of *Lust and Comfort*. *New York Times*, 17 May 1995: C14.

Case, Sue-Ellen. "From Split Subject to Split Britches." In *Feminine Focus: The New Women Playwrights*, edited by Enoch Brater, 126–46. New York: Oxford University Press, 1989.

———. *Split Britches: Lesbian Practice/Feminist Performance*. London and New York: Routledge, 1996.

———. "Toward a Butch-Femme Aesthetic." In *Making a Spectacle: Feminist Essays on Contemporary Theatre*, edited by Lynda Hart. Ann Arbor: University of Michigan Press, 1989, 282–99.

Davy, Kate. "Peggy Shaw and Lois Weaver: Interviews (1985, 1992, 1993)." *Modern Drama*, edited by William Worthen. New York: Harcourt Brace College Publishers, 1995: 1003–8.

Dolan, Jill. *The Feminist Spectator as Critic*. Ann Arbor: UMI Research Press, 1988: 59–81.

Hamilton, Sabrina. "Split Britches and the *Alcestis* Lesson: 'What Is This Albatross?' " In *Upstaging Big Daddy: Directing Theater as if Gender and Race Matter*, edited by Ellen Donkin and Susan Clement, 133–49. Ann Arbor: University of Michigan Press, 1993.

Hampton, Wilborn. "A Sendup of *Streetcar*." Review of *Belle Reprieve*. *New York Times*, 11 March 1991, C14.

Patraka, Vivian M. "Split Britches in *Little Women: The Tragedy*: Staging Censorship, Nostalgia and Desire." *Kenyon Review* 15 (Spring 1993): 6–13.

———. "Split Britches in *Split Britches*: Performing History, Vaudeville, and the Everyday." *Women and Performance* 4, no. 2 (1989): 58–67.

Solomon, Alisa. "The WOW Cafe." *Drama Review* 29, no. 1 (Spring 1985): 92–101.

CARIDAD SVICH

(1963–)

BIOGRAPHY

Caridad Svich, who was born in Philadelphia, is of Cuban, Croatian, Argentine, and Spanish descent. She earned a BFA in theatre-performance from the University of North Carolina at Charlotte (1985) and an MFA in theatre-playwriting from the University of California at San Diego (1988).

She studied playwriting under **Maria Irene Fornes** for four years at the INTAR Hispanic American Arts Center in New York. Svich has held a residency in dramaturgy at the La Jolla Playhouse in La Jolla, California, and has participated in the South Coast Repertory's Hispanic Playwrights Project in Costa Mesa, California, and the Playwrights' Center's Midwest PlayLabs in Minneapolis, Minnesota. She is a member of the Dramatists Guild, the Women's Project and Productions in New York, the Literary Managers and Dramaturgs of the Americas, and PEN Center USA.

Caridad Svich is a translator as well as a playwright. Her translations include Victor Manuel Leites's *Dona Ramona* (partially funded by a Theatre Communications Group Hispanic translation project commissioning grant), Antonio Buero-Vallejo's *The Story of a Staircase* (commissioned by the Classic Stage Company's National Theater Translation Fund), and Federico García Lorca's *Chimera* and his *Love of Don Perlimplin.*

In addition to her theatre work, Svich has taught writing at the University of California at San Diego and playwriting at Yale University. Caridad Svich currently lives and works in Los Angeles.

PLAY DESCRIPTIONS

Caridad Svich's work is a combination of realism and mysticism; a unique poeticism of language captures the deep, almost inexpressible dynamics of need and desire as played out by working people, both Latino and Anglo. *Brazo Gitano* (gypsy's arm) is a collage of music, dance, and short dramatic episodes. The Cuban Americans of Miami and the rituals of Santeria, a West African–Cuban cult religion, are explored in the play.

In quirky, staccato language, Svich's one-act *but there are fires* presents the lives of inarticulate people who want more from love than they can ask for or offer. The play provides a glimpse or a fragment of a relationship between Jeff, his wife, Gina, and their friend, Todd.

Playing off the verb in the title of the one-act *Gleaning/Rebusca*, Svich's work offers a gradual revelation of dramatic information. In a series of short scenes over a six-month period, amid the mundane domestic chores that clutter their lives (ironing, folding laundry, and painting fingernails), roommates Barbara and Sonia share their space and their longings. Parceled out in bits and pieces in between work and dates, their friendship is simultaneously constructed and deconstructed as the play progresses. The on-again-off-again relationships with various men and the vicissitudes of the job control the ebb and flow of the women's relationship and emphasize its ephemeral nature. Their banal chatter continues as Sonia prepares to move in with a new lover, leaving Barbara to fend for herself.

The pattern of seemingly banal conversation used to mask the subterranean forces that propel her characters is extended in Svich's full-length *Any Place but Here*. This gritty, slice-of-life play depicts the dysfunctional relationship of two couples: Lydia and Chucky and Veronica and Tommy. The play, set in an amorphous working-class area of New Jersey, shows how the ties that bind these characters slowly disintegrate. In a series of alternating scenes or snapshots, we are introduced to the beer-swilling Chucky, who cannot seem to hold onto a job, and his wife, Lydia, who works double shifts at the factory to make ends meet. In contrast, Tommy's bar business takes all his efforts, leaving little time for Veronica; in her search for solace, Veronica has been sleeping around and now finds herself pregnant. The constant arguing and passive-aggressive control games escalate because none of the characters is able to give or get what each one needs. Svich's play is a study of entropy—it portrays people who cannot seem to make things work—and she uses a series of props (heaters, televisions, teeth, hair) to objectify this condition. A glimmer of hope is suggested at the end. With Chucky's death, Lydia is able to take the pickup truck and a plant, and she sets off for a new beginning, destination unknown. Tommy has purchased glasses and can now see to mix drinks at the bar. Veronica has walked out of his life.

Whereas *Any Place but Here* seems firmly rooted in the physical, tangible "things" of this world, *Alchemy of Desire/Dead-Man's Blues* explores the more intangible realms of the spirit. Simone, a young woman in her late twenties, is mourning the death of Jamie, her husband of one month who died in an undisclosed war in some country the characters cannot remember. The community of women who surround Simone (ranging in age and experience from late teens to a seer in her late fifties or early sixties) perform a choric function, helping the young widow grieve and exorcising the troubled spirits that haunt Simone. The play is an evocative study of memory and mercy that juxtaposes the mundane rituals of daily life (cutting food, sweeping) with powerful, poetic images of the four elements of ancient cosmology.

SELECTED PRODUCTION HISTORY

Waterfall
   Production, Open Circle Theatre, Goucher College, Baltimore, 1983

Chimera (translation of Federico García Lorca's play)
   Production, Drama League of New York, Circle Repertory Studio, New York, 1989

Gleaning/Rebusca
   Reading, INTAR Hispanic American Arts Center, New York, 1989
   Reading, Women's Project and Productions, New York, 1990
   Workshop, South Coast Repertory Hispanic Playwrights Project, Costa Mesa, California, 1990
   Production, Beyond Baroque Literary/Arts Center, Venice, California, 1991

Dona Romona (translation of Victor Manuel Leites's play)
   Reading, INTAR Hispanic American Arts Center, New York, 1991

but there are fires
   Production, Women's Project and Productions, New York, 1991

Shelter
   Reading, Alice's Fourth Floor, New York, 1991
   Workshop, Playwrights' Center, Minneapolis, Minnesota, 1992
   Reading, Latin American Theatre Artists, American Conservatory Theatre, San Francisco, 1993
   Reading, INTAR, New York, 1996

Any Place but Here
   Reading, Audrey Skirball–Kenis Theatre, Beverly Hills, California, 1992
   Production, INTAR Hispanic American Arts Center, New York, 1992
   Production, Latino Chicago Theatre Company, Chicago, 1993

Alchemy of Desire/Dead-Man's Blues
   Reading, Audrey Skirball–Kenis Theatre, Beverly Hills, California, 1993
   Workshop, Playwrights' Center, Minneapolis, Minnesota, 1993
   Reading, Royal Court Theatre, London, 1994
   Production, Cincinnati Playhouse in the Park, Cincinnati, Ohio, 1994

Scar (solo piece)
   Production, Stage of Their Own Latina Theatre Festival, Cincinnati, Ohio, 1994
   Production, TWEED New Works Festival, New York, 1994

Away Down Dreaming
   Workshop, Playwrights' Center's Midwest PlayLabs, Minneapolis, Minnesota, 1995
   Reading, BRAVA! for Women in the Arts, San Francisco, 1995

Brazo Gitano
Reading, Voice and Vision, New York, 1996

PLAY AVAILABILITY

Any Place but Here is published in *Plays in Process*, vol. 13, no. 12. New York: Theatre Communications Group, 1993.

Gleaning/Rebusca is published in Linda Feyder, ed., *Shattering the Myth: Plays by Hispanic Women*. Houston: Arte Publico, 1992.

Scar is published in Lilian Manzor-Coates and Alicia Alarcon, eds., *Latinas on Stage: Criticism and Practice*. Berkeley, California: Third Woman Press, 1996.

Other scripts may be obtained from the playwright at: 4601 Tweedy Blvd., Suite H, So Gate, California 90280; (213) 566–8369.

AWARDS

Open Circle Theatre Playwriting Award, Goucher College, 1983

Chancellor's Associates Grant, University of California at San Diego, 1987–1988

La Jolla Playhouse Residency in Dramaturgy, La Jolla, California, 1987

Playwright in Residence, INTAR, New York, 1988–1992

Stanley Drama Award, Wagner College, New York, Finalist, *Brazo Gitanto*, 1989

Jane Chambers Playwriting Award, Finalist, *Gleaning/Rebusca*, 1991

California Arts Council Fellowship in Playwriting, 1991

Rosenthal New Play Prize Cincinnati, Ohio, *Alchemy of Desire/Dead-Man's Blues*, 1993–1994

Jane Chambers Playwriting Award, Honorable Mention, *Alchemy of Desire/Dead-Man's Blues*, 1994

Royal Court Theatre Exchange Residency, London, 1994

Pew/TCG Travel Grant, 1994–1995

Playwright Fellow, Latino Theatre Initiative, Mark Taper Forum, Los Angeles, 1995–1996

DESCRIPTIVE AND CRITICAL RESPONSES

Barnidge, Mary Shen. "*Any Place but Here.*" Review of *Any Place but Here*. *Reader* (Chicago), 12 February 1993, 41–42.

Crothers, Don. "Unholy Bones." Review of *Alchemy of Desire/Dead-Man's Blues*. *American Theatre* (July/August 1994): 12–13.

Demaline, Jackie. "Playhouse's 'Alchemy' Beguiles." Review of *Alchemy of Desire/ Dead-Man's Blues*. *Cincinnati Enquirer*, 1 April 1994, 22.

Jones, Chris. "*Alchemy of Desire/Dead-Man's Blues.*" Review of *Alchemy of Desire/ Dead-Man's Blues*. *Variety*, 18–24 April 1994, 73.

REGINA TAYLOR

(n.d.–)

BIOGRAPHY

Regina Taylor was born in Dallas, Texas, where her mother, a poet and painter, raised her daughter by working for the Social Security Administration. Taylor studied journalism and acting at Southern Methodist University in Dallas, but after graduation, she moved to New York City and began performing off-off-Broadway. She became associated with Joseph Papp's Public Theatre, where she played crowd scenes and small parts before she worked her way up to leading roles in Shakespeare's *Romeo and Juliet* (Taylor has the distinction of being Broadway's first black Juliet) and *As You Like It*.

In addition to her stage work, Regina Taylor was creating a career in film and television, beginning with a role in *Crisis at Central High*, a dramatization of the integration of Arkansas schools in the 1950s. She appeared in the film *Lean on Me* and in the television movie "The Howard Beach Story." However, she is best known to television audiences as the strong and compassionate maid Lilly Harper on the acclaimed series "I'll Fly Away," a role that garnered her a Golden Globe Award for Best Actress in a Drama and an Emmy Award nomination.

Regina Taylor adapted two one-act plays by German playwright Franz Xavier Kroetz (*Ghost Train* and *Sty Farm*) which were workshopped at the Public Theatre in New York. She has also been commissioned by the Alliance Theatre in Atlanta to write the book for a musical based on the Fisk Jubilee Singers, and she is an associate artist at Chicago's Goodman Theatre.

PLAY DESCRIPTIONS

Regina Taylor's plays utilize a freedom of dramatic form and structure to examine powerful personal, social, and political issues. This unique combination creates a distinct African-American voice that melds Lorraine Hansberry with Eugène Ionesco. In *Watermelon Rinds*, she creates an absurdist view of a family reunion run amuck. The Semple family has gathered for a celebration of Martin Luther King's birthday. Willy, the host, is surrounded by packing boxes as he prepares to make good on his promise of giving his family a better life. His wife, Liza, is busily preparing a feast in the kitchen and joins the group only to provide progress reports. Their daughter, Lottie, is a precocious fourteen-year-old who is straining at the restrictions imposed on her by her father. Willy's parents, Mama Pearl and Papa Tommy, are comic contrasts of each other and of their earlier lives as a vaudeville team. Jes the Joker, Pinkie the perennially pregnant, and Marva the bleached and successful sister round out the family. Occasionally Willy packs one of the others away in a box. As the memory of King's "I Have a Dream" speech is evoked, each character's dreams and frustrations are revealed. Couched in comedy, Taylor's family mirrors timely topics such as racial prejudice within the black community and the raging violence that affects all of us.

Escape from Paradise was a one-person performance piece in which the actress starred. Structured as a nonlinear montage of past and present, memory and dream, the play chronicles Jennine's journey, both physical and emotional, to Venice, Italy. Influenced by the surrealist painter René Magritte and Giorgio De Chirico, her mental landscape is peopled with friends and relatives (her cousin who is a mortician, her displaced sister) whose dreamlike incarnations are fused with the adventures of the European trip.

Mudtracks creates a fluid structure within the constraints of a more chronological approach to storytelling. Taylor alternates scenes between past and present to depict the events leading up to Ben's suicide and the aftermath in the lives of those who survived. Jessie, who had lived with Ben for two years, leaves him only to be tracked down and tortured in her motel room. The catastrophe rejoins her mother with her grandmother and grandfather, who all have different ways of responding to Jessie and the incident. They are eventually united, however, in their common experience of escaping from stiffling relationships or being abandoned. The play is a vivid imprint of the messy tracks that those relationships leave on the individual.

Inside the Belly of the Beast is a short, dark comedy in the tradition of "machinal/adding machine/metropolis/eraserhead," which depicts the transformation of Walter, a businessman, into the proverbial beast. The play is constructed as a series of short scenes played in a variety of locations along Walter's journey. The dehumanization of Walter's world is signified by the change from character names (Langley and Sheldon) to increasingly generic types (Child, Malice).

SELECTED PRODUCTION HISTORY

Watermelon Rinds (performed in a double bill entitled *Various Small Fires*)
  Production, Humana Festival, Actors Theatre of Louisville, Louisville, Kentucky, 1993

Escape from Paradise (previously titled *Jennine's Diary*)
Production, Humana Festival, Actors Theatre of Louisville, Louisville, Kentucky, 1993
Production, Circle Repertory Company, New York, 1994
Production, Goodman Theatre, Chicago, 1995

Inside the Belly of the Beast (one act)
Production, Goodman Theatre, Chicago, 1994

Mudtracks (one act)
Production, Ensemble Studio Theatre, New York, 1994

Between the Lines
Production, Actors Theatre of Louisville, Louisville, Kentucky, 1995

Transformation 6 (conceived by Taylor)
Production, Goodman Theatre, Chicago, 1997

PLAY AVAILABILITY

Between the Lines is published in Marisa Smith, ed., *Humana Festival '95: The Complete Plays*. Lyme, New Hampshire: Smith and Kraus, 1995.

Mudtracks is published in Marisa Smith, ed., *EST Marathon 1994: One-Act Plays*. Lyme, New Hampshire: Smith and Kraus, 1995.

Watermelon Rinds is published in Marisa Smith, ed., *Humana Festival '93: The Complete Plays*. Newbury, Vermont: Smith and Kraus, 1993; Howard Stein and Glenn Young, eds., *The Best American Short Plays 1992–1994*. Garden City, New York: Applause, 1993, 1995.

Watermelon Rinds and *Inside the Belly of the Beast* are published under the collective title *The Ties That Bind* by Dramatic Publishing Company, P.O. Box 129, Woodstock, Illinois 60098.

DESCRIPTIVE AND CRITICAL RESPONSES

Anderson, Porter. "The Good Diva." *Village Voice*, 22 February 1994, 92.
Brantley, Ben. "On the Run, Seeking that 'Something.' " Review of *Escape from Paradise. New York Times*, 18 February 1994, C19.
———. "Sexual Relationships through 3 Generations." Review of *Mudtracks. New York Times*, 23 May 1994, C13.
Christiansen, Richard. "Strong Ties." Review of *The Ties That Bind* (collective title of *Watermelon Rinds* and *Inside the Belly of the Beast*). *Chicago Tribune*, 19 April 1994, 1, 24.
Hayward, Jeff. "The Write Talent." *Chicago Tribune*, 21 May 1995, 6, 8.
Winn, Steven. "Regina Taylor's Passionate Theatre." *San Francisco Chronicle*, 5 April 1995, E3.

CARMELITA TROPICANA

(1957–)

BIOGRAPHY

Carmelita Tropicana is the stage persona of Cuban-born writer and performance artist Alina Troyano. In the early 1980s, Troyano "went to WOW [New York's lesbian performance space] looking for girls and found something more long-lasting: theatre" (Román, 84). In 1983 she appeared in **Holly Hughes**'s *Well of Horniness* where the challenge of playing a man and a butch girl helped free Troyano from cultural expectations and led to the creation of Carmelita. "Through Carmelita I could be whoever I wanted to be. It didn't matter if I transgressed certain expected behavior" (Román, 92).

Working in collaboration with filmmaker Ela Troyano, her sister, and Uzi Parnes, Carmelita Tropicana was soon performing in Club Chandelier, the WOW Cafe, La Mama, P.S. 122, and other downtown spaces in New York. It was not until 1987 that Carmelita had a name for what she was doing, when, at Ela Troyano's urging, Carmelita Tropicana applied for and won a New York Foundation for the Arts Fellowship for Performance Art. Since then she has performed her unique blend of politics and humor throughout the United States and abroad. Excerpts of her plays and short stories have appeared in the *Michigan Quarterly Review*, *Latinas on Stage*, and *Semiotexte*. With Ela Troyano she coauthored the screenplay *Carmelita Tropicana: Your Kunst Is Your Waffen*, which aired on Public Broadcasting Service in 1995 and was shown in numerous film festivals. It won Best Short at the Berlin Film Festival and toured Germany as a double feature with the Cuban film *Strawberry and Chocolate*. Tropicana currently serves on the Artists Advisory Board of the New Museum of Contemporary Art and on the Avant-Garde-a-Rama Committee of Performance Space 122; she is a member of Actors Equity.

PLAY DESCRIPTIONS

Carmelita Tropicana's multimedia spectacles combine film, slides, music, and live performance (using bilingual texts) to illuminate the experiences of Latinos transplanted to the United States, as well as to reflect upon gender, sexual, and cultural stereotypes of all kinds. The solo piece *The Boiler Time Machine* is a fantastic musical voyage charting Carmelita's time travels through history (and herstory) in search of her faithful Charlie Chaplin–like butler, Ferdinando. After Ferdinando is transported from the East Village to a bull ring in 1912 Spain, Carmelita goes in search of her factotum, the one person who gives her unconditional worship. Carmelita ends up in gay Paris at the Rue Madeleine in the company of Gertrude Stein, Pablo Picasso, Maurice Ravel, and Mata Hari. When she eventually remembers her true purpose, she finds her way to Spain in time to soothe the charging bull with a song and save Ferdinando.

The more complex *Memories of the Revolution*, a parodistic mélange of Tropicana nightclub revue and mystery-thriller drama, introduces many of the performer's recurring characters and themes. The first act is set in the Havana of 1955 where Carmelita's brother, Machito, is trying to assassinate the sadistic chief of police, Capitan Maldito. His revolutionary zeal is mitigated only by his overwhelming desire to seduce two young American tourists, Brendah and Brendaa, an urge that frequently prevents him from following the plot. Carmelita makes an arms deal with Lota Hari, Mata Hari's granddaughter, just as her brother is captured by the police. Act 2 takes place in a rowboat while Carmelita, Lota, and Marimacha, Machito's companion, escape from Cuba. En route, Carmelita is visited by the Virgin Mary who announces that Carmelita has been chosen to be "the next hottest Latin superstar." Act 3 takes place eight years later in 1967 at Carmelita's Tropicana-a-Go-Go Club in New York. Brendah and Brendaa are reunited with Machito who writes Happenings; Marimacha incessantly chants mantras; and Nota, Lota and Carmelita's adopted daughter, is a folksinger. Maldito is thwarted in his plans to turn them in when his punch is spiked with drugs, which transforms him into a chicken. In the end, this zany family of refugees is united in the singing of "Guantanamera."

Milk of Amnesia retains the comic spirit of the earlier works but continues simultaneously to underscore its serious autobiographical and political dimensions. The solo work uses Alina Troyano's 1993 trip to Cuba, part of a dialogue between Cuban and Cuban American artists sponsored by the Dance Theatre Workshop's Suitcase Fund, as the defining event around which the artist explores the issues of identity. Using voice-overs of the artist interspersed with some of Troyano's stage personas, the play weaves the past and present, memory and reality, into a poignant account of her very real conflict between assimilation into her new American culture and efforts to retain her Cuban heritage and past.

SELECTED PRODUCTION HISTORY

The Boiler Time Machine (one-act solo performance)
  Staged reading, INTAR, New York, 1986
  Production, La Mama, New York, 1989
  Production, P. S. 122, New York, 1990

Memories of the Revolution (cowritten with Uzi Parnes)
  Production, WOW Cafe, New York, 1987
  Production, P. S. 122, New York, 1987

Candela (cowritten with Uzi Parnes and Ela Troyano)
  Production, Dance Theatre Workshop, New York, 1988
  Production, Kimo Theatre, Albuquerque, New Mexico, 1988
  Production, P. S. 122, New York, 1989

Carnaval (multimedia operetta in progress)
  Production, P. S. 122, New York, 1991

The Conquest of Mexico as Seen through the Eyes of Hernando Cortez's Horse
  Production, P. S. 122, New York, 1992

Milk of Amnesia (one-act solo performance)
  Production, P. S. 122, New York, 1994
  Production, Women's Theatre Festival, Philadelphia, 1995
  Production, Institute of Contemporary Art, London, 1995
  Production, Centre de Cultura Contemporania de Barcelona, Spain, 1995

Sor Juana (with Ela Troyano)
  Reading, Dixon Place, New York, 1996

PLAY AVAILABILITY

The Boiler Time Machine is published in Nayland Blake, Lawrence Rinder, and Amy
  Scholder, eds., *In a Different Light: Visual Culture, Sexual Identity, Queer Practice.*
  San Francisco: City Lights, 1995.

Carnaval is excerpted in the *Michigan Quarterly Review* (Fall 1994): 732–47.

Milk of Amnesia is published in *The Drama Review* 39, no. 3 (Fall 1995): 94–111.

AWARDS

New York Foundation for the Arts Fellowship in Performance Art, 1987

New York Foundation for the Arts Fellowship in Screenwriting/Playwriting, 1991

Cintas Foundation Fellowship, 1995

DESCRIPTIVE AND CRITICAL RESPONSES

Manzor-Coats, Lillian. "Too Spik or Too Dyke: Carmelita Tropicana." *Ollantay Theater
    Magazine* 2, no. 1 (Winter/Spring 1994): 39–54.
Muñoz, José Esteban. "*Choteo*/Camp Style Politics: Carmelita Tropicana's Performance

of Self-Enactment.'' *Women and Performance: A Journal of Feminist Theory* 7, no. 2–8, no. 1 (1995): 38–51.

———. ''No es facil: Notes on the Negotiation of Cubanidad and Exilic Memory in Carmelita Tropicana's *Milk of Amnesia.''* *The Drama Review* 39, no. 3 (Fall 1995): 76–82.

Román, David. ''Carmelita Tropicana Unplugged.'' *The Drama Review* 39, no. 3 (Fall 1995): 83–93.

ALICE TUAN

(1963–   )

BIOGRAPHY

Alice Tuan was born in Seattle and grew up in California's San Fernando Valley. After she studied economics at UCLA, where she received a BA in 1987, she went to the southern Chinese city of Guangzhou to teach English. Although Tuan describes her experience in China as "part Peace Corp, part *Roots*," she "realized the Chinese were more fascinated by ice-cube-dispensing refrigerators and Disneyland than the socialist ideals she went there to embrace. In the eyes of the Chinese, she would always be American in the same way America would always view her as Chinese."

After she returned to the United States, Tuan went to California State University at Los Angeles to study teaching English as a second language (ESL) and received her master's degree in 1991. In addition to her ESL instruction of Central American and Korean students, Tuan conducted a writing workshop with teenage prison wards at the Fred C. Nelles School from 1993 to 1995. Two plays with music, *Four Corners* and *Four Corners Revisited*, have emerged from this multicomponent program under the auspices of UCLA Artsearch. Alice Tuan is a member of the Taper Mentor/Playwrights Program and the Dramatists Guild, and she had a fellowship for the 1995–1996 academic year at Brown University's Graduate Playwriting Program.

PLAY DESCRIPTIONS

Alice Tuan's theatricalism, coupled with a wild imagination, creates plays that explore the darker sides of human relationships. *Dim Sums* is an expressionistic tale "about eating and being eaten." The collage of characters either work in or frequent Jimbo's Chinese restaurant in Los Angeles's Chinatown.

Bunny Ling, one of the restaurant's dim sum "cart girls," has been smuggled into the country and is virtually enslaved. Her economic constraint is paralleled by the dumplings who appear throughout the play as Dumpling Ghost, Muse, and Dr. God. Confined to their shells without arms, their limitation reflects their struggle to survive in a harsh landscape. Bunny's perverse world is peopled with characters who do not think twice about using and abusing each other: Charlie, a sleazy waiter with contempt for white people and a penchant for porn; Cook, the cook whose dumplings are concocted in a dark basement from secret ingredients including bodily fluids; and Joyce, a homeless woman addicted to the special dumplings. Tuan's play offers a nightmarish vision of contemporary society.

In *Last of the Suns*, Tuan's imaginative style creates a play about Yeh Yeh, a 100-year-old man, who assesses his life before passing on to the next. A colorful mélange of myth, storytelling, and flashback show us a war hero who has outlived his time and place. Yeh Yeh is surrounded by the ghosts from his past as well as his very real dysfunctional family: Sonny, a grandson who is the quintessential Valley Dude pumped up on steroids and a denizen of the ubiquitous Los Angeles malls; Ni Lee, his daughter-in-law who is unable to get past the reality of her own daughter's failure as an ice skater; Ho Ping, his patronizing son; and Twila, his ice-skating granddaughter who returns home after a five-year absence. Yeh Yeh's reconciliation with death corresponds with the reconciliation of his family members with each other.

Tuan's *Crown Goose* uses a Sunset Boulevard strip bar, the Crown Goose, as the crucible for her characters' psyches. Trixie Chan and Jay Sepastapol enter the bar and join its zany crew of characters after Trixie's car has broken down outside. Jay is attracted to Deavere Nicole, a stripper who is trying to reconcile her two personas (intelligent, asexual Anna Deavere Smith, with sexy bimbo Anna Nicole Smith). Bos, a man quietly waiting for Patty the Firegirl to return to the bar so that they can drive to Mexico, is attracted to Trixie. Bos is also accompanied by Sexual Conscience, who acts out Bos's desires. After a night of drinking and ingesting a mysterious rock, a night that Trixie can only hazily remember, she is stripped of her illusions and facades. Although she had previously been only with white men, she and Bos drive off to Mexico.

SELECTED PRODUCTION HISTORY

Dim Sums
  Reading, Mark Taper Forum, Los Angeles, 1992
  Reading, Cast Theater, Los Angeles, 1993

Last of the Suns
  Reading, Mark Taper Forum, Los Angeles, 1993
  Production, Berkeley Repertory Theatre, Berkeley, California, 1995
  Reading, Public Theatre, New York, 1995 and 1996

Crown Goose
  Reading, Cast Theater, Los Angeles, 1994

Kitpor (25 short plays of Go, Fa, Em, and Da)
  Reading, Mark Taper Forum, Los Angeles, 1994

Ikebana
  Workshop, New Plays Festival, Brown University, Providence, Rhode Island, 1996
  Reading, New Works Now!, Public Theatre, New York, 1996
  Production, East West Players, Los Angeles, 1996

PLAY AVAILABILITY

Alice Tuan's plays are available from her agent: Joyce Ketay, 1501 Broadway Suite 1910, New York, New York 10036; (212) 354–6825.

AWARDS

Playwriting Fellowship, Mark Taper Forum Mentor-Playwrights, 1992–1994

Playwriting Fellowship, Brown University, 1995–1997

DESCRIPTIVE AND CRITICAL RESPONSES

Harvey, Dennis. "Magical Idealism." *San Francisco Bay Guardian*, 11 January 1995, 33.
Lu, Alvin. "Secret Stories." *San Francisco Bay Guardian*, 11 January 1995.
Michel, Sia. "Inter the Dragon." *San Francisco Weekly*, 11 January 1995.
Roca, Octavio. "A Young Playwright's Bright Horizon." *San Francisco Chronicle*, 29 December 1994, E1.

EDIT VILLARREAL

(n.d.–   )

BIOGRAPHY

Edit Villarreal, who was born in Texas, received an AB in theatre from the University of California at Berkeley and an MFA in playwriting from the Yale School of Drama. In addition to her theatre work, Villarreal has written the film *La Carpa* (1993) for "American Playhouse." She is currently an assistant professor at the UCLA School of Theatre, Film and Television in Los Angeles where she serves as head of the MFA Playwriting Program. Her current projects in film, television, and theatre include *Foto-Novelas* in development with the Public Broadcasting Service and two play commissions: *Minus Four* for the Mark Taper Forum in Los Angeles is a generational piece, and *Horacio Alvarez* for the South Coast Repertory Theatre in Costa Mesa, California, is a Horatio Alger story set at the turn of the century. Villarreal also reviews theatre, fiction, and nonfiction on a regular basis for the San Jose *Mercury News*.

PLAY DESCRIPTIONS

Edit Villarreal's work blends her Mexican heritage with her American identity. Her bicultural backgrounds are blended thematically and structurally in the plays, adding a touch of Latino "magic realism" to more traditional stories and structures. In *My Visits with MGM (My Grandmother Marta)*, Villarreal has reconciled several oppositions to create a touching family portrait. Within a compact framework, the playwright has painted an epic tale of her grandmother's life. Using flash-forward and flashback, we get to know and understand Marta Grande (from age fifteen to eighty) as seen through the eyes and memory of her granddaughter, Marta Feliz. The fluidity of time and space achieved through the nonlinear structuring device allows the playwright to show the simultaneous clashing and merging of the two cultures in several eras and under numerous circumstances. Marta Grande is shown as a strong-willed Mexican woman who left her native country and family to escape the insanity of the 1910 Mexican revolution. On her lifelong quest for independence, Marta Grande is accompanied by her sister, Florinda, who is the obverse of Marta Grande. Marta Grande's willingness to entertain new options and ideas is contrasted to Florinda's complete dependence on and subservience to the Catholic Church. Florinda's negative, life-negating attitudes are opposed to Marta Grande's life-affirming strength and joy of life. Marta Feliz was raised by her grandmother, and, in the course of the play, comes to realize the lessons that her grandmother's life and experience have taught her. By the end of the play, Marta Feliz is ready to leave her home and seek a destiny of her own making.

The blending of cultures is even more evident in *The Language of Flowers*, which is a "free adaptation" of Shakespeare's *Romeo and Juliet* with music. Without deviating from the original plotline, Villarreal has created a contemporary tale of intra-Latino love and conflict. Romeo Martinez is an illegal alien who has lived in the United States since he was ten years old; now a romantic youth of eighteen, Romeo is trying to raise himself above the violence and frustration that inflame the barrio. Juliet Bosquet is an innocent young girl who is being bartered by her father, Julian Bosquet. Julian, a financially successful Los Angeles businessman, thinks nothing of trading his daughter in marriage to law student Stanley Peterson in exchange for a partnership in a Mexican business venture with Peterson. Julian, a second-generation Mexican American who fiercely denies his ethnic and cultural background, finds Peterson the ideal husband with his WASP background and his business and law connections. The interfamily conflict not only operates on the more abstract levels of economics and culture, but is exacerbated by the lethal feud between Benny Martinez, Romeo's cousin, and Tommy Bosquet. The young, ill-fated lovers are aided in their affair by Father Lawrence, a New Age priest who is also an avid researcher of rain forest plants, and Maria, a maid-cum-mother-figure in the Bosquet household. The play takes place over three days—October 31 (Halloween) and November 1 and 2 (the two Mexican Days of the Dead)—which allows the traditional love story to be freely intermingled with images of death and dying; *calaveras* (skeletons) populate the stage and interact with the living.

SELECTED PRODUCTION HISTORY

Crazy from the Heart
  Production, Winterfest VI, Yale Repertory Theatre, New Haven, Connecticut, 1986
  Staged reading, Old Globe Theatre, San Diego, 1989

My Visits with MGM (My Grandmother Marta)
  Staged reading, Los Angeles Theatre Center, Los Angeles, 1989
  Staged reading, South Coast Repertory Theatre, Costa Mesa, California. 1989
  Workshop, Borderlands Theatre, Tucson, Arizona, 1990

Production, San Jose Repertory Theatre, San Jose, California, 1992

Production, Milwaukee Repertory Theatre, Milwaukee, Wisconsin, 1992

Production (touring), New Mexico Repertory Theatre, 1993

The Language of Flowers (full-length play with music)

Staged reading, South Coast Repertory Theatre, Costa Mesa, California, 1991

Production, Contemporary Theatre, Seattle, 1995

PLAY AVAILABILITY

My Visits with MGM (My Grandmother Marta) is published by in Linda Feyder, ed., *Shattering the Myth: Plays by Hispanic Women.* Houston: Arte Publico Press, 1992.

All other plays are available from the playwright: Edit Villarreal, 1970 North Monon Street, Los Angeles, California 90027; (310) 206–6876 (office).

AWARDS

Susan Smith Blackburn Award, Nominee, *Crazy from the Heart*, 1986

Joseph O. Kesselring Award, Nominee, *My Visits with MGM*, 1992

Susan Smith Blackburn Award, Nominee, *My Visits with MGM*, 1992

Kennedy Center New Plays, Nominee, *My Visits with MGM*, 1992

Playwright Fellow, Latino Theatre Initiative, Mark Taper Forum, Los Angeles, 1995–1996

DESCRIPTIVE AND CRITICAL RESPONSES

Huerta, Jorge. "Professionalizing Teatro, an Overview of Chicano Theatre during the 'Decade of the Hispanic.' " *TheatreForum* (Spring 1993): 54–59.

Huerta, Jorge, and Carlos Morton. "Chicano Theatre in the Mainstream: Milwaukee Rep's Production of a Chicana Play." *Gestos* 8 (November 1993): 149–59.

Koehler, Robert. "To Grandmother's House She Returns." *Los Angeles Times*, 30 May 1992, F10.

Mason, Susan. "Romeo and Juliet in East L.A." *Theatre* 23, no. 2 (Spring 1992): 88–92.

Morales, Ed. "Shadowing Valdez." *American Theatre* (November 1992): 14–19.

PAULA VOGEL

(1951–   )

BIOGRAPHY

Born to a Jewish father from New York and a Catholic mother from New Orleans, Vogel received her BA from Catholic University in 1974 and did advanced degree work at Cornell from 1974 to 1977. She taught at various colleges and universities before going to Brown University in 1984, where she heads the MFA Playwriting Program, which has achieved esteem and national visibility through the caliber of her graduates. She also teaches a theatre workshop for women in the maximum security Adult Corrections Institute in Providence, Rhode Island.

Vogel enjoyed a productive relationship with the Circle Repertory Company in New York in the early 1990s where three of her plays, *Desdemona*, *Baltimore Waltz*, and *And Baby Makes Seven*, were produced. She has worked frequently with director Ann Bogart, who directed the premiere of *Balitmore Waltz* in 1992, which has susequently had more than sixty regional productions. Her screenplay *The Oldest Profession* is currently optioned, and Vogel was selected for the Warner Brothers workshop in 1991. She has also written for television.

Acknowledging her debt to **Maria Irene Fornes** and John Guare, she describes the contemporary climate for playwrights as hostile: "This is a racist, misogynist, homophobic society, and after a while it becomes the air you inhale. . . . I believe we have to get out there and write flawed plays that disturb everybody, and change the atmosphere" (Coen, 26). She would resist calling herself a lesbian playwright, saying that "I do not write lesbian plays. I will not speak for all women, and I will not speak for all lesbians" (Coen, 27).

PLAY DESCRIPTIONS

Vogel's plays are characterized by a dark whimsy, an imagination rich and quirky that takes on ordinary subjects from an off-center perspective. She writes from a strong political sensibility and her plays test "assumptions in regard to gender, family, sexual identity, love, sex, aging and domestic violence" (Savran, xiii). An early play, *And Baby Makes Seven*, explores a nontraditional family: lovers Anna and Ruth, and Peter, the father of Anna's child. In the play, reminiscent of Edward Albee's *Who's Afraid of Virginia Woolf?*, Vogel complicates the story by peopling the stage with the family's imaginary children. The playwright makes no judgements nor provides any psychological justification for her family's eccentricities; the audience must evaluate their choices without authorial intervention.

The Baltimore Waltz blends satire and absurdist humor in a witty revisionist AIDS play. Anna, an elementary schoolteacher, has contracted the deadly ATD, Acquired Toilet Disease. Her brother, Carl, insists they go on a European vacation and look up a mysterious urologist, Dr. Todesrocheln, for a rumored new cure. In defiant rebellion against her dying, Anna sleeps her way across Europe, while Carl, carrying a stuffed bunny, has a number of assignations with the furtive Third Man. The play enthusiastically sends up realistic conventions of staging and borrows from film noir and classic satires such as *Dr. Strangelove*, especially in the memorable gloved-hand, urine-drinking scene. The thirtieth and final scene, a realistic turn, is set in a hospital lounge where a doctor attempts to console Anna over the death of her brother from pneumonia. He hands her travel brochures from Europe, and Anna, remembering with difficulty she must speak in the past tense, says, "We would have gone had he gotten better." Vogel manages, in this play, based on the death of her own brother, to castigate the state of AIDS research, medical obfuscation and society's ignorance of the disease without a trace of didacticism or sentimentality and without once mentioning the disease by name.

Desdemona: A Play about a Handkerchief is a rollicking, bawdy, postmodern, feminist reading of Shakespeare's *Othello* with no male characters. Desdemona, a discontented upper-class Venetian, seeks thrills and adventures in her friend Bianca's whorehouse. Desdemona, characterized as sexually adventurous even in her youth, wants the freedom that men enjoy. She marries the exotic, dark-skinned Othello expecting an unconventional life. To her disappointment, he turns out to be as traditional as other men and, perhaps, more confining because of his possessiveness. Emilia, her pious servant, first steals Desdemona's handkerchief for Iago, then, in an act of comradeship and desire to escape a miserable marriage, attempts to help her mistress leave Cypress for Paris. The play ends when Desdemona, made acutely aware of her husband's jealously, plans to feign sleep, believing "Surely he'll not . . . harm a sleeping woman." Classism is indicted, as well as sexism, as an inhibiting factor for women.

SELECTED PRODUCTION HISTORY

Meg
  Production, American College Theatre Festival at the Kennedy Center, Washington, D.C., 1977

Production, ANTA-West, Los Angeles, 1978
Production, Central Florida Civic Theatre, Orlando, 1979

And Baby Makes Seven
Production, Theatre Rhinoceros, San Francisco, 1986
Production, Perseverance Theatre, Juneau, Alaska, 1989
Production, Los Angeles Theatre Center, Los Angeles, 1990
Production, Wellfleet Harbor Actors Theatre, Wellfleet, Massachusetts, 1991
Production, Alias Stage, Providence, Rhode Island, 1992
Production, Central Works, San Francisco, 1992
Production, Circle Repertory at the Lucille Lortel, New York, 1993

The Oldest Profession (screen play and stage play)
Production, Hudson Guild Theatre, New York, 1981
Production, Theatre Network and 25th Street Theatre, Edmonton, Alberta, Canada, 1988
Production, Company One, Hartford, Connecticut, 1991

Desdemona: A Play about a Handkerchief
Workshop, Shakespeare and Company, Lenox, Massachusetts, 1989
Production, Bay Street Theatre, Sag Harbor, New York, 1993
Production, Circle Repertory Theatre, New York, 1993

The Baltimore Waltz
Workshop, Perseverance Theatre, Juneau, Alaska, 1990
Workshop, Circle Repertory Theatre, New York, 1991
Production, Circle Repertory Theatre, New York, 1992
Production, Magic Theatre, San Francisco, 1992
Production, Goodman Theatre, Chicago, 1992–1993
Production, Yale Repertory Theatre, New Haven, Connecticut, 1992–1993
Production, Oregon Shakespeare Theatre, Ashland, Oregon, 1992–1993
Production, Milwaukee Repertory Theatre, Milwaukee, Wisconsin, 1993–1994
(This list represents a sampling of productions at major regional theatres; there are numerous others, including college and amateur productions.)

Hot 'n' Throbbing
Workshop, Circle Repertory Lab, New York, 1992
Production, American Repertory Theatre at the Hasty Pudding, Cambridge, Massachusetts, 1993

The Mineola Twins
Production, Perseverance Theatre, Douglas, Alaska, 1996

PLAY AVAILABILITY

The Baltimore Waltz is available from Dramatists Play Service, 440 Park Avenue South, New York, New York 10016; and in Robyn Goodman and Marisa Smith, eds., *Women Playwrights: The Best Plays of 1992*. Newbury, Vermont: Smith and Kraus, 1992.

Desdemona is published in Rosemary Curb, ed., *Amazon All Stars*. New York: Applause, 1996.

Hot 'n' Throbbing is published in Marisa Smith, ed., *Women Playwrights: The Best Plays of 1994*. Lyme, New Hampshire: Smith and Kraus, 1995.

Meg is available from Samuel French, 45 West 25th Street, New York, New York 10010–2751.

The Baltimore Waltz, And Baby Makes Seven, The Oldest Profession, Desdemona: A Play about a Handkerchief, and *Hot 'n' Throbbing* are published in Paula Vogel, *The Baltimore Waltz and Other Plays*. New York: Theatre Communications Group, 1996.

Other plays may be obtained through her agent: Peter Franklin, William Morris Agency, 1350 Avenue of the Americas, New York, New York 10019; (212) 586–5100.

AWARDS

American College Theatre Festival Playwriting Award, 1976

Samuel French Award, 1976

ANTA-West Playwriting, 1977

MacDowell Colony Fellow, 1979

Actors Theatre of Louisville, Louisville, Kentucky, commissions, 1979 and 1980

National Endowment for the Arts Playwriting Fellow, 1980 and 1981

Bunting Fellow, Radcliffe College, 1990–1991

AT&T New Play Award, *The Baltimore Waltz*, 1991

National Endowment for the Arts Playwriting Fellow, 1991–1992

Bellagio Fellow, Summer, 1992

Yaddo Fellow, 1992

Obie, Best Play, *The Baltimore Waltz*, 1992

Pulitzer Prize nomination, *The Baltimore Waltz*, 1992

McKnight Fellow, 1992–1993

Joseph Calloway Prize, Young Dramatists, *The Baltimore Waltz*, 1993

Fund for New American Plays, *The Baltimore Waltz*, 1993

Fund for New American Plays, *Hot 'n' Throbbing*, 1993

Senior Artist Residency, Pew Foundation, 1995

Rhode Island Governor's Arts Awards, 1995

DESCRIPTIVE AND CRITICAL RESPONSES

Brantley, Ben. "*Desdemona: A Play about a Handkerchief.*" *New York Times*, 12 November 1993, C20.

Coen, Stephanie. "Paula Vogel." *American Theatre* (April 1993): 26–27.

Dolan, Jill. "Introduction to *Desdemona.*" In *Amazon All Stars*, edited by Rosemary Curb, 437–40. New York: Applause, 1996.

Erstein, Hap. "Playwright Takes Comic Waltz with AIDS Topic." Review of *The Baltimore Waltz*. *Washington Times*, 17 April 1992, E1.

Gussow, Mel. *New York Times*, 7 May 1993, C5.

Kelly, Kevin. "ART's Startling, Scorching 'Hot.' " Review of *Hot 'n' Throbbing*. *Boston Globe*, 19 April 1994, 23.

King, Robert L. *"The Baltimore Waltz." North American Review* 278 (November–December 1993): 44–48.

Roman, David. *"The Baltimore Waltz." Theatre Journal* 44 (December 1992): 520–22.

Savran, David. "Loose Screws: An Introduction." *The Baltimore Waltz and Other Plays*. Paula Vogel. New York: Theatre Communications Group, 1996: ix–xv.

Sommers, Pamela. "Shall We Dance? Playwright Paula Vogel's *The Baltimore Waltz*, Born out of Love and Loss." *Washington Post*, 22 May 1994, G14.

LUCY WANG

(1963–   )

BIOGRAPHY

Lucy Wang was born in Taipei, Taiwan, but moved with her family to Akron, Ohio, two years later. Her father was a Goodyear chemist and taught Chinese at the University of Akron. Her mother taught social studies, science, and math at an Akron junior high. As a young girl, Wang's first dream was to become an actress, so she took acting classes and participated in the high school drama club.

The paucity of roles available to Asian American women prompted her to pursue a more practical career, and she graduated from the University of Texas at Austin with highest honors in Asian studies and economics. She then earned an MBA in finance from the University of Chicago. While completing her graduate studies, Wang worked as a research economist at the Chicago Board of Trade and then moved to Wall Street where she was a bond trader for three years with Kidder, Peabody. In 1989 she left the frenzy of the trading room and tried her hand in various part-time jobs, ultimately taking a staff position in Mayor Dinkins's administration.

It was during this post–Wall Street period that Lucy Wang returned to her earlier interest in the theatre, as a playwright, however, not as an actress. She is an active member of the Dramatists' Guild and received an honorable mention from the 1994 Home Box Office New Writers' Project. Wang has also published several short stories.

Lucy Wang is married to Thomas Halpern, who is currently attending Stanford Law School, and they make their home in California.

PLAY DESCRIPTIONS

Lucy Wang feels an "obligation to tell compelling stories, and these stories contain characters of every stripe." While some plays are written for an all-

Asian cast, others have mixed casts. Her ideas for future plays have characters where ethnicity is "irrelevant." Whether her characters are Asian or Anglo, Wang is interested in testing the boundaries of roles and definitions. She is, however, pleased "if my plays add to the number of quality roles for Asian actors" (Bolia, 15).

Number One Son is a full-length play about a gay male investment banker's attempts to please his traditional Chinese father by unconventional means. *Mah-Jongg* is a full-length play that explores the struggle of a Chinese American woman and a Jewish American man to redefine identity and family within an interracial, interreligious marriage.

Bird's Nest Soup is a "slightly biographical" coming-of-age play. Set in Akron, Ohio, during the mid-1970s, the play explores the turbulent home life of Julie and Mark, two Chinese American teens, and their Chinese-born parents, Daisy and Henry. The play opens with the Lims celebrating their American citizenship, but problems arise when each member of the family tries a version of the American dream. Henry is driven to work at several jobs (including teaching Chinese at the local college), foregoing the simple pleasures of the moment in pursuit of material success. Despite his geographical location in the heart of mid-America, Henry is unwilling to relinquish many of his traditional Chinese values. Daisy, on the other hand, has become assimilated into the American mainstream without difficulty; she tutors people in English and hosts her own television cooking show. When Henry realizes that Daisy's show would require her to be away from home frequently, he forbids such liberated behavior. Caught in the middle of this cultural conflict are the teenage children. Mark's dream to become a rock musician and Julie's desire to become an actress are dismissed by their father who has his own plans for their future. Unwilling to compromise her freedom of choice, Daisy divorces Henry and seeks an equitable marriage in Australia. Julie must also leave home to escape her father's harsh, patriarchal domination.

Wang's *Junk Bonds* is a study in American greed and mistrust. The play traces a young Chinese American woman's initiation into the testosterone-laden world of bond trading. Diana, an eager young MBA, is hired at Tapir, Inc. Her colleagues are a group of jaded young men who deal with people's feelings as blasély as they trade with people's money. Pumped by the pressure, as well as by their seven- and eight-figure incomes, they are determined to preserve their all-male domain. Assaulted by dialogue peppered with racist slurs and sexist jabs, Diana quickly learns how to survive in their world. Eventually she can dish out the insults and invective with the best of them, and she proves it when Hiro, a young Japanese trader, joins the Tapir team. Diana's real lesson comes, however, when she learns that Connor, her mentor, has conned the company out of a fortune before moving on to a bigger and better job. Unable to sustain the financial loss, Tapir is taken over by the Japanese, and Diana's promised promotion and raise are granted only when she threatens to sue. With her trust in her friends and her employers shattered, Diana goes back to work on the trading floor.

Antarctica, inspired by Shakespeare's *Othello*, recounts a Japanese American man's need to prove himself to the world by probing the issues of affirmative action, mixed marriage, racism, and the auto industry. *Just Friends* explores a mother and daughter as they seek to define their relationship. Set in Australia, this play is a sequel to *Bird's Nest Soup*. The two manifestations of *Trayf* are the ten-minute version, which uses the Yiddish word *trayf* as a metaphor for happiness, and the full-length version, which interweaves two love triangles—past and present. The first triangle involves a Chinese American woman and two Jewish American men; the second triangle relates the famous love triangle between Simone de Beauvoir, Nelson Algren, and Jean-Paul Sartre.

SELECTED PRODUCTION HISTORY

Number One Son
    Staged reading, New Federal Theatre, New York, 1992
    Staged reading, Asian American Theatre Company, San Francisco, 1993

Mah-Jongg
    Staged reading, New Federal Theatre, New York, 1993

Bird's Nest Soup
    Staged reading, New Federal Theatre, New York, 1994
    Staged reading, Playwright's Preview Productions, New York, 1994
    Workshop, New Works Festival, Mark Taper Forum, Los Angeles, 1994
    Production, Urban Stages, New York, 1994–1995
    Production, West Coast Ensemble, Los Angeles, 1997

Junk Bonds
    Production, Home for Contemporary Theatre, New York, 1994
    Production, Cleveland Public Theatre, Cleveland, Ohio, 1995
    Production, Capital Repertory Theatre, Albany, New York, 1996

Trayf (ten-minute play)
    Reading, Tandem Acts Festival, Women's Project and Productions, New York, 1995

PLAY AVAILABILITY

Lucy Wang's plays may be obtained from her agent: Peter Franklin, William Morris Agency, 1325 Avenue of the Americas, New York, New York 10019.

AWARDS

National Playwrights Conference, O'Neill Theater Center, Waterford, Connecticut, Finalist, *Number One Son*, 1991

L. Arnold Weissberger Playwriting Competition, New Dramatists, New York, Finalist, *Number One Son*, 1992

White-Willis Theatre New Playwrights Contest, Fort Lauderdale, Florida, Finalist, *Number One Son*, 1993

PlayLabs, Playwrights' Center, Minneapolis, Minnesota, Finalist, *Mah-Jongg*, 1993

Cleveland Public Theatre, Festival of New Plays, Finalist, *Bird's Nest Soup*, 1994

PlayLabs, Playwrights' Center, Minneapolis, Minnesota, Finalist, *Bird's Nest Soup*, 1994

Kennedy Center Fund for New American Plays, Washington, D.C., Winner, *Junk Bonds*, 1994

Catherine and Lee Chilcoat Foundation Award for Best Play, Winner, *Junk Bonds*, 1995

The James Thurber Playwright-in-Residence, Columbus, Ohio, 1997

DESCRIPTIVE AND CRITICAL RESPONSES

Bolia, Steven. Interview with Lucy Wang. *Pollen: A HERE Publication* 1, no. 2 (November/December 1994): 14–15.

Herring, Hubert B. "A Truly Prophetic Bit of Wall Street Swear-and-Tell." *New York Times*, 20 November 1994, F7.

Meglbow, Randi. "Strife and Lies in *Junk Bonds*." *Washington Square News*, 4 November 1994, 7.

Musarra, Russ. "Big Dividends from her *Bonds*." *Akron Beacon Journal*, 25 December 1994, E1, 22.

CHERYL L. WEST

(1965–)

BIOGRAPHY

Cheryl L. West was born in Chicago and lived for years in Markham, a black working-class suburb of that city. She holds three academic degrees, one from the University of Illinois at Champaign-Urbana. Before giving herself permission to write, West supported herself by teaching and social work because those were professions she could "fall back on." After completing her first play in 1986, she was determined that if she was not making a living by writing by the time she was thirty-five, she would relegate it to a hobby. Her subsequent success assured West that she did not have to give up writing when she turned thirty-five. To date her best known play, *Jar the Floor*, has had over fifteen productions since 1991 and has won numerous awards.

Her screenwriting is equally promising. Her play *Before It Hits Home* is under option by Spike Lee. She is also doing a film adaptation for Home Box Office and an original screenplay for Paramount Studios.

Cheryl West makes her home in Champaign, Illinois, where she is able to live on her "own terms." West feels that it is important to maintain her Midwestern sensibility, since it is the heritage from which her voice springs.

PLAY DESCRIPTIONS

Cheryl West's family plays have an intensity reminiscent of Lorraine Hansberry. Her dialogue and characterizations simultaneously create uniquely distinctive families and evoke universal emotions. In *Before It Hits Home*, she explores the timely issue of AIDS and its effect on a black family. Wendal, a bisexual in his early thirties, must deal with the personal repercussions after he is diagnosed with AIDS. In the first half of the play, Wendal struggles with his own denial. His inept announcement to Douglass, his married male lover, and his failure to inform Simone, the woman who believes that Wendal intends to marry her, provide vivid insight into Wendal's view of himself and his sickness. After cutting himself off from friends and lovers and with his health deteriorating, Wendal returns to the family he sees only once a year. Although estranged from his father, who wants more for his oldest son than the gypsy life of a musician, he is his mother's favorite. As his condition is revealed to his family, the reactions range from disgust and rejection to considered acceptance and love. The familial concept of unconditional love is tested and, in some instances, is found wanting.

Jar the Floor also focuses on the family; this time, however, the family consists of four generations of women. As the daughters and granddaughters gather to celebrate the ninetieth birthday of MaDear, the matriarch of the family, the secrets and resentments that fuel the characters are gradually revealed and possibly cleansed from their lives. Lola, MaDear's sixty-five-year-old daughter, is as flamboyant as Maydee, Lola's forty-seven-year-old daughter, is reserved. As Maydee awaits a phone call announcing the college's decision about her tenure, Lola awaits a call from her man of the moment. MaDear slips in and out of senility, imagining herself in the company of her husband who has been dead for years. All three women, however, eagerly anticipate the arrival of Maydee's twenty-seven-year-old daughter, Vennie. As the reunion progresses, their frustrations and dreams begin to collide. Sacrifices (both real and imagined) are used as weapons while selfishness provides a shield. For example, neither Maydee nor Lola appreciates the import of the phone call that the other awaits; Vennie's decision to give up school and pursue a singing career is criticized as being shortsighted. Only through Vennie's friend, Raisa, who is dying of cancer, are they able to see their lives in a reasonable perspective.

The definition of family is challenged in West's *Holiday Heart*, a tale of love and survival within the bosom of a nontraditional family. Set in Chicago's brutal South Side, the play walks the tightrope between situational comedy and hard-bitten reality. In the play, narrated by the precocious and strong twelve-year-old Niki Dean, West's initial family consists of Niki's high-strung mother, Wanda, and their football-sized drag queen neighbor, Holiday Heart. Their familial accommodation is shaken when Wanda's new lover-cum-pusher, Silas, moves into the picture and is clearly contemptuous of Holiday's flamboyance. The family is shattered, however, when a rehabilitated Wanda slips back into a crack habit after receiving one too many rejection letters from publishers. Back on the streets to earn money as a prostitute, Wanda leaves Silas and Holiday to be Niki's surrogate parents. Thrown into each other's "family" and confronted with the task of raising an emerging adolescent daughter, the two men come to respect each other and find out that home and family are defined by love and caring.

SELECTED PRODUCTION HISTORY

Before It Hits Home
   Workshop, Seattle Group Theatre, Seattle, 1989
   Production, Arena Stage, Washington, D.C., 1991
   Production, Second Stage/Public Theatre, New York, 1992

Jar the Floor
   Production, Empty Space Theatre, Seattle, 1991
   Production, Arena Stage, Washington, D.C., 1991
   Production, South Coast Repertory, Costa Mesa, California, 1994
   Production, Cincinnati Playhouse, Cincinnati, Ohio, 1995
   Production, Penumbra Theatre Company, St. Paul, Minnesota, 1997
   Many regional productions in the United States

Puddin 'n Pete
   Production, Goodman Theatre, Chicago, 1993
   Production, Old Globe Theatre, San Diego, 1995

Holiday Heart
   Production, Syracuse Stage (coproduction with Cleveland Playhouse and Seattle Rep),
      Syracuse, New York, 1994
   Production, Manhattan Theatre Club, New York, 1995
   Production, Arena Stage, Washington, D.C., 1995

Play On! (book by West with the songs of Duke Ellington)
   Production, Brooks Atkinson Theatre, New York, 1997

PLAY AVAILABILITY

Before It Hits Home is published by Dramatists Play Service, 440 Park Avenue South,
   New York, New York 10016.

Jar the Floor is published in Robyn Goodman and Marisa Smith, eds., *Women Playwrights: The Best Plays of 1992*. Newbury, Vermont: Smith and Kraus, 1992.

Contact West's agent for further information: Carin Sage, CAA, 9830 Wilshire Boulevard, Beverly Hills, California 90212; (310) 288–4545.

AWARDS

Susan Smith Blackburn Prize, Cowinner, *Before It Hits Home*, 1990

AUDELCO Award for Outstanding Play, *Before It Hits Home*, 1991

Helen Hayes Charles McArthur Award, Winner, Outstanding New Play, *Before It Hits
   Home*, 1992

Beverly Hills/Hollywood National Association for the Advancement of Colored People
   Best Play, *Jar the Floor*, 1995

National Endowment for the Arts Playwriting Award, 1995–1996

DESCRIPTIVE AND CRITICAL RESPONSES

Haithman, Diane. "Hitting Home in the Heartland." *Los Angeles Times*, 23 October 1994, CAL 50.

Kilian, Michael. "The Voice of West: A Powerful New Playwright, Born in Chicago, Makes a Mark in the East." *Chicago Tribune*, 24 January 1992, V3.

McGee, Celia. "Fortress Family for the Brutal City." *New York Times*, 19 February 1995, II6.

Preston, Rohan B. "A Late Entrance." *Chicago Tribune*, 18 October 1992, V3.

Rich, Frank. "A Black Family Confronts AIDS." Review of *Before It Hits Home. New York Times*, 11 March 1992, C17, 22.

Richards, David. "A Surrogate Father in a Mother's Guise." Review of *Holiday Heart. New York Times*, 21 January 1994, C3.

Shirley, Don. "Stage: Cheryl L. West." *Los Angeles Times*, 1 January 1994, F6.

ELIZABETH WONG

(1958–   )

BIOGRAPHY

Elizabeth Wong grew up in Chinatown, Los Angeles, and received her BA from the University of Southern California in 1980. She received her MFA in 1991 from New York University's Tisch School of the Arts. For ten years she worked as a journalist before she decided in 1988 to pursue a career as a playwright. Wong now teaches playwriting at the Henry David Hwang Playwriting Institute in Los Angeles, at the University of California at Santa Barbara, and at the University of Southern California.

Elizabeth Wong was awarded a 1991 residency at Yaddo in Saratoga Springs, Florida, and a 1992 residency from the Ucross Foundation in Clearmont, Wyoming. During 1992 and 1993, she was a Disney Fellow in the Touchstone Television Division, and in 1994 she did dramaturgical work for the Actors Theatre of Louisville's Humana Festival in Louisville, Kentucky. She was a staff writer for the American Broadcast Company's sitcom "All American Girl." Wong's extensive nondramatic works are published in *American Theatre*, the *Los Angeles Times*, and numerous college texts.

Wong is a member of the Mark Taper Forum Mentor Program, the Circle Repertory Theatre Playwrights' Project, the West Coast Ensemble Playwrights' Group, and the Women's Project. She is a member of the Dramatists Guild, the Asian Pacific Alliance for Creative Equality, and the Alliance of Los Angeles Playwrights. She lives in Los Angeles with the memory of her black cat, Crusher. In the fall of 1996, Wong was Playwright in Residence at Bowdoin College, Maine.

PLAY DESCRIPTIONS

Elizabeth Wong's work is a masterful combination of highly charged political topics interwoven with a sense of wit and fun. Her best-known work, *Letters to a Student Revolutionary*, is a stylized, nonnaturalistic play that chronicles the burgeoning friendship between a young Chinese American woman, Bibi, and her youthful Chinese counterpart, Karen. They meet by chance in Tiananmen Square while Bibi is on vacation in China as that country begins to open its doors to the West in the late 1970s. Their ten-year correspondence allows Wong to delineate the evolution of these two women who share a common ancestry but who are worlds apart, both geographically and politically. The flip and cynical Bibi is contrasted to the eager and initially naive Karen. As their friendship grows, each comes to a greater understanding of the concept of freedom. The play ends after the June 1989 Tiananmen Square massacre when Bibi loses touch with Karen, one of the student revolutionaries.

Wong's *Kimchee and Chitlins* is a riotously funny political satire. Suzie Seeto, a tenacious Chinese American television reporter, is plunged into the morass of modern American race relations. Seeto must cover the escalating unrest between blacks and Koreans while she tries to unravel the mystery of "what really happened" inside a neighborhood Korean grocery store in New York City. The play predated by two years the black-Korean tension associated with the Rodney King trial and subsequent riots. Elizabeth Wong's journalistic instincts captured a flashpoint of American culture in this contemporary political play.

Imperial China provides the background for *The Three Kingdoms (The Concubine Spy)*. This full-length work is a revisionist view of a classical Chinese epic drama, *Tales from the Three Kingdoms*. Wong takes San Guo Yen Yi's semifictional account of the struggle to reunify China after the collapse of the Han Dynasty (206 B.C.–A.D. 220) and retells known stories of four Chinese generals as seen through the eyes of the women involved in their lives. Classical operatic techniques are employed in the dramaturgy of the play.

Elizabeth Wong is currently at work on *China Doll*, an extended version of a ten-minute play. This play examines the life of B-movie actress Anna May Wong. The projected *The Love Life of a Eunuch* is a film about bedroom politics during the Ming Dynasty.

SELECTED PRODUCTION HISTORY

Letters to a Student Revolutionary
  Workshop, New World Theatre, Amherst, Massachusetts, 1990
  Production, Theatreworks, Colorado Springs, 1990
  Production, Pan Asian Repertory, New York, 1991
  Production, Northwest Asian Pacific Theatre, Seattle, 1994
  Production, East West Players, Los Angeles, 1994

Kimchee and Chitlins

Reading, Primary Stages, New York, 1992
Reading, Women's Project, New York, 1992
Reading, Mark Taper Forum, Los Angeles, 1992
Production, Victory Gardens Theatre, Chicago, 1993
Production, West Coast Ensemble, Los Angeles, 1994

PLAY AVAILABILITY

China Doll (ten-minute version) is published in Kathy Perkins and Roberta Uno, eds., *Contemporary Plays by Women of Color: An Anthology.* New York: Routledge Press, 1996.

Letters to a Student Revolutionary is available in Roberta Uno, ed., *Unbroken Thread: An Anthology of Plays by Asian American Women.* Amherst: University of Massachusetts Press, 1993; Rosette C. Lamont, *Women on the Verge: 7 Avant-Garde American Plays.* New York: Applause, 1993.

Elizabeth Wong's other plays are available through her agent: Jason Fogelson, William Morris Agency, 1325 Avenue of the Americas, New York, New York 10036; (212) 586–5100.

AWARDS

Humana Festival for New American Plays, Finalist, *China Doll*, 1990

Margo Jones New Play Citation of Merit, 1992

Eugene O'Neill National Playwrights Conference, Invitee, 1993

DESCRIPTIVE AND CRITICAL RESPONSES

Foley, F. Kathleen. "Striking 'Letters to a Student Revolutionary.' " Review of *Letters to a Student Revolutionary. Los Angeles Times*, 13 May 1994, F16, 18.

Gussow, Mel. "Letters across a Cultural Divide." Review of *Letters to a Student Revolutionary. New York Times*, 16 May 1991, C18.

Isherwood, Charles. "Letters to a Student Revolutionary at East West Players." *Back Stage West*, 12 May 1994, 8.

Kim, Jae-Ha. "Hated Hyphens." Review of *Kimchee and Chitlins. Chicago Sun-Times*, 6 May 1993, II, 41–42.

"Prelude to Tragedy." Review of *Letters to a Student Revolutionary. American Theatre* 8, no. 3 (June 1991).

Torres, Vicki. "Prophetic Drama Evokes Some Jitters." Review of *Kimchee and Chitlins. Los Angeles Times*, 26 May 1992, B3.

CHARLAYNE WOODARD

(n.d.–)

BIOGRAPHY

Charlayne Woodard was born and raised in Albany, New York. She attended the Goodman School of Drama in Chicago, but after graduating in 1977, she took $2,000 and her violin and headed to New York City. Within two weeks she had landed a job in the revival of *Hair*. Her next big opportunity was being cast in the original Broadway production of *Ain't Misbehavin'* for which she garnered both a Tony and a Drama Desk nomination. She continued her acting career, landing roles in Joseph Papp's production of *Twelfth Night* and George C. Wolfe's staging of *The Caucasian Chalk Circle*. After acting in the regional theatre circuit, Woodard needed a change of pace, so she and her husband moved to Los Angeles in 1989. Concentrating on film and television after the relocation, Woodard did a stint on "Days of Our Lives" and had recurring roles on "Roseanne" and "The Fresh Prince of Bel-Air." Eager to get back to theatre work, the actress made a deal with the Fountainhead Theatre in Hollywood but had to write the play once they agreed. In a marathon week, Woodard penned her autobiographical piece, *Pretty Fire*. Although Woodard continues her acting career, she has another play in process entitled *I Came to Live out Loud*.

PLAY DESCRIPTION

Living in contemporary Los Angeles with its clearly delimited boundaries between black and white was part of the impetus for Charlayne Woodard's creation of *Pretty Fire*. The actress was determined to provide a window into the lives of ordinary black Americans. Drawing on her own history and biography, Woodard's one-woman show is a series of five monologue vignettes that follow the young Charlayne through the first eleven years of her life and depict a whole cast of characters. *Birth* gives the vivid account of the actress's untimely, premature arrival into the world on her parents' bathroom floor. By combining dialogue and narrative, she introduces us to her young, inexperienced parents and the Woodard clan. *Nigger* contrasts her loving, supportive home with the racial hostility that she encountered during a foot race at school. *Pretty Fire* continues the thread of racial bigotry with a reminiscence about a particular visit to her grandparents' home in the South. Her idyllic memories of those summer vacations are clouded by the harsh reality of watching a cross burn on a neighbor's front lawn. *Bonsey* concerns her close encounter with sexual harassment and possible rape when she is tormented by one of the bigger, lowlife boys in the neighborhood. *Joy* relates the spiritual power and ecstacy unleashed when she fulfills her grandmother's dream and sings her first church solo. Although the play is rooted in the personal experience of Woodard herself, the playwright has successfully explored universal experiences and emotions.

SELECTED PRODUCTION HISTORY

Pretty Fire (full-length one-woman play)
   Production, Fountainhead Theatre, Hollywood, California, 1992
   Production, Odyssey Theatre, Los Angeles, 1992
   Production, Manhattan Theatre Club Second Stage, New York, 1993
   Production, Sylvia and Danny Kaye Playhouse, New York, 1993

Neat
   Production, Seattle Repertory Company, Washington, 1997
   Production, Manhattan Theatre Club, 1997

PLAY AVAILABILITY

Pretty Fire is available in Charlayne Woodard, *Pretty Fire*. New York: Plume, 1995.

DESCRIPTIVE AND CRITICAL RESPONSES

Breslauer, Jan. "A Living Work in Progress." *Los Angeles Times*, 21 August 1994, CAL 7.
Gussow, Mel. "2 One-Woman Plays, Each Starring the Author." Review of *Pretty Fire*. *New York Times*, 16 April 1993, C19.
McGee, Celia. "An Actress's Journey to an Unexpected Place." *New York Times*, 5 December 1993, II8.

MARIAN X

(1944–   )

BIOGRAPHY

Marian X (Marian Warrington) was born in a taxi on the way to the hospital in Trenton, New Jersey. Although raised primarily by their father in Baltimore, Marian and her sister were frequently shuttled among various relatives. Marian's writing career can be traced to her role as official letter writer where she was not above embellishing the tale. When her father's spirit collapsed after his delicatessen was burned by a group of angry white men, Marian and her sister were placed in foster care. Marian was chosen to attend an integrated junior high school and was one of the token blacks at a girls' high school. At the age of fifteen she was recruited into the youth division of the National Association for the Advancement of Colored People where she "marched, picketed, sang my hope and righteous indignation." She won scholarships to several schools and eventually attended Morgan State University where she received a BA in English. Marian was married at the end of her freshman year and had two sons with her husband. However, she "never could get the hang of traditional marriage." After years of being a journal keeper and unpublished poet, she began her playwriting career with a graduate degree in theatre from Villanova University. In addition to her playwriting, Marian teaches English at the G. W. Carver High School for Engineering and Science in Philadelphia, and she has written *Are You With Me Now?*, a public service short for AIDS Films, Inc. She holds memberships in the Dramatists Guild, Sangoma (a collective of African American women theatre artists at the Crossroads Theatre Company in New Brunswick, New Jersey), the Black Theater Network, and the Philadelphia Dramatists' Center.

PLAY DESCRIPTIONS

Marian X's plays are family dramas that explore thorny issues of identity, friendship, love and loss. In *Dream Variations*, Dr. Sengali Rama Ra, a prominent endocrinologist, returns to the United States to accept a university position, the last stop in a career that has seen better days. His return, however, brings his identity into question, even for his wife of fifteen years. Others have known him as Paul Gray, an African American who had a love child (Syreeta) with the recently deceased Estelle, his childhood sweetheart. As his past encroaches on his present, Ram/Paul is goaded by his Shadow-self and finds himself at an emotional and spiritual crossroads.

Wet Carpets is a comedy-drama with music about the midlife crises of three women who were raised as sisters. They have come together at the family home to prepare for the birthday and high school graduation celebrations for Darlene, whom they all claim as their daughter. The smell of wet carpets drying for Darlene's big day evokes past memories and painful dreams: Camille, the woman who has raised Darlene as her own, is trying to purge the memory of her husband's suicide; Nedra is fleeing from a failed career as a singer; and Tutelia is escaping from the romantic entanglements of her most recent job. Their confrontations with themselves and each other allow them to graduate beyond the hurt to the healing.

The Mayor's Wife depicts Dora's spiritual struggle after her incarceration in a women's prison. In a series of flashbacks and surrealistic scenes, Dora's history as an abandoned child, campus activist, and eventually the wife of the mayor is played out. Turning to her college soulmate for sustenance ultimately results in the deaths of both her husband and her lost love. It is only in prison with the guidance of Faisa, an older cellmate, that Dora is able to reconnect with her *umuada* (her chain of female kinship) which provides her with the strength and groundedness that she has sought for so long.

The Screened-in Porch is a mood piece that tells a story of friendship, sexuality, and loss. Lucille Withers, a university instructor and pseudonymous author of erotica, and Hattie Rains, a recently widowed mother of four grown children, are reunited as friends after thirty-five years when Lucille moves into the apartment next door. Their relationship, however, deteriorates when Lucille's friendship with Aleta, Hattie's daughter, impacts the mother-daughter bond. Miss Mary Woodson, Hattie's elderly neighbor, also disapproves of Lucille. As each of the two women approach middle age, the responsibilities and obligations of friendship are reexamined.

SELECTED PRODUCTION HISTORY

Idella (one act)
  Production, Villanova University New Play Festival, Villanova, Pennsylvania, 1983
Dream Variation

Production, Theatre Center, Philadelphia, 1986
Production, Kumba Theatre, Chicago, 1987

Wet Carpets (play with music)
Production, Theatre Center, Philadelphia, 1987
Production, Crossroads Theatre Company, New Brunswick, New Jersey, 1988
Production, Autumn Production Encore Dinner Theater, Baltimore, Maryland, 1989
Staged reading, Oakland Ensemble/Upstart Stage, Oakland, California, 1990
Production, St. Louis Black Repertory Company, St. Louis, Missouri, 1991
Production, Paul Robeson Theater, Buffalo, New York, 1991
Production, Oregon Stage Company, Portland, Oregon, 1995

The Mayor's Wife (play with dance)
Production, Theatre Center, Philadelphia, 1990
Production, Villanova University Sesquicentennial Festival, Villanova, Pennsylvania, 1992

Warrior Stance (Or Sex, A Comedy) (fable)
Production, Penumbra Theatre Workshop, Minneapolis, Minnesota, 1992
Production, Freedom Theatre, Philadelphia, 1993

The Screened-in Porch
Reading, Philadelphia Dramatists Center, Philadelphia, 1994
Reading, Crossroads Theatre Company, New Brunswick, New Jersey, 1994
Production, Crossroads Theatre Company, New Brunswick, New Jersey, 1996
Production, Horizon Theatre Company, Atlanta, Georgia, 1997

PLAY AVAILABILITY

Marian X's plays are available through her agent: Ellen Hyman, 90 Lexington Avenue, Apartment 10–J, New York, New York 10016; (212) 689–0727.

AWARDS

New Professional Theatre Playwriting Award, New York, *Wet Carpets*, 1992
The Kennedy Center/ACT Festival XXV Region II, Winner, *The Mayor's Wife*, 1992
Commision, Historic Philadelphia, Inc., 1997

DESCRIPTIVE AND CRITICAL RESPONSES

Campbell, Bob. "Top-Drawer Acting Enlivens 'Wet Carpets.' " Review of *Wet Carpets*. *Star-Ledger* (Newark, N.J.), 3 May 1988.
Doran, Terry. "Marian Hammonds Warrington, Writing from Home." *Buffalo News*, 17 November 1991, G1, 5.
Haywood, Laura. "Crossroads Play Doubly Gratifying." Review of *Wet Carpets*. *Daily Trentonian*, 2 May 1988.
Klein, Alvin. "*Wet Carpets* at the Crossroads." Review of *Wet Carpets*. *New York Times*, 8 May 1988, XII 8.
Nelson, Nels. "A Fable of Love and War between the Sexes." Review of *Warrior Stance (Or Sex, A Comedy)*. *Philadelphia Daily News*, 10 February 1993, 39.

————. " 'Mayor's Wife' at Theater Center." Review of *The Mayor's Wife*. *Philadelphia Daily News*, 9 August 1990, 3.

Pollack, Joe. "Sisters and Surprises Make a First-Rate Play." Review of *Wet Carpets*. *St. Louis Post-Dispatch*, 13 February 1991, E5.

WAKAKO YAMAUCHI

(1924–   )

BIOGRAPHY

Born in California's Imperial Valley, Wakako Yamauchi was one of four children born to Issei (Japanese-born American) parents who made their living from farming. The young Wakako turned to reading and writing to escape the solitude and isolation of farm life. Her high school education was interrupted with the outbreak of World War II when she and her family were placed in the internment camp at Poston, Arizona. Her father died in the camp, but Wakako was eventually able to leave for Chicago where she went to art school and attended plays for the first time.

After marriage to Chester Yamauchi in 1948, she gave up hopes of a career in commercial art and design to devote herself to her family. In 1955 Yamauchi gave birth to her only child, Joy. It was following the birth of her child that she began to write, as one way to pass on the Japanese culture of her own mother to her daughter. Later she took a correspondence course in short-story writing at the University of California at Berkeley.

Her short story "And the Soul Shall Dance" was published in the 1974 landmark anthology of Asian writing, *AIIIEEEEE*, where it gained the attention of Mako, the artistic director of the East West Players of Los Angeles. He convinced Yamauchi to turn the short story into a play, and her career as a playwright began. Since then she has written eleven additional plays and received four Rockefeller Foundation playwriting awards.

Wakako Yamauchi is also a prose writer; many of her short stories have been published in anthologies and textbooks. A collection of her writing, *Songs My Mother Taught Me*, was published by the Feminist Press at City University of New York in 1994.

She currently lives in Gardenia, California, near her daughter's family.

PLAY DESCRIPTIONS

Wakako Yamauchi's first two plays share a similar tone and scope; they focus on moments of crisis in the lives of ordinary Japanese Americans struggling to survive on the California farms during the Great Depression. *And the Soul Shall Dance* is the poignant tale of two farming families and the lessons in life that the young daughters in each family are forced to learn. Masako, the eleven-year-old daughter of Murata and Hana, learns that, despite their financial difficulties, she is blessed with a loving family. In contrast are their neighbors, Oka and his wife Emiko, who have difficulty relating to other people. Unhappy with their lives together, Oka and Emiko each long for what they do not have: Oka for his deceased first wife and Emiko for her true love in Japan. They both drink and fight to cope with their disappointment, which is exacerbated by the arrival of Kiyoko, Oka's fourteen-year-old daughter who has been raised in Japan. Masako watches as Emiko escapes farther and farther from reality through alcohol and the dances inspired by her music.

Like the earlier play, *The Music Lessons* is a touching coming-of-age tale in which a young girl is tutored in the realities of life. Fifteen-year-old Aki lives on a farm with her widowed mother, Chizuko, and her two brothers where the family ekes out a precarious existence. Although only in her late thirties, Chizuko has been hardened by the physical labor needed to keep food on the table. The arrival of Kaoru, an itinerant worker a few years younger than Chizuko, appears to ease her burden around the farm. During the course of his stay, Chizuko's crusty exterior begins to soften as she allows herself the luxury of feelings and fantasies for the first time in years. The artistic Kaoru also affects Aki, whose youthful romanticism mistakes his attentions for love. When the relationship between Aki and Kaoru verges on the physical, Chizuko exiles Kaoru from the farm, leaving the family saddened and embittered by the encounter.

Yamauchi continues to explore her own past, begun in the previous two plays, in *12-1-A*. The time frame has changed from the Depression to World War II where families not unlike Aki's and Masako's are now incarcerated in internment camps. Mrs. Tanaka struggles to hold her uprooted family together as they learn to adjust to life in the camp. The daily tribulations and triumphs of camp life provide the background through which to explore larger political and social issues: the ideas of family versus kin and the meaning of citizenship and democracy. As in the earlier plays, the realities offer harsh lessons to young and old alike.

The Chairman's Wife is a departure from Yamauchi's earlier portrayals of simple people going about their lives. Based on the life of Chiang Ching, the widow of Mao Tse-tung, this play fluidly moves between past and present. Set in the spring of 1989 with the Tiananmen uprising as the backdrop, the play expressionistically explores the mind and memory of Madame Mao. The once powerful woman who helped shape Chinese history is now seventy-five years old and confined to a prison hospital. The play traverses time to show the rise of this one-time actress into the world of politics, passion, and power and their effects on present-day China.

SELECTED PRODUCTION HISTORY

And the Soul Shall Dance
Production, Northwest Asian American Theater, Seattle, 1974
Production, East West Players, Los Angeles, 1977 and 1996
Production, Pan Asian Repertory Theatre, New York, 1979
Production, Asian American Theater Company, San Francisco, 1980
Production, Pan Asian Repertory Theatre, New York, 1990

12-1-A
Production, East West Players, Los Angeles, 1982
Production, Asian American Theater Company, San Francisco, 1982
Production, Kumu Kahua Theatre, Honolulu, 1990

The Music Lessons
Production, Asian American Theater Company, San Francisco, 1982
Production, Cal State Asian American Theatre, Los Angeles, 1982
Production, East West Players, Los Angeles, 1983
Production, Public Theatre, New York, 1984

The Memento
Production, Pan Asian Repertory Theatre, New York, 1984
Production, East West Players, Los Angeles, 1986
Production, Yale Repertory Theatre, Winterfest, New Haven, Connecticut, 1987

The Chairman's Wife (A Gang of One)
Staged reading, East West Players, Los Angeles, 1989
Production, Kumu Kahua Theatre, Honolulu, 1990
Production, East West Players, Los Angeles, 1990

Not a Through Street
Production, East West Players, Los Angeles, 1991

PLAY AVAILABILITY

And the Soul Shall Dance is published in Misha Berson, ed., *Between Worlds: Contemporary Asian-American Plays.* New York: Theatre Communications Group, 1990.

12-1-A and *The Chairman's Wife* are published in Velina Hasu Houston, ed., *The Politics of Life: Four Plays by Asian American Women.* Philadelphia: Temple University Press, 1993.

The Music Lessons is published in Wakako Yamauchi, *Songs My Mother Taught Me.* New York: Feminist Press at The City University of New York, 1994.

Wakako Yamauchi's other scripts and production information are archived in the Asian American special collection. Additional information may be obtained by writing to the following: Roberta Uno, Fine Arts Center, University of Massachusetts, Box 31810, Amherst, Massachusetts 01003–1810; (413) 545–1972.

AWARDS

Rockefeller Playwright in Residence, East West Players, 1976

American Theater Critics Regional Award, Outstanding Play, *And the Soul Shall Dance*, 1977

Rockefeller Playwright in Residence, Mark Taper Forum, 1979

Rockefeller Foundation Playwriting Fellowship, 1979

Rockefeller Foundation Playwriting Fellowship, 1985

Brody Art Fund Fellowship, 1988

DESCRIPTIVE AND CRITICAL RESPONSES

Arnold, Stephanie. "Dissolving the Half Shadows: Japanese-American Women Playwrights." In *Making a Spectacle: Feminist Essays on Contemporary Women's Theatre*, edited by Lynda Hart, 181–94. Ann Arbor: University of Michigan Press, 1989.

Berson, Misha. "Wakako Yamauchi." In *Between Worlds: Contemporary Asian-American Plays*, edited by Misha Berson, 128–31. New York: Theatre Communications Group, 1990.

Houston, Velina Hasu. "Wakako Yamauchi." In *The Politics of Life: Four Plays by Asian American Women*, edited by Velina Hasu Houston, 33–43. Philadelphia: Temple University Press, 1993.

Uno, Roberta. "Wakako Yamauchi." In *Unbroken Thread: An Anthology of Plays by Asian American Women*, edited by Roberta Uno, 53–58. Amherst: University of Massachusetts Press, 1993.

SHAY YOUNGBLOOD

(1959–   )

BIOGRAPHY

Shay Youngblood was born in Columbus, Georgia, received her BA in mass communications from Clark-Atlanta University in 1981 and an MFA in creative writing from Brown University in 1993. Youngblood has held a number of jobs in the public relations field, including public information assistant for WETV in Atlanta and agriculture information officer with the Peace Corps in Dominica, Eastern Caribbean. Since 1984, however, Youngblood has worked as a freelance writer in Atlanta, New York, Paris, France, and currently works in Providence, Rhode Island, and her poetry and short fiction have been published in numerous magazines and anthologies. Her *Big Mama Stories*, published by Firebrand Books, is a collection of short fiction; *One Red Shoe*, published by Raging Redhead Press, is a collection of Youngblood's poetry. Her short story ''Born with Religion'' won the Pushcart Prize for fiction. Youngblood has written, produced, and directed two short videos, and she wrote the feature-length screenplay adaptation for her play *Shakin' the Mess Outta Misery*, optioned by Sidney Poitier for Columbia Pictures in 1992. Youngblood has taught creative writing at the Syracuse Community Writer's Project, Wells College Feminist Women's Writing Workshop, and several other venues. She has also been a playwriting instructor at the Rhode Island Adult Correctional Institution for Women and at Brown University.

PLAY DESCRIPTIONS

Shay Youngblood's vivid female characters spring to life on stage from the playwright's own Southern roots. Her innate sense of storytelling, combined with warmth, humor, and colorful language, creates vibrant characters. *Shakin' the Mess Outta Misery* is a young black woman's coming-of-age tale. Daughter, a young woman in her middle to late twenties, functions as a narrator in this exploration of black Southern womanhood. Daughter returns to her childhood home after the death of Big Mama, the woman who raised her, and her reminiscences provide the rationale for a series of flashbacks. These scenes, which span the period from the 1920s to the present, allow us to meet the community of women who share their lives, their knowledge, their frustrations, and even, on occasion, their men. There is the snuff-dipping Miss Corine, a professional maid and hairdresser, who nearly caused a racial incident when she spit from a bus window into the face of a white woman; there is Miss Tom, a carpenter and Prayer Circle member, who taught Daughter how to fish and the lesson that her love for Miss Lily is just one of the many forms of love; there is Aunt Mae, who runs a liquor business out of her kitchen and keeps company with Mr. Otis, Miss Lamama's second husband. The love and wisdom of these and many other women gently lead Daughter into adulthood.

Talking Bones explores a surreal world of magic and sacred mysticism set amid the bookshelves of Ancestors Books and Breakfast. Founded on the belief that one must feed the mind as well as the body, the bookstore is a repository of African American history and culture. Despite its unique approach to life and knowledge, the bookstore is languishing for lack of business. Baybay, the middle-aged manager, is on the verge of selling the store to Mr. Fine so that she can pursue her own dreams and missed opportunities. Opposed to the sale is Ruth, Baybay's mother, who hears voices through her broken hearing aid and who is adept at interpreting the "talking bones," a West African method of divining the future. She is aided in her cause by Eila, her granddaughter, who has begun to hear the voices and returns to learn to understand her gift. To honor her ancestors and her heritage, Eila takes over from her dying grandmother the responsibility of building a bridge between the worlds of past and present.

In *Square Blues*, lesbian art activists, interracial couples, and a contemporary revolutionary use a colorful, epic wall mural, the blues, rituals, and dreams to discover the intergenerational influences on their lives. *Black Power Barbie in Hotel de Dream* traces the painful memories evoked in the therapy sessions of the surviving children of murdered African American revolutionaries. Set in an urban funeral parlor, *Communism Killed My Dog* is a contemporary farce about expatriates, political exiles, immigrants, and illegal aliens. *Amazing Grace* is the full-length adaptation of a children's picture book about a young girl who acts out the characters from storybooks and tales told to her by her West Indian grandmother.

SELECTED PRODUCTION HISTORY

Shakin' the Mess Outta Misery
    Production, Horizon Theatre, Atlanta, 1988
    Over thirty regional productions since the premiere

Communism Killed My Dog
Workshop, Seven Stages Theatre, Atlanta, 1991

Talking Bones (full-length play; formerly *Movie Music*)
Workshop, Bay Area Playwrights' Festival, San Francisco, 1992
Reading, Circle Repertory Theatre, New York, 1994
Reading, Public Theatre, New York, 1994
Production, Penumbra Theatre Company, St. Paul, Minnesota, 1994
Production, Frontera Theatre, Austin, Texas, 1994
Production, Theatre X, Milwaukee, Wisconsin, 1994

Square Blues
Reading, Women's Project and Productions, New York, 1992
Staged reading, Theatre Exchange, San Francisco, 1993
Workshop, Bay Area Playwrights' Festival, San Francisco, 1993

Black Power Barbie in Hotel de Dream (formerly *Heroes*)
Production, Seven Stages Theatre, Atlanta, 1992
Reading, Dixon Place, New York, 1993
Workshop, Public Theatre, New York, 1994
Production, Frontera Theatre, Austin, Texas, 1995

Amazing Grace (full-length children's play)
Production, Children's Theatre Company, Minneapolis, Minnesota, 1995

PLAY AVAILABILITY

Shakin' the Mess Outta Misery and *Talking Bones* are published by the Dramatic Publishing Company, P.O. Box 129, Woodstock, Illinois 60098.

AWARDS

Fanny Lou Hamer Award, 1986

Susan Smith Blackburn Playwriting Prize, Finalist, *Shakin' the Mess Outta Misery*, 1989

Hollywood National Association for the Advancement of Colored People Theatre Awards, Best Playwright, *Shakin' the Mess Outta Misery*, 1991

Kennedy Center's Lorraine Hansberry Playwriting Award, *Talking Bones*, 1993

21st Century Playwrights Festival, Edward Albee Honoree, *Square Blues*, 1995

Paul Green Foundation, National Theatre Award, *Square Blues*, 1995

Youngblood has also received numerous Individual Artist Grants, awards for fiction, and artist colony fellowships

DESCRIPTIVE AND CRITICAL RESPONSES

Allen, Diane. "Shay Youngblood Urges Teachers to Nurture Students' Imagination." *Language Arts* 68, no. 2 (February 1991): 166.
Blanchard, Jayne M. "Penumbra's 'Talking Bones' Has Plenty Magical to Say." *Pioneer Press* (St. Paul, Minn.), 31 January 1994.

Erstein, Hap. ''Every Mother's Daughter.'' Review of *Shakin' the Mess Outta Misery*. *Washington Times*, 25 November 1992, E5.

Sommers, Pamela. ''The Pleasures of *Misery*.'' Review of *Shakin' the Mess Outta Misery*. *Washington Post*, 24 November 1992, E2.

Winn, Steven. ''Peninsula's Tribute to Black Matriarchy.'' Review of *Shakin' the Mess Outta Misery*. *San Francisco Chronicle*, 1 May 1992, D9

Appendix A
Playwrights by Cultural/Ethnic Grouping

AFRICAN AMERICAN

Anderson, Valetta
Cleage, Pearl
Collins, Kathleen
Corthron, Kia
Franklin, J. e.
Gibson, P. J.
Hines, Kim
Holland, Endesha Ida Mae
Jackson, Marsha A.
Johnson, Michael Angel
Jones-Meadows, Karen
Jordan, June
Kennedy, Adrienne
Martin, Lynn
McCauley, Robbie
Medley, Cassandra
Nottage, Lynn
Parks, Suzan-Lori
Rahman, Aishah
Shange, Ntozake
Smith, Anna Deavere
Smith-Dawson, Beverly
Taylor, Regina
West, Cheryl L.
Woodard, Charlayne
X, Marian
Youngblood, Shay

ASIAN AMERICAN

Alfaro, Rosanna Yamagiwa
Barroga, Jeannie
Chan, Eugenie
Chen, Kitty
Fiagao-Hall, Linda
Hagedorn, Jessica
Houston, Velina Hasu
Iizuka, Naomi
Kim, Susan
Lee, Cherylene
Louis, Nikki Nojima
Meyer, Marlane
Miyagawa, Chiori
Morizono, Lesli-Jo
Rodgers, Sandra
Son, Diana
Tuan, Alice
Wang, Lucy
Wong, Elizabeth
Yamauchi, Wakako

LATINA

Alvarez, Lynne
Astor del Valle, Janis
Chávez, Denise
Chavez, Theresa
Cruz, Migdalia
Fernandez, Evelina
Fornes, Maria Irene
Gonzalez, Gloria
Gonzalez S., Silvia
Loomer, Lisa
López, Josefina
Moraga, Cherríe
Palacios, Monica
Portillo-Trambley, Estela
Prida, Dolores
Sanchez-Scott, Milcha
Svich, Caridad
Tropicana, Carmelita
Villarreal, Edit

LESBIAN/BISEXUAL

Allen, Claudia
Anderson, Jane

Astor del Valle, Janis
Boesing, Martha
Chafee, Claire
Chambers, Jane
Coss, Clare
Five Lesbian Brothers
Fornes, Maria Irene
Galloway, Terry
Garner, Terry
Grahn, Judy
Hammond, Wendy
Hines, Kim
Hughes, Holly
Jenkins, Mercilee M. (Lee)
Jensen, Julie
Jordan, June
Kane, Honour
Landau, Tina
Miller, Susan
Moraga, Cherríe
Nagy, Phyllis
Olnek, Madeleine
Palacios, Monica
Prida, Dolores
Ryan, Kate Moira
Schenkar, Joan
Split Britches (Peggy Shaw and Lois Weaver)
Tropicana, Carmelita
Vogel, Paula
Youngblood, Shay

Appendix B
Additional Playwrights

AFRICAN AMERICAN

Carlos, Laurie
Dickerson, Glenda
Dove, Rita
Evans, Karen L. B.
Green, Fanni
Jackson, Cherry
Jackson, Elaine
Jackson, Judith
Jones, Jake-ann
Jones, Lisa
Lewis, Ellen
Mason, Judi Ann
McGhee-Anderson, Kathleen
Montgomery, Carolyn Cole
Parris-Bailey, Linda
Perry, Shaunielle
Porter, Regina
Quinn, Nicole
Sanchez, Sonia
Sebastian, Ellen
Vance, Danitra
Williams, Granvilette

ASIAN AMERICAN

Aoki, Brenda Wong
Dizon, Louella

Lim, Genny
Narita, Jude
Sharif, Bina
Tsufura, Donna A.

LATINA

Bonet, Wilma
Brito, Sylvia
Esparza, Laura
Fox, Ofelia
Fusco, Coco
Garcia, Amparo
Gomez, Marga
Llamas, Lorraine
Lowinger, Rosa
Portillo, Rose
Rivera, Carmen
Saenz, Diana
Sanchez, Rose
Simo, Ana Maria
Valdez, Socorro

LESBIAN/BISEXUAL

Gomez, Marga
Harris, Ann
Larkin, Joan
Moed, Clair Olivia
Moore, Honor
Prandini, Adele
Ransom, Rebecca
Schulman, Sarah
Stryk, Lydia
Wagner, Jane

NATIVE AMERICAN

Colorado, Elvira and Hortensia
Glancy, Diane
Gomez, Terry
Hogan, Linda
McCullogh, Mary Millner
Spiderwoman

Appendix C
Nominators—Theatres

Actors Theatre of Louisville, Louisville, Kentucky
American Place Theatre, New York, New York
Arena Stage, Washington, D.C.
Berkeley Repertory Theatre, Berkeley, California
Bilingual Foundation of the Arts, Los Angeles, California
BRAVA! for Women in the Arts, San Francisco, California
Cincinnati Playhouse, Cincinnati, Ohio
Circle Repertory Theatre, New York, New York
Cleveland Public Theatre, Cleveland, Ohio
Cricket Theatre, Minneapolis, Minnesota
Hartford Stage Company, Hartford, Connecticut
Horizon Theatre, Atlanta, Georgia
Illusion Theatre, Minneapolis, Minnesota
INTAR, New York, New York
Jomandi Productions, Atlanta, Georgia
Long Wharf Theatre, New Haven, Connecticut
Magic Theatre, San Francisco, California
Manhattan Theatre Club, New York, New York
Milwaukee Repertory Theatre, Milwaukee, Wisconsin
New York Theatre Workshop, New York, New York
Northlight Theatre, Evanston, Illinois
Odyssey Theatre Ensemble, Los Angeles, California
Pan Asian Repertory, New York, New York
Philadelphia Festival Theatre for New Plays, Philadelphia, Pennsylvania
Primary Stages, New York, New York
Public Theatre–New York Shakespeare Festival, New York, New York
Repertorio Español, New York, New York
Seattle Repertory Theatre, Seattle, Washington
Second Stage, New York, New York

Streetfeet Women's Touring Company, Putnam, Vermont
Theatre Rhinoceros, San Francisco, California
TheatreWorks, Palo Alto, California
Women's Project and Productions, New York, New York

Appendix D
Nominators—Individuals

Rosemarie Bank, Kent State University, Kent, Ohio
Elin Diamond, Rutgers, the State University of New Jersey, New Brunswick, New Jersey
Jill Dolan, City University of New York, New York, New York
Nicolas Kanellos, University of Houston, Houston, Texas
Tiffany Lopez, University of California at Riverside, Riverside, California
Sydné Mahone, Crossroads Theatre Company, New Brunswick, New Jersey
Chiori Miyagawa, New York Theatre Workshop, New York, New York
Patricia Montley, Chatham College, Pittsburgh, Pennsylvania
Elizabeth Ramirez, University of Oregon, Eugene, Oregon
Patti Schroeder, Ursinus College, Collegeville, Pennsylvania
N. J. Stanley, Agnes Scott College, Decatur, Georgia
Paula Vogel, Brown University, Providence, Rhode Island

Selected Bibliography

GENERAL REFERENCE

Berney, K. A. and N. G. Templeton, eds. *Contemporary Women Dramatists*. London: St. James Press, 1994.

Betsko, Kathleen and Rachel Koenig. *Interviews with Contemporary Women Playwrights*. New York: Beech Tree Books, 1987.

Canning, Charlotte. *Feminist Theatres in the U.S.A.* New York: Routledge, 1996.

Contemporary Authors. Series. Detroit: Gale Research.

Contemporary Black Biography. Detroit: Gale Research, 1992.

Coven, Brenda. *American Women Dramatists of the Twentieth Century: A Bibliography*. Metuchen, N.J., Scarecrow Press, 1982.

Davidson, Cathy N., Linda Wagner-Martin, and Elizabeth Ammons, eds. *The Oxford Companion to Women's Writing in the United States*. New York: Oxford University Press, 1995.

Dictionary of Literary Biography. Vol. 38, *Afro-American Writers after 1955: Dramatists and Prose Writers*. Detroit: Gale Research, 1985.

Gavin, Christy. *American Women Playwrights: An Annotated Bibliography*. New York: Garland, 1993.

Notable Asian Americans. Detroit: Gale Research, 1995.

Notable Black American Women. Detroit: Gale Research, 1992.

Notable Hispanic American Women. Detroit: Gale Research, 1993.

Notable Native Americans. Detroit: Gale Research, 1995.

Peterson, Bernard L., Jr. *Contemporary Black American Playwrights and Their Plays: A Biographical Directory and Dramatic Index*. New York: Greenwood Press, 1988.

Redfern, Bernice. *Women of Color in the United States: A Guide to the Literature*. New York: Garland, 1989.

Savran, David. *In Their Own Words: Contemporary American Playwrights*. New York: Theatre Communications Group, 1988.

Who's Who among African Americans. New York: Gale Research, 1997.
Who's Who among Asian Americans. Detroit: Gale Research, 1994.
Who's Who among Hispanic Americans. Detroit: Gale Research, 1994.

PLAY COLLECTIONS

Case, Sue-Ellen. *Split Britches: Lesbian Practice/Feminist Performance.* London and
      New York: Routledge, 1996.
Curb, Rosemary K., ed. *Amazon All Stars: Thirteen Lesbian Plays.* New York: Applause,
      1996.
Feyder, Linda, and Denise Chavéz, eds. *Shattering the Myth: Plays by Hispanic Women.*
      Houston: Arte Publico, 1992.
Frank, Leah D. *Facing Forward.* New York: Broadway Play Publishing, 1995.
Helbing, Terry, ed. *Gay and Lesbian Plays Today.* Portsmouth, N.H.: Heinemann, 1993.
Houston, Velina Hasu, ed. *The Politics of Life: Four Plays by Asian-American Women.*
      Philadelphia: Temple University Press, 1993.
Hughes, Holly. *Clit Notes: A Sapphic Sampler.* New York: Grove Press, 1996.
Kanellos, Nicolas, and Jorge A. Huerta, eds. *Nuevos Pasos: Chicano and Puerto Rican
      Drama.* Houston: Arte Publico, 1989.
Lamont, Rosette C., ed. *Women on the Verge: Seven Avant-Garde American Plays.* New
      York: Applause, 1993.
Lane, Eric, and Nina Shangold, eds. *The Actors Book of Gay and Lesbian Plays.* New
      York: Penguin, 1995.
Mahone, Sydné, ed. *Moon Marked and Touched by Sun: Plays by African-American
      Women.* New York: Theatre Communications Group, 1994.
Miles, Julia, ed. *The Women's Project: The American Place Theatre.* New York: Per-
      forming Arts Journal, 1980.
———. *The Women's Project 2: The American Place Theatre.* New York: Performing
      Arts Journal, 1984.
———. *Playwriting Women: 7 Plays from the Women's Project.* Portsmouth, N.H.:
      Heinemann, 1992.
Osborn, M. Elizabeth, ed. *On New Ground: Contemporary Hispanic American Plays.*
      New York: Theatre Communications Group, 1987.
Perkins, Kathy A., and Roberta Uno, eds. *Contemporary Plays by Women of Color: An
      Anthology.* New York: Routledge, 1996.
Shewey, Don, ed. *Out Front: Contemporary Gay and Lesbian Plays.* New York: Grove,
      1988.
Smith, Marisa, ed. *Humana Festival '94: The Complete Plays.* Lyme, N.H.: Smith and
      Kraus, 1994.
———. *Humana Festival '95: The Complete Plays.* Lyme, N.H.: Smith and Kraus, 1996.
———. *Women Playwrights: The Best Plays of 1992 [1993 and 1994].* Lyme, N.H.:
      Smith and Kraus, 1992 [1994 and 1995].
Uno, Roberta, ed. *Unbroken Thread: An Anthology of Plays by Asian-American Women.*
      Amherst: University of Massachusetts Press, 1993.
Wilkerson, Margaret B., ed. *Nine Plays by Black Women.* New York: Mentor, 1986.

CRITICAL WORKS

Arnold, Stephanie. "Dissolving the Half Shadows: Japanese-American Women Playwrights." In *Making a Spectacle: Feminist Essays on Contemporary Women's Theatre*, edited by Lynda Hart, 181–94. Ann Arbor: University of Michigan Press, 1989.

Baker, Houston A., Jr., ed. *Three American Literatures: Essays in Chicano, Native American and Asian-American Literature for Teachers of American Literature*. New York: MLA, 1982.

Brown-Guillory, Elizabeth. *Their Place on the Stage: Black Women Playwrights in America*. Westport, Conn.: Greenwood Press, 1988.

Dolan, Jill. *Presence and Desire*. Ann Arbor: University of Michigan Press, 1993.

Fabre, Genevieve. *Drumbeats, Masks and Metaphor: Contemporary Afro-American Theatre*. Cambridge, Mass.: Harvard University Press, 1983.

Fletcher, Winona L. "Consider the Possibilities: An Overview of Black Drama in the 1970's." In *Essays on Contemporary American Drama*, edited by Hedwig Bock and Albert Wertheim, 141–60. Munich: Hueber, 1981.

"Giving Freshness to the Weary." *Time* 132 (11 July 1988): 83.

Gray, John. *Black Theatre and Performance: A Pan-African Bibliography*. New York: Greenwood Press, 1990.

Hart, Lynda and Peggy Phelan. *Acting Out: Feminist Performances*. Ann Arbor: University of Michigan Press, 1993.

Horno-Delgado, Asuncion, ed. *Breaking Boundaries: Latina Writing and Critical Reading*. Amherst: University of Massachusetts Press, 1989.

Huerta, Jorge A. *Chicano Theatre: Themes and Forms*. Ypsilanti, Mich.: Bilingual Press, 1982.

Kanellos, Nicolas, ed. *Hispanic Theatre in the United States*. Houston: Arte Publico, 1984.

Kenyon Review 15.2 (Spring 1993).

Martinéz, Julio A., and Francisco A. Lomeli. *Chicano Literature: A Reader's Encyclopedia*. Westport, Conn.: Greenwood Press, 1985.

Miller, Jeanne-Marie A. "Black Women Playwrights from Grimke to Shange: Selected Synopses of the Works." In *All the Women Are White, All the Blacks Are Men but Some of Us Are Brave*, edited by Gloria T. Hull, Patricia Scott, and Barbara Smith, 280–96. Old Westbury, Conn.: Feminist Press, 1982.

Moy, James S. *Marginal Sights: Staging the Chinese in America*. Iowa City: University of Iowa Press, 1993.

Pottlitzer, Joanne. *Hispanic Theatre in the United States and Puerto Rico*. New York: Ford Foundation, 1988.

Sanders, Leslie Catherine. *The Development of Black Theatre in America: From Shadows to Selves*. Baton Rouge: Louisiana State University Press, 1988.

Seller, Maxine S., ed. *Ethnic Theatre in the United States*. Westport, Conn.: Greenwood Press, 1983.

Takaki, Ronald. *A Different Mirror: A History of Multicultural America*. Boston: Little, Brown, 1993.

Theatre 25.2 (1993).

The Drama Review 33.1 (Spring 1989).

Wilkerson, Margaret B. ''Music as Metaphor: New Plays of Black Women.'' In *Making a Spectacle: Feminist Essays on Contemporary Women's Theatre*, edited by Lynda Hart. Ann Arbor: University of Michigan Press, 1989: 61–75.

Williams, Mance. *Black Theatre in the 1960's and 1970's: A Historical-Critical Analysis of the Movement.* Westport, Conn.: Greenwood Press, 1985.

Yarbro-Bejarano, Yvonne. ''The Female Subject in Chicano Theatre: Sexuality, 'Race' and Class.'' In *Performing Feminism: Feminist Critical Theory and Theatre*, edited by Sue-Ellen Case, 131–49. Baltimore: Johns Hopkins University Press, 1990.

Index

Page numbers in **boldface** refer to main entries.

About the Authors

JANE T. PETERSON is Assistant Professor in the Department of Broadcasting, Speech, Communication, Dance, and Theatre at Montclair State University, New Jersey.

SUZANNE BENNETT is Artistic Associate at the Women's Project and Productions and a director and dramaturge in New York City.

ISBN 0-313-29179-9

90000>

9 780313 291791

HARDCOVER BAR CODE